# A Thirst for Souls

# A Thirst for Souls

## The Life of Evangelist
## Percy B. Crawford (1902–1960)

Dan D. Crawford

Selinsgrove: Susquehanna University Press

Associated University Presses
2010 Eastpark Boulevard
Cranbury, NJ 08512

The paper used in this publication meets the requirements of the American National Standard for Permanence of Paper for Printed Library Materials Z39.48-1984.

Library of Congress Cataloging-in-Publication Data

Crawford, Dan D., 1941–
    A thirst for souls : the life of evangelist Percy B. Crawford (1902–1960) /
Dan D. Crawford
        p. cm.
    Includes bibliographical references (p. ) and index.
    ISBN 978-1-57591-140-3 (alk. paper)
    ISBN 978-1-57591-148-9 (alk. paper) (paperback)
    1. Crawford, Percy B. (Percy Bartimus) 2. Evangelists—United States—Biography.
3. Religious broadcasting—Christianity—History—20th century. 4. Religious
broadcasting—United States—History—20th century. I. Title.
    BV3785.C69 A3 2010
    269'.2092—dc22
    [B]
                                                                        2010007945

*To my parents, Percy and Ruth, who showed me
what it means to live a life of service*

# Contents

# Preface

DURING THE SPRING SEMESTER OF 2001, ON A LEAVE OF ABSENCE FROM the University of Nebraska where I held a teaching position in philosophy, my wife and I were working in the library of the Episcopal Divinity School in Cambridge, Massachusetts. During a break, I found myself browsing the library's holdings on fundamentalism to see if any of them said anything about my evangelist father, Percy Crawford. It had been forty years since my father's death—I was nineteen at the time—after which I had gone on to get my doctorate in philosophy and had been teaching at the college level for thirty years. I had always assumed that my father had been a major force and a pioneer in the fundamentalist movement during his active ministry in the 1930s, 1940s, and 1950s, but had never made any serious attempt to assess his place in, and contribution to, that movement or the larger evangelical tradition from which it sprang.

I was pleased to find that several historians brought him into their accounts of that period and recognized his importance. The book that grabbed my attention immediately was Joel Carpenter's *Revive Us Again,* in which I found an entire section devoted to my father and his "protégé" Jack Wyrtzen, as leading figures in a "fundamentalist youth movement." I read with fascination Carpenter's thesis that "historians of American religion and culture have almost totally ignored fundamentalism's career between the winding down of its antimodernist crusades in the 1920s . . . and the rise of Billy Graham and the 'new evangelicals' in the 1950s," and I soon realized that Percy was seen by Carpenter to be one of the key players in what he referred to as the "reawakening of American fundamentalism" during this period.[1]

Although Carpenter gave an accurate and vivid picture of my father's "distinctive style" and "unconventional" ministry, he had scant resources to work from. I was surprised that he had found out as much as he did, since most of my father's personal papers were still in my family's possession. (He said to me a year or so later in conversation: "I couldn't find much about your father.") By far the most helpful source accessible to him was an article my father wrote for Donald Barnhouse's popular magazine *Rev-*

*elation,* entitled "A Modern Revival," in which he described his open-air meetings on Washington Square in Philadelphia in the summer of 1931 and their leading to the first broadcast of his radio program, the *Young People's Church of the Air,* in October of that year. Beyond that piece, there was very little in the way of primary sources. Percy had not published much himself: all that was available was a collection of sermons and a little handbook laying out strategies for soul-saving work, *The Art of Fishing for Men*— neither of which Carpenter cites. Most of his biographical information came from a sketch of Percy's life, written shortly after he died by a young devotee of Percy's, Bob Bahr, which contains some useful information, but has proved to be more of a eulogy than an accurate account of his life.[2]

My reaction to Joel Carpenter's stimulating work was that I believed that I had something very important to add to it. I began to feel strongly that the full story of Percy's unique life and ministry needed to be told and that I had at my disposal the necessary materials to do that. I could greatly expand his rather sparse account of my father's life and ministry with a wealth of detail drawn from primary source materials and my own recollections. I thought that I could locate my father within the web of relationships and interactions he had with other fundamentalist leaders of that time, such as Reuben Torrey, William Bell Riley, Oliver Buswell, J. Gresham Machen, Jack Wyrtzen, and Billy Graham. I could also trace his conflicted relationship with the Presbyterian Church and his determined effort to achieve independence from that (and all other) institutional authorities. And I thought it important to move beyond Carpenter's time frame, into the late 1950s, and show how Percy attempted to break the stranglehold that the commercial broadcasting industry had over evangelical broadcasters by establishing a Christian broadcasting network. In short, I thought that by reconstructing the life and character and multiple ventures of one of the driving forces of the fundamentalist movement at this important juncture in its history, I could at once throw light on the movement and also secure my father's place in it.

However, I felt ill equipped to take on such a project, having spent my entire professional career working in philosophy. The tools I had acquired were those of argumentation and the critical analysis of opposing positions on various philosophical topics. I was accustomed to seeking answers, with my students, to the "big questions" that philosophy posed. I had done a lot of work in the history of philosophy, especially twentieth-century philosophy, but my emphasis was on the philosophical thought of the people I was writing about and not on their lives or their historical context.

But now I had a good reason to do writing of a different kind. Fortunately, it was an opportune time in my career for me to take on a new and different project. And my wife, Sidnie, who is also an academic, trained in the history of the ancient Near East, helped me in converting my writing style and research methods into a historical mode.

I began to gather materials that were distributed among family members. There were boxes of papers, documents, printed sermons, photographs, correspondence, and memorabilia, all heaped together in no particular order. Fortunately, Percy had saved items that were significant to him, including a few early photograph albums he had made and all of his date-books from 1930 to the late 1940s, which proved invaluable. My oldest brother, Don, had already retrieved many of the hundreds of recordings and films of the radio and television broadcasts. I visited the schools Percy had attended and sifted through their records. I ran across a few saved issues of a magazine Percy edited and published early in his ministry, *Young People Today,* and managed to find a (nearly) complete run of it at Westminster Seminary, uncatalogued and therefore inaccessible to the general public. A second magazine, *Christian Newsette,* was also unearthed.[3]

I made contact with dozens of individuals who knew my father and worked with him—many of whom I was acquainted with as a youth. Quite a few members of his quartets and former employees were still living and spoke candidly with me about the rewards and the difficulties of traveling and working with him. A new and more complex picture of my father emerged; I could see more clearly what drove him, the full extent of his ambitions, the strengths he drew on to accomplish his goals, and the weaknesses that prevented him from fully succeeding.

I soon realized that it would be more difficult to reconstruct my father's theological beliefs. I had heard him preach a thousand times when I was growing up, and I knew the doctrines that he considered fundamental to the faith, but he had nowhere expounded on these central doctrines or tried to interrelate them in any systematic fashion. I needed to put them into some order so that I could see their interconnections and how they supported his commitment to evangelism. What helped me in this task were the thirty or so sermons that have survived in various printed forms and the little book, *The Art of Fishing for Men,* which I found contained a rich theology in fairly explicit form.

I have tried to reformulate my father's beliefs in a constructive and sympathetic way, and doing so has heightened their significance for me. Indeed it has required some imaginative effort on my part to enter into his theological thought and to discern the reasons he had for holding those core beliefs and for being so convinced of their truth. This was particularly true of his belief in a literal hell of eternal conscious torment for unbelievers. Where my own beliefs differ from his, I have tried to keep them very much in the background, only permitting myself on occasion to raise some questions about his views (or his conduct)—questions that I might have put to him then if I had thought to do so.

What has emerged from this eight-year project is, I hope, an account of Percy's life and contribution that is accurate and objective. I am acutely aware of the pitfalls and the dangers that lurk when one tries to write about someone he knew intimately, especially if that person is his own father. I have tried to strike a balance between the extremes of being overly charitable or overly critical. On the side of being charitable, I am helped by always having had a strong admiration and affection for my father and a deep respect for his work. On the other hand, I have not followed his path; the fundamentals of my faith are not the same as his; and this divergence in my beliefs together with the passing of more than four decades has, hopefully, given me enough distance from him that I can look at his life and thought with an impartial eye.

This book is not a memoir relying chiefly on my personal experience. A great deal of research has gone into it. I have my place in the book alongside my siblings as a member of the family and a loyal member of his evangelistic team—singing with my brothers from the age of three at meetings and on the radio and television broadcasts. Later, as a student at The King's College—the college he founded—I enter into the story more, because I played a part in triggering his rethinking of "a Christian education" and whether philosophy and open inquiry should be a part of it.

I am quite sure that many of my readers who knew Percy and whose lives he touched will feel that I have missed something of crucial importance about his mission or his message or have not done justice to the particular piece of his ministry they participated in. To them I would say that any biography is selective and that I have inevitably written about the things that I found to be the most definitive and expressive of his person and his faith. I ask only that these devotees read my story sympathetically and with an open mind, and if they do I believe they will recognize in it the Percy they knew and loved.

For those readers who did not experience Percy and his work in their lives, but who want to enter into the living history of that important period in the fundamentalist/evangelical tradition, I offer them a close-up look at one of the movers and innovators who helped to shape and redirect that tradition at a critical time in its history.

# A Thirst for Souls

# 1
# Introduction

IT WAS IN THE FALL OF 1921 THAT AN AMBITIOUS AND ADVENTUROUS YOUTH left his home in Vancouver, Canada, crossed the border and headed for Portland, Oregon, with the intention of getting the high school diploma that he knew would help him make a living in the United States. Nineteen-year-old Percy Crawford finished the high school equivalency course at the YMCA rather easily, and decided he would continue on in school, now with the goal of a possible professional career. Fascinated by reports he had heard from relatives living in Southern California, he set out for the alluring city of Los Angeles where he planned to attend the University of California. When he arrived in Los Angeles, he took a room at the YMCA which happened to be situated in the building complex of the Bible Institute of Los Angeles. Three days later, after getting a good taste of the city's night life, Percy's entire life course was turned around when he accepted Christ at a Sunday morning service at the Bible Institute's associated church, the Church of the Open Door. And within a year, the young convert was enrolled at the Bible Institute, eager to study the Bible and grow spiritually among like-minded, born-again Christians.

Without knowing it, my father had stumbled into one of the centers of the burgeoning fundamentalist movement. The Bible Institute of Los Angeles (BIOLA) was a training ground that was sending hundreds of young men and women into the foreign field and into "home" missionary work in churches, schools, and missions across the land. Students at BIOLA were united in their commitment to the mission of spreading the gospel to all the world. Percy found there a cohesive community of fundamentalist Christians knit together by an intensive program of Bible study and daily devotional activities, aggressive evangelistic work in the city with the express purpose of saving souls, and an active and wholesome social and recreational life. He thrived in this new environment.

Sixty-eight-year-old evangelist and educator Reuben A. Torrey was the guiding light of the Institute. He had come there as dean twelve years earlier at the invitation of founder and superintendent T. C. Horton to set up a curriculum similar to the one he had established at Moody Bible Institute

in Chicago. Torrey also became the first pastor of the Church of the Open
Door. He very quickly became Percy's mentor and spiritual model as he
grew into the role of professional evangelist.


## FUNDAMENTALISM IN THE 1920s

By the time Percy came on the scene at the Bible Institute in the mid-1920s,
fundamentalists had already become an identifiable subgroup within Protestantism. The movement had taken definite shape in the previous decade
(1910s) as various strands of conservative evangelical Protestantism coa-
lesced into a cohesive unit. The groups that comprised the new movement
formed a loose coalition of forces, without any central organization, and
operated partially within the established Protestant churches, and partially
outside of them. The general tendency, however, was away from the institutional church, and toward independent, *non*denominational status. BIOLA,
for example, functioned almost entirely outside the mainline Protestant
churches, even though it drew most of its students from those churches and
sent many of its graduates back to them.

To understand fundamentalism in the 1920s, we must look back at least
as far as the preceding half century, roughly from the post–Civil War period
into the first two decades of the twentieth century (1870–1920). Some of
the main contributing factors that led to its formation during this period
were: First, the gradual formulation of a set of doctrines (fundamentals)
that were deemed essential to the faith. Second, the building of institutional
structures around these doctrines—the Bible Institutes and other schools,
Bible conferences, clubs and youth organizations, mission boards, publishing houses, and alliances with existing independent organizations, most
notably the Young Men's Christian Association (YMCA). Third, an intense
period of urban mass evangelism with a heavy emphasis on soul winning.
And lastly, opposition to modernism and liberalism within the church.
What unified and motivated fundamentalists more than anything was their
vehement rejection of the modernist tendencies that were gradually taking
hold in the established churches. By the 1920s, fundamentalists were at
"war" with modernists, whom they saw as abandoning the central tenets of
the true biblical faith.

Historians of American religion have traced the beginnings of modernist
thinking to a split that was occurring within the Protestant churches as early
as the 1870s between a progressive party within the liberal wing of the denominations and an opposition party on the conservative side. Progressives
wanted to adapt Christian ideas and teachings to new intellectual trends in

the modern world, and to the particular social needs and problems of American society. Conservatives, on the other hand, strove to retain the traditional emphasis on basic doctrines and the salvation of souls. Progressives were responding to societal changes occurring in the intellectual sphere of science and philosophy and in the social sphere of industrial and urban growth. A theological perspective was developed to accommodate these modern ideas, and a social gospel movement emerged to meet the special needs of the industrial age.[1]

In the intellectual realm, the unifying idea around which new theories in science and philosophy were organized in the nineteenth century was the idea of development, and along with it the idea of progress toward some more perfect state or condition. Darwin's theory of the evolution of all life forms fit neatly with the notion of progress, and progressives accepted it while conservatives resisted the whole idea of progress—both biological and social. Darwin's evolutionary theory would become a focal issue in the split between modernists and fundamentalists. Other modern ideas coming from biblical scholars in German universities were even more threatening. These scholars applied a critical methodology to the biblical texts that challenged traditional views about the authors, dates, and sources of the books of the Bible, and tended to interpret the texts as products of their human authors. Liberal theologians were drawn to modern biblical criticism and tried to find ways to accommodate its results in their interpretation of Christian belief and doctrine. But conservative biblical scholars and theologians reacted strongly against these ideas which seemed to undermine the doctrine of the divine authorship and infallibility of scripture.

The Social Gospel movement, whose most prominent representative was Walter Rauschenbusch, pastor of the Second German Baptist Church in Manhattan, called on Christians to address the problems of the urban poor and an exploited working class with the goal of building the kingdom of God on earth. The social gospelers did not deny the important place of soul winning in the church's mission, but argued that before personal evangelism could be successful, the evil and corrupting influences of the social environment had to be changed. Rauschenbusch believed that the system of American democracy afforded the best chance of achieving the kingdom of God, and even thought that it was taking shape in his time.

This hope was shattered by the horror and destruction of World War I, and so, by the 1920s, the Social Gospel movement had largely disappeared. But fundamentalists had been opposed to the social gospel even before the Great War mainly because they could never accept the idea that the redemption of society was more important than the saving of individual souls. For them, social problems were the result of the sinful choices of unregenerate men, and the only remedy for society's ills was the salvation of souls and the effects of the moral transformation that ensued in the lives of those who experienced the new birth.

For fundamentalists, the liberal church, for all its efforts to embrace modernity, was clearly out of touch with the modern world. Those churches that had "gone modern" had departed from the true faith with the result that liberalism had no message that could meet the real spiritual needs of the post–World War I generation, and the sense of hopelessness that prevailed. Worse still, modernism, with its false teachings, was a positive threat to genuine faith. Fundamentalists, therefore, would do their best to identify and oppose modernistic tendencies in their churches and schools in order to protect the faithful from their corrupting influence.

## THE REVIVALIST TRADITION

Over and against the liberal, modernist party we have just described, a conservative reaction was developing that eventually split the Protestant churches. Three movements within evangelical Protestantism came together to form the fundamentalist movement in the fifty-year period we are considering: the Holiness movement, Millenarians and Dispensationalists, and Revivalists. In addition, a small but influential group of theologians from Princeton Seminary allied themselves with the fundamentalist forces. More will be said about these different strands of fundamentalism in a later chapter, but in this introduction to Percy Crawford's life and work, we will focus on some key developments in the Revivalist tradition that my father would soon become part of.

It was a requirement for admission into BIOLA that new converts had to wait a year before entering the Institute so that they could gain some experience and maturity in the Christian life. Percy spent the year getting oriented at BIOLA by attending weekly Bible classes taught by superintendent T. C. Horton, and also by joining Horton's Fishermen's Club whose purpose was to go out into the city's streets, jails, and missions to do "personal work" with the aim of bringing men and women to Christ.

It was not until the end of his first year as a student at BIOLA that Percy began to have some success in winning souls. Soon thereafter, he realized that he had a gift for preaching and a calling to evangelism. In his second year, he formed a quartet and took on speaking engagements, and then did a summer tour with his team up the California coast to Vancouver. As a budding evangelist, he was following in the footsteps of his spiritual guide,

Reuben Torrey, who in turn had launched a successful ten-year period of worldwide evangelism after the death of his mentor and guide, Dwight Moody.

Saving souls was the watchword at BIOLA—the very reason for its being. Torrey's book *How to Bring Men and Women to Christ* was a best seller in the Biola Book Room. Percy practically memorized it. And for the students at BIOLA, especially during Torrey's tenure, Dwight Moody was the highly revered forebear they looked back to as the hero and archetype of evangelism.

Moody had achieved national fame after embarking on a two-year evangelistic tour of the British Isles with his song leader and soloist Ira Sankey in 1873. After their return to America, the Moody-Sankey duo conducted extended citywide campaigns all over the Northeast and Midwest until his death in 1899. Moody brought mass evangelism to a new level, garnering support for his meetings from prominent churchmen, businessmen, and civic leaders, and exploiting major newspapers for press coverage. In addition, although he himself was not formally educated, Moody made an outstanding contribution to the field of education by establishing the Moody Bible Institute in 1889 in Chicago, which soon became the model for the Bible training of Christian workers and missionaries. He also instituted a series of summer conferences at his home in Northfield, Massachusetts, some of which were aimed specifically at getting the younger generation of students to commit their lives to missionary activities.

It has become clear to me that even though Percy rarely made reference to Moody, his own evangelistic career followed closely the pattern set by this influential leader. In the graduation speech he gave at BIOLA, Percy looked back to Moody as an example of what God could do with a life that was "fully yielded" to him. Percy took on this same challenge on behalf of his classmates: "So we tonight . . . desire to be fully yielded to Him that He may use us to present His claims to men." He went on in his own career, albeit unconsciously, to emulate Moody in every facet of the latter's ministry—conducting youth rallies throughout the country, starting a summer Bible conference and camps (Pinebrook), and founding a Bible-based Christian college (The King's College).

Moody had succeeded in elevating professional evangelism to a high standard of respectability with his moderate preaching style that emphasized the positive effects of salvation—the victorious life—rather than the negative consequences of rejecting Christ—eternal punishment in hell. But other revivalists who followed in his wake reverted to more extreme doctrines and scare tactics in getting conversions, and in so doing, badly tarnished the reputation of evangelists. As Percy would later write: "In our day professional evangelism has been spoiled by men who have exploited this high and sacred calling. They have brought it into ill repute."[2]

Billy Sunday, the ex-professional baseball player turned evangelist, was the most famous of those revivalists who damaged the public image of evangelism. Although Sunday was amazingly successful at winning souls, his vaudeville theatrics on the platform, and his slangy and often offensive vocabulary and delivery tended to reduce the preaching of the gospel to the level of pure entertainment. In fact, Billy Sunday and his many imitators had brought revivalism to such a low point that some critics within the church declared that evangelism was dead, and looked for other ways to carry out the church's mission.

Sunday's most active period of revivalist preaching was from 1912 to 1921—the same time that fundamentalist forces were coalescing into a movement. During this formative period, as fundamentalists narrowed their doctrines in opposition to modernism, and separated themselves from the surrounding secular culture, the moderate and irenic spirit that Moody had fostered gave way to an attitude of dogmatism and defensiveness. More and more, fundamentalists felt themselves to be alienated from the world—isolated, embattled, and disregarded. And the world, for its part, increasingly viewed fundamentalists with suspicion, as a minority Protestant sect, prone to narrow-mindedness and bigotry in their beliefs, and extremism in their tactics. The bad publicity received at the infamous Scopes "monkey" trial in Dayton, Tennessee, in 1925, where fundamentalist William Jennings Bryan suffered a humiliating defeat at the hands of agnostic Clarence Darrow, only reinforced this doleful image.

But it would be hard to describe the mood at BIOLA as in any way defeated or dispirited by the Scopes debacle. The students there never lost their zeal for soul winning or the belief that evangelistic revivalism was the only real hope for America. Indeed, Percy and his classmates would likely have thought that the next Dwight Moody or Billy Sunday would be a member of their own class.

And yet, notwithstanding this evangelistic fervor so evident in the Bible Institutes, the reputation of the new movement was severely damaged—a problem made even worse by the controversy and dissension that was rife within its own ranks. Fundamentalists were warring among themselves, accusing each other of heretical, modernist beliefs and of straying in one way or another from the true faith.

When Percy came on the scene in the mid-1920s, he saw right away that these internal disputes and external wars were weakening the movement and diverting its energies from the primary task of winning souls. He saw himself as belonging to a new generation of evangelists who would preach the same old-time religion, but in a new way. First, he changed the tone of the evangelistic service by introducing a light, humorous touch into all of his meetings. Then he followed Moody in steering clear of all theological controversy and consistently refrained from making negative attacks on individuals and groups, even the groups that fundamentalists unanimously opposed—communists, Catholics, and evolutionists. And more importantly, he livened up his meetings with new, peppy songs and choruses and (relying on Ruth, his wife and full-time partner in evangelism) developed a high-quality musical program. He preached a simple gospel message in a hard-hitting, punchy vocabulary that sounded a lot like Billy Sunday, but without the vulgarity. But like Torrey and Sunday, and unlike Moody, he preached hell and God's judgment of sinners because he was convinced that this is what the Bible plainly said.

Percy was especially concerned about the young people of his generation who were drifting away from the church into a life of sin and reckless pleasure. He had been moving down that road before his conversion and understood its attraction. He tried to reach the youth not by admonishing them or condemning their lifestyle, but by persuading them that the decision to commit their lives to Christ took more courage than choosing a life of worldly pleasure, but in the end promised more satisfaction.

By the time Percy began his full-time ministry in 1931 after seven years of schooling and part-time evangelism, the world had changed dramatically, and the exuberant preacher had to adjust his message and his style to meet the particular demands of his time. The country was then deep in the Great Depression and suffering not only severe economic hardship, but the sense of helplessness and despair that it engendered. To those who felt buffeted by larger social and economic forces they could not control, he offered a message of hope and told them it was in their power to make a decision that would change their lives and determine their eternal destiny.

But the most significant change in the cultural landscape for evangelism in the early 1930s was the advent of radio as a form of mass communication. Even as a student, preaching on BIOLA's station KTBI and Moody Bible Institute's WMBI, Percy recognized the power of radio as a vehicle for communicating the gospel. He had seen how other preachers and Bible teachers had successfully used radio to further their cause—R. R. Brown in Omaha, Aimee Semple McPherson in Los Angeles, Paul Rader and Wendell Loveless in Chicago, and Donald Barnhouse in Philadelphia. Percy started his own radio ministry in October 1931 on one station in Philadelphia with a program he called the *Young People's Church of the Air,* and within a decade would be reaching a national audience on more than four hundred stations. He firmly believed from the beginning that radio was the instrument God would use to bring revival to the nation and the world, and he even dared to believe that he was on the leading edge of such a "modern revival." Percy's ministry in the 1930s and 1940s was significant in as much as he helped to reenergize the fundamentalist movement when it was languishing and move it forward into the "great harvest days" of the *Youth for Christ* and Billy Graham era of the 1940s and 1950s.

Another of Percy's distinguishing qualities that shaped his work as much as any other was his entrepreneurial and adventuresome spirit. He took as a motto for his life the Scripture verse in which Jesus commands Simon the fisherman to "launch out into the deep" (Luke 5:4). Percy spent his entire life creating new strategies and new avenues for reaching lost souls. Beginning with his radio broadcast which he later took onto network television with the first coast-to-coast religious program, *Youth on the March,* he branched out into many satellite enterprises: fishermen's clubs and tract clubs, the summer Bible conference and camps, bookstores and book clubs, two magazines, a liberal arts college (The King's College), the Victory Center for service men and women, new types of youth rallies, a whole musical entourage, a foreign mission, and his boldest venture, a Christian broadcasting network.

Percy was motivated in this last venture of building a network of stations by what he considered to be the unfair policies and arbitrary decisions of the profit-driven network managers and station owners—especially toward independent evangelical broadcasters like himself. Accordingly, in the last five years of his life (1955–60), he was able to acquire and operate a network of six radio stations (with two more pending) and a television station. With this ambitious project, he dared to take hold of one of the important levers of secular power and thereby open up new channels of communication for the cause of evangelism.

Percy was a pacesetter for the fundamentalist/evangelical movement in a critical period of its history. In the 1930s, when it was beleaguered and held back by hostile cultural forces, he was one of the "young men on fire"[3] who reinvigorated the movement and kept mass evangelism moving steadily forward. And in the 1950s, his contribution lay in changing the thinking and the attitudes of fundamentalists toward the broadcasting industry. By competing with opposing forces in the commercial realm for a share of the power they wielded over him, he opened the door for more aggressive strategies in the use of the media to carry the gospel to the nation and the world.

# 2
## Conversion in Los Angeles

LOOKING BACK AT HIS YOUTH, PERCY DESCRIBED HIS TEENAGE YEARS, prior to his conversion at age twenty, as a time of revolt—revolt against his parents' strict rules (one of which was that he attend church regularly) and against the "dry religion" he was getting at his home Baptist church in Vancouver, British Columbia. He said that his father used to whip him and his brothers whenever they missed church. And yet he went to church and Sunday school and even received a Bible for regular attendance.[1]

By all accounts, Percy's youth was full of physical activities and adventures with his pals. In one of the few references to his boyhood, Percy recalled: "When I was a boy, 12 or 13 years of age, I palled with a boy that I thought was terrific and enjoyed his presence more than anyone else."[2] But he and his pals had a penchant for mischief making. There was the time when he wanted to be a cowboy and got caught roping and riding the neighbor's dairy cows. The dairyman led Percy and his brother to their home and wanted compensation from their father, Tom, because the cows weren't giving any milk. Percy's cousin, Barr Crawford, who told this story, added that his Uncle Tom "settled with Percy in the woodshed that night."[3]

He started working as a child, selling newspapers on the street corner, because "we needed the money." After his father left his mother and the three children, Percy had to drop out of school and work in order to supplement the family income. As the youngest of three boys, he was expected to help support the family while his older brother Alph prepared for medical school. His first salaried job was driving a delivery truck for a wholesale hardware firm. "At the end of the first week I went home with a total of $23.50 for my pay. I thought I was a millionaire."[4] Later he helped his mother, Margaret, run her small grocery store. But as soon as he was able to pay for his room and board, he announced one day to his mother that he would do what he wanted about church. This was the time when he started looking to have "a good time" and when he openly disobeyed the household rules by smoking and hanging out at the local pool hall and going to the dance hall. And he stopped going to church.[5]

While still in his teens, he left what must have been a rather unhappy home life, living with his puritanical and high-strung mother who was deeply offended and embittered by her husband's leaving her, and migrated to the United States. In his minisermon "My Testimony" (which first appeared in print twenty years later), Percy recounts the events that led to his conversion in Los Angeles. He says that he "drifted around the Pacific coast." But there is little evidence that he did any drifting. He moved across the border to Portland, where he had some relatives, got a job, and enrolled in the Oregon Institute of Technology, taking the full equivalency of high school courses in the College Preparatory School. He finished the program in eighteen months, graduating along with twenty-five others in May 1923, at the age of twenty. The school was referred to as "the local YMCA school" according to the newspaper clipping he saved announcing his graduation, and so he spent a good deal of time at the "Y" and may even have lived there while attending the Institute.[6] The principal of the College Preparatory School, Dale B. Worthington, took a special interest in Percy and counseled him to make use of his ability and go on to university. This was the good advice and moral support that he had not gotten from his family, and it was at this time in his life that he realized he did have the ability to succeed in school and decided to go on and get his college degree.

The photographs from his time in Oregon that Percy collected in his scrapbook show that he had an active social life with lots of friends and that he liked to ham it up and make funny poses in front of the camera. But there are clear indications of moral seriousness, as in this pact made with a classmate the month before they were to graduate from the Institute. The "Pledge," dated April 22, 1923, written in Percy's own hand, states that

> We, Percy B. Crawford and Frank D. Chambers, in order to govern and control our activities, insure [against?] domestic interferences, limit our financial re[s]ources (including moving picture shows), and better ourselves in every respect, do here ordain and agree to this document which governs our weaknesses, between the dates of April 22 to June 1, 1923. This cannot be amended.
>                          Signed, Percy B. Crawford. Frank D. Chambers[7]

At a time when it was natural to be celebrating their accomplishment, these two young men were thinking about controlling their appetites, not overspending on entertainment, and improving themselves. And so, in this spirit of moral earnestness and correct living, Percy submitted a letter of application to the University of California, Southern Branch—soon to be renamed the University of California, Los Angeles—for entrance in the fall of 1923. He may have been drawn to Los Angeles because his mother's sister, Vera, had moved there from Vancouver, and had brought back glowing reports of that fabulous city and its many attractions.

Percy worried about what vocation to choose and was genuinely perplexed about what his life's course would be. In a letter to older brother Alph in the fall of his last year at the Oregon Institute of Technology, he had suggested the possibility of a law degree and asked for advice. Alph, who was finishing his medical degree at McGill University, suggested pharmacy, with the idea that they might form a partnership since (he noted) Percy had good business skills and he had none; Alph also proposed dentistry. It is doubtful that Percy took these suggestions to heart, but it must have pleased him that Alph was taking his professional aspirations seriously. And just in case other options failed, he kept the name and number of the school of dentistry in his address book as he headed south.

It is also clear that when Percy left home he did not sever his ties with his family. His correspondence with Alph shows that the brothers were on good terms. In fact, while he was putting himself through school, Percy continued to help pay for Alph's medical schooling.[8] Alph was Percy's best man (and only relative) at his wedding, and my parents visited Alph and his family periodically over the years. Percy always admired his older brother and lauded him for his professional accomplishments as a doctor; but after Percy's conversion the brothers moved into their different worlds and gradually lost touch with one another.

Percy's mother had a very strong influence on him in these early days. Margaret was of Scottish Irish descent, born in Ontario, Canada into a large Methodist family of eleven children. Her strict pietism certainly contributed to her son's good moral character, but it also stifled him and triggered his rebellion. After his father, Tom, separated from Margaret and the family, Percy was the one who took on the role of protector of his mother. He was fond of her and never lost his feeling of sympathy and affection for her. Margaret never forgave Tom for leaving her and was bitter and resentful toward him all her life; and her young son also developed a deep resentment toward his father that he never got over. But Percy was eager to get out from under his mother's rigid standards and overbearing personality, and after he left home he always managed to keep his distance from her.

And so we have the picture of a twenty-year-old youth, with diploma and character reference[9] in hand, setting off for Los Angeles—adventurous, ambitious, and a little heady over what he had already achieved on his own, industrious and serious and yet wanting to have a good time, and bound for a major university where he was determined to find his life's work. He would find it all right, and in a very short time, but he would find that he was going in a direction that he never dreamed that he would go in.

## THE DECISION

Percy arrived in Los Angeles on Thursday, September 20, by boat, fully expecting to attend fall classes at the University of California. But he never
made it to the university campus, because three days later he had a conversion experience that would change the course of his life. He has given
us a vivid description of what happened on that Sunday morning in "My
Testimony," which he must have given hundreds of times before it took its
final shape as the opening piece in *Salvation Full and Free,* a collection of
"radio messages" published in 1943. The following excerpts from this account reveal how he came to understand that all-important event and also
illustrate his crisp, colorful style, tinged with humor, so suitable for short
radio sermons:

> I had traveled to Los Angeles on a boat and as I walked down Broadway, with
> my two suitcases, not knowing where to go, I met two young women I had been
> dancing with on the trip. They looked at me and said, "Haven't you got a room
> yet?" I said "No." "Well," they said, "why don't you try the Bible Institute?
> They have a hotel for men and women." I thought, Bible Institute? And that did
> not appeal to me, but they persuaded me to try it.

It is understandable that he would have taken the girls' suggestion to stay
at the Bible Institute because that was where the YMCA was located, and
Percy had been comfortable in that setting at the "Y" school in Portland.
When he arrived at the "hotel," the man at the desk asked him if he was a
Christian. Percy was taken aback: "Well, I had not come to be interviewed
and besides I was no heathen, and since I thought I was a good deal better
than many Christians I knew, I said I was a Christian. I thought because I
had not killed anyone or held up any banks, I was entitled to call myself a
Christian." He had thought that being a Christian was a matter of not committing crimes and being a morally good person (which he was). He would
later say of his preconversion self: "My life, when I was a youngster there
in our community, my life was a good, clean, moral life for a young man."[10]
But his good character notwithstanding, he soon came to look upon his life
as hopelessly "sin-stained" and in need of a Savior.

It was only natural, however, that the young adult, about to turn twenty-
one and completely on his own, would want to have some fun and get a
taste of the night life that was on offer in the big city. It would have been
hard for him to resist the glamour and the lights of Los Angeles in those
roarin' times. Although naturally shy, he was sociable and wanted to begin
to find friends as he had in Portland. And so he found the dance halls:

Thursday I went to a dance: Friday, I went to a party; Saturday, I went to the Cinderella Roof Dance Hall, two blocks away from the Bible Institute. On Sunday morning I thought it would be nice to go to church, to keep up the spiritual side of my life as well as the social. Dr. R. A. Torrey was then pastor of the Church of the Open Door. It is a large church, seating over 4000, and I knew no one would know me. I sat fairly near the door just in case I did not like the preacher.

Not being accustomed to so much partying in such a short time, he must have felt jaded and disoriented after his big weekend. Percy had not completely abandoned the spiritual side of his life; he still had the "scent of religion" about him (as he later said), and so it was not surprising that he decided to attend services at the Church of the Open Door, which was on the ground floor of the dormitory he was staying in. Besides, this was no ordinary church. When Reuben Torrey had come to the Bible Institute of Los Angeles twelve years earlier, he came on the condition that the Institute would annex to its main building a church auditorium with seating for four thousand in the sanctuary and balcony for his evangelistic services. And the sheer scale of what was going on in the street below his dormitory window—the automobiles and thousands of people converging on this magnificent structure—would have been more than enough to lure the curious sojourner inside:

> I waited for the preacher, for Dr. Torrey was away. Out came a man in a blue serge suit. I afterwards learned his name was William P. Nicholson. And did he preach! I never heard anything like it in all my life. I was used to a nice, sweet, soothing voice. I was used to poetry and book reviews and I could sleep well under that kind of sermon. But there was no sleep for me that morning.
>
> Mr. Nicholson preached on hell and heaven and sin and Christ, and he told me Christ was the One I needed. He seemed to pick me out of that huge congregation and speak directly to me.

Willie Nicholson was a fiery Irish itinerant evangelist whom Billy Graham once described as a "blood and thunder preacher [who] could preach every night for a solid month on 'Hell.'"[11] He caught Percy at a time of emotional vulnerability when he was searching for something to devote his life to:

> God knows I was at the crisis, the crossroads. God knows I was going one hundred per cent for the devil or for Jesus Christ that morning, so at the close, when the invitation was given, I raised my hand and took it down quickly for fear someone would see me. They sang a hymn and asked those who raised their hands to come forward. But I would not. However, a converted Jew came to me,

put his arm around me and walked up to the front with me. That was September 23, 1923. Oh, what a joy the Lord Jesus has been to me ever since.

Willie Nicholson had impressed upon my father that in spite of his best efforts to lead a good clean life he was still a sinner in God's eyes and needed to be saved. He also realized that accepting Christ as his Savior meant that a radical change was taking place in his life and that it was now incumbent on him to go in a new direction, and that if he was serious about this he would have to make a total (100 percent) commitment to his newfound Savior.

But it would take Percy some time before he would get this life-changing experience into its proper theological perspective and see that the events that led him to his meeting with Willie Nicholson, although seemingly accidental, were all part of a divine plan. God had singled him out and brought him to this crossroads. God was using Willie Nicholson and the converted Jew to convert him. As he writes, in a passage reminiscent of Augustine's *Confessions:* "All this time I had been in rebellion against God. Although I was not interested in Him, He was interested in me. Although I had forgotten Him, He had not forgotten me."[12] But he had no idea yet where God was taking him.

Percy's own singular conversion experience became for him the archetypic model of what it meant for someone to be born again and of what he would try to achieve in the lives of the unsaved. As an evangelist, he would offer them the same chance for salvation. He would convict them of their sin and make them see that Christ was the only answer. He would ask them to raise their hand and "come forward" as an outward sign that they were accepting him. He would instruct them to mark the date on which they were born a second time. And he would send them on their way, resolved to become "real Christians" from that day forward.

September 23, 1923, was the day that marked a turning point in my father's life. He immediately gave up seeking "worldly pleasures" and began to live the new life he thought was required of him as a Christian. He would withdraw his application to the University of California and rethink his long-term professional goals. And he would begin to look for a way to enter into Christian service.


A THIRST FOR SOULS

The year following his conversion was a transitional one for Percy in which he took time to reorient himself and ease his way into Christian service. He needed to find employment to support himself and took a job with a building contractor and also did janitorial work. At the same time, in order to develop spiritually, he began to explore the rich opportunities for an active Christian life that were afforded by the Bible Institute and the closely affiliated Church of the Open Door. Naturally he returned to the church where he was born again for more nourishment and became acquainted with its charismatic pastor, Reuben Torrey. Searching for companionship with like-minded Christians and ways to nurture his faith, he heard about T. C. Horton's Fishermen's Club, whose weekly meetings, held at the Bible Institute, attracted 150 to 300 men. "Daddy" Horton, as he was affectionately known, had formed the Fishermen's Club in 1906 initially as a Bible study group while he was an assistant pastor at Immanuel Presbyterian Church of Los Angeles. It had a twofold objective: "The study of God's word, and the doing of active, aggressive personal work for the Lord Jesus Christ."[13] As a neophyte Christian eager to rediscover the Bible, Percy would have been a regular at Horton's Monday evening meetings. And it was in this setting that he first became aware of personal evangelism and its prominent place in the fundamentalist faith and practice of that time.

Horton also conducted a training class for Sunday school teachers and printed pertinent lessons and tips for presentation in a quarterly magazine.[14] One of Percy's first acts of service was to volunteer to teach a Sunday school class of boys, which he did with enthusiasm, but found himself handicapped by his lack of knowledge of the Bible.[15]

Daddy Horton, who was in his mid-seventies at this time, certainly influenced Percy more than anyone in this early formative phase of his Christian life and became to him both a teacher and a shining example of what it meant to be a totally committed Christian. (A photo in Percy's scrapbook shows Horton looking admiringly at the young man with his arm around his shoulder; the handwritten caption reads: "Daddy and one of his boys. The Lord was good in allowing me to know Daddy and used him to lead me out into full time Christian Service.")

## THOMAS CORWIN HORTON

Thomas Corwin Horton (1848–1932) never had any formal theological training. He was a successful businessman for twelve years before accepting a call to become secretary of the Indianapolis YMCA, taking a considerable cut in pay. For the next twenty-eight years, before moving to Los Angeles, he held positions at several YMCAs and churches. It was while serving as associate pastor of Bethany Presbyterian Church in Philadelphia that he made a systematic study of the Bible under the tutelage of A. T. Pierson. Later, in St. Paul, he started an independent church in the city center, known as the Gospel Tabernacle, and built it from scratch into a large congregation. Over the years, he became dissatisfied with the YMCA (and the YWCA), seeing the organization as having lost its original purpose of soul saving and putting in its place "merely social work and the betterment of the body."[16] Horton moved to Los Angeles in 1906 and three years later saw the need for a Bible training school and, with the financial backing of businessman Lyman Stewart, founded the Bible Institute of Los Angeles and served as its superintendent for seventeen years.

Horton was obsessed with the urgency of winning souls and impressed upon his students their grave responsibility to go out and save the lost. In 1922 he published a book entitled *Personal and Practical Christian Work,*[17] which he dedicated to the Fishermen's Club of Los Angeles. Percy would have been thoroughly acquainted with this book—especially the part of it that laid out strategies for dealing with the various types of objectors and resisters that one might encounter when witnessing. Horton begins the book with a personal testimony:

> For forty years it has been my privilege and delight to teach and practice the art of soul-winning. [After mentioning some of the rewards of having served as a pastor, he continues:] But the supreme joy of my life has been found in clasping the hand of a man who has looked me in the eyes and said, "I will take Jesus Christ to be my Saviour, and I will confess Him before men."
>
> If the pages of this book are used to lead others to engage in soul-saving service in which they will find unspeakable joy, it will not have been written in vain.

Later in the book Horton counsels the reader:

> There are but few soul-winners in the church, and yet *soul-winning* is the *work* committed to the Church and the work for which the Holy Spirit desires to qualify every believer. You can be a soul-winner if you will. If you are not, you are failing in the *one thing* which above all others should and does characterize the true follower of the Lord Jesus Christ, who came to seek and save that which was lost.[18]

He warns the reader: "You may have failed; you may feel that you are not called to do personal work. Be on your guard lest Satan shall beguile you and spoil your Christian life by depriving you of the most blessed of all Christian experience. Christ says in Matt. 4:19 'I will make you fishers of men.' Go at it and keep at it."[19]

Percy was one of those who thought that he lacked the natural ability to do personal work. But he took Daddy Horton's advice and persevered until he was successful. In his own book on personal evangelism, *The Art of Fishing for Men,* Percy wrote: "I recall that when I began to do personal work I thought I would never be able to succeed. I was timid and backward and unable to open my mouth before people, but gradually, after many attempts and many apparent failures, the art was acquired."[20]

Percy started with the most elementary technique of passing out Gospels of John, using the special edition of the gospel that Horton had designed "to assist Christian workers in their personal endeavor to win souls." The Bible Institute ran full-page ads for the "Little Red Gospel of John, specially arranged for use in soul-saving and soul-strengthening work."[21] It included supplementary sections such as "God's Plan for Saving Sinners," "Teaching concerning the Fundamental Doctrines in the Gospel of John," and "Jesus as a Fisher of Men," as well as an invitation to the reader "to receive Jesus Christ as your Saviour [and] confess Him before men" (by signing on a dotted line). Eight hundred thousand copies had been printed by 1926. Percy continued to use Horton's Gospel of John for many years in his ministry before printing his own simpler version. One 1950 edition of Horton's gospel that Percy used advertised thirty million copies printed.

I have come to see that my father's first acquaintance with fundamentalist theology came through T. C. Horton's teaching and specifically his formulation of God's plan of salvation in the Gospel of John "made plain" (as he said). This interpretation of John stressed the doctrines of substitutionary atonement and the new birth and was reduced in Horton's text to three essential points:

1. God sent His Son into the world that He might take the sinner's place. When Jesus died on the cross as God's Lamb, He took the punishment that belonged to the sinner. (John 3:16–17; 1:29)
2. When we acknowledge ourselves to be sinners, and take Jesus Christ as our Saviour, God gives us a new nature. We are born from above. (John 3:3, 7)
3. By our acceptance of Jesus Christ as Saviour and Lord, we receive eternal life. (John 1:12; 3:36; 5:24)[22]

This blending of Johannine and Pauline theologies was the milk and message that Percy carried to the unsaved, and it constituted for him a foundational set of beliefs from which he never deviated.

Percy tells us that in the year following his conversion, he took steps to change his attitudes and improve his character. Letters were written in an attempt to right the wrongs of the past. He also had to give up his desire for money and eliminate greed. He began to tithe.[23] And all the while he was doing his very best to win souls. At last, he experienced his first victory:

I was working for a contractor in Hollywood as a carpenter's helper. I had recently taken Christ as my Saviour and had a longing to reach others, but thought I was not qualified. One day a young Swede, over six feet tall, came on the job with us. We worked together until about 11:00 o'clock, when it began to rain. We had to stop work, so we sat in my old, broken-down Ford. As we sat there I thought, "Here is my chance to 'fish' for this fellow." We talked about everything under the sun but religion, until finally, very hesitantly, I handed him a Gospel of John; then I read to him from it. I pointed out that God saw our lost condition in sin, and that God had provided a Sin-Bearer. I asked him if he would recognize these facts, and that big Swede put out his hand, grasped mine, and said, "Yes." My, what joy! I went back on that job thrilled through and through. The joy of leading one soul out of darkness into light is unspeakable.[24]

He had approached his fellow laborer somewhat nervously, but expectantly, and was overjoyed when the man said yes to his appeal. He had won him. He was beginning to acquire that thirst for souls that (he later said) God had given him. And yet he was still a long way from knowing what his life's work would be. This is expressed in what he adds to the above account in a slightly different telling of the same story: "I was so thrilled, to think that I led my first soul to Christ. That gave me a thirst and a desire to become a fisherman. But never in all this world did I expect to become a preacher. This was the farthest thing from my mind."[25]

But even though Percy was deadly earnest about his Christian commitment, he did not stop trying to have some fun in beautiful southern California. He had a car and probably ferried his friends to many outings at the beach and in the mountains. Pictures from his scrapbook usually show him clowning and having a good time on these occasions. Percy had a real fondness for the automobile; and he went for practicality in his cars, but also showiness. In December 1923 he took a week off and toured southern California and Arizona, apparently by himself. His datebook from that year includes a record of the total miles covered on the trip (1,143) and the amount spent on gas and oil ($8.16 one way). No expenses are listed for lodging, indicating that he either slept in his car or under the stars. He was adventuresome, and he liked being on the road.

It is not surprising that he decided to enter the Bible Institute in the fall of 1924. The Institute was a familiar and nurturing environment to him. The weekly Fishermen's meetings were held there in the ample lower auditorium. And the Church of the Open Door was next door to it. More importantly, he tells us, he hungered for more Bible training. And so, he decided to postpone once again his plan to attend the university and, by enrolling at the Institute, moved ineluctably toward full-time Christian service.

# 3

# The Roots of Fundamentalism

WHEN PERCY CAME ON THE SCENE AT THE BIBLE INSTITUTE OF LOS ANGE-
les in 1923, fundamentalism as an identifiable movement was still in its in-
fancy, and yet in Percy's experience it was well-established and had a clear
sense of its place in the broad spectrum of American Protestantism. BIOLA
had taken its place as one of the two main nondenominational educational
institutions (along with Moody Bible Institute) that was giving the new
movement its character and purpose. And T. C. Horton and Reuben Torrey,
though nearing retirement, still provided strong leadership and direction at
the Institute.

The aim of this chapter is to trace in some detail the historical roots and
antecedents, extending back into the previous half century (1870–1920),
that gave fundamentalism the particular shape it had when my father encountered it as a new convert. In the introduction, we identified the main
movements or groups that came together to form the new entity—the Holiness movement, Millenarians and Dispensationalists, Revivalists, and a
small group of Reformed theologians and scholars at Princeton Seminary;
we will explore more fully in this chapter the contribution to fundamentalism of each of these four strands. We noted too the split that was occurring
in the (northern) churches between a liberal party that wanted to adapt
Christian ideas to modern intellectual trends and address the social problems of that time, and a conservative party that clung to the fundamental
truths of the Bible and gave primary importance to evangelism and the salvation of souls. The *Modernist* movement emerged out of the liberal group,
and *Fundamentalism* sprang from the conservative camp. What unified the
various fundamentalist forces more than anything, as they formed themselves into a single unit, was their opposition to Modernism and its influence in the churches. In heated exchanges and debates with modernists, the
fundamentalists forged their own belief system and established their separate identity. Since fundamentalism emerged to a great extent as a reaction
to modernism, it will be important in understanding the formative elements
of the movement to specify some of the main points of disagreement between the two groups.

## The Roots of Modernism

Modernism was perhaps not sufficiently organized to be called a movement; it was rather an intellectual shift toward a liberal theology, initiated in books and articles written by relatively obscure seminarians, but also popularized by a few well-known "celebrity clerics" such as Henry Ward Beecher, Lyman Abbott, and Harry Emerson Fosdick.

As indicated, the liberal, progressive elements in the denominational churches wanted to adapt Christian ideas and teachings to societal changes occurring in the intellectual sphere of science and philosophy, and in the social sphere of industrial and urban growth. A "new theology" was devised to accommodate these social and cultural shifts, and a social gospel movement emerged that addressed the special problems brought on by the industrial age.

In the intellectual realm, the broad metaphysical idea that guided the formation of new theories in science and philosophy in the nineteenth century was the idea of development, growth, and progress. Modern science was developing new theories of an evolving universe, and modern philosophers constructed theories of an advancing social and political order. Significant gains in knowledge were occurring in the areas of physics and chemistry, and in the new fields of psychology and sociology. In biology, Darwin proposed his bold evolutionary theory of the origin of all life forms by means of a natural process that had no place for divine interventions. Darwin's theory would become one of the central issues that divided modernists and fundamentalists. The very idea that new species evolved from earlier ones by a gradual process of change challenged the traditional idea that individual species were fixed forms created by God in separate acts.

In philosophy, the systematic thought of the German idealist Hegel predominated in this country, with its concept of the Absolute (God) as immanent in the world and advancing through human history toward completion. By the early decades of the twentieth century, European influences were fading and the rival American school of pragmatism, advanced by C. S. Peirce, William James, and John Dewey had nearly supplanted Hegelianism. Pragmatism tended toward naturalism, and correlated with it, a much humbler view of human knowledge, maintaining that all knowledge is fallible and open to revision—never absolute.

When Darwin's theory was introduced to America, it did not initially create controversy among evangelicals. Protestant theologians and clergymen generally accepted biological evolution in some form and thought it could be made consistent with the Genesis account of creation. They interpreted Darwin as saying that the evolutionary process was progressing toward higher and more perfect beings, culminating in man, and they assumed that God was needed to guide the process toward that end. Some religiously motivated biologists, such as Harvard's Asa Gray, even thought that God had to be brought into the biological process, guiding and channeling the creative advance—a view that Darwin explicitly rejected in correspondence with Gray.

Further, Protestants were attracted to the popular variant of Darwinism known as Social Darwinism, advanced by the English philosopher Herbert Spencer, which applied Darwin's law—that the "fittest" individuals win out over the weaker in the competitive struggle for survival—to the social and political realm. This concept was palatable to Protestants because it cohered with their own ideas about American individualism and the free enterprise system.[1] Although the Social Darwinist principle continued to hold sway among evangelicals, Darwin's biological theory would soon be rejected by the fundamentalist subgroup as it became increasingly clear that the theory did not have any place at all for God in the evolutionary process. The origin and development of species, including man, was determined entirely by chance variations and the contingent circumstances in which organisms found themselves, together with the laws of natural selection and the struggle for existence. Thus Darwin's theory was seen as a direct challenge to Genesis, and indirectly, to the authority of scripture.

In addition to the Darwinian theory, there were other modern ideas emanating from Europe that were even more threatening to fundamentalists. Biblical scholars in German universities were proposing a new approach to the Bible and its origins. This critical methodology, known as *higher criticism,* attempted to understand the biblical texts in light of the historical and social context in which the authors wrote them, and thus tended to view them as human artifacts. Scholars who adopted this method challenged traditional views about the authors, dates, and sources of the books of the Bible. One of the most controversial hypotheses, put forward by Julius Wellhausen and others, was that the Pentateuch was not a single work written by Moses, but rather the work of unknown editors who combined several different sources. Another explosive result of the biblical critical analysis of texts was that the book of Isaiah was composed by two different authors (or possibly three) writing in different time periods. Liberal theologians generally accepted the conclusions of modern biblical criticism and tried to incorporate them into their interpretation of Christian doctrine. But conservative biblical scholars reacted strongly against these ideas that threatened to undermine their belief in the Bible as the spoken Word of God, valid for all times and places.

In the social sphere, modernists were responding to the situation they were in. The last quarter of the nineteenth century was the Gilded Age, a time of general prosperity across the land which saw huge fortunes amassed by industrial and business tycoons, as well as a decent standard of living for the rising middle class. The prevailing mood at the time was one of optimism and continuing progress.

But there was a darker side to this phenomenal growth. The greater prosperity brought with it a widening gulf between rich and poor—especially the poor immigrant populations that were pouring into the cities and providing the cheap labor needed to keep the factories, mines, railroads, and sweatshops operating. Most of these new immigrants were Catholics, Jews, and Orthodox, from Ireland, and eastern and southern Europe, who moved into the cities and displaced established Protestant communities, driving them out of their beautiful inner-city churches into the suburbs. Protestants were losing their monopoly on religion in America.

These massive movements and dislocations in society inevitably gave rise to the perennial urban problems of crime, poverty, ignorance, exploitation of labor, unemployment, alcoholism, prostitution, and corruption in government, together with accompanying feelings of despair and hopelessness. Progressive evangelicals wanted to address these social problems and saw this social agenda as very much in keeping with the whole history of evangelicalism in America. Thus there emerged at the end of the century the Social Gospel movement, whose most articulate and prominent representative was Walter Rauschenbusch, theologian and pastor of the Second German Baptist Church adjacent to the impoverished "Hell's Kitchen" section of Manhattan. In his 1907 book, *Christianity and the Social Crisis,* Rauschenbusch called on Christians to address the problems of the urban poor and an exploited working class in order to promote the kingdom of God on earth. (The epigraph of his book reads: "Thy Kingdom Come! Thy Will Be Done On Earth!") Rauschenbusch and the social gospelers did not deny the importance of evangelism in the church's mission, but argued for the necessity of dealing first with the corrupting influences of the social environment. The sins of society must be renounced along with the sins in the individual's past life.

> To repent of our collective social sins, to have faith in the possibility of a divine life in humanity, to submit the will to the purposes of the kingdom of God, . . . this is the most intimate duty of the religious man who would help to build the coming Messianic era of mankind.[2]

All of Jesus' actions and teachings "receive their real meaning" when viewed in relation to the kingdom of God, "the ideal human society to be established."

Instead of a society resting on coercion, exploitation, and inequality, Jesus desired to found a society resting on love, service, and equality. These new principles were so much the essence of his character and of his view of life, that he
lived them out spontaneously and taught them in everything that he touched in
his conversations or public addresses.[3]

The coming of the kingdom and the very survival of civilization depended
on whether Christians could summon the "moral strength" to deliver the
world from "social strangulation and death."

We are actors in a great historical drama. It rests upon us to decide if a new era
is to dawn in the transformation of the world into the kingdom of God, or if
Western civilization is to descend to the graveyard of dead civilizations and God
will have to try once more.[4]

Implicit in these remarks is the idea that God's redemptive work is not finished in the life and sacrificial death of Christ; the spirit of Christ continues to enter humanity as humans carry on his work of building the kingdom.
God is a copartner with us in our struggle to combat evil and the corrupting influences of society. Rauschenbusch was optimistic in his belief that
social reform and the building of the kingdom of God on earth could be
achieved within the framework of American democracy and that it was in
fact being realized in his time.

But this vision for the future of civilization was shattered by the horror
and destruction of World War I, and so, by the 1920s the Social Gospel
movement had largely disappeared. But fundamentalists, or rather their
forerunners, had never endorsed the social gospel. It was not that they had
abandoned all efforts to reform society.[5] Rather they could not accept the
idea that the salvation of individual souls somehow depended upon the redemption of society. This was backward. For them, social problems were
a consequence of the sinful choices of fallen man, and the only solution for
society's ills lay in the conversion of enough individuals to the new life in
Christ to make a difference in the affairs of men. Moreover, fundamentalists were skeptical about the ability of humans to advance the kingdom by
their own efforts. Society was in irreversible moral decline, and only a cat-
astrophic act of God at the end of time could redeem it.

Further, fundamentalists reacted strongly to the Christology implicit in
Rauschenbusch's theology. As they interpreted scripture, Christ came to
earth and gave his life to redeem sinners, not to improve society or ame-
liorate human suffering. The task he had given Christians was the Great
Commission—to preach the gospel to all the world. Liberal theology, they
claimed, weakened the divinity of Christ and the special significance of his

atoning death on the cross. Only if Jesus Christ is God incarnate can he be our savior. God acted once and for all in the death and resurrection of his son. There is nothing more for God to do except continue to offer the free gift of salvation to any who will repent of their sins and confess Christ.

In spite of the creative efforts of liberal Protestant theologians and pastors to engage with the world in thought and in practical social work, liberalism was losing ground by the 1920s. The efforts of modernists to accommodate scientific naturalism, and their willingness to let go of any supernatural interventions in human history seemed to be losing sight of an essential element of religion, namely that God is the creator and ruler of the universe who relates to humans in special revelatory acts. Moreover, the emphasis on the social gospel had made the church virtually an arm of the civil government, cooperating with state agencies to carry out social services on a voluntary basis. Even leaders within the Protestant fold came to recognize the failures of modernism. In 1935, H. Richard Niebuhr of Yale Divinity School warned that "the church is imperiled not only by an external worldliness but by one that has established itself within the Christian camp." This has happened because the church "has made compromises with the enemy in thought, in organization, and in discipline." A growing number within the church, he continued, "had heard the command to halt, to remind [themselves] of its mission, and to await further orders."[6] Niebuhr seemed to be in agreement with fundamentalists that the liberal church, in gutting orthodox belief, had relinquished what was distinctive about evangelical Christianity.

For fundamentalists, the liberal church was out of touch with the modern world. It had compromised the true meaning of the gospel to such an extent that it had no vantage point from which to call the world back from sin, and no message that could meet the real spiritual needs of the post–World War I generation and the sense of hopelessness and disillusionment that prevailed. Moreover, modernism posed a positive threat to Christians insofar as its teachings were based on a humanistic perspective that undermined their faith and trust in the revealed truths of scripture. Percy would continue to decry the pervasive influence of modernism in the churches throughout his ministry, even though, by the 1930s there was hardly anyone willing to call himself a modernist. Percy used the term as a catch-all to refer broadly to those pastors that denied, or did not give prominence to, the doctrines that were for him essential to the faith, or to those who preached that a person could get to heaven by doing good deeds or by some means other than accepting Christ as one's sin-bearer. For him, many of the nominal Christians on the Protestant church rolls needed salvation just as much as the unchurched, and a major part of his evangelistic efforts was aimed at reaching them. But the danger for fundamentalists was that by narrowing their doctrinal stance and distinguishing it so sharply from that of their modernist "enemies," they would fall into unyielding dogmatism and an inability to find common ground from which they could reason with their more moderate brethren who professed to be followers of the same Christ.

## THE ROOTS OF FUNDAMENTALISM

We have distinguished three movements within evangelical Protestantism that came together to form the fundamentalist movement: the Holiness movement, Millenarians and Dispensationalists, and Revivalists—supported by theologians from Princeton Seminary. These different groups overlapped in various ways and were not always in agreement on essential points, as we will see. Also, some groups (or some of their members) remained steadfastly within the denominational traditions while others were wholly independent. It will be helpful to give a brief sketch of each of these four strands of fundamentalism.

*

The Holiness movement emerged out of Wesleyan Methodism with its emphasis on piety and righteous living, but was also prominent among the Presbyterians and Baptists. It was also closely allied with the Keswick movement that started in England and came to this country in 1913. The adherents of holiness teachings looked for a "second experience" (after justification) called the "baptism of the Holy Spirit" in which the believer is empowered by the indwelling Spirit to become wholly surrendered to God and attain victory over sin. Some of the fundamentalist leaders associated with the Holiness and Keswick traditions were evangelist Dwight Moody and his younger associates, A. J. Gordon and Reuben Torrey, C. I. Scofield, who published the widely used Scofield Reference Bible in 1909, Charles Trumbull, editor of the popular magazine the *Sunday School Times,* and Robert McQuilkin, founder of Columbia (South Carolina) Bible School. Torrey in his writings and his sermons placed a strong emphasis on what he called the "baptism *with* the Spirit," and claimed that Moody had had such an experience and had asked Torrey, on many occasions, to preach his stock sermon on that subject.[7]

The Pentecostal movement, which achieved its own separate identity in the early 1900s, had roots in the Holiness tradition. Although it had much in common with fundamentalism in attitude and doctrine, the two movements differed sharply on the matter of the "gifts of the spirit" mentioned in the New Testament, especially physical healing and speaking in tongues, with the consequence that they developed independently along parallel tracks. As an example of this separation, BIOLA had virtually no interaction with Pentecostal Aimee Semple McPherson's Angelus Temple which practiced both faith healing and tongues and her Bible Training School, even though the two schools were geographically next-door neighbors.

\*

The millenarians had gradually formed themselves into a unitary force in a series of conferences beginning with the Niagara conferences, held at Niagara-on-the-Lake, Ontario, from 1883 to 1897, and the concurrent Bible and Prophecy Conferences, held intermittently from 1878 until the 1919 conference when the name of the prophecy conference was changed to the World Conference on Christian Fundamentals and its emphasis shifted from prophecy to defining and defending the fundamentals of the faith. According to one historian's account, fundamentalism acquired its identity (and its new name) as a result of this conference.[8]

The millenarians of this era stressed prophecy and the imminent coming of Christ and his kingdom. They embraced the *premillennial* doctrine—that Christ's return would precede the establishment of his thousand-year reign on earth—a doctrine that had come to the fore after the Civil War, and that by the turn of the century had almost completely replaced the *post-millennial* view that had prevailed in American religion since the time of Jonathan Edwards. Premillennialists tended to be pessimistic about the course of human history, believing that society was on a downward slide morally and spiritually, and that there was little that humans could do to reverse this trend before Christ's coming. Christians could take comfort in the "blessed hope" that Christ would soon return to earth and establish a just social order. Postmillennialists on the other hand believed that the coming reign of Christ would occur after humans had done much of the work to advance the kingdom.

The Dispensationalist theological view, propagated in this country by the Irish clergyman John Nelson Darby in the 1870s, held that human history was divided into seven ages or dispensations, and that God operated differently in each age. According to Darby's interpretation of scripture—a few passages in the books of Ezekiel, Daniel, and Revelation—the current age, the Age of the Church, was coming to an end with the church in ruins, and was passing into the final millennial age. Darby also advanced the novel idea of a "secret rapture" of true believers that would occur before the period of great tribulation that will precede Christ's coming. One of Darby's converts was C. I. Scofield, who incorporated dispensational-ism into the notes of his Reference Bible, giving it an aura of authority. Many fundamentalists who read the Scofield Bible (myself included) never realized that there was any distinction between Scofield's timeline and in-terpretive notes and scripture itself. By the 1920s, the dispensationalist-premillennialist synthesis had become one of the pillars of the funda-mentalist faith.

\*

Another partner in the alliance of fundamentalist forces was a group of con-servative Presbyterian theologians at Princeton Seminary. These men, led by the young New Testament scholar John Gresham Machen, gave the movement some measure of intellectual respectability. Machen was the lat-est in a century-long succession of theologians that included Archibald Alexander, Charles Hodge, his son A. A. Hodge, and Benjamin Warfield, reputed for their scholarly defense of the essential doctrines of the Re-formed (Calvinist) tradition, especially the doctrine of the verbal inspira-tion and inerrancy of scripture. Charles Hodge had also published a decisive rejection of Darwin's evolutionary theory in an important essay "What is Darwinism?" (1874), arguing that the hypothesis of natural se-lection was implicitly naturalistic and atheistic, and therefore incompatible with the supernaturalist Genesis account.

Although the Princeton traditionalists were in accord with fundamental-ists on some key points, they disagreed with them on other central doctrines such as premillennialism and the role of the individual's free decision in accepting or rejecting God's grace. However, these disagreements were overshadowed by the shared perception of both groups that they were in a life and death struggle with liberalism in the church, and that the historic, orthodox faith was in danger of being lost altogether. In his 1923 book, *Christianity and Liberalism,* Machen joined the ranks of the militant fun-damentalists, arguing strenuously that liberal theology had relinquished es-sential elements of the faith and should no longer be called Christian.

## Revivalism

The strong revivalist movement that swept through the country in the form of urban mass evangelistic efforts from Dwight Moody (1837–99) to Billy

Sunday (1862–1935) played a major role in the formation of fundamentalism. Dwight Moody has been called by one historian of this era the "principal progenitor" of the fundamentalist movement.[9] Moody moved to
Chicago in 1856 at the age of nineteen where he joined both the YMCA
and the Plymouth Congregational Church, and worked with children in the
church's Sunday school program. He soon loosened his ties with the church
and within two years erected a Sunday school building of his own for the
children of a Chicago slum area. A few years later, he founded the nondenominational Illinois Street Church (later known simply as Moody Church),
and acted as its pastor for two years until he could persuade the members
to hire a regular pastor. By this time, Moody was fully engaged in the community activities of the Chicago YMCA, rising to become its president in
1866.

With only limited experience in revivalist preaching, Moody decided in
1873 to accept an invitation to conduct revival meetings in England. He
thought it would help his meetings if he took a song leader with him
and finally settled on the music director at his church, Ira Sankey. He could
not have found a better partner; Sankey led the congregation in the singing
of old favorites and new choruses, and his own singing of inspirational
hymns softened the audience and prepared their hearts for Moody's con-
victing sermons.[10]

The Moody-Sankey duo began the tour in York and ended two years later
with five months of revival meetings in London, having held meetings in
just about every major city in the British Isles. The American press took
notice of the success of these innocents abroad, and when they returned to
the United States they were given a hero's welcome. Evangelical leaders
and church committees clamored to book them for revivalist meetings in
their cities.

Over the next two years, Moody and Sankey conducted a series of campaigns—in Brooklyn, Philadelphia, New York City, Chicago, and Boston
—that brought them national fame and raised mass evangelism to a new
level, drawing hundreds of thousands to the tabernacles and halls erected
especially for these meetings. To illustrate the scale of the meetings, the
Boston campaign ran for thirteen weeks at the Boston Tabernacle from
January to April 1877. Moody preached more than a hundred sermons to
the more than one million people who gathered to hear them with little
more than a sounding board to amplify his voice. An estimated six thousand souls were saved and many more rededicated their lives to God; these
converts (it was hoped) would go back and revitalize the spiritual life of
their churches and communities.[11]

Many church leaders at the time questioned whether Moody's spectacular results did contribute effectively to the revival of the local churches; and journalists and city officials wondered if the large number of conversions would have any lasting effect on the very real physical and social needs of their cities. It seemed to them that Moody had not done much to relieve the miserable conditions that rapid urbanization had caused for the impoverished and working-class people in the cities. Historians, too, have asked whether Moody was able to penetrate the large immigrant populations—mostly Catholics and Jews—living in the cities. The vast majority of his audiences (and his converts) were middle-class Protestants of rural background.[12]

In fact, Moody was putting the emphasis right where he wanted it to be—on the salvation of souls. He was far more interested in the eternal destiny of the individuals in his audience than in their earthly, temporal needs. This emphasis on individual salvation and neglect of social problems was strongly reinforced by his commitment to the premillennial doctrine. Moody did not expect to see the cities transformed to the shape of the kingdom by human effort. The best that men and women could do would be to take care of their own souls, and wait for Christ's coming, at which time a new order would begin.[13] As he once put it (in an oft-cited remark): "I look upon this world as a wrecked vessel. God has given me a lifeboat and said to me, 'Moody, save all you can.'"[14]

Moody's preaching style was moderate in tone, given to homely, sentimental illustrations that emphasized family ties as typified by a mother's love for her wandering child. Strongly influenced by the Holiness and Keswick teachers, he preached the positive message that the Christian could achieve victory over sin. Moody narrowed the definition of sin to those personal vices over which the individual had some control, such as drunkenness, profanity, gambling, and breaking the Sabbath, and tended to ignore social evils and injustices. If sinners would just come home, he declared, they would be transformed and become responsible family members and hardworking citizens, able to overcome temptation and contribute to society.

Theologically, Moody stressed God's love, and did not preach hell or God's wrath. "Terror never brought a man in yet," he said.[15] He was not doctrinaire or dogmatic and made it a point never to enter into theological controversy. He was definitely opposed to the theory of evolution and the higher criticism of the Bible, but restrained in his criticism of these views. He once said about the biblical critics: "Couldn't they agree to a truce, and for ten years bring out no fresh views, just to let us get on with the practical work of the kingdom."[16]

Although lacking any formal education himself, Moody took very seriously the need to train up young people for Christian service and urban evangelism. To this end, he founded a girls' school at his home base in Northfield, Massachusetts, and later, a school for boys. But his most important contribution educationally was the founding in 1889 of what came to be called the Moody Bible Institute, whose purpose was to train lay persons to do aggressive soul-saving work in the cities. Moody called these Christian workers "gap men" or "irregulars," because they were being trained to do what the educated clergy would not do—"lay their lives alongside of the laboring class and the poor and bring the gospel to bear upon their lives."[17] In addition, Moody initiated a series of summer conferences beginning in 1880 at his home in Northfield, that brought together educators and speakers from all over the world. At one of these conferences, dedicated to students, a hundred young collegians made a commitment to missionary service leading to the formation of the Student Volunteers Movement, which would send thousands of men and women to the foreign field.

When Moody suffered his fatal heart attack in 1899 during a campaign in Kansas City, Reuben Torrey, his chief associate, rushed out to finish the meetings. At the time, Torrey was superintendent of the Bible Institute and pastor of Moody Church. Two years later in 1901, Torrey received an invitation to conduct revival meetings in Australia and took this to be a sign that he had a calling to carry on Moody's evangelistic work. For the next ten years, he conducted mass revivalist meetings in the United States and abroad with hundreds of thousands in attendance and tens of thousands of souls saved. During one four-year round-the-world tour (1901–5) with soloist and song leader Charles Alexander, Torrey reported having won 102,000 converts.

Unlike Moody, Torrey had a first-rate education—at Yale College and Yale Divinity School, and studied for a year in Germany where he was exposed to the higher-critical methods of studying the Bible. However, he totally repudiated higher criticism and became an ardent defender of the old time religion and what he claimed were the literal, plain truths found in the Bible.

Torrey was more aggressively dogmatic than Moody in defending the faith, and more strident in attacking the enemies of the faith. He denounced science, evolution, philosophy, and modern progressivism, usually with superficial and crowd-pleasing arguments. His career as an evangelist came to a rather abrupt end after his song leader, Charles Alexander, left him and joined another of Moody's evangelist associates, J. Wilbur Chapman. Torrey retired from evangelism in 1911 in order to become dean at BIOLA, and Chapman became the new frontrunner in urban mass evangelism.

Beginning in 1905, Chapman promoted a new method of citywide evangelism which he called the Chapman Simultaneous Evangelistic Campaign. It consisted of dividing a city into a number of districts each of which was to conduct a revival simultaneously with every other. To achieve this he had to assemble a team of co-evangelists and singers who traveled with him from city to city. One of these assistants was Billy Sunday. In 1909, Chapman used a corps of thirty evangelists and thirty choristers in Boston for the most successful campaign of his career. In twenty-three days, over 750,000 attended a total of 990 services, with close to 7000 decisions.[18]

Chapman tended to be more intellectual than Moody, and more moderate than Torrey. He was one of the few evangelists who did not employ hard-hitting, fiery techniques in his sermons, but rather made a more pleading appeal. He did not preach hell. One journalist noted an element of pathos and tenderness in his sermons. He wanted to be known as a man who brought "spiritual dignity and grace" to revivalism.[19] Chapman and Alexander conducted successful urban campaigns and worldwide tours until 1918, but by then, Billy Sunday had taken over the top spot in evangelism in America.

Billy Sunday, the former professional baseball player, began conducting his own revivalist campaigns in Garner, Iowa, in 1896. At first, Sunday tried to imitate the dignified manner of his mentor, but very soon found that this style did not fit his personality. Instead, he cultivated his own slangy vernacular that often slipped into vulgarity and offensiveness. Sunday was a showman who introduced drama and excitement into his sermons by pounding the pulpit, standing on a chair, doing handsprings, and jumping on top of the pulpit waving an American flag.[20] He preached what one observer called a "muscular Christianity." Jesus "was no dough-faced, lickspittle proposition," he declared. "Jesus was the greatest scrapper that ever lived." The implication for prospective converts was this: "Let me tell you, the manliest man is the man who will acknowledge Jesus Christ."[21] And he preached hell, and did not hesitate to state publicly which individuals and groups were going to end up there.

Sunday perfected Chapman's techniques for the efficient management of his campaigns. He used business principles to run his organization, hiring a staff of some twenty experts to handle different aspects of his evangelistic work. The "Sunday Party" included a private secretary, advance agent, publicity manager, research assistant, assistant ministers working with special groups, chorister, soloist, and pianist.[22] He introduced various schemes aimed at increasing the free will offerings he collected at the end of each campaign, and the amounts paid to him by organizers. He angered many by getting rich from his profession.

But there was no getting around the fact that Sunday got results from the methods he used—both in saving souls and in generating religious fervor in places and churches that had gone dead. During the course of his career, Sunday claimed, he preached to one hundred million people and converted one million of them.[23] This success in soul-winning is what impressed my father about Billy Sunday more than anything else. Shortly after Sunday's death in 1935, Percy gave a sermon on the radio in which he reported having once attended one of Sunday's meetings and referred to him as "a mighty instrument in the hands of God for pulling men back from the road that leads to Hell. . . . Preached like I wouldn't preach, and I criticized him, I know it. I saw him give an invitation one night and he was boxing in the pulpit, standing there shadow-boxing, . . . but my, there were three hundred young people coming up to the altar and that's something I've never done! So I keep my mouth shut and I say only what a great man he was."[24]

There was, however, a price to pay. Sunday's theatrics and vulgar style, and his handling of finances badly damaged the image of evangelism. And the hundreds of evangelists who followed Sunday and imitated him brought the profession into even greater disrepute. Sunday's popular appeal began to fade by about 1918, although he continued to hold meetings in smaller cities and towns for another decade. (He conducted his last campaign in Mt. Holly, New Jersey, in 1930.) Many church leaders and pastors who had originally supported his evangelism gradually came to think that the negatives outweighed the positives and openly criticized him. One of these, the Methodist Episcopal bishop, Joseph F. Berry, even pronounced that "Vocational evangelism is dead."[25] William McLoughlin, in his history of modern revivalism, supports this view, arguing that "the flamboyant and high-pressure attempts to 'get results' at any cost [employed by Sunday, Chapman, Torrey, and others] had deprived the revival tradition of its last shreds of authority," and as a result, "the one hundred year tradition of modern revivalism subsided into a relatively unimportant and unsung role in the evangelical churches for thirty years after 1920."[26]

*

My father, who came to the realization that he was called to be an evangelist for the cause of Christ as a twenty-three-year-old Bible student, would not have agreed with McLoughlin's assessment of modern revivalism. He had no reason to believe that professional evangelism was dead, or even subsiding. Rather, he and his classmates at BIOLA would have thought that evangelistic revivalism was the only real hope for a "lost world" and a church that had gone astray. And like his predecessors, Percy would rely on the newest forms of mass communication to further the cause of evangelism. Just as Moody had utilized journalism and press coverage to promote his revivals, and Chapman and Sunday had employed business principles in marketing their campaigns, he and others in his generation would exploit the new mass medium of radio (and later television) to communicate the gospel, and in so doing, give new impetus to the revivalist tradition and keep mass evangelism alive. Percy never took a church as a regular pastor. Instead, from the very beginning of his ministry in 1931, his vision was to build a radio church. Radio was the instrument God would use to bring revival to the nation and the world. Billy Sunday had taken the gospel to a hundred million people in his lifetime; but Percy Crawford (*Young People's Church of the Air*) or Charles Fuller (*Old Fashioned Revival Hour*), or Walter A. Maier (*Lutheran Hour*), at the height of their ministries, could reach that many in four or five broadcasts.

# 4
## Reuben Torrey's Bible Institute

Percy ENTERED THE BIBLE INSTITUTE OF LOS ANGELES (BIOLA) IN THE FALL semester 1924, eager to find fellowship with other born-again Christians and to deepen his spiritual life. At the time of his conversion, a year earlier, the Institute was flourishing under the direction of T. C. Horton, the school's founder and superintendent, and dean Reuben Torrey. From the beginning, Horton and Torrey were in perfect agreement about the fundamentals of the faith and about giving the highest priority to soul winning, and they shaped the program accordingly.

However, by the time Percy entered the Institute, both Horton and Torrey were stepping down from their offices, and their place was being taken by Torrey's longtime friend and coworker John MacInnis, whom Torrey had just brought to the Institute (in 1921), no doubt with his own retirement in mind. Torrey also resigned as pastor of the Church of the Open Door at the same time (June 1924). During his two student years, Percy kept in close contact with Daddy Horton by staying active in the Fishermen's Club, but his main contact with Torrey was through the latter's occasional preaching and lecturing in the church and school. Torrey undoubtedly maintained a strong presence in both. Percy did become familiar enough with Torrey to have taken a snapshot of him, under which is inscribed (in his scrapbook) simply "Rev. R. A. Torrey, 1924"; but he never became friendly with Torrey in the way he did with Daddy Horton. That he held Torrey in high esteem is evident from the recognition given him in the preface to his 1935 handbook, *The Art of Fishing for Men:* "The writer is deeply indebted to the teachings of Dr. R. A. Torrey. . . . The influence of this great man of God on the writer's life was tremendous." Percy even named his second son, Richard Torrey Crawford, after this great man of God.

### REUBEN ARCHER TORREY

Reuben Archer Torrey (1856–1928) achieved eminence in the evangelical world in his several roles of preacher-evangelist intent on carrying on the

revivalist work of D. L. Moody, of Bible teacher and educator, and of pro-
lific author of semipopular religious books. He was educated at Yale College and Yale Divinity School and later studied theology for a year in
Leipzig and Erlangen, Germany. He was ordained by the Congregational
Church but very soon lost any denominational affiliation. (Once, when Torrey was asked: "What church do you belong to?" he replied without a moment's hesitation "I am an Episcopaleopresbygationalaptist.")[1] He took a
pastorate at the Open Door Church in Minneapolis and was superintendent
of the Minneapolis City Missionary Society when in 1889 Moody asked
him to be the first superintendent of his Bible Institute in Chicago. During
his tenure there he became pastor of Moody Church. When Moody suffered
his fatal heart attack during a campaign in Kansas City in 1899, Torrey went
there to finish the meetings. Soon thereafter, he decided that he would devote himself to carrying on Moody's evangelistic work and for the next ten
years conducted mass revivalist meetings in the United States and overseas
in which many thousands of souls were saved.

His pulpit manner was solemn, scholarly, and pontifical. He never joked,
and his delivery could be as stiff and austere as the wing-collar he wore;
but he was capable of animated outbursts when dealing with such urgent
matters as God's judgment and hell. Nonetheless, people flocked to his
meetings.[2]

In 1912 Torrey was persuaded to come to Los Angeles to build another
curriculum and institution in this progressive urban center like the one he
had created at Moody Bible Institute, and the Bible Institute of Los Angeles quickly became the equal in influence of Moody.[3] He stayed until 1924,
when, at age sixty-eight, he decided to devote the rest of his life to evangelistic and Bible conference work.

Torrey played an important role in formulating the core doctrines and
public stances that shaped fundamentalism in the first quarter of the twentieth century, even before the movement was called by that name. He was
one of three editors of *The Fundamentals: A Testimony to the Truth* (published 1910–15), a twelve-volume series financed by Lyman Stewart and
sent out free of charge to every pastor, missionary, theology professor and
student, YMCA and YWCA secretary, Sunday school superintendent, and
religious editor in the English-speaking world. Some three million individual volumes were sent out altogether. Torrey himself was one of the
sixty-four authors who contributed essays to these volumes.[4]

Further, Torrey played a leading role in organizing the important 1919
World Conference on Christian Fundamentals in Philadelphia, which
marked the beginning of the movement as a cohesive unit. Other key leaders at that conference were William Bell Riley and Charles Blanchard, and

it is noteworthy that each of them represented independent schools—
Torrey, as Dean at BIOLA, Riley, president of the Northwestern Bible and
Missionary Training School in Minneapolis, and Blanchard, president of
Wheaton College. Planning for the meeting took place at Torrey's summer
home at the Montrose, Pennsylvania, conference grounds the previous
summer, and he and Riley each delivered two of the twenty-five addresses
at the conference. Riley used the occasion to form the World's Christian
Fundamentals Association, which took as its immediate goal the continuation of revivalism across the nation. And Blanchard drafted a nine-point
doctrinal statement, which articulated fundamentalist beliefs, and some
version of which soon became the accepted creed of many fundamentalist
schools, including BIOLA and Wheaton.

In the previous decade, conservatives generally had accepted as their
creed the five-point statement adopted by the General Assembly of the
Presbyterian Church in 1910, in which the following doctrines were declared to be essential: the inerrancy of scripture, the virgin birth of Christ,
the substitutionary atonement of Christ, the bodily resurrection of Christ,
and the miracle-working power of Christ.[5] Along with these, the nine-point
statement affirmed the sinful nature of all human beings, the experience of
the new birth for "all who receive by faith the Lord Jesus Christ," the "personal, premillennial, and imminent return" of Christ, and "the everlasting,
conscious punishment of the lost."[6]

By the 1920s, Torrey had earned a reputation as an outspoken and militant defender of the faith in the famous fundamentalist-modernist "wars."
Heated exchanges were occurring between leaders of the two camps. Fundamentalists aimed their most pointed attacks at the two leading representatives of modernism, Shailer Mathews, Dean of Chicago Divinity School,
and his colleague, Shirley Jackson Case. In addition, Harry Emerson Fosdick, pastor at First Presbyterian Church in New York City, provoked in-
dignant responses from many quarters with his 1922 sermon "Shall the
Fundamentalists Win?" which condemned fundamentalists for their intol-
erance.

In 1917, Torrey had entered the fray with the modernists at the Chicago
Divinity School by writing a stinging refutation of a pamphlet that Shailer
Mathews had published entitled "Will Christ Come Again?" which denied
the literal second coming of Christ. Torrey's rebuttal, entitled "Will Christ
Come Again? An Exposure of the Foolishness, Fallacies and Falsehoods of
Shailer Mathews," denounced Mathews the man, and accused him of du-
plicitous motives. Mathews's tactic of substituting his own interpretations
and meanings for "the plain and crystal clear teaching of the Bible," Torrey exclaimed, is a "sneaking and cowardly infidel method," and can only

be taken as "dishonoring" and "discrediting" the words of Christ and the apostles. Torrey concluded that the pamphlet, as a whole, is a "mass of il-logical arguments, gross misrepresentations, demonstrable falsehoods, and rank blasphemies."[7] This was the sort of invective that my father grew accustomed to hearing from Torrey. Although Percy liked his teacher's hard-hitting, denunciatory language, he knew that it was not helping the fundamentalist cause and was clear in his own mind that he had to take a very different tack.

## THE CITY OF ANGELS

We may wonder why Torrey was drawn to Los Angeles. It may be that he simply wanted a new challenge after a twenty-two-year relationship with Moody Bible Institute; but it seems that another reason for leaving Chicago was the lure of the city of Los Angeles. This is suggested by his descrip-tion of the city in the 1923 BIOLA Bulletin where he lists for prospective students the "Advantages and Privileges" of attending the Institute. The primary advantage is the school's location. He mentions first the "health-ful climate" of the region: "Many coming to Los Angeles in run-down physical condition, soon regain abounding health." (The corpulent, over-stressed Torrey may have been one of these.) He goes on to extol the city's other attractions, placing them in the context of the opportunities they af-ford for Christian work. Students will be able to work among a heteroge-neous population—"Spanish-speaking people of Mexico, Central and South America, and among Koreans, Chinese, Japanese, and Hindoos." He concludes that there is no "other city on the globe where there is at the pres-ent time so great a need on the one hand, and on the other, so great an op-portunity and promise, for sound and solid Bible work and aggressive Christian effort."

What Torrey does not mention, however, is that the rapid growth of the city and the influx of diverse populations had made Los Angeles a fertile ground for religious enthusiasts of all stripes. The population had increased tenfold between 1890 and 1920—from fifty thousand to over five hundred thousand, and it would rise to over a million by the end of the decade. These newcomers were people of varying ethnic, religious, and cultural back-grounds, all trying to better themselves in some way by exploiting the rich opportunities that this booming frontier city proferred. They came in pur-suit of health or fortune, or just a more comfortable environment in which to live out their days. They would have expected to have more excitement in their lives in this entertainment capital of the world. Most of these seekers were, like my father, in need of something that would bring a sense of permanence and stability to their lives.

Preachers and revivalists were passing through and Angelenos flocked to hear them, as much to be entertained as to be spiritually uplifted. New sects and independent churches were being formed regularly, especially among Holiness and Pentecostal groups. In 1906, the sensational African American Pentecostal preacher, William Joseph Seymour, received national attention with his revival meetings on Azusa Street, where an interracial group of worshipers practiced the New Testament "gifts of the Spirit" and made overt displays of ecstatic experience that led critics to refer to them as "Holy Rollers." The uneducated, ex-slave Seymour, who was himself capable of powerful eruptions on stage, shared the pulpit with his followers, and looked on as black and white men and women prayed, preached, wept, quaked, hugged and kissed each other, and spoke in tongues. Even some Pentecostal clergy worried that Seymour's brand of worship was excessive.[8]

Another Pentecostal who came to Los Angeles in the early 1920s was the itinerant evangelist and faith healer, Aimee Semple McPherson. The Canadian-born McPherson had conducted revivalist meetings in tents and tabernacles all across North America and in Australia before finally deciding to make Los Angeles her permanent base of operations. She had previously held successful campaigns in Los Angeles, including one in 1917 which was the last leg of a cross-country tour in her "gospel car" from New York to Los Angeles. On January 1, 1923—the same year that Percy arrived in Los Angeles—McPherson dedicated her fabulous dome-shaped, fifty-three-hundred-seat Angelus Temple, built at a cost of $1.2 million dollars. A few months later she opened the Evangelistic and Missionary Training Institute, whose curriculum, doctrinal statement, and overall mission was practically identical to BIOLA's.[9]

McPherson's charismatic personality and dramatized sermons set against elaborate Hollywood-type props, together with her faith-healing services, soon drew a large and devoted following. The response was so overwhelming that the evangelist could write in the church's magazine, *The Bridal Call,* just three months after the opening of the temple:

> We are now living in the very heat of a most mighty and notable revival. Its power and influence are flowing out through the community, city and state. . . . Like great tidal-waves that eddy and surge, the multitudes throng Angelus Temple at Echo Park and go forth, His praise to swell.[10]

Yet Torrey and the fundamentalists at BIOLA seemed utterly oblivious to the whirl of religious activity going on around them. Even though Aimee

Semple McPherson proclaimed the same gospel message, adhered to the same doctrines (including premillenialism), denounced the same enemies, railed against the same social evils, emphasized the baptism of the Holy Spirit, and most importantly, made conversion and the salvation of souls the main point of her preaching, still the Biolans would not cooperate with her church or her Bible school, or even so much as acknowledge their existence. The chief obstacle to any cooperation, I believe, lay in McPherson's practice of faith healing and her condoning of tongues.[11]

We can get some idea of the official position at BIOLA regarding tongues from an article written by A. C. Dixon for *The King's Business* in 1922, "Speaking with Tongues: The Plain Replies of the Word of God to some Modern and Dangerous Views of the Matter." Dixon was another one of Dwight Moody's protégés and a colleague of Torrey on the BIOLA faculty from 1919 to 1921. In the article, he tries to minimize the importance of tongues by pointing out that the Word of God "places the gift of tongues at the bottom of the list of the Spirit's gifts and plainly tells us that it is not one of the best gifts; that speaking God's message in a language that can be understood is better" (I Corinthians 12:28, 14:5). Further, "seeking a spectacular display of the Holy Spirit's work is not of God," because the Bible warns against "disorderly confusion" (I Corinthians 14:40, 14:33); and moreover such seeking is unnecessary since "the Holy Spirit is with us all the time, ready to use us just as we yield ourselves to Him."

Dixon concludes with a revealing passage indicating one way in which fundamentalism tended to discount emotionalism and uphold rationalism: "There is an experience of ecstatic, rhapsodical joy [he states] which is inexpressible in connected language." It is a purely personal experience "between the soul and God," but the one who has it "knows the reasons for such exuberant joy and should be able to give those reasons to others," that is, express them in intelligible language to others.[12] While Dixon, in this article, may have succeeded in arming the Biolans with scripture verses that justified their stand against spectacular displays of emotion, his claim that the practices of the Pentecostals are not "of God" surely went too far and simply illustrates how narrowly the fundamentalists at BIOLA were defining their faith.[13]

\*

Torrey's influence on my father came mainly through his preaching and his writings. Percy was able to hear him preach at the Church of the Open Door for more than two years before Torrey left Los Angeles and moved to Ashville, North Carolina. During that period, his sermon topics ranged widely, but most of them had a practical "how-to" emphasis with such titles as "The Way of Salvation Made as Plain as Day," "How to Pray so as to Know That Your Prayer Is Heard and the Thing Granted even before You Obtain It," "Everyone Who Professes to Be a Christian Should Make Soul-Winning the Principal Business of His Life," and (on Easter) "Seven Tremendously Important Facts Proved by the Resurrection of Jesus Christ." His farewell message on Sunday evening, June 22, 1924, was entitled "Goodbye to the People of Los Angeles: How to Get Joy Unspeakable and Full of Glory."

Percy responded to Torrey's style and his message as he had to Willie Nicholson's. He liked the way Torrey could communicate the meaning of the gospel in simple, unequivocal terms. Torrey believed that it did not take any special training or insight to understand scripture; "In ninety-nine out of a hundred cases [he wrote] the meaning that the plain man gets out of the Bible is the correct one."[14] Torrey was decisive and seemed to have answers to every question and every problem based solely on what was contained in the Bible. Eager to learn, Percy quickly came to see him as an authority and as the model of what it meant to be an educated Christian scholar.

Percy also delved into some of the voluminous writings of Torrey that were available cheaply in the BIOLA Book Room. At the top of the list was his *How to Bring Men to Christ* (1893), a manual that laid out the general conditions that one must satisfy in order to achieve "real success in bringing men to Christ."[15] In his zealous efforts to win souls, Percy made good use of Torrey's classification of the types of respondents one might encounter in personal work and strategies for dealing with them. Another resource was Torrey's grand theological treatise, *What the Bible Teaches* (1898), which would have been required reading for every Torrey student. This book arranged thousands of Scripture verses under "propositions," which were then subsumed under the general headings: What the Bible Teaches about God, Christ, the Holy Spirit, man, angels, and Satan. Percy received his first introduction to systematic theology from this book, and it gave him the general framework he used to study the Bible throughout his entire ministry.

A third writing, in which the budding evangelist would have had a keen interest, was the booklet *Why God Used D. L. Moody* (1923), which set out the qualities Moody possessed that explained why he "had that power of God so wonderfully manifested in his life."[16] Torrey describes Moody as one who was a fully surrendered man, a man of prayer, a deep and practical student of the Bible, a humble man, free of the love of money, consumed with a passion for the salvation of the lost, and endued with power from on high. Percy would make a deliberate effort to cultivate these traits during his time at the Institute in order to make himself a fit instrument for God's use.

## THE CALL TO EVANGELISM

The Bible Institute of Los Angeles was a Bible school that advertised itself as offering "an unparalleled opportunity to obtain thorough, practical and efficient Bible training and a practical knowledge of missionary work," both at home and in the foreign field.[17] The 1923 bulletin that Percy would have used in making his decision to attend BIOLA outlined the Institute's goals and the basic program of study. The overall objective was to send out men and women with these characteristics:

1. genuine and thorough consecration
2. intense love for souls
3. a deep and comprehensive knowledge of the Word of God, and especially of how to use it in leading men to Christ
4. willingness to endure hardness as good soldiers of Jesus Christ
5. untiring energy
6. well balanced common sense, especially along religious lines
7. enduement with power by the filling with the Holy Spirit[18]

These goals were roughly coordinate with the conditions that were necessary to be successful in bringing people to Christ and with the qualities that enabled Moody to be used of God. The Institute attempted to instill these qualities in its students through its Bible-based teaching and by creating the sort of atmosphere in the students' daily lives that would encourage them.

In the two-year program that Percy (and every regular student) enrolled in, the core course extending over both years was called the "Doctrinal Study of the Bible." The course had always been taught by Torrey but was now taken over by his successor John MacInnis. In addition to Bible doctrine, other required courses (all of which appear on Percy's official transcript) included "Bible Analysis," "Bible Synthesis," "Bible Chapter Summary," "Origin and Development of the Christian Religion," "Philosophy of the Christian Religion," and a comparable number of practical courses, including "Evangelism" and "Personal Work." The only surprising class on the transcript is Conducting I, in which he received an A–.

Another section of the bulletin describes the "devotional life" that was fostered among the resident students. Definite times before and after meals were set aside for prayer, testimony, and devotional Bible study. "[One] daily feature of great helpfulness is the corridor prayer meeting. The students on each corridor gather in a student's room at whatever hour is most convenient to discuss their perplexing personal problems and to present them to God for solution. It is here, as perhaps at no other gathering, that definiteness in prayer is learned."[19]

Further, there was a requirement of "practical work": "Students are required to attend and assist in missions, street meetings, tent meetings, to visit people in their homes, to conduct adult Bible classes and Sunday school classes, and to engage in various other forms of aggressive Christian work, and always with their eyes open for opportunities for personal work."[20]

For young Percy, the requirement of practical work simply meant a continuation of the witnessing and personal work he had been doing with the Fishermen's Club. But the Institute afforded him the opportunity to try other forms of service, and in his first year he joined the Men's Glee Club under the direction of John Bissel Trowbridge; over the Christmas holidays the choir toured up the Pacific Coast as far as Portland, performing a rich selection of vocal and instrumental music at twenty-five churches and schools. The concert tour was valuable to Percy in giving him exposure to excellent musical performance and also the experience of going on the road with an evangelistic purpose.

Percy continued to do personal work and gradually improved in his ability to preach. But going out and preaching in the street was not always easy; often these ventures ended in disappointment and failure. Percy wrote about this time in his life:

> I recall how God tested me a few years ago in Los Angeles. I had to show Him that I was willing to set aside my pride and go out on the street corner by myself with the cornet and have my own street meeting. I didn't love it! I was laughed at, but God was testing me. It was the road up, for to be used of Him we must be humble as the Son of God Himself.[21]

In order to bring unregenerate people to Christ, he had to find a way to get their attention and hold it long enough to convey to them the simple gospel message. A few trying experiences with his cornet probably convinced him early on that he should go out with musicians who could attract an audience and set the stage for his preaching. This he did, and he began to win some souls.

Faculty members and students at the Institute put a lot of stress on whether one was "fully surrendered" or "fully yielded" to God. Torrey in particular emphasized this as one of the preconditions of being "filled with the Holy Spirit," as in this passage from *How to Bring Men to Christ:*

> The condition of the gift of the Holy Ghost here stated [Acts 5:32] is that we "obey Him." Obedience means more than the mere performance of some of the things that God bids us do. It means the entire surrender of our wills, ourselves and all we have, to Him. It means that we come to Him and say from the heart, "here I am, I am thine, thou hast bought me with a price, I acknowledge thine ownership. Take me, do with me what thou wilt, send me where thou wilt, use me as thou wilt." This entire yielding of ourselves to God is the condition of our receiving the Baptism of the Holy Spirit, and it is at this point that many fail of this blessing.[22]

Percy wrestled with this injunction to be fully surrendered to God. He tells us that he felt buffeted by the many different "lessons" that were being taught at the Institute and then goes on to describe how they led him to an important second experience of rededication:

> Missionary messages were heard from time to time and the Lord began dealing with me as to whether I was willing to go. I felt I could not be in the place of usefulness unless I was seriously willing to go to Africa. Africa was selected because it was thought in my mind to be the hardest field in the world. Finally one day I was reading in my New Testament (it was a day of prayer and I had decided that day to read the whole New Testament through in one day) . . . where it says "Launch out into the deep." . . . That was what I needed. . . . Was I willing to go to Africa? There in my room, alone and on my knees I said "Yes" to the Lord. What a joy came over my soul. I went up to the library and got books on Africa, *Thinking Black* by Dan Crawford,[23] and other wonderful books, but God didn't let me go. But it was only when I was willing to go that He was ready to use me. Before, I had gotten a soul here and a soul there, but now when I went out and gave my testimony, quite a difference. It seemed the Spirit of God had filled me, and blessed the message as never before. God was giving me a dozen souls here and a dozen souls there.[24]

It was not until the summer of 1925, after finishing his first year at the Institute, that Percy preached his first sermon. We know this from the inscription written under a picture of himself, taken at about that time, which says: "August 16, my first sermon, 500 congregation." That picture shows the aspiring preacher, dressed in a nicely fitting suit and bowtie, looking cheerfully optimistic and very satisfied with himself.

It was about this time that Percy organized a quartet and started going out to meetings on Sundays. The team also appeared on BIOLA's radio station, KTBI, giving Percy his first experience preaching to a radio audience.[25] The Institute had started a radio station on March 10, 1922, which it claimed was "the first strictly religious broadcasting station to be licensed in the United States, if not in the world."[26] In 1924 the ten-watt station was increased to 750 watts power and for more than a year was "the most powerful broadcasting station west of the Mississippi river." In 1923 the station manager reported that their signal could be heard clearly from Canada in the north to Mexico in the south and from Hawaii in the west to New Hampshire in the east.[27]

Both Torrey and Horton had questioned the advisability of starting a radio station at the Institute when it was first proposed to them, but they finally acceded. Eighteen months after the station went on the air, in an editorial in *The King's Business* (September 1923), Horton outlined seven reasons why he thought radio should not be used as a medium to advertise the gospel, arguing that "the devil is the prince of the power of the air," but concluded by giving a cautious endorsement.

Percy did not share these misgivings. He never thought that radio was the special province of the devil. He saw it as just another marvelous invention that could be used to propagate the gospel. His view of radio reflected more the outlook of Aimee Semple McPherson, who had launched her radio station KFSG (FourSquare Gospel) on February 6, 1924, a year after the inauguration of the Angelus Temple. The opening ceremonies for the station with its two 125-foot towers "reaching to heaven" were conducted in an atmosphere of celebratory joy. An impressive lineup of the city's civic and religious leaders were present and taking part in the dedication. The first words heard over the air were those of the evangelist reading from scripture (John 3:16).

In a series of articles in *The Bridal Call* leading up to the grand opening, McPherson explained to her followers what the new invention would mean for her ministry. Radio would carry the gospel to vast new audiences that otherwise would never hear it—over land and sea, mountain and desert, to the hospital patient and the cripple in the wheelchair, to the business man as he sits at his luncheon, and to the housewife as she sweeps the floor and washes the dishes.[28] She deplored the fact that Hollywood had already co-opted the "moving pictures" and asked:

> Shall we let them have the Radio too? Or shall we say: "No, this is Father's Air and Earth, and we will send the Message upon its breezes to spread the Gospel in this wholesale and miraculous manner.[29]

And she marveled at the new medium and its potential for evangelism:

These are the days of invention! The days when the impossible has become possible! Days more favorable than any that have ever been known for the preaching of the blessed Gospel of our Lord and Saviour, Jesus Christ!

Here it stands beside me; and my soul is thrilled with the possibilities which I see in it.[30]

Percy would have been fascinated by Aimee Semple McPherson as a personality, and the sensational events she was caught up in while he was in Los Angeles; but he would have had great difficulty acknowledging her authority as an evangelist. Temperamentally, he needed a more masculine version of the Christian message, and a more aggressive style of delivering it, than McPherson offered. And theologically, he preferred Torrey's version of God the Father, who judged and chastened his children, to McPherson's loving Father of air and earth.[31] But it is hard to see how Percy could have avoided listening to her station and hearing her captivating sermons during his time there. And I imagine that he took more from this celebrity preacher than he realized, including his appreciation of the amazing potential of radio to carry the gospel to the unsaved.

*

Percy's commitment to evangelism and his clear sense of purpose were evidenced in the speech he gave at graduation representing the thirty-one "men graduates" of BIOLA's class of 1926. In it, the twenty-three-year-old reminded his classmates that the first and necessary condition of a life of service is to be totally surrendered to God. He looks back to Moody as his model and inspiration:

When Mr. D. L. Moody was a young man, someone said to him, "The world has yet to see what can be done through a life fully yielded to Jesus Christ." Moody replied, "By the grace of God I'll be that man." So we tonight . . . have been saved through faith in Christ as Saviour and Lord, and now desire to be fully yielded to Him that He may use us to present his claims to men.[32]

He suggests that the mission to which these men are called is somehow new and great:

We have no desire, as the apostle Peter had, to go back to the old nets, nor have we merely a desire to be hewers of wood and drawers of water, as the Midianites of old. Ours is a great calling, namely to "Go into all the world and preach the gospel" pointing lost men and women to the Lamb of God that taketh away the sin of the world.

And they would be empowered in carrying out this mission by Christ himself: "Just as he said to his disciples before His ascen[s]ion, He has said to us, 'But ye shall receive power, after that the Holy Ghost is come upon you; and ye shall be witnesses unto me.'" And then, speaking just about himself, he describes (in the third person) how he had come to Los Angeles and "found himself in the midst of strangers." But "the Lord led him to the Bible Institute and within three days God graciously saved him and tonight he leaves this Institution with a great desire in his heart that God may use him in His great vineyard." One senses in the young man's remarks not only a zealous commitment to serve the Lord, but a great hope and expectation that God would use him in some special way to accomplish his work.

In the summer of 1926, after graduation, Percy took his gospel team on the road. His quartet consisted of fellow students Harlan Fischer, Ward Altig, I. A. Moon, and William Shipcott. Calling themselves the Los Angeles Quintet, they did a ten-week tour up the Pacific Coast, covering fourteen hundred miles in a Dodge touring car, with meetings in forty-two towns and cities. The team crossed over into Canada and held some meetings in Vancouver, British Columbia, where the spiritually reborn Percy was reunited with family and friends. The tour was by all counts a huge success. One bulletin from the Whitman Memorial Church in Seattle said:

> The visit of the Los Angeles Bible Institute Gospel Team is drawing large audiences and we expect capacity crowds today. We wish the "Boys" could have remained longer but their schedule for this month is filled. They form a splendid evangelistic group and all our people have been delighted with the songs rendered and testimonies and addresses given. The chief speaker, Percy Crawford, proclaims gospel with no uncertain sound. We have felt the presence and power of God in these services and are sure much good has been accomplished.

And Percy, on this his first evangelistic tour, must have been buoyed up by a letter received from a contact person in Ellensburg, Washington, where the team's reputation evidently preceded them; it read in part:

> Sunday night our pastor is booking you here at the big Chautauqua tent. They have wired Portland to call off Billy Sunday and want you boys. They will announce it every night at Chautauqua and yours will be the crowning event. Billy S. was here two years ago but gave sort of a lecture and no altar call. The ministers here are evangelistic and long for a spiritual awakening, and the low ebb of spirituality here is the burden on their hearts. . . . The Lord is paving the way and this is an opportunity for you.[33]

But for Percy and the gospel team, by far the most important measure of success, and indeed the only one that really mattered, was the number of souls saved. Percy was counting, and the number of professions he recorded for that tour (in his calendar book) was thirteen hundred. There is no way of verifying the accuracy of this figure, but even if it is inflated, it is an astonishingly large number of professions for a neophyte preacher, speaking at largely evangelical churches. By the end of this tour, only three years after his conversion, Percy knew that he had a gift for evangelism and that this is how God would use him. And he was chafing at the bit to do more of it.[34]

\*

Percy's experience at the Bible Institute from 1924 to 1926 had a profound effect on him. First, he received the deep immersion in the Bible he was looking for. Second, he absorbed the particular set of beliefs that characterized what was coming to be known as fundamentalism—mainly through Reuben Torrey's and T. C. Horton's instruction. In addition, he cultivated there the attitudes fostered by the fundamentalistic outlook—a fully surrendered life and a passion for souls. In the process, it became clear to him who the opponents of the faith were: within the church it was the modernists and liberals; and without, it was secular science—in particular, evolutionary theory based on a false philosophy of social progress.

Finally, and most importantly, the Institute, with its strong practical orientation, was an ideal training ground where Percy could hone his skills and find his direction. It afforded him the opportunity to go out into the street, into missions and jails, and acquire the art of fishing for men. It gave him his first exposure to radio in its earliest phases and how it could be used for evangelism. It guided him in formulating his message and the manner in which he would present it. Indeed, by the time he left the Bible Institute in September 1926, the contours of his thinking and the style of his preaching were in place and would not undergo any significant change throughout his life.

# 5

## UCLA: "Atheism Was Rampant"

WHEN IT CAME TIME TO LEAVE THE SAFE HAVEN OF THE BIBLE INSTITUTE, Percy had to decide whether he would continue with his education or go directly into full-time evangelistic work. He must have been tempted by the latter course, because he knew that he was called to evangelism and he was confident of his ability to preach and win souls. But in fact he had no trouble making the decision (as he said) to seek "more preparation before entering active Christian work." He often gave this analogy to explain his decision:

Awhile back when I . . . was at the point when I was considering a college education, Dr. Chafer, of Dallas [Theological Seminary], gave me a very striking illustration that mean[t] a great deal in shaping my plans for life. He said in the olden days at the sound of the fire bell in a fire house the horses would automatically rush to the front of the fire house and stand until the harness was dropped upon them and then they would dash off to the fire pulling the fire engine with them. Suppose, said he that the horses were quite anxious to get to the fire one day and instead of waiting for the harness to fall on them and be buckled, just as soon as the doors swung open they should dash to the fire alone, only to find out upon arrival at the fire that they had nothing to fight it with. This is what a lot of young people do today.[1]

Although Percy was fully satisfied with the Bible training he had received at the Institute, he realized it was not enough. Later on, in a sermon he gave after he had founded his own Christian college, he looked back on his motives for going on to the university and then seminary and graduate school. The sermon was on the topic of hell:

I used to preach on this subject shortly after I was converted and people used to belittle me. Some would say, "Oh, he's just a Bible School student. He doesn't know any better. . . ." Others said, "He's not a college man. He doesn't know that men of intellect do not believe in a hell." "Well," I said to myself, "I'll get an education, cost what it may." [He then described the educational path he took.] I tell you that purposely so that you cannot rate me down, for what I am going to say I have weighed very carefully and studied for the past fifteen years.[2]

Clearly, Percy thought his message would be discounted, and therefore less effective, if he did not have a college degree. He wanted the respect that comes with having good credentials. "History proves that the men God used were educated men," he would say later, probably thinking of Torrey.[3]

Further, Percy wanted to have the knowledge that would enable him to give authoritative answers to questions and challenges. He had learned from Torrey and MacInnis that the philosophy of the Christian religion was the most rationally defensible of all systems of belief, and he wanted to be able to marshal the evidence and give the arguments himself that would show this. He wanted to put his theological convictions on a solid intellectual footing. In another sermon, speaking about his seminary training, he said this: "The Bible either *is* or it *isn't* the Word of God. One reason why I took so much time to study the Greek, and went to Seminary and dug into chapter after chapter, [was] so that I might prove to myself that it *is* wholly the Word."[4]

But in order to be an "educated man," he needed to get his bachelor of arts degree at the university. And he chose to go across town to the University of California[5] along with his close friend and fellow BIOLA graduate, Harlan Fischer, who had been a member of his gospel team.[6] It is harder to explain why Percy chose to go on at a secular university. He knew what he would find there—an approach to learning that gave no special privilege to his belief in God, the redeemer of humanity, and would probably even be disdainful of the idea. The prestige of the university may have been a factor; Percy always intended to take on the challenge of the best education available to him. But there was also the element of fascination, of wanting to find out what the secular world had to offer, and to put his own beliefs to the test, to see if they could stand up against secular alternatives. In a word, Percy entered UCLA expecting to encounter a hostile environment and prepared to do battle with it. And he got just what he was expecting.

He describes what he found there in one of his earliest surviving sermons, "Did the University Make Me an Atheist?," written while he was still in seminary: "Atheism was rampant. It seemed as though the whole student body was hostile to the things I loved."[7] He goes on to describe the atheistic views of some of his professors and the way they attacked Christian beliefs, which he saw as a concerted effort on their part to undermine his faith. He tells of a particularly intense encounter he had with a psychology professor that affected him deeply and became for him a kind of symbol of his whole university experience:

The courses were arranged so as to throw the incoming students off their guard. The President of the University personally saw to it, in his Psychology class, that the freshmen were enlightened and given the proper perspective. We were taught that we should ever keep an open mind; never to allow ourselves to become narrow and bigotted by set beliefs of our forefathers. . . . [The President] instructed us, in commenting on the prodigal son, that the idea of the new birth was all wrong for we had advanced far beyond that today. We now see that such primitive ideas are false. Such was his subtle attempt to attack and undermine our Christian position.

The course Percy describes was a one-credit course required of all freshmen called "The Psychology of Study," taught by Dr. Ernest Carroll Moore, whose training was in the fields of education and philosophy. Percy saw his professor's emphasis on putting all of one's beliefs in question as a direct challenge to the certainty of the new birth, and the brazen freshman would not stand for this:

This continued until one day, in class, I felt constrained to object. . . . I stood to my feet and said "Gladstone once said, 'Give me one illustration, and it is better than a thousand reasons.' So it is," said I, "with the new birth. When you see men taken out of the gutter and transformed through the power of Christ, who is any little frenchman [an unidentified authority the professor had referred to] that he should deny it. The fact remains that God does work miracles by transforming lives." To my amazement, the whole class of seven hundred burst out clapping much to the chagrin of the President.

For this experienced personal worker, the results he had witnessed of actual cases of conversion were far more credible than any general reasons the professor might give for doubting the Bible and its truth. The lowly freshman had rebutted the learned professor, and the class applauded him, probably more for his courage than the cogency of his argument. But this was not the end of it; the exchange became even more confrontational in a follow-up letter:

His atheistic philosophy continued. He taught that the modern scientific mind doubted everything. . . . I replied by way of letter saying that there were certain things God had been pleased to reveal to man which man would not have known otherwise. These, I felt, should be treated with respect if not reverence and not doubted till there was some reason for doubt. "Would you," I asked, "doubt the purity of your own mother?" . . . It seemed to me that his aim was to dislodge us from our position of trust in the scriptures and to place ourselves over them as a judge. I would object to the virtue and truthfulness of my friend being interr[o]gated without cause so I believed I had much more reason to object to the doubting of the words of my Lord who said "Thy word is truth." Doubt would destroy confidence and without confidence I would be hopelessly at sea.

. . . Basic in all the courses was the idea that man was autonomous and must sit in judgment on all the facts even on God himself.[8]

Much is revealed in this account about my father's beliefs and his approach to education. In the first place, I believe, he correctly identified what is the hallmark of a liberal arts education—that one should be willing to hold *any* of one's beliefs open to rational scrutiny. This tradition of rational inquiry has come down to us in the West from the ancient Greeks and also from the Enlightenment thinkers of the eighteenth century. It is a tradition that was embraced by most evangelical and Reformed theologians in the nineteenth century and strongly influenced Reuben Torrey in particular. Percy fully accepted from Torrey the idea that the basic tenets of his faith, such as the divine authority of Scripture, were rationally provable by the standards of natural reason. Indeed it is noteworthy that Percy does not simply reject the professor's views as those of an atheist or an infidel, but attempts to counter them with arguments for his own contrary position. In doing so, he is playing by the university's rules of entering into rational debate and giving reasons. Nevertheless, he rejects the idea that all our beliefs should be put in question until they are certified or grounded in reason. He makes the point that there are many things that we accept without proof on the basis of some authority or testimony and that it is reasonable to do so as long as there is no reason for doubting them. (Would you doubt the integrity of a friend without cause?) Similarly, it is not unreasonable, he claims, for Christians to trust in the Scriptures and accept the things that God has revealed in them, as long as there is no good reason to doubt them.[9]

Percy had accomplished a great deal in this exchange with Dr. Moore. He had stood up to an authority figure who represented for him the modern, atheistic, scientific worldview and had successfully countered his position with an argument that safeguarded the Christian's right to believe the Bible's claim to truth. He had now put the burden of proof on his opponent to produce reasons for doubting or disbelieving the authenticity of the Bible. As we will see in a later chapter, Percy thought that he could answer and refute any of the skeptic's counterarguments, and he attempted to do so in the little book he wrote eight years later on fishing for men.

\*

After the close fellowship and spiritual warmth that prevailed at BIOLA, Percy found the atmosphere at UCLA cold and barren. He tried out for the tennis team, thinking that "it would be a real honor among six thousand students to make the team" and that this would enhance his Christian witness, but he failed to make the team.[10] He lacked motivation in his studies because all of his classes seemed to be couched in an atheistic framework. Harlan Fischer recalled those first weeks: "We felt crushed and hemmed in by this anti-Christian spirit that permeated the campus. We needed the warmth and friendship of other Christians. Everything was pulling the opposite way. We needed each other."[11]

So Percy and Harlan and another BIOLA grad, James Carter, started meeting at the noon hour at the YMCA near the campus for prayer and Bible study. Soon they were joined by a few others. Since this initial group was made up of soul winners, Percy apparently made some initial moves to organize the group into a Fishermen's Club. But the idea was short-lived because, after only a few weeks, Percy became so dissatisfied with his situation that he officially withdrew from the university (September 30) and repaired to BIOLA. Carter also returned to BIOLA, leaving the club and its mission in the hands of Harlan Fischer who was doing a much better job of functioning in a secular environment. Harlan found some others who were interested in Bible study, and soon they started talking about forming a Greek letter fraternity. Over the Christmas holidays, Harlan brought together some sixteen men, and that group decided that their organization would gain "more prestige and influence on the campus" if they established a fraternity than if they remained a Christian club. Out of that meeting came the Alpha Gamma Omega Christian fraternity, still in existence today.[12] The first official meeting of the fraternity was held at the beginning of the second semester, February 25, 1927, with twelve men signing on as charter members. Harlan Fischer was elected president. However, Harlan wrote, "One [of the twelve] dropped out as he did not agree with our purpose. Percy returned for the second semester so we made him a charter member and gave him the number 12."[13] So it is not clear whether Percy took part in these organizational meetings.

The prospect of being involved with this new Christian fraternity may have been a factor in Percy's decision to reenter UCLA for the second semester. He signed up for roughly the same schedule of courses: geology, philosophy, history, public speaking, military science, and, as required, another dose of Dr. Moore's psychology class. Things went a little better for him this time around. He was active in the fraternity, which held regular meetings with guest speakers and sponsored social events with a Christian sorority. Later on, during his ministry, Percy often boasted about the fraternity in his sermons and his part in its formation (which was not very great). He mentioned it in order to show how university students who excelled in sports and academics still had the courage to "show their colors" and take a definite stand for Christ, even while they met with ridicule and scorn from their classmates. He was emphasizing that it takes courage to be a Christian. In one sermon, he told the story of the time he and Harlan were walking down a street in Los Angeles carrying their Bibles and noticed that "everybody was looking at us, peeking around at us." Harlan (who, Percy noted, was a boxer) commented: "You know what it makes me feel like doing? It makes me feel like getting a bigger Bible when they laugh at us." Percy added: "What we need is one who'll walk down the street with the Bible under his arm and show the gang that he's not afraid or that he's not ashamed of the Word of God."[14]

Percy also attended the fraternity's first father and son banquet in May of that year. Estranged from his own father, Percy brought to the banquet a man by the name of Mobley, who had been wonderfully saved through the Bible Institute. In a radio sermon given eight years later, Percy harked back to this event and the example of Mobley as a powerful illustration of what it meant for someone to be "in Christ" and born again, and at the same time, he reveals how he viewed what had happened in his own life:

I took as my father a man by the name of Mobley. . . . Poor Mobley, after he came into the United States after serving with our army in the Philippines for twenty years, was pensioned and came back. He came into the United States at San Francisco so rotten and vile the government took steps to keep him out. He was a reproach to any community. He stayed in and came down to Los Angeles and went into a Gipsy Smith meeting. When the invitation was given, he raised his hand. Nothing happened. Went out as drunk as usual. He came up to a meeting where I was. Daddy Horton was preaching. . . . He also gave an invitation. Once again Mobley raised his hand, and Mobley went up to the front. Something had happened. He was in Christ. He accepted Christ as his personal Saviour and Mobley stood there. . . . I was up in Mobley's room once, when he showed me the gashes in his wrists where he had tried to take his life before he knew Christ. I tell you, he was down.

I took him there among all those university men. I was proud of him. I know his face had the marks of sin. . . . Mobley stood there before those men. I'll never forget his look. Tears in his eyes. Oh, he was thinking of the past. He stood there and gave his testimony. He said, "Men, I stand here by the grace of God."

. . . You say, you're not talking to me, I've never been drunk. Neither have I . . . but I tell you, God did as much for me as He did for poor, dirty, rotten, drunken Mobley. He took my life, even though I had a little scent of religion about me, and transformed my life when I came IN Christ. He made me a new creature. He transformed my life.[15]

There is another part of the fraternity lore about my father that bears mentioning, namely his love of pranks and stunts. Bill Hoffman, the national president of Alpha Gamma Omega from 1962 to 1990 relates this story, which may be apocryphal: Percy and Irwin Moon (a classmate at BIOLA who traveled with Percy's 1926 gospel team) "were encouraged to leave BIOLA because of their pranks," one of which was doing handstands on an I-beam that joined the thirteen-story dormitories to the central auditorium above a recessed court.[16] It sounds preposterous, but there may be truth in it. I realized this when I remembered a picture of my father doing a handstand on the beach at a family outing—a very unlikely thing for a fifty-year-old man to do, unless it was for him a throwback to an earlier time.

I stumbled across another prank from this period as I examined a large rolled-up photograph he kept of the entire student body and faculty of the Institute (1925 or 1926). To my surprise, I found two Percys in the photo, one in the back row of men on the left, and one standing behind the women on the right. So either there was a mysterious doppelganger at BIOLA or Percy was having some fun racing the "panoramic" camera as it moved on its tripod from right to left. Percy loved to do stunting and clowning and incorporated it in various ways into his ministry as a way of attracting attention and loosening up his audience.

*

At the end of the school year, Percy decided to leave UCLA—one feels, deeply disillusioned. His grades were poor—mostly C's. About the only thing he could boast of academically was the A he received in Dr. Moore's psychology class. Percy may have thought he could prosper at a secular institution while resisting the attacks on his faith, but it soon became apparent that the whole experience, on balance, was unprofitable, and so he sought a more hospitable climate. He probably chose Wheaton College because of its high standing among Christian liberal arts colleges. Also the new president of Wheaton, Oliver Buswell, had been a guest speaker at the fraternity in January, and Percy may have responded to his vision of a Christian education.[17]

But even while he struggled at UCLA Percy had not stopped doing evangelistic work, and throughout the year he was planning his next evangelistic venture, a summer tour that would take him across the entire country. He put together another gospel team of BIOLA students made up of two former members (Harlan Fischer and Ward Altig) and two new ones (Harold Pugh and Harry Neufeld) and worked up a two-and-a-half-month schedule that would take the team through seventeen states and forty-five towns and cities from San Diego (June 16) to Baltimore (August 28). The organizational and promotional work required by such an undertaking must have been tremendous. Although the Extension Department of BIOLA gave assistance, Percy did most of the planning and correspondence himself. A copy of one of the letters of inquiry that he sent to a prospective pastor said in part:

> Our programs include lively songs by the quartet, including Negro Spirituals, Baritone Solos, Saxophone, Banjo, Steel Guitar and Violin Solos. All the young men give ringing testimonies, after which a short Gospel message is given. Our aim is to uphold Christ that the young people like ourselves, as well as the older ones, may come to know Him whom to know is life eternal.

The cross-country tour in Percy's sturdy Dodge, carrying five people with baggage and instruments, must have been grueling and at times comical (as pictures reveal). Besides these photos, the only other surviving mementos from the trip are the itinerary, and Percy's rough calculation in his datebook for the year 1927–28 (which included the summer of 1927) of fifteen hundred professions for Christ. It was on this tour that the team held services at R. R. Brown's Gospel Tabernacle in Omaha, Nebraska (June 18–19). Brown is famous for having broadcasted the first nondenominational service on the radio on April 8, 1923. By the time Percy arrived there, Brown's Sunday broadcast, Radio Chapel Service, had mushroomed to become the "World Radio Congregation" with official membership cards and a listenership of more than one hundred thousand.[18] Percy would have been a keen observer of Brown's novel radio church and congregation. Four years later, he would launch his own radio church in Philadelphia, calling it the *Young People's Church of the Air,* and he too issued membership cards to his new congregants, asking "charter members" to contribute a $2 annual fee.

By the end of this trip, I believe my father had no doubt about the direction of his life; his calling was to do evangelistic work on the home front. He had logged thousands of miles and preached almost every day of the tour. He was beginning to make good on the promise he made to the Lord after he was saved: "I'll burn myself out for you."[19] But in spite of his eagerness to keep going, he remained steadfast in his commitment to get more preparation before moving into full-time service.

# 6

## Training at Wheaton

W HEN PERCY ARRIVED AT WHEATON COLLEGE IN THE FALL OF 1927, HE found himself in a setting as congenial to him as the one he had left behind at the Bible Institute. Once again he was in the company of fellow Christians who shared the same beliefs, the same social and behavioral standards, and the same enthusiasm for spreading the gospel. Further, he was in a place where there would be similar opportunities for evangelistic work, with Chicago only twenty miles away. Percy was in his element again; he could shine in this environment.

A nondenominational college founded in 1843, Wheaton sought to put "accredited college training . . . on a distinctly Christian basis."[1] The chief difference, however, between Wheaton and BIOLA was that Wheaton was a liberal arts college with a curriculum that centered on the arts and sciences. Only eight hours of Bible courses (approximately three courses) were required of all students. Moreover the academic program was rigorous. Percy would encounter well-trained professors who valued clear and objective thinking and were dedicated to teaching their special fields of learning. The new forward-looking president, Oliver Buswell, who had been at the helm a little more than a year, was taking definite steps to improve the accreditation of the college and strengthen the faculty by increasing the number of PhDs.[2]

But what mattered most to Percy about the curriculum at Wheaton was that all of his instructors were professing Christians; all of them had signed a nine-point statement of faith, instituted in March 1926, affirming the same fundamentalist doctrines that BIOLA had endorsed.[3] This meant that all of his courses were taught from a perspective that presumed the truth of the Bible and that all subject matters would be judged in the light of whether they were in accord with the Bible.

This is exactly what Percy was looking for. He was prepared to read and absorb secular writings and knowledge, but he could digest these goods only if they were wrapped in the cloth of a Bible-based theology. He strongly believed that his studies in the liberal arts and sciences should be not only consistent with the Bible's claims, but that they should strengthen

70

and reinforce those claims and his faith in them. Evidently he was satisfied with the educational blend that he received at Wheaton; at the end of his first year, he sent this glowing report back to the alumni office at BIOLA:

B.I. [BIOLA] has surely been on my heart lately, and I have remembered dear old B.I. to the Lord. Wheaton College has been great. I can look back over this past year and thank God for sending me to such a College that not only is for Christ and his Kingdom [Wheaton's historic motto] but has a high educational standard.

Best Wishes to you all.

*

Even though Percy was able to transfer (from BIOLA and UCLA) only about one-quarter of the credits needed for graduation, he was determined to finish his degree program in two years. To make up the difference, he took an overload of courses in all four semesters and took summer school classes after his first year. Since he was able to transfer ten hours of Bible courses from BIOLA, he did not take any of Wheaton's Bible offerings (thus missing the chance to study with Edith C. Torrey, the daughter of R. A. Torrey, who had come to Wheaton in 1925 as the first full-time Bible instructor).[4] As a history major, he was required to take twenty hours of history courses. And to meet his general studies requirements, he took the full complement of humanities and science courses, including psychology, English poetry, Latin (two years), Spanish (two years), rhetoric (under the renowned Darien Straw), algebra and trigonometry, and in the natural sciences, geology, botany, and chemistry. Courses in theism and ethics, required of all seniors, would have been largely a repeat of the material covered in John MacInnis's classes at BIOLA. Percy probably took chemistry with the distinguished L. Allen Higley, who had come to Wheaton with a PhD from the University of Chicago in 1925 as "the first full-time faculty member to hold that advanced degree."[5] Higley helped to establish Wheaton's reputation in the sciences by promoting the development of field work in geology and biology.[6] (Fifteen years later, Allen Higley would cross over into my father's sphere by accepting a position as dean and head of the science program at the Christian college he founded in 1938, The King's College.)

The Christian context in which Percy's courses were taught made all the difference for him, and his performance improved dramatically; his average grade was 90, and he had only one grade below 80 (75 in English poetry). Thus he was able to prove to himself, after the debacle at UCLA, that he could handle college-level work and that he had the capability to continue his education after college if he so desired.

\*

Percy was eager to participate in the social life of the college and the many extracurricular activities that Wheaton offered. He also wanted to recapture the spirit of fun and camaraderie that he had enjoyed at BIOLA. (It would seem that he succeeded in doing so, as is indicated by the quotation cited under his senior yearbook picture: "A little nonsense now and then, Is relished by the wisest men.") Since he was four or five years older than most of his classmates and had a proven track record in evangelistic work, he had the self-assuredness and maturity that equipped him to be a student leader. His main extracurricular activities were the debate team and the gospel team—both of which were prestigious organizations on the Wheaton campus. He also played interclass tennis (but not varsity tennis). He was active socially, and among the women he dated was Allen Higley's daughter, Evelyn, a recent Wheaton grad and chemistry lab assistant who was closer to him in age.[7]

Confident of his reasoning and rhetorical skills, Percy joined the debate team, coached by a young history professor, Herbert Moule.[8] In his first year of intercollegiate competition, his four-man team took the affirmative side of the question: "Resolved: that United States should cease to protect by armed force capital invested in foreign countries, except after a formal declaration of war." The next year, he became president of the Debate Union and aided in expanding the program by joining two new intercollegiate leagues and in promoting the organization's visibility and prestige on campus by sponsoring a very lively interclass debate.[9] One high-ranking member of the debate squad, whom Percy knew well and who occasionally debated with him on the same team, was Stephen Paine, who went on after Wheaton to become president of Houghton College.[10]

Percy also played an active role in the fervent spiritual and devotional life on Wheaton's campus, where "outbreaks of revival and renewal were frequent."[11] One student from that era, Anne Howard, recalled Percy's student days at Wheaton in a letter to my mother after his death: "When I was a freshman I remember very vividly the Student Prayer Meeting that Percy led. He was a senior at the time. Many of us raised our hands that night—indicating our surrender to the Lord. It was a very important turning point in many lives."[12] On a similar note, Stephen Paine wrote to my mother: "All of us respected him, even back in those years, for the gift of soul winning with which the Lord had endowed him."[13]

Of course Percy went to Wheaton with every expectation of continuing his evangelism, and it was not long before he formed his own gospel team, the Wheaton Quintet, and held meetings in nearby towns and in Chicago. The team consisted of Percy and quartet members Frank Pickering, Wilton Nelson (who also played saxophone), John Neuenschwander, and Willard Price (first tenor and song leader). A poster with a photo of the group gives the following advertisement:

> You'll Want to Hear Them
> Wheaton College Quintet
> For Christ and his Kingdom
> Male Quartet and Instrumental Music
> Negro Spirituals and Wide-Awake Testimonies
> Admission Free
> Silver Offering

During the Easter vacation, the team did a ten-day tour with fourteen meetings in Iowa, Minnesota, and Wisconsin, including a stop at William Bell Riley's Northwestern Bible School in Minneapolis. Percy's calculations show 4,570 people in attendance at these meetings and 191 professions.[14]

In his second year (1928–29) the quintet continued to hold meetings with two replacements—George Ferris and Clarence Wyngarden, who was also a cornetist—joining Price and Nelson. The Wheaton yearbook (*Tower*) reported that the quintet was in such demand that year that the meetings of the regular gospel team "practically ceased" midway through the year.[15] It goes on to say:

> The Quintet has broadcasted several times from Chicago and has also held many services in this vicinity. At a recent service in Chicago, about one thousand attended the meeting. Scores responded to the invitation at the close. The following Sunday twenty of these applied for church membership on profession of faith. This was the largest group that has ever been taken into the membership of this church at one time. Needless to say, the Quintet was invited back.[16]

The radio broadcasts referred to were done on the Moody Bible Institute station WMBI, where Wendell Loveless was program director and chief announcer. It was at this time that Percy made his first contact with Loveless, who would later become a regular song leader and speaker at his Pinebrook Bible Conference.[17]

It was during this year, too, that Percy established a relationship with a church that had close ties with Wheaton—the First Baptist Church of South Chicago. The pastor of this church was Martin Luther Long, a classmate of

Percy's at UCLA and a fraternity brother of Alpha Gamma Omega. Percy and his team had such an impact on this church that Rev. Long and his congregation decided to ordain him a Baptist minister. The process of ordination into the Baptist Church (Northern Convention) would have been easy at this time since individual churches, applying the precept of "local church autonomy" were at liberty to ordain their own ministers. Percy took advantage of this opportunity to obtain a credential that would raise his status as an evangelist until he was able to finish seminary.

In the summer of 1929, after graduating from Wheaton, Percy took his team on the road again for an eighty-one-day tour of the Central and Northeastern states. His typed itinerary remains, and it is daunting. It begins in Elkhorn, Wisconsin, moving to Minnesota, Nebraska, Iowa, Kansas, Missouri, Illinois, Ohio, Michigan, New York, and New Jersey, with meetings in Boston, New York City, Philadelphia, and Baltimore; returning to Wheaton with stops in Pennsylvania, Ohio, and Indiana. At least one meeting was scheduled for each day of the tour, and there was an occasional radio broadcast. In his Philadelphia meetings, Percy made his first contact with some key pastors whom he would connect with again in the following years as a seminary student: O. R. Palmer (Berachah Church), William Wells (Olney Presbyterian), and George Palmer (Maranatha Tabernacle). Percy seems to have used three sermons on this tour, marked on his itinerary as "Whither Goest [Thou]," "Rich [Young] Ruler," and "Marriage Supper" (all of which became staples in his repertoire). The first was his stock sermon, with the others interspersed or used when more than one service was held in a given location. It proved to be another spectacular tour, with eight hundred professions.

One humorous incident that took place on this trip was related by Clarence Wyngarden many years later in an alumni publication. While driving through Massachusetts, the team got the idea of trying to sing for former President Calvin Coolidge. When they arrived at the Coolidges' Northampton home, "dressed like ragamuffins," Percy knocked on the door, and the maid informed them that the Coolidges were not home but that "Mrs. Coolidge should be back from her walk soon if you'd like to wait." "Sure, we'll wait," Percy said. Mrs. Coolidge returned, and after a few minutes of pleasant conversation with her on the front porch, Wyngarden wrote:

A model A pulled up. Mr. Coolidge stepped out in a black coat and derby. He ascended the walk with his head held high, affording us only a glance. Mrs. Coolidge jumped in, "Mr. Coolidge, we have some boys here from Wheaton College in Illinois. They are traveling the country singing, and they thought it would be nice if they could have the privilege of singing a song for you." He yanked his derby down over his eyes. "Uhgg," he grunted and marched up the steps into the house. Mrs. Coolidge turned to us. "Well, boys, I guess Mr. Coolidge is not in a very musical frame of mind today."[18]

I would venture to add to this account that if Mr. Coolidge had been willing to listen to their song, he would have found himself being asked if he knew Christ as his personal Savior.

Percy took more control over this quartet than he had at BIOLA. In both years he had each member of the quartet sign a contract agreeing "to recognize as leader of the quartet Percy Crawford"; other members were designated manager and treasurer. It was spelled out that any funds from offerings left after expenses were split equally among them. The practice of having quartet members sign contracts (which he continued throughout his ministry) was clearly a way of establishing his authority over the group and signaled that he now saw himself as the team leader and organizer. It was no longer a gospel team of coequal members, it was *his* evangelistic party.

## THE MACINNIS AFFAIR

It was during his final year at Wheaton that Percy started to get reports that all was not well at BIOLA. John MacInnis, his former teacher, who had replaced Torrey as dean of the Institute in 1924, was being charged with heresy. William Bell Riley, pastor of the First Baptist Church in Minneapolis and self-appointed guardian of fundamental belief in the schools and seminaries, had found some passages in MacInnis's new book, *Peter the Fisherman Philosopher: A Study in Higher Fundamentalism,* that smacked of modernism, and was putting pressure on the board to let MacInnis go. However, after a careful review, the board backed MacInnis and his book.

John MacInnis, a former Presbyterian minister and a moderate, wanted to turn BIOLA's emphasis away from controversial issues such as premillennialism and evolution, and build better relations with the Protestant churches. Earlier, he must have angered Riley with a comment he made in an interview with the *Los Angeles Times,* reported a day after assuming his new position as dean. When asked about the evolution issue, he said that theologians and scientists are in agreement that God made the world, but "as to His method of creation, and the time involved, no one can be certain." He continued:

In my opinion, it is foolish to consume valuable time in argument over things which no one knows much about—and which might not make a lot of difference if we did know—when there are so many vital issues to be solved in the lives of individuals and of the nation.[19]

But Riley had consumed a great deal of valuable time arguing about such things, and no doubt under the assumption that he knew quite a lot about them. In fact, two years earlier in June 1925, while MacInnis was dean, he had debated evolution with Maynard Shipley, president of the Science League of America, before a packed house at the BIOLA auditorium.

To make matters worse, Torrey, who was MacInnis's close friend and colleague, and was responsible for his coming to BIOLA, became alarmed at some of the changes his successor was making in the curriculum—in particular, MacInnis had turned the Bible *major,* which had been BIOLA's only academic offering, into a *program* leading to a degree in Philosophy, Psychology, and Religious Education. Also, the title of MacInnis's book, referring to Peter as a "fisherman *philosopher,*" was disturbing to Torrey, who had a profound distrust of philosophy. MacInnis wrote a series of articles for *The King's Business* on "The Christian Philosopher," explaining that Christian faith and practice "involves a comprehensive philosophy of the world and history," but it didn't help.[20] After reading the book, Torrey notified Riley that he would not endorse it.

Further compounding his problems, MacInnis had alienated Horton when he took over as editor-in-chief of *The King's Business.* In setting out his editorial policy, he announced that his intention was to eliminate the accusatory tone of the magazine: "In all our writing we shall earnestly desire the triumph of God's truth rather than the downing of an enemy."[21] Horton came to believe that the Institute's course of study under MacInnis was in violation of the school's charter and threatened legal action.

The board finally bowed to the pressure put on it by Riley and another prominent fundamentalist leader, Charles Trumbull, editor of the influential *Sunday School Times,* who dropped BIOLA from his published list of "Bible Schools that are True to the Faith." In a split vote, the board finally accepted MacInnis's resignation, declared that it had been a mistake to publish his book, and ordered the printing plates destroyed. Four of the ten board members then resigned, along with several key faculty members including the world-renowned Bible teacher, G. Campbell Morgan.[22]

Percy must have been surprised and puzzled by the whole episode. He respected his former teacher, and would have responded favorably to his moderate approach. But by remaining silent in the controversy, he tacitly accepted Riley's (and the board's) judgment. (In the ensuing years, he would align himself with Riley and the hardliners.) I imagine, however, that he must have felt deeply sorrowful that fundamentalist strife and discord had struck at the very heart of the institution he loved.

*

Percy's experience at Wheaton had deepened his spiritual life and given him new opportunities for evangelism. In his two years there, he was able to make contacts with key individuals, churches, and institutions in Chicago and other cities in the Northeast, where fundamentalism was thriving. Academically, Wheaton moved him along in his quest for educational respectability by giving him exposure to the history of Western ideas and culture. He now knew more about Gladstone and Disraeli, Milton and Pope, Locke and Spinoza. And yet it seems to me that he never assimilated these ideas into his active thoughts or attempted to integrate them into his theological beliefs. It was as if he kept this new knowledge in a separate compartment of his mind. Hence, the effect of his studies in the arts and sciences on the message that he was carrying to the world was virtually nil. He shied away from subjects like English and philosophy that required that he grapple with other (non-Christian) viewpoints and ideologies. For him, the Christian philosophy was the only one worth considering, and it comprised the whole truth; other viewpoints were either false (because they rested on humanistic premises) or unimportant. Additionally, his experience on the debate team sharpened his forensic skills and made him even more confident of his ability to defend the faith against all opposing views. And so, ironically, his exposure to the liberal arts, instead of opening his mind to new ideas and insights, ultimately had the effect of narrowing his perspective and making him more dogmatic in his beliefs.

On the other hand, his academic experience at Wheaton convinced him that liberal studies could be couched in a framework of God and God's great plan of redemption; they did not have to be taught from an atheistic or naturalistic perspective. Whatever knowledge was obtainable in the arts and sciences fell neatly into place within the larger framework of God's truth as revealed in the Bible. Thus the instruction that Percy received at Wheaton became for him a model of Christian education. He saw firsthand how it should be done—in his psychology classes, in his science classes, and in his philosophy classes.

Soon after finishing seminary in Philadelphia, Percy would begin to make plans to start his own Christian liberal arts college, which he anticipated would be "the Wheaton of the east." He had in mind a re-creation of the Wheaton College of his own experience. That vision would come to fruition nine years after graduating from Wheaton, when The King's College opened its doors.

Meanwhile, he never wavered in his determination to continue his education. Looking back on this period in his life, he said that he knew that God had some purpose for his life, but he did not yet know what it was. He added: "I always felt in my soul that I was different, . . . [and hence] that God was preparing me for greater things."[23] All he could do, then, was try to make himself a fit instrument for the Lord's use; and he was convinced that seminary training was an essential step in this direction.

# 7

# A Westminster Man

Pᴇʀᴄʏ ᴀɴᴅ ᴛʜᴇ Wʜᴇᴀᴛᴏɴ Qᴜɪɴᴛᴇᴛ ᴇɴᴅᴇᴅ ᴛʜᴇɪʀ 1929 ꜱᴜᴍᴍᴇʀ ᴛᴏᴜʀ ɪɴ Vincennes, Indiana, on September 1, after eighty-one days of continuous evangelistic meetings, and made the short trip back to Wheaton to recuperate briefly before the beginning of the school year. Although the boys in the quartet would stay together at Wheaton, Percy was moving on, farther east—to Princeton Seminary, where he planned to complete the next phase of the educational program he had laid out for himself.

Princeton was a logical choice for Percy. For one reason, he was becoming familiar with that region of the country and had made some contacts there on his tours. More importantly, Princeton was the foremost Presbyterian seminary, with a solid reputation for sound scholarship and conservative theology. Among fundamentalists, Princeton stood out as an institution that upheld the essential doctrines of the faith—and particularly the doctrine of the inerrancy of Scripture. In addition, its leading New Testament scholar and theologian, J. Gresham Machen, had published an important semipopular book in 1923, *Christianity and Liberalism,* which mounted a sustained attack against liberal theology, arguing that it could not be viewed as a true Christian theology. The book would have been available to Percy in the BIOLA Book Room during his student years there. Finally, although the seminary was entirely separate from Princeton University, it enjoyed some of the glamour and prestige of its great Ivy League neighbor, and this was something that would have appealed to my father, who wanted to obtain the best academic credentials.[1]

But why a Presbyterian seminary? Percy had been nurtured by the nondenominational wing of fundamentalism at BIOLA and Wheaton and had no loyalty to any particular denomination. Part of the explanation is that the independent institutions that he attended tried very hard to maintain good relations with the mainline denominations. (Wheaton sent a steady stream of its graduates to Princeton.) Moreover, the Presbyterian Church in the U.S.A. had been dominated up to this time by conservative elements who had allied themselves with the "Princeton theology." Further, in 1923 the General Assembly of the Presbyterian Church had reaffirmed the five points considered essential to the faith (first adopted in 1910) that conformed so closely to fundamentalist belief: the inerrancy of Scripture, the virgin birth of Christ, the atonement of Christ, the resurrection of Christ, and the miracle-working power of Christ.[2]

But what Percy probably did not know was that in the mid-1920s conservative voices in the church were beginning to lose control as moderates and liberals won key battles culminating in a report to the 1927 General Assembly that effectively rescinded the requirement that the five points be accepted as a condition for licensing and ordination of clergy. And within Princeton Seminary, the same split was occurring between conservatives (led by Machen) and moderates (led by President J. Ross Stevenson) who wanted to make the seminary more inclusive and representative of the spectrum of views within the larger church.

It is doubtful that Percy was tuned in to the controversy that was raging at Princeton during the two-year period he was at Wheaton. But he may well have noticed in the September 1927 issue of the *Moody Bible Institute Monthly* an article entitled "Professor J. Gresham Machen, D.D., Declines the Presidency of Bryan University," which cited the open letter Machen sent to the board of the new university formed to memorialize Williams Jennings Bryan, in which he declared:

> Princeton Theological Seminary is an institution which for a hundred years, and never more successfully than now, has been defending and propagating the gospel of Christ. It is now passing through a great crisis. If the re-organization favored by the General Assembly which has just met at San Francisco is finally adopted next year—if the proposed abrogation of the whole constitution of the seminary and the proposed dissolution of the present board of directors is finally carried out . . .—then Princeton Theological Seminary, as it has been so long and so honorably known, will be dead, and we shall have at Princeton a new institution of a radically different type.[3]

In the meantime, Machen went on to say, "the seminary is still genuinely and consistently evangelical," and he pleaded that "the right of thoroughgoing conservatives in the Presbyterian Church to have at least one seminary that clearly and unequivocally represents their view may still be recognized and Princeton may still be saved."[4] But the reorganization was adopted by the 1928 General Assembly and as a result Machen decided that he could not in good conscience remain at Princeton and resigned in mid-June 1929. One month later, with the backing of a group of laymen and clergy in Philadelphia, Machen announced the formation of a new seminary that would, he vowed, adhere faithfully to the historic principles of the old Princeton.

But Percy was just setting out on his summer tour when Machen resigned. And when the *New York Times* ran a story on June 18 under the headline "Machen Proposes a New Seminary," Percy and the Quintet were in Marshfield, Wisconsin, on their way to St. Paul, Minnesota. And when the decisive meeting took place in Philadelphia on July 18 in which the decision was made to proceed with the founding of Westminster Seminary and to open in the fall,[5] the team was en route from Cleveland to Meadville, Pennsylvania. It is quite possible that he did not hear about Westminster until the Quintet got to Philadelphia in late August.

Percy does not record anywhere what took place after he arrived at Princeton and what led to his decision to withdraw and enter Westminster.[6] But it is not hard to reconstruct his thinking. He would have learned upon his arrival that three professors and twenty students had left the seminary over the issue of maintaining the historic principles and doctrines of the Presbyterian faith and that a new board had been formed by decree of the same General Assembly that had just effectively made void the five essential points of Christian belief. Percy's sympathies would undoubtedly have been with the dissidents whom he would have seen as standing up for the fundamentals of the faith against the growing tide of liberalism within the church.

And if these doctrinal issues were not enough to move him, another factor would have been the greater opportunity he would have for evangelistic work in the urban setting of Philadelphia. Having just spent two years on the quiet, sheltered campus of Wheaton, the prospect of three more years in a small university town must have been dismaying. He longed to be nearer to the masses of men and women—in the missions, the docks, the prisons, the bars, the streets—who were desperately in need of a Savior. And so Percy joined the ranks of the fifty new students who were willing to cast their lot with J. Gresham Machen and his fledgling institution.

## WESTMINSTER SEMINARY

In eloquent and passionate tones, Machen laid before his constituents the "purpose and plan" of the new Westminster Theological Seminary at the opening ceremonies on September 25, 1929. Percy would have responded to the opening theme of the address—the unpopularity of the gospel—a theme that he would accentuate throughout his ministry:

> Westminster Theological Seminary, which opens its doors today, will hardly be attended by those who seek the plaudits of the world or the plaudits of a worldly church.

... Our new institution is devoted to an unpopular cause; it is devoted to the service of One who is despised and rejected by the world and increasingly belittled by the visible church, the majestic Lord and Saviour who is presented to us in the Word of God. From him men are turning away one by one. His sayings are too hard, his deeds of power too strange, his atoning death too great an offense to human pride. But to him, despite all, we hold.

Machen then began to lay out the basic plan of the curriculum at Westminster; it would be centered on God's revealed word:

We believe . . . that God has been pleased to reveal himself to man and to redeem man once for all from the guilt and power of sin. The record of that revelation and that redemption is contained in the Holy Scriptures, and it is with the Holy Scriptures, and not merely with the human phenomenon of religion, that candidates for the ministry should learn to deal.

But, he went on to say, "if you are to tell what the Bible does say," you must master the languages in which it is written: "We may sometimes be tempted to wish that the Holy Spirit had given us the Word of God in a language better suited to our particular race, in a language that we could easily understand; but in his mysterious wisdom he gave it to us in Hebrew and in Greek." This was one of the main reasons Percy had gone to seminary— to study the Bible in the original languages in which God had revealed it to its authors.

Machen then struck a chord that would have reminded Percy of his former teacher, Reuben Torrey; he spoke of a "new Reformation" in biblical exegesis that would "be a return to plain common honesty and common sense." "There will be a rediscovery of the great Reformation doctrine of the perspicuity of Scripture; men will make the astonishing discovery that the Bible is a plain book addressed to plain men, and that it means exactly what it says." However, the plain meaning of the Scriptures is not right on the surface. In order to uncover it, it would be necessary to "come into contact with the truly fine exegetical tradition of the Christian church."

Percy may have thought that Reuben Torrey had already accomplished the goal of deciphering the plain meaning of the Bible in his great work *What the Bible Teaches* and that he had achieved this by the application of the most scientific inductive methods. Still, he would have been curious to learn what the "truly fine exegetical tradition" of the church had to say about Scripture.

I imagine that my father had some misgivings when Machen got to the part of Westminster's purpose that it would instruct its seminarians in that "system of theology" that was found in "the Reformed Faith, the Faith commonly called Calvinistic, which is set forth so gloriously in the Confessions and Catechisms of the Presbyterian Church."[7] This would have sounded too sectarian and confessional to his nondenominational ears, and he probably hoped that this part of the curriculum could be kept to a minimum.

Machen closed his remarks with a statement of the three main principles on which the new seminary would be founded, which may have seemed to Percy to summarize exactly the way his own educational goals were subordinated to his evangelistic mission:

> We believe, first, that the Christian religion, as it is set forth in the Confession of Faith of the Presbyterian Church, is true; we believe, second, that the Christian religion welcomes and is capable of scholarly defense; and we believe, third, that the Christian religion should be proclaimed without fear or favor, and in clear opposition to whatever opposes it, whether within or without the church, as the only way of salvation for lost mankind. . . . Pray that the students who go forth from Westminster Seminary may know Christ as their own Saviour and may proclaim to others the gospel of his love.[8]

*

Percy entered into his studies in the first year with great enthusiasm, eager to take on the academic challenge that Machen had set before him. All eighteen members of his first-year "junior" class had a bachelor's degree—a requirement for admission; four were from Wheaton, four from Asbury College, and two from Taylor University. (Members of the upper classes of this first cohort, whose paths would later intersect with Percy's were Carl McIntire [middle class] and Harold Ockenga [senior class].) He took a full schedule of six courses each semester in his first year with some first-rate scholars and teachers—Cornelius Van Til in apologetics and systematic theology, Oswald Allis in Old Testament, Paul Woolley in church history, Ned Stonehouse in Greek. (He could not take any New Testament courses with Machen that year since they all required a preliminary knowledge of Greek.) The stage was set for Percy to take hold of the educational opportunities that Westminster afforded.

But unfortunately, he was unable to seize that opportunity and use it to his full advantage. He was not drawn into any of his new fields of study, nor did he find a true mentor and friend among his professors. He soon realized that getting hold of the basic grammars of Hebrew and Greek was tedious and unrewarding. And he had never had any liking for systematic theology and now found Van Til's brand of Calvinism unpalatable.

As a result, his grades suffered: on a scale of 1 to 5 (where 1 was high honor, 2 was honor, 3 was medial, 4 was passing, and 5 was failure), except for a one-credit course in public speaking in which he earned a 2, he received grades of 3 or lower in all of his classes, including a 5/4 in Van Til's systematic theology, which meant that he flunked the course on the first try and later retook the final exam and passed it.[9] He ended the first year with a general standing of 3.24 (roughly equivalent to a C– in a letter grade system). Percy realized that his scholastic abilities were being questioned, but he did not know whether to blame himself or Westminster. In any case, a message was being sent from his teachers that he could hardly have missed: if you want to succeed at Westminster, then you are going to have to make a far more serious commitment of time and hard work to your studies.

Part of the problem was that Percy had taken on too much. In addition to six courses at the seminary, he had decided to enroll in a master's program at the University of Pennsylvania and was accepted into the history department. Evidently he was in a hurry to finish his education and thought that if he was going to have to spend three years in seminary, there was no reason why he could not fit a master's degree into the same time frame. So he took on two additional yearlong courses at Penn. All together, this was an extremely heavy load of coursework, and it is not surprising that he had trouble handling it all.

During this year, as well, he began the process of making contacts and opening doors for evangelistic work in the area, but invitations were sparse and for the first (and only) time in his Christian life he experienced a lull in his ministry. He took advantage of this brief interlude by being more socially active, getting to know some of the women who associated with the Westminster men, and also by going on one-day excursions to attractions in Philadelphia and surrounding areas.

Overall it was a satisfactory school year. Percy could still recommend Westminster to his friends at BIOLA (Harlan Fischer and Jimmy Blackstone) and at Wheaton (Jimmy Price); all three of them entered the class of 1934, overlapping with him for one year. Percy seems not to have been too distressed by his poor performance in the classroom. He looked forward to his New Testament courses with Machen in his middle year and hoped they would enliven his whole experience at Westminster.


## Pastoring at Rhawnhurst Church

In the summer of his first year, Percy took a church. He was assigned by the Philadelphia Presbytery, as summer supply, to the Rhawnhurst Presbyterian Church in northeast Philadelphia. The Rhawnhurst church had been in existence for only a year and did not yet have a regular pastor. Percy would be shepherding a handful of motivated people who had persuaded the Philadelphia Presbytery to purchase land in Rhawnhurst on which they constructed "a small wooden structure." His responsibilities as student-pastor included two Sunday services, morning and evening, from the first week of May to the last week of September (twenty-two weeks), conducting Wednesday night prayer meeting, and "calling" in the neighborhood three days each week. For this he was offered $10 a week with board, or $20 without. He chose to be fed.

By all measures, Percy was extremely conscientious about preparing his sermons and carrying out his other pastoral duties. He listed seventeen of the many sermons he gave in his calendar book, and although none survive in their original form, a sampling of the titles indicate some of the themes and motifs that were occupying his mind: "Playing the Fool," "Three Views of Peter," "Can a Person Dance and Be a Christian?," "Blood Guilty," "Is There a Hell?," "The Victorious Life," "The Unpardonable Sin," "The New Birth," "Soul Winning." He gave invitations at least some of the time, and had one memorable convert who would go into full-time Christian service—Walter Haman, a Pennsylvania state trooper who became a Secret Service agent assigned to two presidents and who later established the New Life Boys Ranch in Harleysville, Pennsylvania, for delinquent boys.[10] (Percy would invite Haman to speak and give sharpshooting demonstrations at many of his meetings over the years.)

All in all, his time at Rhawnhurst was well spent. By the end of the summer, the congregation had doubled in size and Sunday school had tripled, and in October the church dedicated its "first permanent stone building."[11] Percy liked the people there and stayed in contact with them after he left. And they liked him, even to the extent that they were willing to come to his aid a year later with financial assistance when he was in dire need of it for his radio broadcast. Although he must have found it limiting in the extreme to work with one small congregation and conduct five months of preaching at one location, he did it cheerfully and enthusiastically. Baptist minister Tony Campolo remarked to me recently that, as a young person, he heard Percy preach and was struck by his being just as emotionally involved when preaching at a small church as he was when he spoke to thousands at large rallies. Percy never lost the feeling of excitement over winning just one soul. He labored mightily at Rhawnhurst, and perhaps because it was his first (and only) church, he always had a fondness for the people there.

*

Percy was occupied with other things besides pastoring that summer. Naturally he continued to do personal work. In *The Art of Fishing for Men* he recalled this period of his life: "When I was in Seminary and had a small church and rode to it, I used to get out of an elevated car at one station and climb into another, giving out tracts in each car as I went through it. This was an opportunity to preach to many. I know it is hard when people stare at you and think you are a radical, but it is an opportunity that should not be missed."[12]

But the bulk of the summer was taken up with summer school. At Westminster, he arranged a two-credit independent study course in which he wrote a "thesis" entitled "Calvin and Free Will." In addition, he took three more graduate courses at Penn, making a big push to get the bulk of his coursework finished while his schedule was still relatively light. We may well wonder why Percy was doing graduate-level work at all—and why at a secular university? One reason was that it was part of his master plan to prepare himself to be maximally used of the Lord; and to this end, a graduate degree from an Ivy League school would be an impressive credential. Another motivation was that he wanted to finish what he had failed to accomplish at UCLA—to meet the challenge of the secular university and prove to himself that he measured up to its standards. But it is hard not to believe that his studies at Penn meant little to him, since they had virtually no visible effect on his thinking and preaching. The most that can be said is that Percy thought it a valuable discipline to go through the process of getting a graduate degree; (he encouraged quite a few King's College graduates to go on for their master's at Penn). But I cannot see that he took anything from that process that changed him or improved him in any way.

Ironically, it was a philosophy professor at Penn, Gordon Clark, with whom Percy had the most rapport and who was most sympathetic to his evangelism. He took a summer course in modern philosophy with Clark in which he got a good dose of the writings of Descartes, Spinoza, and Leibniz—names that Percy often rattled off in his sermons to show that he was familiar with the worldly philosophers. Percy invited Clark to give a testimony at one of the series of open-air meetings he conducted the following summer in Philadelphia and stayed in touch with his professor until he left Penn and took a position in philosophy at Wheaton.

Meanwhile, in his middle year of seminary, Percy was taking courses with the luminaries of the Westminster faculty—J. Gresham Machen in New Testament studies and Robert Dick Wilson in Old Testament. His first course with Machen was gospel history, in which he was finally able to bring to bear his studies in Greek on the original gospel texts. He would take four more courses with Machen in the remaining semesters—"John," "II Corinthians," "Paul & His Environment," and "Apostolic History"— all of which held great promise.

Percy liked Machen as a person and had great respect for him as a scholar and teacher. It helped that "Dassie," as his students nicknamed him, shared Percy's fondness for jokes and good fun. He was known to spend the first class of every course loosening up his students with stories and stunts.[13] He played tennis with students, invited them to social gatherings at his apartment where they could challenge him to checkers or chess, and took them to Penn football games. (Later on, Percy followed suit with his associates in all of these activities, except that he substituted the game of caroms for chess.) It is not known whether Percy ever participated in any of Machen's social activities (none are recorded in his datebooks), but it is known that he took part in the annual "stunt night" on campus and even helped organize it one year, sending Machen a bill for expenses of $11.10, which was promptly paid.[14] And it is probably no accident that stunt night would be a regular feature of every week at Pinebrook Bible Conference during the entire twenty-seven years that Percy ran it.

But he was still dissatisfied with his general standing, which improved slightly in the second year to 2.79 (approximately C+).[15] Tension was mounting. His teachers thought that he was putting more time and energy into evangelism than into making preparation for it. But Percy began to feel as though he was being criticized personally for his evangelism and that his character was being impugned because of it. Looking back to this time (in a later sermon), he expressed the frustration he felt with the confining atmosphere at Westminster and spoke of his urge to get away and preach to the unsaved:

> When I was attending seminary I didn't get opportunities to preach very much, for the "powers that be" were against it, but I used to sneak away on Saturdays especially and preach; for I longed to make known the story of Jesus and his love. I went down on a Saturday night to a mission for sailors right near the waterfront. The fellows had just come off the ships and were gathered there for a meeting. . . .[16]

Percy even had fleeting thoughts of leaving Westminster and completing his degree elsewhere and began to think that his career might have been better served if he had stayed at Princeton. His decision to begin a weekly radio program in October 1931, at the beginning of his third year was reason enough for him to stay in Philadelphia. But by the end of that year, he and his radio quartet were booking meetings three and four nights a week.

Some light is thrown on his relationship to the seminary by an exchange he had with Machen about the prospect of going on the radio. It was a faith venture, and the expenses of $100 per week plus equipment rental had to be raised on a week-by-week basis. Percy tried to garner funds from every possible source and apparently felt secure enough about his relationship with Machen to ask for assistance. In a letter dated August 5, 1931, he explains that during the previous summer, while ministering at the Barnes Memorial Community Center of the Philadelphia Presbytery,[17] he had conducted open-air meetings at nearby Washington Square and now wanted to begin a radio broadcast in the auditorium of the Barnes Center. He writes:

> The Lord has surely blessed. We have just closed a sixteen day campaign and He has given us close to two hundred professions and we trust a goodly number of those people really possessed Him.
>
> Now here is what I want to ask you. This broadcast will cost me $100 a week. Due to the fact that I would be a Westminster man and that I would be using Westminster talent constantly, the Seminary would indirectly be kept before at least 100,000 Philadelphia people every week. I asked Dr. Stevenson [Lecturer in Pastoral Theology] if he thought Westminster would help me any. He suggested a possible $10 a week for some eight weeks. This has been the only concrete encouragement I have had as yet. I was wondering what you would think of it and if you would think it a worthwhile investment say for eight weeks till I get on my feet. I feel sure the money would be well invested.
>
> . . . I have the young people of some eight churches back of me. I have the auditorium and the equipment. Now the question is to get the backing.
>
> I hope to sign the contract this week and I trust I may be encouraged by a favorable reply from you. Sincerely yours,

Machen's reply, from the family's summer residence in Maine, was polite and to the point:

> I am very greatly interested in the good report of your work this summer and in your plans during next year. Unfortunately my resources are taxed very heavily for the cause of Westminster Seminary, so that I do not feel able to help you in a financial way. Ordinarily, I do not think that it is wise for a man to enter upon so extensive a program until he has completed his Seminary course, since it seems to me that a thorough acquaintance with the message logically precedes the proclamation of it. But I can well understand your enthusiasm because of the open door which seems to have been placed before you, and I trust that you may have the guidance and the blessing of God in the great work of preaching the gospel. . . . Very sincerely yours.

Machen's turndown probably added to Percy's feeling that Westminster was against him, but he should have been encouraged by his professor's positive comment about the radio ministry, even though the professor knew, and seemed to care, that it meant the loss of one of his students.

*

Machen's lukewarm endorsement of my father's evangelistic work reflected his own qualified acceptance of evangelism generally. He had expressed himself on this subject (sixteen years earlier) in correspondence with his mother, reporting on two of Billy Sunday's mass evangelistic meetings during a two-month campaign in Philadelphia in January 1915. The impression made upon him after the first meeting by the former baseball player-turned-evangelist, notorious for his theatrics on the platform, was largely positive. As a scholar, accustomed to writing books for an unseen audience, he was overwhelmed by the dimensions of the meeting: "An audience of 20,000 people or more under the same roof is simply overpowering. . . . [And] when you consider that in the [Billy] Sunday meetings it is a matter of daily occurrence for two months—and indeed two or three times daily—the thought is even more overpowering." After the second meeting he wrote:

> The sermon was old-fashioned evangelism of the most powerful and elemental kind. Much of it, I confess, left me cold . . . but the total impact of the sermon was great. At the climax, the preacher got up on his chair—and if he had used a step-ladder, nobody could have thought the thing excessive, so dead in earnest were both speaker and audience! The climax was the boundlessness of God's mercy; and so truly had the sinfulness of sin been presented, that everybody present with any heart at all ought to have felt mighty glad that God's mercy is boundless. In the last five or ten minutes of that sermon, I got a new realization of the power of the gospel.[18]

Later that same year, the faculty of Princeton Seminary invited Billy Sunday to speak there. Although both the president and the dean of Princeton University (fully separate from the seminary) vehemently opposed the evangelist's coming to Princeton and refused to allow the use of Alexander Hall, the only auditorium in town large enough to accommodate the anticipated crowd, Machen was fully supportive of the idea. In a long letter to his mother prior to the event, he reveals his views of the close relationship between evangelism and his own endeavors as an educator. "Princeton is in a tremendous tempest over Billy Sunday," he begins. After describing the controversy between the seminary and the university, he offers further reflection:

> The result of the whole thing is to make me more and more enthusiastic for the work that Billy Sunday is doing. His methods are as different as could possibly be imagined from ours [the seminary's], but we support him to a man simply

because, in an age of general defection, he is preaching the gospel. We are not ashamed of his "antiquated theology"; it is nothing in the world but the message of the cross, long neglected, which is manifesting its old power. . . . Despite all the trouble, however, I am glad that the Seminary in this public way is giving the right hand of fellowship to a man who is doing the Lord's work. There ought to be the closest kind of cooperation between real evangelism and the type of theology that we represent—indeed the two things are absolutely necessary to each other.

In a final letter relating to the event, sent the day before Sunday's arrival, Machen indicates the kind of close cooperation he envisions between "Billy Sunday evangelism and Princeton theology": the converts who have been moved by the evangelist's words must be brought to an understanding of what has happened to them. "There is going to be an increasing need for pastors who are really able to teach the people; in Philadelphia for example the ground has been broken in a wonderful way, and the question is whether the seed is to be planted." He is referring, he says, to "the intellectual interests which are awakened—though of course not satisfied—by the Sunday campaigns."[19]

Machen, then, cannot have been opposed to Percy's evangelism per se, but probably had mixed feelings about him since he was supposedly in training to become one of the "pastors who are really able to teach the people." Percy's strong predisposition for evangelistic work and his below-average performance in the classroom may have signaled to Machen that this was not to be. His instructors would work with him as best they could, even if he was not entirely the kind of Westminster product they hoped for. But there was little doubt in anyone's mind that spreading the gospel and winning souls had won out over reading Calvin and mastering Greek.

There were, moreover, other differences of a theological nature that Percy had with the seminary (and its founder): (1) the Calvinist doctrine of divine election (predestination), (2) the doctrine of premillennialism, and (3) the practical question of living "the separated life." The doctrine of premillennialism—that Christ will return after a time of great tribulation to establish his kingdom for a thousand years—was considered a fundamental of the faith at BIOLA and Wheaton. So it was a matter of concern to him that the faculty at Westminster as a whole rejected it. In *Christianity and Liberalism,* Machen had acknowledged that there were differences among Christians concerning "the order of events in connection with the Lord's return." He went on to say with characteristic bluntness:

That [premillennialist] belief, in the opinion of the present writer, is an error, arrived at by a false interpretation of the Word of God; we do not think that the prophecies of the Bible permit so definite a mapping-out of future events. The Lord will come again, . . . so much is clear—but that so little will be accomplished by the present dispensation of the Holy Spirit and so much will be left to be accomplished by the Lord in bodily presence—such a view we cannot find to be justified by the words of Scripture.[20]

Of greater concern to Percy was the Calvinist doctrine of divine election—that God has preelected those who are destined for eternal salvation. Percy struggled with this doctrine as a student because he saw that it was in conflict with the premise of his entire evangelistic ministry—that the individual must accept or reject Christ as Savior and that this choice would determine his or her eternal destiny. The doctrine that this choice was already determined and that the individual contributes nothing to it would, if true, make a mockery of all that he was doing.

As we have seen, Percy chose to do a summer independent study course for which he wrote a paper entitled "Calvin and Free Will," hoping that he could resolve the problem. The thesis has not survived, but we can surmise that, in it, he laid out the grounds for both sides of the issue, but could not see a satisfactory way of reconciling them. This, anyway, is the burden of a poem he wrote, probably that summer, to clear up the matter in his own mind, and which he published six years later in a short editorial piece in his magazine, *Young People Today,* under the heading "Calvinism." He writes:

> After facing the ultra-Calvinism of Westminster Seminary and thrashing through the "ins" and "outs" of the whole thing—one day in my room I wrote the following:
> The question of God's will and mine,
>   Is far too much for me.
> That God selects is on each line,
>   And yet men's will seem[s] free;
>
> So this I'll do and falter not,
>   To make his gospel known.
> I'll preach His word, the life He bought
>   'Til all my breath hath flown,
>
> I'll plead with men their hearts to yield,
>   Or else their souls they'll lose,
> And trust to God that from the full
>   His very own He'll choose.[21]

In the end, he could not accept the "ultra-Calvinist" position if it meant giving up his belief in the sinner's free choice. He would continue to "plead

with men their hearts to yield" as if the decision was their own. And even
if he could not see a way of making his belief in free will compatible with
the doctrine of election, he would not let this intellectual difficulty stand in
the way of his commitment to making the gospel known "'til all his breath
had flown."

However, in spite of these disagreements, relations at the seminary remained cordial and Percy continued to take part in various functions on
campus, even while his calendar was filling up with more and more speaking engagements.


## MACHEN'S INFLUENCE

Machen's influence on my father is difficult to trace because Percy never
refers to him or credits him with anything in his sermons and other writings. I have found only one allusion to Machen's writings in all of my father's materials—a long quotation that he typed out from his book *What Is
Faith?* and put in a file folder full of anecdotes and sermon illustrations
taken from a variety of sources. The passage describes the believer's stance
of faith and the risks that it involves and is worth citing in full:

> This world is a dark place without Christ [Machen writes]; we have found no
> other salvation either in ourselves or in others; and for our part, therefore, de-
> spite doubts and fears, we are prepared to take Christ at His word and launch
> forth into the deep at His command. It is a great venture, this venture of faith;
> there are difficulties in the way of it; we have not solved all mysteries or re-
> solved all doubts. But though our minds are still darkened, though we have at-
> tained no rigidly mathematical proof, we have attained at least certitude enough
> to cause us to risk our lives. Will Christ desert us when we have thus commit-
> ted ourselves to Him? There are men about us who tell us that He will; there are
> voices within us that whisper to us doubts; but we must act in accordance with
> the best light that is given us and doing so we have decided for our part to dis-
> trust our doubts and base our lives, despite all, upon Christ.[22]

Percy would have resonated with the idea that faith is a risky proposition that overcomes doubt. It is a venture, a launching out into deep waters,
despite all difficulties and uncertainties. But Percy would have downplayed
the idea that we affirm our faith in Christ "though our minds are still darkened" and our doubts unresolved. For him, the risk involved in the act of
faith had less to do with intellectual uncertainty and more to do with the
Christian's venturing into an uncertain and hostile world that would put obstacles in his way. Percy's taking on the radio broadcast without financial

backing would have been for him a prime example of a faith venture. On the other hand (as we have just seen in the poem he wrote on Calvinism), Percy was enacting Machen's idea of faith when he made a commitment to "preach His word" and "make His gospel known" in spite of his inability to resolve the intellectual question of "God's will and mine." This was a decisive act of faith in Machen's sense of acting in the face of unresolved doubts.

Further, Machen's teaching had a significant effect on Percy's theological beliefs by enabling him to ground them more firmly in the biblical texts and in the historical contexts in which the New Testament authors lived and wrote. Percy also learned from Machen's technique of drawing sharp contrasts between liberalism and what fundamentalism stood for and of showing how liberal interpretations conflicted with what the Scriptures actually say. For example, in the following passage, Machen castigates the liberal portrayal of Jesus as an unoffending moral teacher as being unfaithful to the "real Jesus" set forth in the Gospels:

> Does the teaching of Jesus form any exception to the otherwise pervasive presentation of the wrath of God in the Bible? Well, you might think so if you listened only to what modern sentimentality says about Jesus of Nazareth. The men of the world, who have never been born again, who have never come under the conviction of sin, have reconstructed a Jesus to suit themselves, a feeble sentimentalist who preached only the love of God and had nothing to say about God's wrath. But very different was the real Jesus. . . .
>
> Where do you find the most terrible descriptions of hell in the whole of the Bible? . . . It is Jesus who speaks of the worm that dieth not and the fire that is not quenched; . . . Just let your mind run through the teaching of Jesus, and I think you will really be surprised to find how pervasive in His teaching is the thought of hell. . . .
>
> Let not anyone who thinks that fear of hell should be put out of the mind of unregenerate men ever suppose that he has the slightest understanding of what Jesus came into the world to say and do.[23]

Percy seized on the idea that Jesus spoke of hell in terms of literal fire and often in his sermons on hell pointed to the fact that Jesus used the (Greek) word *gehenna,* meaning "a place of perpetual burning," eleven of the twelve times it is used in the Bible. But the pupil differed from his teacher over how Jesus' words should be interpreted. For Percy, the plain meaning of his words was that hell was a place of literal fire and conscious torment. Machen, however, was willing to allow that this language might be figurative, as in the interpretation he gives of Matthew 7:23: When Jesus pronounced upon sinners the sentence: "Depart from me, ye that work iniquity," he said quite definitely that they "would be cast into hell." The meaning of this is "perfectly plain," Machen declared, namely, that "hell is designated in our passage as being banishment from Jesus."[24] On this view, what was terrible about hell was that it was separation from God; but for Percy, it was the fires and torment that quickened his imagination.

Finally, Machen may have reinforced Percy's belief that the social gospel was something that fundamentalism did *not* stand for. The good news of the gospel was first and foremost news about Christ's atoning death and only secondarily about Jesus as a moral teacher who can be used as a model for solving social problems. The only hope for society was through the transformed lives of men and women who have been reborn:

> If we really love our fellowmen we shall never be content with binding up their wounds or pouring on oil and wine or rendering them any such lesser service. We shall indeed do such things for them. But the main business of our lives will be to bring them to the Saviour of their souls.
>
> It is upon this brotherhood of twice-born sinners, this brotherhood of the redeemed, that the Christian founds the hope of society. He finds no solid hope in the improvement of earthly conditions, or the molding of human institutions under the influence of the Golden Rule. . . . The true transformation of society will come by the influence of those who have themselves been redeemed.[25]

## PARTING OF WAYS

Percy's amicable and respectful relationship with his teacher continued after he finished at Westminster. A few months after graduating, Percy invited him to speak to his young people at the Barnes Community Center, and Machen gave a talk there entitled "What Must I Do to Be Saved?" Percy wrote him the next day thanking him for his "splendid message," adding that "many spoke of it with real blessing."[26] And two years later, when Percy had started his magazine, *Young People Today,* one of the first issues included a long editorial (written by coeditor and fellow Westminster graduate Robert Strong) praising Machen as "perhaps the greatest living Christian scholar."

But while my father continued to have a favorable opinion of Machen, this was not the case for his seminary. Even at the time Percy graduated, he had developed a negative feeling toward Westminster. A few years later, in an editor's column on Calvinism (December 1936), he expressed extreme disapproval of the seminary because of the effect it was having on many of its students: "I know of many preachers-to-be who have lost all love for souls after one year at Westminster Seminary because of their ultra-

Calvinistic position."[27] If a doctrine could affect this all-important aspect of a person's faith in this way, then it was dangerous and should not be taught.[28]

A few months later, he announced his parting with the seminary over the issue of "the separated life." This had been a concern of Percy's in his student days, but now it had erupted internally when one of its original faculty members, Allan MacRae, resigned because of it. Percy wrote: "What a shame it is that Westminster Seminary has missed the great opportunity of becoming a great Seminary. I just read in the papers—'Founder of Fundamentalist Seminary Charges Drinking by Faculty.' This I feel is a shame. When the charge was made by Dr. Allan MacRae no denial of the charges [was] made."[29]

Allan MacRae had been on the faculty as a professor of Semitic philology at Westminster from its inception. Percy had taken courses with him in Hebrew, Old Testament, and archeology. MacRae resigned from Westminster in April 1937, shortly after Machen's death, charging that "practically every member of the faculty has entered upon a rigorous defense of an asserted right to use intoxicating liquors—a defense occasioned by the fact that certain faculty members themselves use intoxicants." Westminster was simply following the lead of its church (Machen's newly founded Presbyterian Church of America, later the Orthodox Presbyterian Church) in not condemning all use of alcohol, although it did not allow drinking on campus. R. B. Kuiper's reply to MacRae on behalf of the faculty stated in part: "The Biblical teaching against intemperance is very emphatic, but the Bible does not permit of a teaching which would make our Lord's example sinful."[30]

But for Percy this stance was "certainly one of compromise." Although he recognized that the Bible did not unequivocally condemn drinking, he thought a person who had accepted Christ should abstain from alcohol because of its associations with a worldly and sinful life. He had encountered too many lives for whom being saved from sin meant being saved from alcohol to condone it in any form.

And so Percy was through with Westminster. He had not reckoned with the strong denominationalism and confessionalism of the seminary from the start, and in the end, when he saw the practical effects of its official teaching and stance on its students and their "love for souls," he felt obliged to withdraw his support. But, characteristically, his criticism was mild; it was just "a shame" that Westminster was failing. He had no desire to "tear down" the seminary or denigrate any individuals; there was nothing to be gained from that. He would simply steer would-be-preachers to other more fundamental seminaries.[31]

# 8

## Early Ministry in Philadelphia

IN THE SUMMER OF 1931, AT THE END OF HIS MIDDLE YEAR AT WESTMIN-
ster, Percy's evangelistic career took off. It began with his summer assignment as director of the Barnes Mission, which led to his open-air meetings
on Washington Square in Philadelphia, out of which came his radio broadcast on a single Philadelphia station. Within a period of five months, Percy
had laid the foundations of a new "church of the air" with a congregation
of thousands of radio listeners. He embarked on this course initially within
the institutional framework of the Presbyterian Church in the U.S.A., but
gradually loosened his ties with the church and built a completely separate
organization.

As a seminary student, the usual process was for him to work with the
Philadelphia Presbytery to do summer supply preaching, and this had led to
a very positive experience at the Rhawnhurst Presbyterian Church after his
first year. In his middle year, Percy had done quite a lot of preaching at local churches, and now he wanted a summer assignment that would give him
more flexibility to do evangelistic work outside the walls of a single parish.
Mission work seemed to be the answer, and so he put in a request for the di-
rectorship of the Barnes Memorial Mission and Community Center at Seventh and Spruce Streets and was approved for the job on April 8. The church
official he dealt with was Rev. William P. Fulton, who had been superintendent of city missions and church extension for many years and was about
to begin a one-year term as moderator of the Philadelphia Presbytery.

Percy would have been attracted to the Barnes Mission because of its
shifting population and the opportunity it afforded (he thought) to work
with the street people of south Philadelphia. He had already done some
preaching at various missions in the city and was comfortable in this sort
of setting. Also, as director of the community center activities, he would
have a chance to work with young people.

Fortunately, we have Percy's own account of his first few months at the
Barnes, in an article that appeared a year later in Donald Barnhouse's *Revelation* magazine that described how his radio ministry was launched. Con-

sidering that the Barnes was to be his home base for more than five years, he gives a rather bleak description of his first encounter with it: It was "an old community center in the downtown district of Philadelphia. There was nothing there but a run down dilapidated building. It seemed a wreck—a derelict, and we hesitated to accept the work."[1]

However run-down the Barnes had become, it was a splendid structure when it was constructed thirty-five years earlier (in 1896). It was built by the adjacent First Presbyterian Church (which faced onto Washington Square, at Seventh and Locust Streets), in order to meet the changing needs of the community. In the mid-1880s, a new wave of immigrants had moved into the area south of First Church, including Jewish refugees from Russia, Italians, and East Europeans, and many Protestant churches were closing their doors or were being sold to Roman Catholic and Jewish congregations. Enrollment at First Church was in decline. The Barnes, built in memory of Albert Barnes, pastor of First Church from 1830 to 1867, was financed by a wealthy Philadelphia merchant, George Griffiths, at a cost of $50,694. It was equipped with modern steam heat and electric lighting and had ample space for Sunday school, adult classes, a playroom for younger children, as well as a gymnasium, library, reading room, and meeting spaces for Girls' Sewing School, Mothers' Meeting, Mission Board, and so on. It also had an auditorium used for various entertainments. It was in every sense a community center serving its neighborhood.[2]

In 1928 First Church merged with Calvary Presbyterian Church and left vacant the historic site that had sheltered the first Presbytery, the first Synod, and the first General Assembly in America. In 1931, the Barnes Memorial was still owned and overseen by First Church, but was supervised and funded to a large extent by the Presbytery.

Percy was put in charge of the mission work, which meant that he was expected to conduct Sunday services, Bible study classes, and daily vacation Bible school. He took his charge at the Barnes seriously and even took over some community activities, such as taking the Boy Scouts on regular outings.

Although he would eventually build up a lively ministry at the Barnes, his initial experience there must have been demoralizing in the extreme for an evangelist with a burning desire to win souls. He wrote: "At the first service there were fourteen present, boys and girls, and a few older folk. This went on for a few weeks, but there was no pleasure in preaching the Gospel to old walls and saints that had been sanctified years before I ever saw the daylight."

After this first dismal Sunday evening service, Percy immediately took steps to revitalize his congregation. The very next day he began to contact groups of young people from the various churches where he had been preaching and seeding the previous year, to bring them to the Barnes to participate in the evening service. He started with his good friends, Tom White and Walter Haman, at Rhawnhurst, and two weeks later, a "delegation" from Rhawnhurst came to the Sunday meeting. Over the summer and in the following year, delegations from all over Philadelphia would come to the Barnes for services. He also began to assemble the musical talent that he had been scouting for two years to sing and play at these services. In less than three weeks, he had assembled enough of an entourage to move his services outside the Barnes and conduct an "open-air meeting." He wanted to hold services on Saturday and Sunday evening around the corner, on the front porch of the old First Church that looked out onto Washington Square, and accordingly requested permission of First Church (through Rev. Fulton) to do so.

Percy had every reason to expect that the appropriate church boards and committees would cooperate with him. After all, the old First Church was just sitting there, empty and falling into disrepair. Moreover, the Presbytery was actively sponsoring summer evangelistic work through its Summer Evangelistic Committee, which had been in existence for thirty-three years, with Rev. Fulton taking an active supervisory role. That summer, the committee was exploring the feasibility of using "automobile loudspeaker equipment" to conduct open-air meetings at various locations around the city, and eventually two vehicles were equipped with sound equipment and $600 was committed to a twenty-four-day campaign using local volunteer ministers.

But in his article, Percy portrays the committee "who had charge of outdoor evangelistic work" as being hostile to him. "Immediately there was opposition. They said, 'Why, there is no good of your holding services from the porch of the First Church, for you will never get an audience. All you will have to preach to will be the trees in the park, and a dozen or so people.'"

There was hardly time to get official approval, but Percy did manage to gain access to First Church and permission to use the porch. We can best appreciate his own sense of what was happening at these first open-air meetings and of what God was accomplishing through him from his own narrative:

> But we asked for no money, and the meetings had been announced, so we went ahead and attempted this work for our Lord and Saviour Jesus Christ.
> A piano was moved from the Barnes Memorial around to the First church porch. The old communion platform was pulled out from the unused church, and braced under the rail of the porch, so that one end projected out over the street some ten or twelve feet below, like a diving board. Trumpet players came

voluntarily to assist. A choir of fifty or sixty young men formed to sing for the meetings. A number brought musical instruments and formed an orchestra.

The first service was held on a hot Saturday night in June [the 13th]. Some two hundred gathered in the street below and in Washington Square across the street. Sunday evening a still larger crowd attended. These Saturday and Sunday night meetings continued for two or three weeks until real conviction of sin was seen in the audience. The crowd was a motley one, made up of drunkards, dope fiends, gangsters, and bandits from the hardest quarters of South Philadelphia, but they listened attentively to the songs and to God's Word as it was boldly declared from the diving board platform. Young people's groups prayed daily for the services, and came to do personal work and give out tracts.

Percy had of course invited these volunteer musicians and personal workers to be there, drawing them from local churches and from Westminster. Female soloists and trios were regulars. Percy also obtained sound equipment from the same company that had equipped the gospel cars for the Presbytery, the Sound Amplification Company, and had three loudspeakers rigged to the church pillars. What the "audience" was getting was a full-scale rally with plenty of fine music and testimony, all of which was a prelude to the evangelistic sermon. Personal workers were in the audience ready to speak to anyone who made a decision.

The crowds kept growing. Hundreds stood below in the suffocating heat and listened attentively.

At the close of each service the choir sang an invitation hymn, and a call was given in no uncertain terms for those who would trust Christ as their Saviour to raise their hands. Scores responded. Then I climbed down the ladder to the street, and said, "If you meant business with Jesus, walk across the street and let me have a word of prayer with you." Scores marched over, night after night. Night after night we would interview and have personal prayer with them, giving each a Gospel and a word of invitation. In this way hundreds were led to Christ. The Moderator of the Philadelphia Presbytery visited a service one night and said that he was amazed to count sixty who had marched across the street that night to take Christ as their Saviour.

After four weekends of outdoor services, Percy capped off the series with a two-week campaign (July 11–26) which, he said, was inspired by "the apparent moving of the Spirit and the deep conviction so noticeable among those listening." By Percy's estimates, audiences ranged from 75 to 500, averaging 250 over twenty-four services for a grand total of about 6,000 in attendance. He counted 200 in all who made professions.

He goes on (in his account) to give further evidence of the moving of the Spirit by describing three individuals who were converted—a gang leader in south Philadelphia who had been shot in the stomach by the police in the act of robbing a house "and who came, leaving his gang, walking clear across the street with hat off, and bowing there in prayer. Before many nights he was up on the porch singing hymns with us"; another man who had spent nineteen years in the penitentiary, whom Percy dealt with after the meeting and who said "I see it, I see it, I'm saved, I'm saved!" and "left rejoicing"; and a church member who "came down off the platform where he had been with the others who were helping with the meeting, and stood with the drunks and down and outers in the gutter to take Christ as his own Saviour." He also describes the case of a man who trailed him after the service as he was returning to his room. Although the man would not accept Christ he was greatly convicted of sin, raising his hands toward heaven and crying, "Oh God, help me, help me, Oh, my sin, my sin" before disappearing into the night.[3]

Percy tended to look back on these outdoor meetings as having a very special significance in his ministry. We may wonder why since a few thousand people in attendance and two hundred professions is small even compared to the results he had gotten on his summer tours at BIOLA and Wheaton.

First, the open-air meetings were significant for him personally. This was not a prearranged tour with pastors and congregations waiting to receive him. He was reaching out to the unsaved and the unchurched and seeing many social dropouts make public professions and life-changing decisions. Further, the results that he witnessed were for him a vindication of evangelism. God was still working through "the declaration of the simple Gospel story" to save the lost. Percy had something to prove to the "powers that be" at Westminster where he felt that his evangelistic fervor was being discredited. Even his own fundamentalist brethren were raising doubts. He had written in the back of his appointment book, in very small print in pencil, a remark he attributed to Donald Barnhouse: "Evangelism is a thing of past"; and below it, another (from a Dr. Kelsey): "Evangelism is a step backward." Percy evidently took these comments as a personal challenge. His success convinced him that his work had been "singularly owned of God."

Another aspect of the importance of these meetings for the young evangelist was that he was winning souls outside the established church. His act of moving his service outside the walls of his appointed parish was literally an act of separating himself from the church. And his use of the abandoned facility of First Church, with its "gaunt gray pillars, corroded with age," was symbolic of the passing of the old order and the beginning of the new. As anyone could plainly see, the Holy Spirit was absent from that structure and visibly present in what transpired outside it and in the street below. For Percy, his Saturday and Sunday night rallies, culminating in a two-week campaign, were living proof of a "modern revival" in which "tremendous movings of God's Holy Spirit have been seen." "Hundreds of young men and women in Philadelphia are turning to Christ. A great movement toward revival is seen. . . . The doors of Heaven are opening and we are looking for an out-pouring that will sweep over the entire country. God is still on the throne. He longs to save."

\*

But Percy's highly dramatized account of these events tends to be one-sided and distorted, especially regarding his dealings with the Presbyterians. It has the quality of a morality play in which clear lines are drawn between the forces of good and evil, between those who are on the side of preaching the gospel (Percy and his coworkers) and those who are trying to obstruct it (church officials). In his telling, he encounters resistance at every turn and is able to carry out his mission only by sheer boldness and determination. He suggests that Rev. Fulton is one of the skeptics on the Evangelistic Committee who doubts that he can be successful at Washington Square and then, showing up at one of his meetings, has to admit grudgingly that the upstart preacher is having amazing success in bringing men and women to Christ. However, the actual scenario was quite different from this. Although Rev. Fulton and some members of the committee may have been somewhat wary of the brash seminarian, they were generally supportive and agreed to sponsor and give aid to his open-air meetings.

The Evangelistic Committee was made up of representatives from the Presbyterian Social Union, the Presbytery of Philadelphia, and the Presbytery of North Philadelphia. It was organized in 1899 at the suggestion of D. L. Moody who visited the Social Union that year and urged upon them the importance of "city evangelization."[4] Thus the committee had been sponsoring various types of evangelistic endeavors throughout the city—in missions and open-air meetings, as well as Daily Vacation Bible School—for thirty-two years.

Another aim of the committee was to reach with the gospel the various ethnic groups that had settled in Philadelphia. In the 1930 annual report, Rev. Warren R. Ward, pastor of Westminster Church where Percy had been asked to speak on several occasions in the previous year, wrote in an article entitled "The Spirit of the Work":

We are attempting to reach all races and nationalities, having work among Italians, Negroes, Greeks, Poles, Hebrews, etc. God has sent people from the "ut-

termost parts of the earth" to our city and your Committee is seeking to reach
them for Christ. One hundred cents of every dollar given is invested in soul-
saving work. I know of no work more worth while than this work of the Evangelistic Committee.

Percy's request to conduct open-air meetings at First Church would
have been channeled to the "Open Air and Place of Meeting" subcommittee. Serving on the committee (of twelve) was Rev. Fulton, Rev. Merril
MacPherson (who was soon to become one of Percy's closest friends), and
Elder Edgar Frutchey (who later in the year became a member of Percy's
board of advisers for his radio church). As noted, for the summer of 1931,
the Evangelistic Committee was exploring the feasibility of using automobile loudspeaking equipment for outdoor services—something that had
never been tried in Philadelphia. Two cars were furnished by radio station
WCAU, and eighty-seven "gospel car services" were held at various parks
and squares around the city. (In fact, Percy participated in some of these
gospel car services and is pictured conducting one such service at Franklin
Square in the annual report pamphlet.) The committee also sponsored
open-air services at two "Fixed Stations," which included two weeks of
meetings conducted by "Rev. Percy Crawford, Portico of the Old First
Church."[5] The sound-equipped car was sent to three of these meetings at
Washington Square.[6] A midsummer report noted that "the Rev. Percy Crawford, a senior in Westminster Seminary, showed quite unusual talent as a
street evangelist."[7,8]

William Fulton is remarkable for his lifetime of devoted service to the
church. At the November 1931 meeting of the Presbytery, Fulton was hon-
ored on his seventy-fifth birthday, and Merril MacPherson presented him
with forty-one roses—one for each year of service to the Presbytery. Fulton was a strong advocate of evangelism in the church. He had served on
the Summer Evangelistic Committee continuously since 1900 and was its
superintendent for nineteen years (1907–26). In the previous fall (November 1930), he had organized an Evangelistic Convention and pushed it before the Presbytery ministers and elders with the announcement that "we
are exceedingly anxious to make this convention a great success in stimulating evangelistic activity in all the churches of the Presbytery."[9] So there
is every reason to believe that Rev. Fulton had an open and positive attitude toward Percy's evangelistic endeavors and entreaties.

Fulton had encouraged members of the Evangelistic Committee to make
at least one visit to the various outdoor services they were supporting, and
some of them wrote up their impressions for the annual report. Since he
had been working with Percy for over a year, it is not surprising that he at-

tended one of Percy's services at Washington Square. He wrote the following account, which was printed in the 1931 annual report along with photographs of the service:

> On a Sunday evening, the latter part of July, I attended an open-air evangelistic service at 7th and Locust Streets, conducted by Percy B. Crawford, a senior in Westminster Theological Seminary. . . .
>
> Peoples of various nationalities live in the neighborhood. In hot summer evenings many of these emerge from courts, alleys, and narrow streets, and congregate in the open square for a breath of fresh air and for rest under the cooling shade trees.
>
> [That evening] I found Mr. Crawford, with choir and orchestra consisting of many young people and personal workers, assembled on the veranda of the old First Church building, ready to conduct an evangelistic program of vocal and instrumental music, Scripture reading, hymn singing, prayer and sermon. At 8 o'clock, a broadcasting automobile, loaned for this service by the Summer Evangelistic Committee, drew up close to the building, adjusted the microphone on the veranda and the service began. Far out across the square went the sweet strains of music and the clear voice of the speaker. The people came closer and stood on the pavement or sat on the curbing. Mr. Crawford spoke on "the parable of the great supper," and was listened to with rapt attention. The appeal to accept Christ as Saviour was forceful and urgent. Many responded with the uplifted hand. Then the speaker came down from the veranda to the pavement and asked those who were willing to accept Christ as Saviour to come and take him by the hand. Some 50 or 60 responded and remained as Mr. Crawford made plain to them "how to be saved." He then commended them to God in prayer.
>
> I came away from that meeting feeling that there are multitudes in our city who never enter our churches, but who can be reached with the Gospel, if we go to them. "Go out and bring them in," is Christ's command. Are we willing to go?[10]

## THE RADIO BROADCAST

Rev. Fulton was evidently pleased with the work Percy was doing at the Barnes and invited him to continue there for the coming year. Percy's response was to try to strike a deal:

> We replied that we would if they would give us the radio. Having had previous experience in preaching over the radio on stations [KTBI] in Los Angeles and WMBI of the Moody Bible Institute and others, we knew the way in which God would bless that work. The answer was that it would be impossible. They were unable to help in any way towards the broadcasting.[11]

Fulton must have realized that Percy was branching out and doing his own independent work, but cooperated with him nonetheless by allowing him to use the auditorium. However the moderator understandably would have wanted to make it absolutely clear to all concerned that the radio broadcast was not part of Percy's work at the Barnes, that the church was not sponsoring the service that Percy put on the air as it had the open-air service, and that any funds solicited on the program would not be used to support the church or the Barnes activities.

However Percy was not deterred. Even without the church's backing, he would go ahead, trusting that the Lord would supply his need:

> Groups of young people began praying. Prices were gotten on every Philadelphia station. Friends were consulted and money began coming in for a radio fund. A board of five men were selected as advisers. The day before the contract was to be signed, I talked with one of these men, who said, "You had better not sign the contract unless you are underwritten by business men." This was impossible for I did not have the contacts with wealthy business men.
>
> I turned to God's Word for guidance. My Testament opened to Philippians 4:19: "My God shall supply all your need." I said, "Lord, do you really mean it?" I turned to my Greek Testament and read this verse: "My God will make up the deficiency of all your need." This was enough. I said, "Lord, I will trust this promis[s]ory note as my underwriting."

A contract was signed with WIP-WFAN Broadcasting Company for the one-hour service to be aired Sunday afternoons at 5:30 for thirteen weeks beginning October 4, 1931. The fee was $100 per week, plus $75 per week for "rental of speech input equipment and circuits." And so the open-air service and the entire musical ensemble was moved back into the Barnes Memorial auditorium where it became the *Young People's Church of the Air* to be sent out "over the ether waves" to some one hundred thousand Philadelphia listeners.[12] The Sunday broadcast would originate from the Barnes auditorium for the next five years.


## COURTSHIP

As Percy was assembling the cast of vocalists and instrumentalists who would take part in the radio broadcast, he found that he was in dire need of a regular pianist and also a reliable quartet. He had put together a quartet of Westminster men to sing with him at local meetings, but he was not satisfied with them. Always on the lookout for new talent, he heard about a promising young pianist through one of his classmates, Bill Hawks, who happened to be dating an attractive Christian woman, Esther Duvall, from nearby Collingswood, New Jersey. While attending a guest dinner at the seminary one evening, Esther heard that Percy was looking for a pianist and told him about her talented younger sister, Ruth. A visit to the Duvall home was arranged, and soon thereafter Percy and a few of his classmates set out on the short hop over the Ben Franklin bridge to Collingswood to hear Ruth play.

The Duvalls were a large, close-knit, church-oriented family whose roots were in the South. Ruth's father, Rezin Fenton Duvall, was a jeweler by trade who had moved his family to New Jersey in 1913 and then tragically died six years later (when Ruth was only three) in a fall while painting the house. My grandmother, Nancy, did not remarry and so was left with five children, ages three to sixteen, to raise on her own. Esther, the oldest, had to drop out of school and work to help support the family.

Family life in the Duvall household centered in the activities of the First Methodist Church and the larger Holiness tradition. The children could be seen regularly attending seven different services each Sunday: Methodist class meeting and morning worship in the morning, Sunday school and Holiness meeting in the afternoon, and Epworth League (for young people) and evening service in the evening, followed by a hymn sing at various homes (usually the Duvall's). Ruth naturally believed, as did her brothers and sister, that she would one day be leading a life of Christian service in some form.

Mother Duvall was known for having young people gather at her house for lively singing and fellowship, while accompanying on her guitar (later joined by Ruth on the piano). If her visitors were lucky they got to enjoy some of her good southern cooking along with the singing. All the children sang and loved music of all sorts, from gospel music and hymns to folk songs to opera. At the time of Percy's visit, the family was taking part in Gipsy Smith's three-week evangelistic campaign in Collingswood (singing in the choir), which ended on the same day that Percy's radio broadcast began (October 4).

Ruth was a natural on the piano. She had taken lessons from the mother of one of her closest friends, Irene Campbell,[13] but was largely self-taught. At age fifteen, she had already composed a gospel hymn, "The Nail-Pierced Hand," with a piano harmonization that showed unusual chordal complexity. The words to the song were penned by poet-sister Esther, and it found its way into Percy's first songbook, *The YPCA Hymn Book,* put out within the year—the only song in the book not published in other songbooks.

As Ruth prepared herself for her audition with the young, energetic—and *single!*—Philadelphia evangelist and contemplated the possibility of playing on a weekly radio broadcast, she must have been a little overawed by the opportunity that lay before her. And too, she would have wondered deep in her heart, as would any pretty teenage girl, if this dashing fellow could possibly be the one she would love. But she muted these feelings by telling herself she could never be interested in someone with the name "Percy," which she thought was the "worst name" anyone could have.[14]

Ruth's skill as an accompanist shone forth as she played and sang one of her favorite folk songs, the sentimental "Mandy Lee." My father was duly impressed with Ruth's natural musicianship and knew pretty quickly that he wanted her to play on the broadcast. But he was even more impressed with her natural beauty and (as he would later tell it) did make some advances that evening, kissing her outside the house. Many years later, Bill Hawks reminisced about that very evening and wanted to set the record straight regarding Percy's true intentions. In a semiserious letter read at Percy's This Is Your Life banquet, he wrote:

> When you hear Percy Crawford say in that superior way of his that he took pains to take unto himself a wife as sort of a proposition to get a good piano player you can put it down that the pianist part was purely incidental. Why I can still see Percy as the Duvall family drove us back to the bridge on that night of his first trip to the Duvall home; Percy was taking pains all right, and he was working up a lather trying to discover how an old man like himself could ask Ruthie's mama if he could see her daughter again.

The immediate problem the old man faced was that he was nearly twice Ruth's age—he was about to turn twenty-nine and she was just fifteen. What Percy said to Ruthie's mama when he left was: "It's a shame she's so young. As soon as she's old enough to have dates, I'll be back." Fortunately for him, my grandmother, who was no pushover, liked Percy well enough to let him come back to the house (she began to invite him to dinner) and to let the relationship continue.

So Ruth began to play on the radio broadcast right from its very beginning in October 1931,[15] and the duo of Ruth and Percy would continue uninterrupted for twenty-nine years.

An added bonus of finding Ruth for the broadcast was that Percy also got his quartet. When Ruth heard that he was dissatisfied with his Westminster quartet, she urged him to try the quartet at her church, which consisted of her brother, Fenton Duvall, Burdelle "Chick" Hawk, Robert Mortenson, and Vince Joy. Percy liked them and this foursome became his first *Young People's Church of the Air* quartet with Ruth as accompanist.

Two years later, after Ruth finally reached the marrying age of seventeen, she became Percy's life companion and partner in his great work. They were married September 18, 1933, at the Pinebrook Conference, which had just opened that summer. And although her betrothal to Percy was a clear case of his robbing the cradle, it was a marriage that worked in every way. Percy had made it clear to Ruth when he proposed that he could marry her only on the condition that she would "have third place in his life and affections," after the Lord (first place) and the Lord's work (second place).[16] Ruth was head over heels in love with Percy, but in any case she would have had no difficulty putting the Lord and the Lord's work above everything else in her life, and so she gladly accepted the terms of the marriage. One can only say, looking back on the ministry of Percy and Ruth Crawford over twenty-nine years, that my mother did faithfully keep her end of the deal. What is more, she became an equal partner in the work (as we will see), contributing far more to its success through the music than Percy even fully realized.

In a letter Percy wrote to Ruth toward the end of his life (dealing mainly with financial matters), he said to her in his usual terse manner, "You have been a perfect wife." Words of appreciation and affection like that did not flow often from my father's lips (or pen). But what he said was perfectly apt and true.

*

Percy's radio broadcast, almost overnight, made him a popular figure, and one to be reckoned with among fundamentalists in the Philadelphia area. Invitations to preach came pouring in, and he accepted as many as he could (even several one-week campaigns), all the while continuing with his final year of studies at Westminster and Penn. Upon completing both programs in May 1932, he finally felt free to devote himself 100 percent to the Lord's work. With this unburdening came a sense of exhilaration at the possibilities that were opening up before him. That summer, in addition to his duties at the Barnes, he resumed his open-air meetings on Washington Square, sharing the "pulpit" with his good friend from BIOLA, Harlan Fischer, who was then attending Westminster, and continued to conduct evangelistic meetings with Ruth and the YPCA quartet in the greater Philadelphia area. That summer, too, his career got an unexpected boost when fundamentalist leader Donald Barnhouse asked him to be a speaker on his "Revelation Cruise."

## DONALD GREY BARNHOUSE

Donald Grey Barnhouse had come to Philadelphia in 1925 as pastor of Grace Presbyterian Church and two years later moved to the prestigious

Tenth Presbyterian Church at Seventeenth and Spruce Streets, just a few blocks from the Barnes Mission. He had gained a reputation as an outspoken critic of modernist ministers (some within his own Presbyterian denomination), an inspired Bible teacher, and a fearless defender of the gospel. His ministry extended well beyond Tenth Church, as he conducted regular Bible classes and meetings at preaching-stations in Philadelphia and New York and was on the air coast-to-coast with his radio broadcast. Although his contract with the CBS network had ended in the previous year after three-and-one-half years, Barnhouse continued to buy radio time, and in the spring of 1932 was heard on close to one hundred stations nationwide.[17]

Percy and Barnhouse were fundamentalists of the same stripe, both in terms of their theological stance and their zeal in propagating the gospel. They had been on similar educational tracks, with Barnhouse in advance of my father by about a decade. The exceptionally bright Donald had entered BIOLA in 1913 immediately after high school, where he came under Reuben Torrey's powerful sway. While at BIOLA, he too had made a commitment to the Lord to serve as a missionary in Africa (but instead, after the Great War, labored in the fields of Belgium and southern France). From BIOLA he moved to Princeton Theological Seminary, where he was challenged by B. B. Warfield in theology and Robert Dick Wilson in Old Testament, as well as other "younger men," which may have included J. Gresham Machen, who was an assistant professor of New Testament at the time.[18] Later, in Philadelphia, he too took graduate courses in history at Penn. By way of contrast, it is interesting that while Percy earned his bachelor's degree (from Wheaton), his seminary degree (from Westminster), and his master's degree (from Penn), Barnhouse did not complete any of the degree programs he entered after Bible school. And yet the latter was a true intellectual who embraced higher education and was profoundly shaped by it, whereas my father was not an intellectual and was always deeply critical of the secular university.[19]

By the summer of 1932, Barnhouse was reaching out to his junior colleague and inviting him to take part in his various ventures. First, he invited Percy to contribute the article discussed above to his magazine, *Revelation,* describing his open-air meetings of the previous summer and the radio broadcast. Then he was asked to be a speaker on the Revelation Cruise, set to go July 14–21, and after that a speaker at his Revelation Labor Day Conference on September 3–5.

The Revelation Cruise was a bold new venture. The plan was to rent the entire Cunard liner *Transylvania* for a weeklong cruise with stops at Bermuda and then north to Nova Scotia. Barnhouse ballyhooed it in his advertisements as "a dream come true" and "an ideal vacation plan for your summer." "But chiefly it will be a conference, a meeting of God's own to hear His Word, to magnify the Name of our Saviour."[20] There was an impressive lineup of speakers, selected for their reputation of being "true to the Word of God": in addition to speaker-director Barnhouse, the principals were Harry Ironside, Will Houghton, Captain Reginald Wallis, and William Allan Dean; but the final list included four additional speakers: Roy Brumbaugh, Erling Olsen, Shuyler English, and Percy Crawford, as well as song leaders Homer Hammontree and Paul Beckwith. Percy was scheduled to speak at only one evening service (along with Will Houghton), indicating perhaps his lesser stature. But although he may have been somewhat frustrated by the relatively minor assignment he was given, I imagine that he accepted his subsidiary role with grace, while taking advantage of the chance to relax and mingle with the young people.

But an important lesson was brought home to him on the Revelation Cruise. As he watched Barnhouse's people gather around him in a relaxed atmosphere of fun, fellowship, and Bible study, he realized that he too had to find a way to gather together his new flock of young people that was growing by leaps and bounds as a result of his radio ministry. He knew from the mail he received that he was reaching hundreds of individuals who were committing themselves to the Lord and who would need nurturing in the faith as they prepared for a life of service. These young people would have to be brought within some sort of institutional framework where they could receive sound Bible-based instruction. And so, as he sunned and played deck tennis and volleyball, Percy was nurturing his own dream—to start a summer Bible conference for young people, a dream that would come to fruition in the very next summer with the opening of Pinebrook Bible Conference in the Pocono Mountains of Pennsylvania. He already had enough contacts among leading fundamentalists and Bible teachers to make up an attractive roster of speakers; but he would exploit the opportunity the cruise gave him for further networking. Indeed, every one of the invited speakers and song leaders who were on the cruise showed up at Pinebrook in the first couple of years.

Given the remarkable similarities in the backgrounds and beliefs of these two fundamentalist leaders, one wonders why a closer relationship never developed between them. There was the remark that Percy had penciled into the back of his 1931 calendar book: "Barnhouse: Evangelism is a thing of past." Assuming that Barnhouse did make this statement, what could he possibly have meant, since he was certainly no foe of evangelism? He made constant reference to the importance of bringing people to the saving knowledge of Christ and saw his own ministry as instrumental in achieving that end.[21] However, his own preaching was not aimed at getting people to make a decision, but rather at teaching and instructing in the faith. A close associate of Barnhouse, John DeBrine, recalled that he used to say (contrasting himself with Billy Graham): "I'm a pediatrician, not an obstetrician." Thus he rarely gave invitations and altar calls. In fact, he tended to be skeptical about the methods used by evangelists and revivalists in winning souls. "Where will these converts be in ten years?" he asked.[22]

This difference in attitude over the best method of preaching the gospel may have been a sticking point between them. But more likely, it was their personalities that kept them at arm's length over the years. Both men were authoritarian figures who needed to be at center stage in all of their endeavors. Neither had any inclination to be in the other's orbit. But unlike Percy, Barnhouse tended to be a "lone wolf" who alienated friend and foe alike by correcting their errors and then not caring what they thought of him. He wrote about this period of his life: "Early in my ministry I conceived the idea that I must strike out against all error wherever I saw it. . . . If [error] was in some fundamental leader with whom I was in 95% agreement, I swung hard at the 5%."[23]

In the ensuing years, Percy did reciprocate Barnhouse's early support by inviting him to contribute an article to his own magazine, *Young People Today;*[24] and the great Bible teacher did finally come to Pinebrook in its sixth season (for two days instead of the usual one week). At that time, Percy was about to realize his cherished vision of a Christian liberal arts college—The King's College would open its doors in the fall of 1938. Several Pinebrook staffers from that era remember Barnhouse saying to Percy that he was opposed to Christian colleges because he did not think they could achieve the same standards as secular institutions, and if he came back to Pinebrook again, he would have to speak out against Christian education. He was threatening to take a hard swing at my father who decided to duck and did not invite the great man back until much later in their lives.[25]

### PHI GAMMA FISHING CLUBS

Percy's first season of full-time evangelistic work in Philadelphia (1932–33) was marked by new ventures and continuing success. He put the radio broadcast on a second station—WMCA, New York—more than doubling his listening audience and greatly enlarging the field of his evangelistic meetings. He and Ruth and the YPCA quartet began a heavy schedule of meetings, traveling six nights of the week to churches throughout the Northeast.

A good part of his week was devoted to his duties as director and pastor of the Barnes. He enjoyed working with the young boys, of different ethnicities and usually poor, who came to the Community Center. He made a policy that the boys were not allowed to use the gymnasium unless they attended church on Sunday. One boy by the name of Alexander Pantellas, who was Greek Orthodox, recalled attending church at the Barnes when he was about ten and listening to those "powerful sermons"; "it was like he reached right out and was speaking directly to you," he said. Percy noticed that Alexander and his pals were shining shoes on the street and organized them into a singing group called "The Boot Black Quartet." He took them with him to some of his meetings and put them on the radio program.[26]

Percy also started a weekly Bible class at the Barnes, which he called "The Young People's Bible School," and charged a nominal "tuition" fee ($1 per semester). Attendance grew to two hundred by the second year. That year, too, he began looking for a suitable site for a summer conference and putting together a roster of Bible teachers and speakers. Pinebrook Bible Conference would open July 1, 1933, and run for nine weeks.

After the third year of broadcasting the *Young People's Church of the Air* on Philadelphia and New York stations, Percy began to think more about how to give structure and organization to the amorphous congregation that was coalescing around his radio ministry. The problem, as he put it in the August 1934 edition of *Young People Today,* was to find a way in which the young people he was reaching could come together for the purposes of fellowship and Christian service. Presently, he wrote, "we have the names of over two hundred young men and women from eight different states who already are gathering together in their own cities and towns other young men and women of like mind."[27] He had already brought many of these young people together at his summer Bible conference, which was beginning its second season, but his converts were looking for ways in which they could actively serve the Lord in their hometowns. It is not surprising that Percy's way of channeling this spiritual energy was to form fishing clubs whose primary purpose was to win souls. He wrote: "As a result of many conferences with young people's leaders we have decided to band ourselves together through the means of Fishing Clubs."

Percy named them Phi Gamma Fishing Clubs, putting together the two models of soul winning groups he had experienced in Los Angeles—Daddy Horton's Fishermen's Club and the Alpha Gamma Omega fraternity at UCLA. In his initial announcement of the plan, he followed Horton's model closely: the threefold purpose of the clubs would be to "furnish workers for churches, missions, etc.," to ground young people in the faith through Bible study and to "fish for men."

The clubs were to be made up of young men or women separately, or both men and women together; they would be interdenominational and would meet either "in a church or in a private home." His aim was "not primarily to start another organization in or outside of the church," similar to existing young people's groups like the Epworth League or Christian Endeavor; he had no desire to administer a new society. The *Young People's Church of the Air* would be the umbrella organization, but each club would "sink or swim on its own initiative." With regard to the delicate question of how the clubs would be related to the denominational churches, he thought they could be formed either inside or outside of the church, depending on whether the church and the pastor were fundamental; but whether they were in or out, he envisioned that they would supply "consecrated young workers" who would "supplement" other organizations and be a "stimulus" to existing activities.

The proposed requirements for membership indicate what my father thought were the important ingredients in the Christian life: an individual must (1) have experienced the new birth and publicly testified to it, (2) live "the separated life" (described here simply as "abstain[ing] from practices which tend to wasting of time and weakening of body and mind"), and (3) sign an eight-point statement of doctrine.[28] Any group that met these standards would be "taken into the fellowship of the club" and would receive a charter, a chapter number, and "a two and a half foot fish with Phi Gamma written on it."[29] Percy proposed that the clubs meet once a week and that meetings should be "brief and full of life." Club members would want to bring their unsaved friends to their meetings in an effort to win them to Christ.

Clubs would also be interested in carrying the gospel to the outside world. This would normally take the form of distributing tracts and Gospels of John. (Within a few months, Percy had prepared a special edition of the Gospel of John, entitled "The Greatest Love Story Ever Told," "adapted to the needs of the personal work of the Phi Gamma Clubs.")[30] But it might also mean witnessing or conducting a service in prisons, hospitals, and missions. The YPCA office, through a regular column in *Young People Today,* proposed various ideas and strategies for effective soul winning. To illustrate: it offered "question pins" for sale—"to get the folk to bite on, then replying with the gospel of John."[31] Or it encouraged the distribution of packages of tracts wrapped in colorful cellophane (called "Gospel Bombs") and supplied the materials necessary "to roll your own bomb."[32]

Individual chapters were quite ingenious in thinking of ways to spread the gospel. In one instance, a group of nineteen "young ladies" from Immanuel Baptist Church in Chicago dressed in colored cellophane uniforms and gave out fifty-five thousand tracts in one evening. Jack Wyrtzen, a Phi Gamma writing from Woodhaven, New York, reported that over a period of three months, he had given out twenty-one thousand gospel bombs, resulting in fifteen hundred people writing in for a "Reason Why" booklet, and a quarter of these writing in for a New Testament.[33] Another Chicago club distributed tracts pasted to handheld fans. And an innovator from Salem, New Jersey, sealed tracts in bottles (called "Moses Bottles") and set them adrift in lakes, rivers, and the ocean. Some clubs had gospel teams and were able to obtain air time on the radio. Another printed its own magazine, *Good News.*

Percy had little direct contact with club members, communicating with them primarily through his monthly column. He also arranged annual rallies and banquets (in Philadelphia and New York), which brought together the clubs in these regions to meet each other and share ideas.[34] Also, the clubs prompted him to write his little manual on soul winning, *The Art of Fishing for Men,* which went on sale in April 1935 and was "Dedicated to the Phi Gamma Fishing Clubs scattered over the United States." By that time there were 150 chartered clubs with membership ranging from five to ninety, and consequently Percy's first and only book had an instant readership as it was put into the hands of thousands of Phi Gamma members.

The number of clubs peaked about two years after their inception at approximately 250 and held steady at least through 1939. In January of that year, on the basis of responses to a questionnaire, the newly appointed "General Secretary" of the clubs, Charles Lampman, estimated that there were 232 chartered clubs (200 of them active) in twelve states and one Canadian province and 4,835 chartered members. The vast majority of the clubs were located in Pennsylvania, New Jersey, and New York.

In 1939, as the clubs became more and more peripheral in his ministry, Percy tried to revive them by linking them with another similar organization active in high schools, the Bornagainers Clubs, directed by youth worker Brandt Reed. Reed had been working with Jack Wyrtzen's Word of Life organization in New York City. However, within the next few years, the Phi Gamma clubs either faded away or were absorbed into the Bornagainers Clubs.[35] But they were a huge success as long as they lasted (about seven years) and were an important part of my father's ministry. They were one of his earliest initiatives, helping to build infrastructure in his organization and providing a source of new recruits for his other endeavors. Further, the clubs contributed to his larger mission of saving souls by mobilizing thousands of young people into Christian service and steering them into evangelism and "personal work." Percy viewed the hundreds of local Phi Gamma chapters dotting the Northeast as field stations, where cadres of young people were propagating the gospel in the streets and in homes and where he could bring his evangelistic team to build on their efforts. He had gotten from the clubs a big return in souls on a fairly modest investment of his time, energy, and funds.

Percy's family, Vancouver, British Columbia, 1912. Percy stands in between older brothers Willoughby (left) and Alph (right), Margaret and Tom seated.

The Bible Institute of Los Angeles with the 4,000-seat auditorium/Church of the Open Door in the center, flanked by dormitories. Percy stayed in the YMCA located in this building on the first day he arrived in Los Angles and was converted three days later, September 23, 1923, at the Sunday service there.

After his conversion, Percy joined Thomas "Daddy" Horton's bible class and Fishermen's Club where he began to learn the techniques of soul-winning. He wrote under this picture in his photo album: "Daddy and one of his boys."

Percy's inscription: "Rev. R. A. Torrey 1924." Reuben Torrey was the pastor of the Church of the Open Door and the Dean of the Bible Institute. He became Percy's mentor and spiritual model.

Percy took this photo of John MacInnis, who succeeded Torrey as Dean of the Bible Institute and was Percy's primary teacher at BIOLA. He was later ousted for modernist tendencies in his book, *Peter the Fisherman Philosopher.*

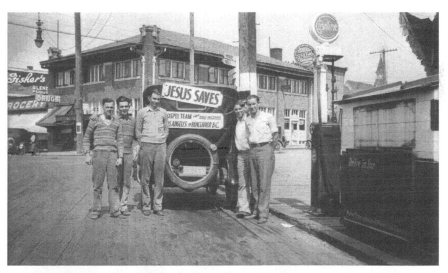

Percy's first quartet from BIOLA and first evangelistic tour, summer 1926, from Los Angeles to Vancouver with meetings in 42 towns and cities.

Percy's open air meetings began in the summer of 1931 from the porch of the abandoned First Presbyterian Church facing Washington Square in Philadelphia. The communion platform was braced under the rail "like a diving board."

Percy conducting a street meeting at Franklin Square, Philadelphia, sponsored by the Presbyterian Church, U.S.A., Philadelphia, 1931. The Evangelistic Committee reported that the senior at Westminster Seminary "showed quite unusual talent as a street evangelist." Image courtesy of the Presbyterian Historical Society.

Portrait of the twenty-nine-year-old radio evangelist.

Donald Barnhouse invited the youth-oriented Percy Crawford
to be a speaker on his "Revelation Cruise," July 1932. Percy
was able to network with the impressive lineup of Bible teachers Barnhouse assembled.

# 9
## The Presbyterians

AFTER FINISHING AT WESTMINSTER SEMINARY, PERCY WRESTLED WITH the question of whether to seek ordination in the Presbyterian Church. The church was regularly accepting Westminster graduates into its parishes and ministries. Two classifications on the roll of ministers were possible at this time—pastor and evangelist. But Percy had mixed feelings about whether to join the Presbyterians. On the one hand, with his appointment at the Barnes, he was already halfway in the church and under its authority. The Barnes was his home base and gave him a place to be. Moreover, he received a salary from the church—$1,950 in 1932 and $1,500 in 1933—and this was no small matter in the early 1930s with the country deep in depression.

On the other hand, he was also halfway out of the church since his radio ministry was entirely independent. Moreover, as we have seen, he was already an ordained Baptist minister, and that gave him all the clerical credentials he needed to further his evangelism. Theologically, he did not view the church as having any special God-given authority; nor did he think that being ordained in the church gave him any special office or spiritual authority. In a later sermon (1936) he said: "Do you think because a lot of men laid their hands on my head and ordained me to the ministry that that makes me any different from you? It certainly docs not; you are no better than I am or I am no better than you, for there is no difference."[1] The church was, in essence, only an institutional framework in which the Holy Spirit might or might not be actively working; and there was much to convince him that the Holy Spirit was not in residence in many of the denominational churches of his day.

Further, he certainly did not want to get tangled up in the politics of the Philadelphia Presbytery and the ongoing battle between liberals and conservatives. He was deeply troubled by Donald Barnhouse's having just been put on trial in the Presbytery, resulting in his being admonished as a "disturber of the peace and purity of the Church of Jesus Christ."[2]

After delaying for a year and a half Percy finally decided to seek ordination and in November 1933 was received by letter of transfer (from First

Baptist Church, South Chicago) into the Presbyterian Church in the U.S.A. The minutes for that meeting of the Philadelphia Presbytery indicate that "after examination in theology, and after answering the Constitutional questions, on motion, his name was placed on the Roll of Ministers of Presbytery" as an evangelist. Without fanfare, he met with the appropriate church officials and, swallowing hard, answered yes to the following eight questions:

1.  Do you believe the Scriptures of the Old and New Testaments to be the Word of God, the only infallible rule of faith and practice?
2.  Do you sincerely receive and adopt the Confession of Faith of this Church, as containing the system of doctrine taught in the Holy Scriptures?
3.  Do you approve of the government and discipline of the Presbyterian Church in the U.S.?
4.  Do you promise subjection to your brethren in the Lord?
5.  Have you been induced, as far as you know your own heart, to seek the office of the holy ministry from love to God, and a sincere desire to promote his glory in the gospel of his Son?
6.  Do you promise to be zealous and faithful in maintaining the truths of the gospel, and the purity and peace of the Church; whatever persecution or opposition may arise unto you on that account?
7.  Do you engage to be faithful and diligent in the exercise of all private and personal duties, which become you as a Christian and a minister of the Gospel . . . ?
8.  Are you now willing to undertake the work of an evangelist; and do you promise to discharge the duties which may be incumbent on you in this character as God shall give you the strength?[3]

He chose not to make the ceremony part of a worship service, with presenters and guests. It was not a very important event in the life of the church or in the life of Percy.

*

Percy's relationship with Rev. Fulton, his closest contact with the church hierarchy, continued to be chilly as it had been from the start. His correspondence with Fulton specifying his assignments were clipped and businesslike. In one letter he lays out his plans for the coming summer and fall in a tone that sounds more like a pronouncement of what he intends to do rather than an asking for permission to do these things. It begins: "So as to have a clear understanding of future plans I might state them briefly." And regarding the important matter of the continued use of the Barnes auditorium for the radio broadcast, he writes: "For next fall I propose continuing the broadcast as at the present time only with additional stations. I shall assume all responsibility for these just as I have in the past."[4] One feels that he was in hard negotiation with his superior, willing to do only what he contracts with him to do and on terms that he specifies.

A partial explanation of his strained relations with Fulton and the church lay in his anti-institutionalism and strong individualism. He was by nature distrustful of all institutions, groups, and bureaucracies, always wanting to strike out on his own and do things his way. He hated having to meet with boards and committees to get their permission to do the Lord's work and tried to circumvent them whenever he could. He viewed them all as unduly restricting his preaching and putting obstacles in his path. This made it difficult for him to be a *member* of the church body and to submit to its rules of governance.

Percy kept his status as minister in the Presbyterian Church for three and a half years, when, in a letter to the Stated Clerk of the Presbytery (published in the June 1937 issue of *Young People Today*), he formally requested that his name be withdrawn from the roll of the Presbytery, thus severing his last connection with that church body. In his letter, he lays out the developments over the previous six years that led to his reversal (it is noteworthy that by this time, Percy was no longer dealing with Rev. Fulton, but with another churchman, John MacCallum, who was much less sympathetic to Percy and his work):

Dear Mr. Shultz:

Last fall when I asked of the Presbytery permission to use the Barnes Memorial Auditorium for our radio services and was refused that privilege, I knew certain members of the Presbytery were out to "trip me up." When Dr. McCallum lost his temper and threatened me by saying that I would "soon find out what power the Presbytery had over me" I knew I certainly was not amongst men of God interested in reaching lost souls for Christ.

The general trend of the Presbytery has been away from the fundamental doctrines such as the Virgin birth, His blood shed on Calvary for forgiveness of sins, a Hell of fire and brimstone for the godless, and His pre-millenial return. Besides this, I have noticed how the Presbytery has acted toward men of God, of like beliefs as myself in these fundamentals of our faith. Such an attitude has been unchristian.

As for our own work, I began my radio services nearly six years ago and the Presbytery made me announce publicly that it had nothing to do with my work. Now, since Dr. McCallum's threat, I have received an ultimatum that I must get permission of the Presbytery before I may solicit funds over the radio. My Board flatly refuses you the authority to delve into matters not your own.

Because I feel my liberty and service for the Master would be hindered by my obeying your mandate rather than God I request that my name be taken from the roll of the Presbytery of Philadelphia.

I thank God for the many true Godly men in the Presbytery who are dear friends of mine, but after praying over the matter I feel led to withdraw.
Sincerely in Him,
Percy B. Crawford

Six reasons are succinctly stated in this letter for withdrawing:

1. That six years earlier, when he began his radio work, the Presbytery had made him announce publicly that it had nothing to do with his work.
2. That church officials had recently demonstrated that they were out to get him by not allowing him to use the Barnes auditorium for his radio broadcast.
3. That he had recently been given an "ultimatum" that he must henceforth get permission from the Presbytery before soliciting funds on the radio.
4. That the Presbytery was moving away from the fundamental doctrines of the faith.
5. That the Presbytery had acted in an unchristian manner toward "men of God, of like beliefs as myself in these fundamentals of our faith."
6. That his "liberty" to obey and serve God was being restricted by the church's power over him.

Evidently Rev. MacCallum had put further restrictions on Percy, which certainly look as though they were intended to force him out of the church. Why did the Presbytery want to force his hand by making the absurd demand that he must get permission to solicit funds for his own work? To see what was going on, we must look back to the events of 1933 when J. Gresham Machen and a band of loyal supporters created the Independent Board of Foreign Missions. Machen took this action because he thought he had overwhelming evidence that many members of the official Presbyterian board, and many of the missionaries it sent out, had deeply compromised the board's mission of carrying the true principles of the Reformed faith to all the world. The church leadership, in response, decided it would not tolerate this renegade board and so issued a "Mandate" that was passed by the 1934 General Assembly, declaring the board unconstitutional and ordering all Presbyterian members of the board to resign or face disciplinary action. Since none resigned, local presbyteries began taking action in 1935 against those ministers and elders on the board who did not comply.

Percy would have been keenly interested in the controversy swirling around Machen and the Independent Board, because seven members of the board were his associates and persons whom he would have counted "men of God of like beliefs as myself in these fundamentals of our faith." Two of these men—Harold Laird and Merril MacPherson—were friends and very close coworkers; the others were Roy Brumbaugh, Wilbur Smith, Oliver Buswell, Charles Woodbridge, and James Bennet. All seven of these men were disciplined by the church (along with Machen) in 1936–37. But well before that, by the summer of 1934, the year of the mandate, all of them were on the "Speaker's List" at Percy's Pinebrook Bible Conference.

## GODLY MEN ON TRIAL

It was the actions taken against his friends Harold Laird and Merril MacPherson that really jolted Percy. He had known Laird since his first year at Westminster, having spoken often at his church in Collingswood and then reciprocating by having Laird speak at Rhawnhurst Church, his open-air meetings, the radio broadcasts, and Pinebrook Bible Conference from its opening in 1933. The trusting relationship that formed between them is evidenced by Laird's being the principal minister who performed Percy and Ruth's wedding ceremony at Pinebrook (in 1933) and who baptized the Crawfords' first three children.

Laird moved from his Collingswood church to the historic First and Central Church, Wilmington, Delaware, in 1933. His trial was initiated by the Presbytery of New Castle in October 1935 and ended six months later with his being "rebuked"—a lesser penalty that would have allowed him to continue to minister in the church, which he chose not to do.[5] Instead, he left First and Central Church and formed the First Independent Church of Wilmington.[6]

The charges brought against Laird indicate how divisive and bitter this matter of the Independent Board had become in the church. Laird's only offense was that he served on the board and would not resign from it, but he was charged with violation of his ordination vows in three respects: acting in defiance of "the government and discipline" of the church; failure to subject himself to his "brethren in the Lord"; and not having been "zealous and faithful in maintaining the truths of the Gospel and the purity and peace of the church." Laird responded in a prepared statement read before his First and Central congregation shortly after being rebuked: "My own conscience is quite clear. I am convinced that in all this matter I have earnestly endeavored to be true to my ordination vows."[7]

Laird felt that he could not in good conscience support the Presbyterian Foreign Missions Board or advise his church members to do so and that he had every right to support nondenominational agencies and even to create an Independent Board that would be faithful to the church's traditional mission of carrying the "pure Gospel" to far-off lands. He saw the main issue

as one of safeguarding his liberty to choose God's word over the General
Assembly's mandate: "The whole issue involves the truth and liberty of the
Gospel of our Lord Jesus Christ. The question is whether members of a certain Christian church are going to recognize as supreme the authority of
men or the authority of the Word of God. . . . I must refuse to obey men
when I believe their commands are contrary to the Bible."[8]

Meanwhile back in the Philadelphia Presbytery, the trial of Merril Mac-
Pherson and four other members of the Independent Board[9] was drawing to
a conclusion at about the same time as Laird's. The official pronouncement
of suspension on June 8, 1936, ended with these solemn words:

> We the Presbytery of Philadelphia, in the name and by the authority of the Lord
> Jesus Christ, do now declare them suspended from the exercise of their office
> of minister in the Presbyterian Church in the USA until such time as they shall
> sever their connection with the Independent Board for Presbyterian Foreign
> Missions and give satisfactory evidence of repentance.[10]

None of the five were present at the ceremony.

MacPherson was called to Philadelphia's Central North Broad Church
in 1930 and was an outspoken and forceful voice for fundamentalism within
the Presbytery. He had stood by Barnhouse during his trial and after his ad-
monishment introduced a resolution commending Barnhouse for his "zeal
and earnestness in preaching the full Gospel of Jesus Christ under the manifest power and blessing of God."

Percy first came into contact with MacPherson in the summer of 1931
when he sought permission from the Summer Evangelistic Committee to
use the porch of First Church. MacPherson served with Fulton on the
"Open Air and Place of Meeting" subcommittee and so would have been
aware of the young seminarian with "unusual talent as a street evangelist."
A year later, MacPherson invited him to his Central North Broad Church
for a series of meetings lasting twelve days. The next summer MacPherson
was invited to be a guest speaker for the opening season of the Pinebrook
Conference; two months later he assisted Laird at Percy and Ruth's wedding, and a lifelong friendship ensued.

A few months before his suspension, in a printed sermon, "The Apostasy and Crisis in the Presbyterian Church, USA," MacPherson pointed to
the growing influence of modernism among church officials and on various boards. This he saw as leading to the destruction of the church:

> If the '36 General Assembly upholds the Mandate of '34, and Godly, Bible-
> believing Christians are forced out, . . . then the real crisis will have been

reached . . . such an action will be a public declaration that the Presbyterian Church, USA, is no longer a true church of Christ, but an apostate, Laodician church, with Christ forced out.

He then issued a call to his fundamentalist brethren remaining in the church, which may have been intended specifically for the ears of his good friends, Crawford and Barnhouse: "When such a crisis is reached, I feel confident that there are thousands of loyal, consecrated Christians in the denomination who will refuse to bow the knee to Baal and will walk out to be with Jesus and his 'Little Flock.' "[11]

Percy surely felt the anguish and frustration of these two "men of God" who were being persecuted by the church in an "unchristian" manner. And he did for them what he could: he befriended them, affirmed the worth of their ministries, and gave them a platform from which they could speak the word—on his radio broadcast, at his summer Bible conference, and (in printed word) in his magazine.[12]

But the pain felt by the two rejected ministers was heightened by their witnessing the downfall of *their* church—the church of the great reformers in which God was particularly manifest to which they had committed their lives and their ministries. It was this God-ordained institution that was falling into unbelief and ruin. To be sure, this pain was lessened by their firm belief that the apostasy of the church was something that God had willed. In their *dispensational* view of history, the ruin of the church signaled the end of the "age of the church" and the ushering in of the end times and the second coming of Christ. Thus, for them, the forming of independent churches was a way of holding together the remnant that made up the "true church" of the faithful, who now had even more reason to expect the Lord's imminent return.[13]

Percy did not have the same degree of attachment to the church as the others, and so he did not feel the same sense of loss over the church's ruin. He certainly shared with his colleagues the belief that modernists were taking control of the Presbyterian Church in the U.S.A., that the church was slowly abandoning the fundamental doctrines, and that this was one sign of the end times;[14] but this tendency only illustrated that many in the church were in need of salvation. Percy was not greatly concerned, as Laird was, about purifying the church and apparently did not view impure elements in the church as a sufficient reason for leaving it. And to MacPherson he might have said: I don't have to "walk out" of the church to be with Jesus and his "little flock" because I am already with him. To his way of thinking, the "true church" was made up not of that faithful remnant who were upholding the essential doctrines of the Reformed faith, but of those who were truly born again and who were thereby Christ's very own.

*

Percy must have felt a good deal of pressure to withdraw from the church at Pinebrook in the summers of 1935 and 1936, as he fraternized with his speakers, many of whom by this time had separated from their denominational churches. In the relaxed atmosphere of the mountain retreat, their conversation would have turned inevitably to their struggles with the church. In addition to the Presbyterians—Laird, MacPherson, and the others[15]—there was also Baptist minister, Bob Ketcham, who began his long tenure at Pinebrook in 1936. Ketcham, the leader of a group of churches that had split from the Northern Baptists in 1932 (the General Association of Regular Baptist Churches), would have pounded my father's ears with the latest word about the modernist and "socialist" takeover of the Northern Baptist Convention.

These dissidents wanted more than sympathy from Percy: they wanted his public backing, and they wanted him to join them. Indeed, it is remarkable that Percy held out as long as he did, in the face of these proddings and pleadings, before finally withdrawing.

As Percy noted in his letter, it was the provocative actions taken by the Philadelphia Presbytery that triggered his final act of separation from the Presbyterians—first, in September 1936, in denying him the use of the Barnes auditorium where he had been broadcasting for five years; and then six months later, in demanding that he must get the church's permission to solicit radio funds. The first action did not evoke a direct response from him, but it was covered by the *Christian Beacon,* where he was reported to have said: "The committee would rather have the building stand idle than have him preaching there."[16] (Percy simply moved his broadcast a few blocks away to the WIP studios in the Gimbel building on Eighth and Market Streets.) The second action elicited a public rebuke in his "Editor Chats" column of *Young People Today,* in which his comments were both lighthearted ("seems to me some of these committees of Presbytery think they have the power of the Pope himself") and deadly serious ("but with it all I promise you I'll not allow any committee of Presbytery or any other committee to direct my work for the Lord").[17] For Percy, as for Laird and MacPherson, it was a question of Christian conscience and not submitting to a human authority that infringed on his preaching of the gospel. Two months later, he published his letter of withdrawal in the same column.

Percy was right that some members of the Presbytery were out to "trip him up." The church was deep into the process of cutting off those fundamentalists who defied its government and discipline and of demanding allegiance from those who remained. Since Percy was overtly giving aid and comfort to the defiant fundamentalists, his own acts were viewed as defiant and requiring discipline. And to his disadvantage, he was no longer dealing directly with Fulton, who at eighty years of age was pulling back, but with others who were hostile to him. He may not have appreciated fully the extent to which Fulton had cooperated with him and shielded him from potential enemies in the Presbytery.

And so he withdrew from the roll of the Presbytery of Philadelphia. He departed, as he had entered, without fanfare or publicity. Not surprisingly, his resignation was reported in the *Christian Beacon,* but otherwise received little attention. Even some of his own associates did not know he had done it.

It is tempting to view his leave-taking as the final step in an inevitable process of gaining independence from the church. But this interpretation, I believe, misses something important about my father and his understanding of his mission. That he delayed as long as he did indicates to me some reluctance on his part, an unwillingness to sever his ties to the church. Percy did not want to leave those "true Godly men in the Presbytery"—William Wells, Warren Ward, Donald Barnhouse, Edgar Frutchey, and others who had invited him to speak, nurtured him, and from whose churches he had drawn a host of young people to assist in his broadcast. As long as they were in the church, God's Spirit was present there. He was not a "come-outer"; he left only when he saw that if he did not he would be forced to compromise his own particular work for the Lord. And when he did finally leave, he did it in the least harmful way that he could—without attacking church officials or denouncing the church.

So I conjecture that he felt some sense of loss, some heaviness of heart, when he sent off his letter to the Stated Clerk. A consoling thought would have been that in cutting his formal ties with the denominational church he was not ending his relationship with those dear friends and their churches; he would continue to minister to them as an independent evangelist.

# 10

## Pinebrook Bible Conference:
## A Mountaintop Experience

Every day with Jesus
Is sweeter than the day before,
Every day with Jesus
I love him more and more;
Jesus saves and keeps me,
And He's the One I'm waiting for;
Every day with Jesus
Is sweeter than the day before.[1]
*(Chorus frequently sung before meals at Pinebrook)*

AFTER THE FIRST YEAR OF STUNNING SUCCESS IN REACHING YOUNG PEOPLE through the radio broadcast, Percy began to realize the need for a summer conference for young people. His "church of the air" was gaining scores of new members each week, many of whom were asking: "Now that I have accepted Christ, where do I go from here?" "How do I live the Christian life?" "Where can I meet other Christians?" "How do I prepare for Christian service?" Percy recognized from the beginning that his radio church had to do more than win souls to Christ; it also had to provide for their nurturing and spiritual growth. Moreover, he had little confidence that the denominational churches, tinged as they were with modernist thinking, were meeting this need.

He had in mind a place of natural beauty where young people could retreat from the world and be physically refreshed and spiritually nourished. He wanted to create an environment in which young Christians could experience the same sort of joyful fellowship and growth that he had known at BIOLA and Wheaton. The first order of business was to find a suitable location.

Percy wrote about the origin of (what was initially called) Pine Brook Bible Conference a few months after the first season ended in a story published in his magazine, *Young People Today*.[2] In the article, we learn about the acquisition of the campgrounds and also something about the personality and the style of the man who acquired them. After describing the need for a conference, he writes: "So one Sunday over stations WIP, of Philadelphia, and WMCA, of New York City, in the course of our regular broadcast, we told of our hopes. It was suggested that perhaps some would care to contribute land for the starting of a Conference. To our surprise, we received over thirty different offers of land."

Many of these sites were inspected and all were unacceptable for one reason or another. A way out of this "quandary" finally came when he received a letter from the Chamber of Commerce of East Stroudsburg in the Pocono Mountains of Pennsylvania offering "several acres of land for such a work." This land too proved to be unsatisfactory. However, while Percy was in Stroudsburg, he met a realtor, Frank LaBar, who showed him a property called Pine Brook Inn that had been a small resort on twenty-seven acres of land, but had recently gone out of business. When Percy saw the property he proclaimed: "This is just what we want. We must have it." There were three main structures on the property, the stately inn and a smaller lodge, which together could accommodate about 100–150 people, and a dance hall. All the rooms had running water supplied by natural springs. There were also several small cabins with outdoor facilities, a springhouse, and a tennis court. Running along the edge of the property was a clear, cool mountain stream, the Brodhead Creek, used for swimming. The tall pines, trout pools, and lake made it a place of quiet beauty. And it was ideally situated, equidistant from Philadelphia and New York City (about ninety miles).

When Percy returned to Stroudsburg to meet with officials of the bank that had taken over the property, he was told by LaBar that they wanted to talk only to buyers who could pay the sale price, $21,000,[3] in cash. Percy's response was, "Well, phone them up and tell them I'm coming down to the bank. We *must* see them." The bank's entire board, which happened to be meeting that day, agreed to see him for five minutes. "In we went before them and told of our desires." Those desires were to put $500 down and be given a few weeks to raise an additional $4,500 cash and obtain a mortgage for the balance ($16,000). "No little debate followed, and they requested me to leave while they thr[a]shed it out." (Another account of these events, written by Charles Lampman, an early associate of Percy's, tells this last part of the story a little differently. He wrote that "when he tried to negotiate, however, Percy was so importunate that he was ejected from the meeting.")[4]

In any case, Percy was called back and told that the bank would accept his offer and that he could have until March 1 to raise the full $5,000. "We left jubilant," but as the deadline approached, Percy realized that he was having some difficulty putting together the required balance of $4500. "Immediately I went to good Christian friends and explained my plight . . . [and] they wonderfully came to my aid. The day the money was due, I walked in and placed it in the bank's hands. Pine Brook had been acquired for God." And too, Percy was having success raising money from his Christian friends and supporters.

To further demonstrate how God's hand had been in the acquisition of Pinebrook, Percy adds this anecdote to his account:

> The day following the purchase of Pine Brook a bootlegger walked into the bank and offered a check for $21,000, saying, "I'll take Pine Brook." The reply was, "It's sold. . . . The Young People's Church of the Air has taken it over." So close had we come to losing it that we gratefully thanked Him all the more for allowing us to have it. The place might have been an unsavory road house.

Percy's own account of his negotiations for Pinebrook reveals that he was a hard-driving businessman determined to win the deal on his terms. Lampman was right that my father was importunate in his business dealings—and aggressively so. Whether negotiating for a piece of land, a used tractor, or a case of soap, he bargained hard. He strongly believed that since it was the Lord's work he was doing, others should be willing to make concessions. These tactics enabled him to swing many good deals in his lifetime, but they also put people off and earned him a reputation among local officials and businessmen in the Stroudsburg area for being pushy and overly demanding.

*

After the purchase of Pinebrook, Percy had only four short months to get the camp up and running and to line up speakers. He had been networking in the East and Midwest ever since his cross-country tour with the gospel team at BIOLA, and now he was making good on these contacts. For the first summer, he managed to assemble an impressive list of Bible teachers. And the *Young People's Church of the Air* quartet and pianist Ruth Duvall, and his brass quartet, the Harmony Trumpeters, would supply in person the same distinctive gospel music that listeners were accustomed to hearing on the radio broadcast.

The conference opened July 1, 1933, and ran for nine consecutive weeks through Labor Day. Guests were encouraged to stay for no longer than a week because only two hundred could be accommodated, and the cost for room and board was "the extremely low figure of $11 per week," due to "a desire to keep the price as near to cost as possible."[5] (In the second year, it was increased to $12 and stayed there until the early 1940s.)[6] These were Depression years and Percy kept prices low because he wanted the conference (and the gospel) to be accessible to all.

From the beginning, Pinebrook was pitched to young people, fourteen years of age and older. It took two years for Percy even to offer "a limited number of double rooms for young married couples at an additional charge of $2 per person." In the same year, he acquired a large tract of land (two hundred acres), that was practically given to him, one mile from Pinebrook, called Shadowbrook. The property had two houses on it separated by a small lake, one of which was a neocolonial mansion. Percy kept the name Shadowbrook, and for two years used it as a facility for "older young people" who wanted to attend the conference, but in a more peaceful setting, where life is "a little more quiet than that found amongst so many young people."[7]

In 1937 the Shadowbrook premises became a camp for boys, six to fourteen years of age, and attracted about fifty boys for each of eight weeks. In the next year, Percy split the property down the middle and opened a similar camp for girls six to fourteen, Mountainbrook. Attendance at the boys' and girls' camp grew steadily and reached about three hundred at each camp in the mid-1950s. The children's camps offered good food prepared by "a motherly woman cook," varied sports and activities, and counselors specially trained to give boys and girls "the very best spiritually and physically." Percy sometimes used giveaways to attract the kids: "A flashlight will be given to every boy/girl who registers during the month of April [1939]. Boy, it's a dandy too."[8]

In the year that Shadowbrook opened (1937), Percy hatched the idea that someone might want to sponsor a boy for a week at camp and he made this appeal to his radio audience. Later this appeal took the form of meeting a specific social need. In a 1952 special brochure entitled "The Heart Line Calls You!" he invited people to sponsor orphans from the Christ's Home Orphanage for a week at camp; they could also sponsor a blind boy or girl (with guide dog) or "help a Teenage Officer (unsaved) from high school have a week's vacation at Pinebrook."[9] One goal was to give the disadvantaged kids a chance to have a summer camp experience ("No Vacation? Ugh!" says a sad-faced boy in the brochure), but the larger purpose was to win more kids to Christ. This program for kids and teenagers was the only one I can recall in which Percy responded to a social need and deviated a little from his firm belief that it was no part of the Christian's business to try to cure social ills or improve society.[10]

Shadowbrook and Mountainbrook were always strictly separated from Pinebrook, in spite of their close proximity. Pinebrook was never a place for children; there were no playgrounds, no portable cribs, and no nursery during services. It was not until the mid-1950s that Percy even began to charge for small children under six ($10/week plus their age). He was willing to forgo the large potential clientele of families because of Pinebrook's mission—to win souls and strengthen them in the faith. Small children and infants could only be a distraction from that all-important goal.

*

Pinebrook was a place of great natural beauty, and Percy used this setting to build an image of the conference as a place where one could escape the troubles of urban life and expect to have a "mountaintop experience" of God. The holiness of the natural surroundings was captured (and romanticized) in this poem by Pinebrooker Ruth M. Withun, published in a promotional piece:

> Pinebrook, most precious hallowed place of beauty,
> So high above the paths we daily trod,
> So far from all the world, its cares and sorrows,
> And oh, so close, so very close to God,
> We love thee for thine every spot is sacred,
> God lives in pow'r upon thy mountain top,
> He walks and talks with us in sweet communion,
> And from our hearts all heavy burdens drop.
> A sheltered nook, a green and shady pathway,
> A lonesome pine beneath the blue of heav'n,
> May be an holy altar where by God's grace
> Some soul has knelt in sin, to rise forgiv'n.[11]

Percy also emphasized the healthy and wholesome atmosphere of Pinebrook. This meant not only clean air and spring water, but also homegrown food. In the first year of operation, a small farm and farmhouse adjacent to the camp were given to him, and he began to think of growing his own vegetables. Two years later, he announced (in his usual folksy manner) that one of the greatest improvements that summer would be in the farm:

. . . orders have been placed for seed in extra large quantities, to insure plenty. String beans, beets, peas, carrots, lima beans and corn are being grown in extra large quantities. . . . A new quartet—rather four pigs, are to be placed in reserve. Two cows on the farm will provide fresh cream and milk for all guests. Uncle Tom [the chef] is all enthused and can hardly wait till he starts serving us those delicious platters.[12]

In the following year, a chicken coop was erected, and "an order has been placed for thirty-three hundred baby chicks so all our guests can taste some of Uncle Tom's famous fried chicken."[13] A few years later, he noted: "Our Chefs make our own bread, muffins, biscuits, puddings and pies."[14] In the mid-1940s, he began raising his own cattle for beef so that he could announce that "Aberdeen Angus, corn-fed beef (raised right at Pinebrook) will provide steak and roast beef each week . . . all on individual platters and plenty of seconds."[15] In the same ad, he ballyhooed the "deliciously roasted turkeys," also raised on Pinebrook's farm.

Percy went to all this trouble to produce his own food, in part because he had a hankering to live off the land and be self-sufficient, and also because he believed that homegrown food was healthier and tastier than store-bought or shipped food.

Isabelle Van Buskirk was the cook at the children's camps beginning in 1953. When she expressed doubts about taking on the task of cooking in such a large kitchen for five to six hundred kids, Percy persuaded her to take the job. "You can do it," he told her. (Percy was a master at spotting talent in people they did not know they had.) Once a week, the farmhands would put half a cow on her counter to be butchered and prepared for the children's meals.[16]

She can also tell you about the turkeys. Out of the blue, Percy approached her and her husband, Carl, who worked in maintenance, and asked if they would raise turkeys for the coming summer. They had never done anything like that, but agreed to give it a try. "How many will we need?" Percy asked. Isabelle estimated four hundred. Percy went right out and bought incubators, lights, feeders and feed, and in February the Van Buskirks were raising four hundred chicks in an upstairs bedroom in a small farmhouse Percy owned near the camp. At two pounds, the chicks were moved outdoors to a shed. At ten pounds, they were killed and sent to the kitchens, where they were "cleaned and drawed" and roasted for the hungry campers—eight or nine per meal, one-quarter pound per person, three hundred turkeys in all. The Van Buskirks did this only one year. Was it worth the trouble? Was it more economical than buying prepared turkeys from Pocono Meats? Probably not. But that did not matter. Percy had managed to start his own turkey farm and (with the help of devoted employees) had made it work.


THE TABERNACLE

In the very first year, Percy hit upon a schedule for Pinebrook that would remain essentially unchanged for the entire twenty-eight years that he operated the camp. The week's activities were quite regimented. The day began with the ringing of the bell at 7:00 a.m. After breakfast there were two morning services at 9:30 and 11:00, with an evening service at 7:30. The entire afternoon was set aside for recreation; in the first brochure, he advertised swimming, fishing, boating, hiking, tennis, golf, volleyball, baseball, and horseback riding; in a few years, shuffleboard, bicycling, ping-pong, and zel ball were added. The few events that took campers off the grounds included an early morning hike up the hill to the "beacon" where one of the staff led devotions and a bus trip to scenic Bushkill Falls.

The meetings in the tabernacle were the heart of the week's activities. Percy took primary responsibility for the evangelistic part of Pinebrook's mission, and the speakers and Bible teachers, whom Percy called "one of the greatest if not *the* greatest group of God's men ever assembled,"[17] were charged with providing sustenance from the Word. Percy's only service in the tabernacle all week—his salvation service on the first morning after the campers arrived—was the pivotal one because it was then that the campers received the invitation to accept Christ. The rest of the week could then be given over to "feasting on good solid Bible teaching" (with no altar calls).[18]

Over the years some two hundred speakers, song leaders, and musicians came through Pinebrook. The core group of regulars came from the Philadelphia area and included Laird and MacPherson, William Allan Dean (Aldan Union Church), Rowan Pearce (billed as a star collegiate athlete),[19] Orson Palmer and Andrew Telford (both from Berachah Church), George Schmeiser (Fellowship Church), Wilbur Smith (Coatesville Presbyterian Church), and author Grace Livingston Hill. Another Philadelphian, Bob Strong, a classmate at Westminster, was one of the younger and more scholarly speakers on the list in the 1930s. From the New York City area came lawyer and lifelong associate James Bennet, businessman Erling Olsen, singer Beverly Shea, and from Calvary Baptist Church, where Percy spoke frequently, Will Houghton and William Ward Ayer.

From the Midwest he corralled a number of leading figures, including William Bell Riley, Harry Vom Bruch, Bob Ketcham, Harry Rimmer, Harry Ironside (Moody Church), and Oliver Buswell (Wheaton College); and from Moody Bible Institute, William Evans, Ralph Stewart, and Wendell Loveless.

From the South, where Percy's ministry penetrated the least, there was Robert G. Lee (Bellevue Baptist Church, Memphis), Vance Havner, and Robert McQuilkin.

And from Percy's native country, Canada, came evangelist John Linton, Albert Hughes, and P. W. Philpott, pastor of Moody Church and later Church of the Open Door, Los Angeles.

Some others of note who came in the latter half of Pinebrook's career were Ruth Stull (evangelist and missionary among the Campa Indians in Peru), Jack Wyrtzen, Mel Dibble, David Allen, Don Lonie, Jim Vaus (a convert from syndicated crime), and John DeBrine (founder of Youthtime in Boston).

Billy Graham was at Pinebrook before he became a national figure and apparently received some mentoring from my father. Speaking at Percy's memorial service in 1960, Graham reminisced about his first time there in 1946:

> I remember the first time [Percy] invited me to Pinebrook. . . . I remember how excited I was and how afraid I was, and how nervous I was to stand and preach in front of Percy Crawford, and how encouraging he was all week long. He would say little things to encourage you. And then I remember I stood around on the last day wondering if he would invite me back next year. And he did, and we went![20]

In a radio broadcast devoted to Billy Graham that Percy made late in his career, he recalled that he had advised Billy to go into "city-wide campaigns." "Maybe you'll starve the first year," he said, "but it's wide open."[21]

Often the speakers and song leaders formed lasting relationships with one another. Graham goes on to say: "And one of the first times that Cliff Barrows and I were ever together was at Pinebrook, and that was the . . . beginning of the warm friendship and relationship and association with Cliff Barrows."

Another association that started at Pinebrook was recounted by Beverly Shea, who happened to be paired with Will Houghton (then president of Moody Bible Institute) in the summer of 1938. At that time, Bev Shea worked for an insurance firm in New York City and had often sung with Percy and Ruth on the radio and at Pinebrook banquets.[22] Shea recalls an encounter with Houghton one afternoon when he and his wife Erma were out walking: "There under those towering pines, we talked. I can still find the spot." Houghton asked him to consider filling an opening at Moody's radio station WMBI. The singer was hesitant at first, but did finally accept the offer, quit his insurance job, and headed to Chicago for full-time service.[23]

\*

Percy selected these speakers on the basis of several loose and highly subjective criteria. First and foremost, they had to be solidly fundamental in their beliefs. Since fundamentalists formed a tight-knit circle with clear boundaries, there was never any danger of going outside of it. In addition, speakers were expected to live "the separated life."[24]

Another general characteristic of the speakers was that they were on the moderate end of the spectrum. Percy deplored controversy and negative attacks, especially when directed at other believers. It was okay to attack modernists, evolutionists, communists, and Catholics (albeit not too harshly), but not fellow fundamentalists, and certainly not by name. Percy himself set the tone. Accordingly, Carl McIntire from Collingswood, New Jersey was never invited to Pinebrook, even though he gave Percy favorable and frequent coverage in his influential newsletter, *The Christian Beacon*. McIntire was too much of a controversialist to fit in at Pinebrook.[25] John R. Rice was never on the list. And Bob Jones Sr. made just one appearance—and that because Percy wanted to repay him for the honorary doctorate he received from Bob Jones College in 1940.

Finally, Percy picked speakers who, he thought, were able to "present [the word of God] to young people in an appealing way."[26] The guests at Pinebrook could expect that the sermons would not be overly intellectual or dry and that they would never exceed a half hour in length. Also in this regard, speakers were expected to be willing to enter into the fun and do some cutting up, or as one quartet member put it: they all had to "shed their dignity."

*

Perhaps the most prominent fundamentalist leader to come to Pinebrook in the 1930s was William Bell Riley. He was there in the first year (1933), at age seventy-two, and returned for two more years. Percy had crossed paths with Riley five years earlier on tour in Minneapolis with the Wheaton Quintet.[27] Riley was a commanding figure, known throughout the land as one of the principal architects of the fundamentalist movement. He was notorious for his rooting out of modernist tendencies in the schools and churches of his own Northern Baptist denomination and for his debates with atheists and evolutionists.[28] We have seen that he played a major role in forcing the resignation of John MacInnis, the dean at BIOLA, and Percy may have wanted to hear from Riley himself some of the specifics concerning MacInnis's heterodoxy.

In his seventies, Riley was still actively fighting for various fundamentalist causes and had become even more extreme in his social and political views; in particular, he embraced a highly questionable theory of an international Jewish-communist conspiracy to undermine capitalism and enslave Christians.[29] Over a two-year period, Riley published seven articles in *Young People Today,* with topics ranging from noncontroversial fundamentals ("The Simplicity of Salvation," "Will Christ Come Again?") to highly tendentious social-political issues ("Evolution—an Unscientific Pretense," "Sovietism in Our Schools," "Is Society Rotting?"). Percy would have been sympathetic with Riley's antievolution stance and to a lesser extent his anticommunist bent, but I believe he would have been very uncomfortable with the more extreme elements of Riley's agenda.

Another important figure on the roster in the early years was J. Oliver Buswell, president of Wheaton College, whom Percy had known in his student days. By the time he arrived at Pinebrook, Buswell had already established his reputation as an educational leader and scholar—having just completed his five-volume treatise, *The Lamb of God.*[30] It was during Buswell's three years at Pinebrook (1934–36) that Percy was putting into action his plan to start a Christian liberal arts college—"a Wheaton of the East"—and he surely would have sought Buswell's counsel for this project.

But Buswell was getting caught up in more and more controversy. Having joined Machen in separating from the Presbyterian Church in the U.S.A. to form the Presbyterian Church of America in 1936, he was already, in that same year, raising issues with Machen and within two years (along with Carl McIntire) would lead a faction that split off to form the Bible Presbyterian Church. It is not clear why Buswell stopped coming to Pinebrook after three years, but it is plausible that he was dropped because he was becoming too heavily involved in disputes with other Christians about matters that Percy may have considered nonessential and distracting from the primary business of winning souls.

Robert Ketcham was a dyed-in-the-wool separationist who, like Riley, was a relentless campaigner against modernism and (in the 1930s) the "growing tendency in [Baptist] Convention circles toward a radical Socialism, and a sort of a 'pink' Communism."[31] By the time he came to Pinebrook in 1936, he was president of a group of churches, the General Association of Regular Baptist Churches (GARBC), that had split from the Northern Baptist Convention in 1932.[32]

Percy and Bob Ketcham developed a friendship and a mutual affection that would last a lifetime. Although Ketcham had no formal education and therefore typified for him the untrained worker who left the firehouse before hitching his team of horses to the fire truck, Percy was drawn to him because of his humble origins, his unassuming manner, and his fun-loving spirit. Ketcham could laugh at himself and joke with Percy—as in this lighthearted, teasing letter sent to Percy and Ruth congratulating them on the birth of their first son Donald:

140                         A THIRST FOR SOULS

Boy, oh boy! Can you imagine Percy Crawford pushing a baby buggy around
over the hills and hummocks at good old Pinebrook, and still trying to pawn
himself off as a young man. Won't be long now before it will be "Grandpa Crawford." . . .

Percy also would have appreciated Ketcham's crusade against modernism in the church and even his exposing of socialist and communist tendencies. Somebody had to keep these threatening forces at bay, and he
had no taste for it himself. This forthright Baptist preacher was a kind of
alter ego to Percy—living proof that it was not necessary to have academic
credentials or even formal training to be an effective preacher and Bible
teacher.

Further, Percy would have admired Ketcham's gutsy readiness to stand
up to the "powers that be" within the church—a trait the fiery Baptist had
amply demonstrated throughout his career. His famous dispute with Baptist officials over denominational authority surely would have been aired
in casual speakers' conversation that first summer at Pinebrook. Seventeen years earlier, in 1919, when the thirty-year-old Ketcham was pastoring the First Baptist Church of Butler, Pennsylvania, his church was
asked to contribute $17,000 to the New World (Missionary) Movement
that was just being launched. The church balked and authorized its pastor to write a twenty-four-page pamphlet pointing to modernist elements
in the church's boards and societies and stating its refusal to participate.
Shortly thereafter he was visited by a committee of the Pittsburgh Baptist Association that demanded that he withdraw the pamphlet and then
tried to bully him into compliance. Ketcham recounts the incident in his
1936 pamphlet:

I will remember that day throughout eternity. Just a young preacher, with my
ministerial career still before me, then and there I had to decide whether my lord
was to be the Lord Jesus Christ or the Denominational Program. . . . I cast my
lot with Him that day, and to the praise of His everlasting glory, what a happy
lot it has been.
   After more than two hours of grilling, the Chairman of that Committee said
"Mr. Ketcham, we may as well tell you that you must withdraw that pamphlet
from circulation, or I will personally see to it that you never get another Church
in the Northern Baptist Convention." My reply was "Brother, $17,000 is too
much money to pay for any Baptist pulpit. I can secure a soap box for a dime."
No sooner were these words out of my mouth than another member of the Committee jumped from his seat, raced across the office, grabbed me by the coat col-
lar, and literally shook the daylights out of me, yelling into my face "You get
down on your knees and tell God to forgive you for that statement."[33]

When Percy heard this story (or read it) in July 1936, it would have struck a deep nerve. He too had been contending with the hostile boards and committees of the Philadelphia Presbytery and in a matter of months would encounter the ill-tempered, "red-in-the-face" Dr. MacCallum, who would threaten him with the words: "You'll soon find out what power Presbytery has over you." When my father exhibited the same defiant attitude toward the churchman, followed up a few months later by his withdrawal from the church, he was perhaps thinking of brother Bob, in making common cause with him against ecclesiastical authority.

## MUSIC AT PINEBROOK

It did not take Percy long to realize that the singing of choruses in the tabernacle was contributing mightily to Pinebrook's success. Ruth compiled a new songbook, *Pinebrook Choruses,* in 1934, with 215 fresh and easy-to-learn songs, and in 1936, *New Pinebrook Songs* followed with 170 more—many of them newly minted and bearing the copyright of Percy B. Crawford.

The YPCA songbooks appeared about every other year—thirteen in all through 1960. Some choir directors and youth leaders of that time have said that these songbooks set the standard for Christian music for young people. There were no repeats in any of the songbooks, although many of the favorites from earlier books kept their place in the song services from summer to summer. Over the years, Percy and Ruth cultivated a new breed of composers who wrote lively choruses that expressed the joyful Christian life and conveyed the simple story of what Christ has done for us. But many of the songs had a more inspirational and moving quality, appropriate for solos or duets.

A few of the main contributors to the chorus books, such as George Schuler, Harry Dixon Loes, and Merrill Dunlop had already made their reputation as gospel songwriters; while others, like Wendell Loveless, Norman Clayton, John Peterson, and Arlene Barnes either launched their careers or established themselves through working with Ruth and the YPCA. But there were a number of composers (in these songbooks) who contributed favorites at Pinebrook; my list would include:

- Wendell Loveless: "Sweeter Than the Day Before," "More Time Alone with Thee, Lord Jesus," "After All He's Done for Me"
- George Schuler: "Have I Given Jesus My Heart," "Oh, What a Day!" "I'm Overshadowed"

- Norman Clayton: "He Holds My Hand," "We Shall See His Lovely Face," "Now I Belong to Jesus"
- John Hallett: "There's No Disappointment in Jesus"
- Merrill Dunlop: "Deep within My Heart," "Wonderful, Marvelous, Yet True"
- Arlene Barnes: "Laudes Christi," "Rose of Sharon"[34]
- Alex Burns: "Christ for Me"
- Evelyn Tarner: "Wedding Prayer"
- John Peterson: "It Took a Miracle," "In His Presence," "The Saviour Brought Sunrise"
- Blanche Osborn:[35] "How Wonderful"

Percy even reached back to his BIOLA days as several choruses by music professor Herbert Tovey ("Rolled Away") were included. He also encouraged speakers and team members to write new songs, and several did, including quartet members Fenton Duvall ("I Will Guide Thee") and Paul White ("Jesus, Wonderful Lord"), and Percy himself composed a few very simple songs and texts.[36] Almeda J. Pearce, the wife of speaker Rowan Pearce, contributed the music and words of the triumphant "When He Shall Come," a favorite of all the quartets.

As singing was becoming the hallmark of the Pinebrook experience, Percy began to include song leaders on the speakers list by the second year. And by the 1936 season, there was a song leader or musician who could lead the singing scheduled for each week. These included former stage comedian Walter "Mac" MacDonald, Wendell Loveless, Beverly Shea, and Homer Hammontree. In 1937 Carlton Booth made the first of several appearances, along with Peter Slack, who arrived "with sixteen instruments" and Hammond organ and who soon became the regular organist at Pinebrook.

In 1940 Grace and Lester Place came on the scene playing marimba, bells, and the magnificent triple octave chimes. Percy had met them in the WIP radio studio, doing their own radio program just before his, and invited them to play on his broadcast. The Places then came to Pinebrook and came back every year thereafter. Also in 1940 Robert Harkness, formerly Reuben Torrey's pianist, showed up, along with former dance band saxophonist Jake Sheetz, who started a long tenure at Pinebrook.

Perhaps the only song leader from the 1950s who was in the same league with "Mac" MacDonald and Wendell Loveless, was John DeBrine, founder of Youthtime rallies in Boston and the radio program *Songtime*. DeBrine could move an audience to great heights with his well-chosen mix of new and old hymns.

In the 1940s and 1950s other outstanding musicians were the Claus Indian Family, the Wigden Trio (one year referred to as "The Wigden Colored Quartet"), Anton Marco (who had sung with the San Carlo Opera

Company), instrumentalists Neil and Pat Macauley, singer Theron Spurr, and organist Clayton Erb. An African American singer who should be mentioned is Jimmy McDonald, who was a dishwasher on the staff when he was not doing stirring solos in the tabernacle. His rendition of "I Stood at Calvary" stands out in my memory.[37]

But it must be emphasized that the prime mover and organizer of the entire musical program at Pinebrook was my mother, Ruth. She played piano at all the song services, giving the song leader complete freedom to switch to any song at any time in any key; she planned the musical portion of every service, selecting the music, arranging most of it, and coordinating it with the guest musicians; she played piano solos, duets, and occasionally sang. But her great gift was as accompanist—she let the singers sing, following their lead, accenting their particular strengths with graceful ornamentation.

Pinebrook was a magnet for young musicians all over the Northeast who wanted to experience firsthand the exciting music they were hearing on the radio. And Ruth and Percy were constantly on the lookout for fresh talent. In the summer of 1937, they thought they spotted some talent in the trombone playing of the eleven-year-old son of speaker Rowan Pearce, Billy, and Percy asked him to play a solo on the Sunday afternoon radio broadcast (recorded at the camp). Bill Pearce recalled: "So, with his wife Ruth as the accompanist, I had my radio debut on the trombone. It was the Gospel song, 'He Lives' (two verses and an extra refrain in B flat—no variations). It was broadcast across the Nation!"[38] Bill would later play with the YPCA brass quartet, the Harmony Trumpeters, in the early stages of what has been a brilliant musical career.

Ruth took the distinctive sound she had created for the radio broadcast and working with fewer forces—the quartet, an organist, what musical talent she could recruit at the camps, the guest artists, and her children—and mixing in the robust congregational singing of choruses, created another original variation of sacred music, appropriate to the Bible conference. Her offering to Pinebrook over the years was this uplifting gospel music that people came from miles around just to hear and participate in.

## THE DIRECTOR

For the three months of the summer that Pinebrook was active, Percy was constantly on the go and pushing everyone on the staff to keep up with his pace. "Let's produce" was the motto he used to prod people into action. Except for the musical program, Percy ran the entire operation at Pinebrook. In addition to setting up the general program and lining up the speakers, he

made all the decisions pertaining to the acquisition of new property, maintenance, and new construction and contracted with the local builders and
firms who did work at the camp. He wrote the brochures and the letters of
appeal for funds and handled all the publicity.

He brought his office staff up from Philadelphia to do secretarial work
and mailings, but the bookkeeping and accounting practices were extremely lax. Jack Wyrtzen recalled his impression of the way my father
handled business matters: "He never had books or anything. I mean he was
as honest as the day was long, but that's the way he ran it—just right out
of his pocket." Wyrtzen sent his business manager down to assist, but "that
lasted about two weeks."[39]

Percy always maintained very tight control of the purse strings. This was
due in part to the frugality bred into him by his Scotch Irish parents; but
also to his wanting to run an efficient operation and keep Pinebrook af-
fordable and accessible. "We have no desire to make a profit on our guests,"
he wrote in a 1950 brochure when the cost for a week at Pinebrook was
only $15. If he could break even at the end of the summer, with enough
profit to make improvements for the ensuing year and pay his salary of
$6,000 (which remained constant throughout his lifetime), he considered
Pinebrook a financial success. And, in fact, the summer camps were the
most consistently solvent operation of any that he undertook.

It was not uncommon to see Percy doing some of the hard physical work
around the grounds. In the early years, he used his carpenter's skills to help
in the construction of new buildings. (There is a famous photograph of him
hammering nails into the new roof of the tabernacle, built in 1937.) He was
not above doing maintenance work in the trenches either: one staff member remembers working side by side with Percy up to their knees in raw
sewage, cleaning out a clogged pipe. He was also an avid sportsman, who
(I am told) could whip anyone on the tennis court with his driving forehand
shot; and he loved to hunt—the bullfrogs that croaked all night in the lake
beside our house, proudly displaying at breakfast the trophies he had
gained in the early morning hours.

Percy's leadership skills were tested in the summer of 1955, the year of
the great flood in which hurricane Connie wreaked havoc on the region. All
of the damage in our area occurred on the night of Thursday, August 18,
when the heavy rains caused a series of dams to break upstream of the
Brodhead Creek, turning it into a raging torrent. There was relatively little
damage done at Pinebrook—a few cabins and a staff house (where the quartet members lived) were swept away, but no one was injured. But the little
camp situated on lower ground across the creek from Pinebrook was not so
fortunate. That night, thirty-seven people from Camp Davis died in the

flood, and only nine of them survived—three of those because they had walked over to attend the evening service at Pinebrook.[40] At the time, Percy was still recuperating from a minor heart "episode" he had suffered a few days before, but as soon as he realized the seriousness of the situation he swung into action. All night long he drove from place to place, barking orders and instructions with a megaphone and shepherding people to safety. The next day, he took part in the recovery operation, sending food across to the survivors who had taken refuge in the farmhouse Pinebrook owned on the other side of the Brodhead. The following day, Percy went on the air to announce that no one had been hurt at Pinebrook. However the camp facilities had been battered, and Percy used the flood damage as a basis for raising enough funds to build two new twenty-room "motels" for the following summer.

Percy was ubiquitous around the campgrounds and highly accessible to the guests. He liked to interact with the young people, sometimes just sitting out on the grounds on a chair or relaxing by the swimming pool, chatting and joking with whomever came by. Sometimes he would clown for them and do stunts like riding a bicycle sitting backward on it or playing with his pet monkey Weezer. He always dressed well; in the early years, he and Ruth could look positively chic, and later on, as he got older, he went in for flashy sport shirts and red or green sport coats.

Although Percy had ceded the tabernacle to the speakers and the musicians, he took full charge of the dining hall and claimed it for his own. Mealtime took on a very special, ceremonial meaning at Pinebrook and became a cherished part of the Pinebrook experience. Sitting at the center of the V-shaped speakers' table just inside the door, where he could monitor the whole room, he presided over the fun and fellowship. In the brochures of the mid-1930s, he highlights the dining room experience: "One of the most delightful periods at Pinebrook is meal time. . . . Not only is the food delicious, but the Christian fellowship is wonderful. The speeches, singing, fun, and joy of meal time make Uncle Tom's cooking taste all the better."[41]

All the meals began with a song and a blessing—"Everyday with Jesus is sweeter than the day before" and "Thank you Lord for saving my soul" were standbys; "Showers of Blessing" was always sung if it was raining. The guests would sing various silly dining hall songs as they waited for their food: "Here we sit like birds in the wilderness, waiting to be fed." The food was served family style and (usually) hot. Percy would egg on the guests over the speaker system with wry comments and one-liners. At breakfast he occasionally read headlines from the newspaper and commented on how badly the Philadelphia baseball team was doing ("the Phillies are only 23 games out of first place.") He would call attention to latecomers as they tried to sneak in the main door unnoticed. And he would play postman, hand delivering telegrams and letters that had sentimental messages on the envelope. Percy liked to single people out and put them on the spot. Often he made them stand "on the chair" in the middle of the dining room—sometimes for fun and games, and sometimes for more serious purposes, if they had something to say to the group.

*

Being in charge of everything also had its downside. Percy became very protective of Pinebrook lest anyone upset the idyllic scene he had so carefully constructed. He took on night watchman's duties around the camp, patrolling the grounds in his car, making sure that campers and staff were in the evening meeting, that no one wandered off the grounds after dark, and that everyone got to their rooms by 10:30. He also played the role of sheriff, warding off local boys trying to pick up our girls. He would often take his grievances and a license plate number to the local magistrate or to the boys' parents and press hard for some retribution. These were real concerns, and my father usually had good reasons for getting tough with offenders.

Percy was also the enforcer of the rules at Pinebrook and did not hesitate to send campers and staff packing if they were caught breaking the rules. If any of his employees stepped out of line or crossed him, his instinctive reaction was to dismiss them. It did not matter who it was or what their job was. "No one is indispensable to the organization," he often said. Charlie Jewett, who had sung with the same quartet and traveled with Percy and Ruth for four years (1934–38), found this out. He related to me the following incident that brought his time with Percy to an abrupt end. As camp was coming to a close in the summer of 1938, Charlie took his summer earnings and went into town and bought a used ten-passenger Buick sedan. He brought it back to camp, piled a bunch of kids into it, and took them into town for ice cream. When Percy heard about it, he approached Charlie and fired him on the spot, saying only, "You're leaving tomorrow morning." And just that quickly, Ruth found herself looking for another second tenor. No explanation was given, and Charlie did not protest. He must have realized he had done something very bad.

But what did he do? There was no rule that campers or staff could not leave the grounds and go into Stroudsburg, although this was not encouraged. There was no rule against having your own car. Why would Percy put himself and Ruth through all the trouble of finding a replacement for a loyal member of a very good quartet over such a seemingly trivial incident? It is difficult to justify his punitive action, but he probably thought that

Charlie had stepped out of line and should have asked permission to take the kids off the grounds. If he allowed this sort of thing to continue, campers would soon feel they could miss meals or (heaven forbid) skip meetings. He wanted on his staff only people who would cooperate fully, who were totally devoted to his mission of carrying out the Lord's work. It was a straight and narrow path, and if anyone strayed from it to satisfy some personal desire, then they did not belong on the team.

But the fact is that this incident is indicative of a not-so-admirable side of my father's character. He was temperamental and prone to impulsive actions. Anyone who crossed him or went against him in any way or was "disloyal" would not be around very long. A pattern developed of disagreements over small matters that led to peremptory firings. He even fired his own son Don, age twenty, after an exchange in which (as Don reports it) the son criticized the father "from top to bottom." Don left camp for ten days and returned only when our mother "effectuated a reconciliation" between them.[42]

The worst offense anyone could commit was to steal from the organization. Percy was always worried that cash contributions in the mails—the "lifeline" of his work—were being pilfered by postal workers. There had been at least one instance of proven theft by one of his office workers, and he was outraged by it. In his eyes, to steal money from his work was to steal from the Lord—it was Percy's own unpardonable sin. He became almost paranoid about the possibility of being cheated. This tendency showed in one of the tactics he used to catch thieves at Pinebrook. One of the duties of the staff member who ran the bookstore was to collect the money that was put in the locked offering boxes at the exit doors of the tabernacle. To see if any of the clerks were pocketing some of those offerings, he would plant a marked twenty-dollar bill in one of the boxes and then see if it came back to him. On one occasion he accused the attendant, a King's student, of pilfering the $20, and even though the young man claimed innocence, and a thorough search of his room and his belongings did not turn up the bill, Percy sent him packing anyway. A few days later, apparently realizing that he had made a mistake, Percy called the individual and asked him if he wanted his job back. He did, and he returned to Pinebrook; and not long after the incident, he was asked to sing in the quartet and became a trusted member of the team.

Percy's actions—or reactions—were often arbitrary and unfair to the person involved. As one quartet member put it: for Percy, "the work was more important than people." He would seldom feel remorse for these actions or make any apologies. He trusted his judgments about people and their fitness for service with him. However (as we have just seen), if he did come to believe that he had acted unfairly, he would make amends and sometimes give the person his job back. I have talked to a number of individuals who were let go by my father and, to my surprise, I found very little bitterness or resentment toward him. Almost all of them had moved on to other forms of service and expressed positive feelings toward him and his work, even though they still believed he had wronged them. Percy did not carry grudges either, and it even happened in several instances that he would come back to people years later and work with them or hire them for another job, as if nothing had ever happened. Sixteen years after Charlie Jewett left the work, Percy and Ruth and the quartet met up with him again on their world tour, in Pusan, Korea, where Charlie was serving as an army chaplain. He was the appointed liaison for Percy's team and facilitated their meetings at the air force and Army bases there.

## FAMILY

We five children spent all of our summer months at Pinebrook. I spent my first nineteen summers at the camp while Percy directed it and three more summers with my brother Richard at the helm. The four boys—Don, Dick, Dean, and myself—dreaded the thought of having to go to the boys' camp, Shadowbrook, and we were often threatened with banishment there. We much preferred to stay at Pinebrook, where we had privileges and were constantly in the spotlight. My recollection is that I spent only the better part of one summer at Shadowbrook, with my cousin Bob Duvall who was my age. I must admit it was not all that bad—I enjoyed the crafts and some of the activities, such as playing "capture the flag" at dusk in the woods. I liked sleeping in a hogan for two; the food was tolerable; and the calisthenics before breakfast were—well, bracing. But on balance, Pinebrook was a lot more fun for a kid who happened to be the son of the director.

In a real sense there was no family life for us boys at Pinebrook. We thought of ourselves as staff members, and we were constantly on public display. Part of our regular duties as children was singing in some of the services and on the morning broadcast. (Starting in 1943, Percy was broadcasting his morning devotional program, *Pinebrook Praises,* every weekday at 8:00 a.m. from the tabernacle.) I had a strong, clear voice as a boy, and I liked singing melody in our "junior quartet." But the pressure of singing solos before a large audience got to be too much for me at an early age. I broke down once in the middle of singing "The Lord's Prayer" at Pinebrook, and after that I rarely did stand-alone solos and only felt relaxed when singing with my brothers.

It was an important part of Percy's idea of family values that we children should work. Work would build character and develop in us a real sense of devotion and loyalty to the camp and its mission. So we were put to work, doing the most menial jobs at a very early age. The first job I can remember having (at about age five) was picking grass out of the clay tennis courts. And my first paying job was swatting flies in the dining hall for a penny a fly.

I recall vividly one incident with my father-boss when I was only nine or ten. My cousin and I had the tedious job that year of picking up litter around the camp grounds for twenty-five cents an hour. We decided one day, in a moment of delusionary self-importance, that we were being grossly underpaid and plotted to get a raise; our strategy was to ask for twice as much as we thought we could get. We approached Percy, and when he asked how much we wanted, we said seventy-five cents an hour. The boss was genuinely offended and responded indignantly with words I can still hear: "You don't love the place." What bothered him more than the money was our lack of commitment, our unwillingness to make a personal sacrifice for the good of the place. Percy expected others to have the same love for Pinebrook and devotion to its mission that he had. We did not get the raise, and the lesson I learned at a tender age was to do what I was told to do and not to complain about it.

As soon as I was old enough, I was given some real jobs—first, waiting tables in the dining hall, and then the more prestigious job of working behind the registration desk. Eventually I got to be in the real quartet for a couple of summers, singing bass (even though my natural voice was tenor). Our foursome—which consisted of my brothers Don (baritone) and Dick (second tenor), Neil Fichthorn (first tenor), and myself—proudly carried on the rich tradition of gospel quartet music at Pinebrook, but it was not easy following on the heels of the previous quartet of Bob Straton, Sam Seymour, Don Crawford, and Steve Musto—which by general consent was one of the best in YPCA history. I loved singing my mother's quartet arrangements with their robust harmonies that ranged in style from old-fashioned hymnlike ("Man of Sorrows," "Still Still with Thee") to upbeat camp meeting ("The Old Account Was Settled," "Meeting in the Air," "Little David Play on Your Harp") to more modern ("Salvation Time," "Day and Night").[43]

## GRANDFATHER TOM

In the summer of 1948, I had an encounter with a family member I had never met before—my grandfather, Tom Crawford. I was six years old and he was seventy-five, and I have but the dimmest memory of his brief visit.

Our only living grandfather had no place in our family life; Percy rarely mentioned him at home, and then only in disparaging terms. In his testimony and in hundreds of sermons, he had painted his father as a villain who whipped him when he didn't go to church and caused him to revolt against God.

Tom had walked away from what was most probably an unhappy marriage and left Margaret and the three boys to fend for themselves, and as a consequence, Percy spent the next six years of his boyhood working and filling in for his missing dad. Tom dropped out of view after leaving the family scene in Vancouver, but this much is known—that he married again and that he and his wife, Jeanie, settled in Vernonia, Oregon, near Portland, and had a son, Middleton. Tom was successful in business, eventually owning and operating a Ford garage with Jeanie until his death.

Percy's characterization of his father as uncaring and brutish is almost certainly a gross exaggeration. Undoubtedly Tom used corporal punishment on his kids, but that was not unusual, and Percy too was not averse to taking off his belt and giving us boys a "licking" on those few occasions when we did something very bad. But Tom was not a monster. One member of his second family, Middleton's wife Betty Jean, remembers him as a kind man in all his dealings with her family. Certainly it was impossible for me to fit my image of the stern disciplinarian to the gentle and outgoing man who visited us at Pinebrook. Tom thoroughly enjoyed his stay and gladly entered into the meetings and camp activities. He was delighted to be with his four grandchildren and made a point of buying each of us an appropriate gift before he left.

We may wonder why Percy arranged this meeting with his father that summer, after more than thirty years of virtual estrangement from him. And why at Pinebrook? Percy had never invited any of his family members to Pinebrook—including his mother—even though the conference was the crowning achievement of his ministry. (One reason he kept his immediate family away was that he did not want his constituents to know that his parents were divorced. Divorce was considered an egregious sin in our fundamentalist world,[44] and it was especially inappropriate at Pinebrook where so much emphasis was put on moral and spiritual renewal.)

But Percy's main motive for bringing Tom to Pinebrook, I believe, was to give him his best chance of receiving Christ. Pinebrook was the place where this could happen, if it was to happen at all. Time was running out for Tom. Moreover, the sense of urgency for Percy was heightened by the fact that his brother Alph had tragically died in an automobile accident just a few months earlier. For Percy, the real tragedy of his brother's death was that he had died without knowing the Lord.

The situation was even worse: Percy's oldest brother, Will, had also died in the previous year—of multiple sclerosis, and he too had died without the assurance of salvation, having turned down Percy's invitation to accept the Lord when he visited our home in Philadelphia shortly before his death.

Percy felt obligated to do all that he could to enable his father to avoid this same fate. He would put aside his personal feelings of animosity toward his father and give him a definite opportunity to say yes to Christ. While Tom was at Pinebrook, his son dealt with him and asked him to receive Christ as his savior. But as it happened, not everyone who came to Pinebrook got saved. Percy later reported that Tom had declined, saying that he could not make the sort of decision that Percy wanted, but that he did not mean to reject God altogether. However, for Percy, who always saw conversion as an all-or-nothing affair, Tom's answer was a no. He had done what Alph and Will had done before him—he had rejected Percy's savior.

Percy did for his father what he had to do as an evangelist, and Tom had made his choice. The party was over. He went back to Oregon, and Percy's relationship with his father continued to be cold and withdrawn until Tom's death two and a half years later. If there was any longing in my father's heart to reconcile with his father—as I think there was—he did not allow it much of a chance to come to life. Percy had made his choice too; he had not opened himself to a possible loving and forgiving relationship with his father. When Percy had his conversion experience many years earlier, he had found the path to salvation and reconciliation with his heavenly Father in one courageous act of acceptance, but over the course of a lifetime he could not find within himself the wherewithal to return to his earthly father. He simply carried that heavy burden of resentment within him throughout his life.

## THE CAMPFIRE

The week at Pinebrook had a beginning (the salvation service), a middle (the daily meetings), and ended with the campfire service on the last evening, when Percy would try to bring closure to what had taken place during the week. Saturday evening began with the much-loved "stunt night" in which staff, guests, speakers, and quartet would put on funny (and not so funny) skits in the "bowl" in front of the inn.

Some of these, in the early years, involved mock weddings, "knights and fair ladies, beautiful Indian maid and handsome Indian chief," and the "Pinebrook Minstrels."[45] And all the quartets will remember and be remembered for doing a humorous takeoff on the famous quartet from Verdi's opera *Rigoletto* ("Take me where the great big red bananas grow. I want to go, I want to go . . .").

The stunts lasted until dark when everyone made their way a quarter of a mile up the road to a rocky slope at the edge of the campgrounds, and there, under the stars, a bonfire was lit; and Percy, using a megaphone or a sound system, would conduct the service. He wrote about the campfire service in a newsletter he sent out at the end of the 1944 season:

> I wish you could all stand with us around our huge camp fire. . . . Good old hymns are sung and choruses. Then those who have confessed Christ that week step out and give testimony to their faith. Then those come and stand who desire to go on and prepare further. Then those who desire to consecrate themselves 100% to the Lord. Then those come who will volunteer to do the Lord's will and go to the foreign field if He should so lead. Each Saturday night from two to four hundred answered this call. It was thrilling to see them form a huge circle around the fire and sing, "Where He leads me, I will follow."[46]

There were indeed many huge circles around the campfires, and Percy's numbers (two hundred to four hundred) remind us that in addition to the forty or so Pinebrookers who accepted Christ each week, many more responded to the other calls to dedicate their lives in various ways to Christian service. Percy was well aware of the sort of question that was being asked—even by fellow fundamentalists—about the type of conversions and onetime decisions that were being induced at Pinebrook: "Do they really mean it?" and "How long will they last?" He knew that inevitably some of those who professed Christ or who rededicated their lives would not really "mean business." All that he could do was try to ensure that they knew what they were doing and were making a genuine commitment to live for Christ. After this, it was up to the individual to fulfill his or her pledge, with the aid of the indwelling Spirit.

But the mountaintop experiences that occurred around the campfire were very real in the hearts and minds of the individuals who made them, as the following account, taken from a 1947 newsletter and written by someone identified as "Sylvia," makes plain:

> As I looked down at the campfire and thought back on that week [at Pinebrook], I felt closer to God than I had ever before felt. The joy that I had found in walking close to my Lord was greater than I had thought could be found anywhere in the world. I had discovered how the Lord supplies every need, both spiritual and physical, when a life is wholly dedicated to Him. God was very real to me as I gazed up into the heavens. . . . I found myself wishing that everyone might know this Saviour of mine, that everyone might have the joy and peace that I

had found in Him. In that instant, I realized what I wanted my life work to be. I wanted to tell others about Jesus. I didn't know whether God would call me as a missionary to some foreign land, or whether He would give me something to do for Him right here in my own country, but I knew that I wanted Him to use my life wholly for His glory. The people began to sing:

"Have Thine own way, Lord! Have Thine own way!
Thou art the potter; I am the clay;
Mold me and make me after Thy will,
While I am waiting, yielded and still."

That was my prayer that evening; God knew I meant every word of that hymn. As I told Him this, I looked at the campfire. From the glowing embers a bevy of sparks flew overhead. One spark went higher than any other; it went far beyond the stars, carrying with it my prayer of dedication to my Saviour.[47]

The author of this moving account was Sylvia McCutcheon, who at that time was playing harp on the YPCA broadcast. After receiving her bachelor's and master's degrees in music education at the University of Pennsylvania, she married a King's graduate, Bob Ward, and went with him to the Belgian Congo under the auspices of the Africa Inland Mission, where she served at a mission school for nineteen years. Her husband died in Africa at age forty from a blood condition for which he could not get adequate treatment. Sylvia was one of the thousands of individuals whose lives started on a new course on that hillside in the twenty-eight-plus years of Pinebrook's history. How can one even begin to calculate the overall spiritual effects in the interior lives and the outward living of those who made these decisions?

Peggy Claasen Craven was a young person who came to Pinebrook already saved. She was so moved listening to Percy preach, she recalled, that "I almost wished I hadn't been saved so I could do it all over again." Although accepted at prestigious Smith College, she decided to attend The King's College, graduating in 1950, and went into evangelistic work aimed at women's groups. "I have led hundreds and hundreds of women to Christ" she said to me, and "my evangelism has come from Percy."[48]

Another story of two lives that were redirected at Pinebrook is told by Marge and Jack Wyrtzen. In 1933, the year Pinebrook opened, Marge Smith, the adopted daughter of an affluent Brooklyn surgeon, was dating a boy named John Von Casper "Jack" Wyrtzen, also from Brooklyn, who loved music and riding horses. Wyrtzen played horn and drums at Jamaica High School and with the U.S. Cavalry Band and later would direct his own dance band. Marge and Jack had both attended church regularly and were exposed at home to Percy's Sunday radio broadcast over WMCA; however they were not greatly impressed by Percy or the program. Looking back to that time, Wyrtzen recalled: "We'd mock and make fun of Percy Crawford and the testimonies and just laugh at him."[49] Marge's mother, however, liked Percy's program and when she heard on it that he was starting a summer conference in the Pocono Mountains, she talked her daughter into going for a few days—on the condition that they would then move on to some of the more swinging resorts in the area.

When she got to Pinebrook, she was both attracted and repelled. Percy, who was helping in the kitchen, had burned the spaghetti. Then she was asked to help clean the tables. But (according to Wyrtzen) when she got to the evening service, her resistance began to weaken. The quartet had done some "cutting up, and they were having a lot of fun. And she thought: 'well, these are Christians? I can't believe it, they are having so much fun.'" She stayed long enough to hear Percy preach and he reached her, and when the invitation was given, she raised her hand and went forward. But it was not until she got back to her room that she realized what she had done and the tears flowed.

Wyrtzen goes on to say that he and Marge returned to Pinebrook, and they "both dedicated [their] lives to the Lord under [Dr. Albert Hughes's] preaching that summer, and we said: 'Lord, we're ready to go any place'; and I thought sure we were going to Africa, some place like that." Marge returned to Brooklyn and started one of Percy's Phi Gamma Fishing Club chapters for women to complement Wyrtzen's boys' Bible club. Wyrtzen quit his dance band that winter and soon left his job in the insurance business to begin full-time evangelistic work. Though he went on to do great things of his own, he did not forget his debt to Pinebrook; in 1940 he sent Percy a note that said: "Heaven alone will tell what the Lord has done for me at Pinebrook."

If one is to get a grasp of the magnitude of the spiritual effects that flowed out of Pinebrook, one has to realize that there were literally thousands of stories like those of Sylvia McCutcheon, Peggy Craven, Marge Smith, and Jack Wyrtzen.

## HIS BLESSED VINEYARD

Pinebrook Bible Conference was my father's finest achievement. It was initially a place where he could assemble the hundreds of young people that he was reaching over the air and in the Phi Gamma clubs and bring them together into one visible body. It was a safe haven, where young people in nondenominational and mainline churches could retreat from the world, interact socially, and grow in their common faith. At the same time, it offered a highly charged spiritual environment that fostered life-changing experiences of conversion and dedication to Christian service. For speakers, it was a neutral site where fundamentalists of different stripes could lay aside their differences and, in a spirit of tolerance and collegiality, focus on getting youth to commit their lives to the cause of Christ. And for Percy and his team (and family), it was hallowed ground where they could relax a little and enjoy the daily encounters with their congregants.

But even more, Pinebrook was the place where Percy could best express his whole personality—his managerial skills, his showmanship, his love of fun and humor, his familial and nurturing tendencies, and his great gift of evangelism. It was where he was most himself and where he could draw a breath and rest (even while constantly on the go).

Further, it was the place where he had complete freedom to do the Lord's work in the way he thought it should be done. He had no external authority hovering over him, no church officials or committees to answer to. Nor was there any internal review, as the loyalists he appointed to Pinebrook's board of directors failed to exercise any serious oversight. Harold Ockenga once said of Percy that he was "a rugged individualist [who] could not be confined to the restrictions of any denominational hierarchy but took his orders direct from God."[50] This absolute independence my father enjoyed undoubtedly had its positive side—Pinebrook would not have flourished as it did if he had not had the freedom to pursue the vision he had for it. But there were also potential dangers.

First there was the issue of executive power. We have seen how Percy's unchallengeable authority led to some arbitrary and questionable decisions in his relations with staff. Those who may have thought they were treated unfairly had no recourse whatsoever; there was no higher court of appeal. Initially, Percy could exercise this sort of tight control and discipline over his staff without undue consequences; it may even have strengthened his overall operation. But eventually, I believe, his unwillingness to distribute power proved harmful to him and weakened his organization. As we will see, over the years some very good people were let go who could have been used to build the organization and give it added strength and stability.

Moreover there were a few occasions (not only at Pinebrook) in which Percy became overly familiar and fresh with female members of his staff. This too casual attitude toward women—although it may not have been considered sinful in that era—was disrespectful and inappropriate for someone in his position of authority, and was certainly abetted by his feeling that he ruled over his entire organization and everyone in it.

Further, when a single individual has all the decision-making power, without any mechanism for review by some human authority, then he has to assume the risk of making wrong judgments and going astray. But Percy eschewed all human authority and trusted in the Lord to lead him when he made important decisions. The practical rule he adopted was to follow the path on which he thought he was being led, and if God was *in* that work, blessing it—that is, if the necessary contributions were received to carry on the work and if souls were being saved—then he would continue with it. And if God was not in the work, then it would sputter and he would go on to something else. By this measure, there was little doubt that Pinebrook was being blessed. But as we will see, down the road, there would be other ventures in which Percy overextended himself and placed his entire organization in jeopardy.

Another more serious threat stemming from Percy's being in full command at Pinebrook was that he might begin to elevate himself and think of the enterprise as his own doing and not the Lord's. Fundamentalists did not allow a person to claim the glory for himself; one had to give all the glory to God. However, Percy was always acutely aware of this greatest of all temptations and conscientiously guarded against it. Although Pinebrook was in one sense his own creation, I think he would have said that he had provided only the physical setting in which the Holy Spirit could do his work of regenerating souls. Percy would not take credit for what was really happening there in people's lives. The following remark after the 1944 season is typical: "We've worked hard and we thank God that we've had another year to work in his blessed vineyard. What an honor, what a privilege. To think He's willing to use poor miserable sticks like you and me but it seems He just loves to do it."[51]

Comments like this conveyed what was, I believe, a genuine attitude of humility in my father. He admired in others this quality of being humble—in Billy Graham, for example—and tried to foster it in himself.[52] Although he was in many ways a proud and self-assertive man, he was not egotistical; he did not overadvertise himself or zealously seek the praise and adulation of his fellows.

Finally, a serious problem that did emerge at Pinebrook—one that threatened his entire ministry—was that the conference was so centered on and dependent upon his individual person that it would be unable to continue after he was gone. There was no hierarchical structure from which a successor could emerge. Percy was at the top, with everyone else subordinate to him. Toward the end of his life, he tried to groom his children to take over his various enterprises, and he wanted his second son, Richard, to direct the camps. The devoted twenty-one-year-old son became director of Pinebrook after Percy's death and ran the summer conference for three years before leasing it to evangelist Ross Rhoads. Dick gave the program a more youth-oriented and upbeat flavor, but it was a holding operation from the start, and he finally was forced to sell Pinebrook in 1968.[53]

By the mid-1930s, as Pinebrook Bible Conference was taking shape as the flagship enterprise of his ministry, Percy charted his course for the next decade. He would continue the radio ministry of the *Young People's Church of the Air,* gradually extending his coverage to reach a nationwide audience. And he would begin to lay the groundwork for a Christian liberal arts college where his young converts could receive a Bible-based education and train for full-time service. He continued to drive hard, making good on his pledge to the Lord when he said: "I'll give you every drop of blood I have."[54]

The Inn at Pinebrook Bible Conference in the Pocono Mountains of Pennsylvania.

Eighteen-year-old pianist, Mrs. Ruth Duvall Crawford, took charge of the music for the radio broadcast and the evangelistic team.

Percy used the skills he had learned as a "carpenter's helper" in L.A. to help build the new tabernacle at Pinebrook in 1937.

**Percy and Ruth cut a fine figure at Pinebrook, 1934.**

**The brass quartet was featured prominently on the radio broadcast from 1931 to 1949. Left to right: Arol Fesmire, Jack Hoover, Vernon Haupt, and Sam Ayling (1940).**

Percy and Ruth with the quartet that sang together from 1934 to 1938. Left to right: Charlie Jewitt, Horace Davies, Fenton Duvall, and Ken Shick.

The only family photos of Percy's father Tom were taken during his visit to Pinebrook in 1948, shown with Ruth's mother Nancy Viola Duvall.

**Percy referred to these Bible teachers in the second season of Pinebrook Bible Conference (1934) as "one of the greatest if not *the* greatest group of God's men ever assembled."**

Fundamentalist leader William Bell Riley was a speaker at Pinebrook from 1933 to 1935.

Left to right: Speakers John Linton, Rowan Pearce, Will Houghton, Beverly Shea, and Percy in 1938. It was at Pinebrook that Houghton persuaded Bev Shea to quit his job in New York City and come to Moody Bible Institute.

Percy is flanked by Pinebrook speakers and close associates Merril MacPherson (left) and Harold Laird (right), both of whom were thrown out of the Presbyterian Church, U.S.A. Also pictured (left) saxophonist Jake Sheetz and (right) songleader Stan Cook.

Percy cutting it up with Wendell Loveless (left) and Bob Ketcham at a Pinebrook service.

Pinebrook speakers (left to right) Percy, Deak Ketcham, Jack Wyrtzen, and Joe Springer.

Cliff Barrows and a young Billy Graham were together at
Pinebrook in 1946, 1947, and 1949. Graham recalled that
his warm friendship and association with Barrows started
at Pinebrook.

Pinebrook speakers (left to right). Lawrence Wigden, Lehman Strauss, Percy and
Ruth, Ruth and Billy Graham, Walter "Mac" McDonald, and Bob Wigden. By the
time this picture was taken (August 1952), Graham had achieved national prominence.

# 11

## Radio: The Young People's Church of the Air

In HIS 1932 *REVELATION* ARTICLE "A MODERN REVIVAL," AFTER DESCRIBing the success his open-air meetings and the radio broadcast were having in changing lives and saving souls, Percy makes a concluding statement that indicates what he took to be the greater significance of these events. God was using him and his ministry to accomplish a larger purpose. A revival was afoot that would spread across the entire nation:

> The doors of Heaven are opening and we are looking for an out-pouring that will sweep over the entire country. God is still on the throne. He longs to save. He still looks for men and women as empty vessels that He can use. The time is opportune, with other resources gone, and hardship and sorrow on every hand.[1] Hearts are sick of sin; there is no rest.

He then issues a call for Christians to respond to God's leading:

> Oh, that all Christians might reconsecrate themselves and mean business with God. Oh, that they might see that He is willing to save if they stop tying His hands. . . . Let us take courage and not only attempt great things for God but expect great things from Him. Let us prove His promise. "Ask of Me, and I will show thee great and mighty things that thou knowest not."[2]

This was the larger vision that guided my father in those early years. He had a proven track record in evangelism and was now ready and eager to venture forth and attempt even greater things for God. And radio would be the primary vehicle he would use to carry the gospel to a "sin-sick" nation.

When Percy started his radio program, the *Young People's Church of the Air,* on one station in Philadelphia on October 4, 1931, it was a risky proposition for him. The country was deep in economic depression. He was a "poor student" (as he later said) wearing secondhand clothes, with a meager income that consisted of a small salary for his work at the Barnes and whatever he was given or collected in offerings for his speaking engagements. And radio was expensive. When he signed the contract with WIP-

WFAN Broadcasting Company, he was committing himself to a payment schedule that would cost $175/week (or over $6,000 for the entire season), and he had no church or organization or wealthy individuals backing him.

Percy's finances were further strained when his bank, the Franklin Trust Company, closed on the Monday following his first broadcast. (Franklin Trust was one of the largest of the fifty Philadelphia banks that would close in the three-year period after the crash of 1929.) When the bank was closed on October 5, Percy lost whatever money he had been able to raise to get the program going, as well as the money in his personal savings account ($600) that he had built up over the previous eight years. From the start, the broadcast was a "faith venture," which meant that he would rely on God's promise in Philippians 4:19 to "supply all his need."

But the other side of the coin was that radio could be the means of reaching a whole new audience. It could reach those who had turned away from religion and who "never darkened a church door." In the 1930s, radio was becoming a fixture in bars, clubs, and other public venues.[3] When asked once whether radio was doing away with the old-fashioned pulpit, he answered: "No, it is not. It is supplementing the pulpit. It gets into all kinds of places where the preacher can't go himself."[4] At the beginning of a 1936 sermon, he asked the Lord to "make [the broadcast] go into the dives and dens where they're longing to find forgiveness of sin."[5]

Further, the radio was reaching an audience on a scale that could not have been imagined a decade before. Historian Joel Carpenter points out that "fundamentalists' and evangelicals' expanding radio operations were riding a popular wave of immense proportions, for the commercial radio industry was becoming a major source of entertainment in America and even the Depression could not dampen its growth." He goes on to say that between 1930 and 1935, the number of radio sets doubled, numbering over eighteen million and reaching 60 percent of American homes.[6] But in fact, by 1935 radio was approaching total coverage in large cities, where 93 percent of households had radios.[7] In the 1934–35 season, when Percy was about to go on four metropolitan stations, he expected to be reaching four million to five million people with the gospel each week—numbers that his mentor, Reuben Torrey, could hardly have fathomed.[8]

Percy thrust himself into the marketplace of religious broadcasting, confident that he could find a niche in the already bustling lineup of religious programming available on the radio dial. A Philadelphia listener who wanted to tune in a Sunday religious program in October 1931 could choose twenty or twenty-five different offerings representing the major faiths and denominations as well as smaller groups and sects. The Columbia Broadcasting System had just initiated its policy (following NBC) of not selling time to

religious broadcasters, but rather giving "sustaining" (free) time for an in-
terfaith "devotional" program distributed among each of the three major
faiths called *Church of the Air.*[9]

Among fundamentalists, the competition was not so intense when Percy
started his broadcast. Donald Grey Barnhouse was the powerhouse figure
with his half-hour of Bible exposition coming from Tenth Presbyterian
Church at 5:00 p.m. Barnhouse had been on the nationwide CBS network
for three and a half years, but had just been put off the network and was
now buying time on close to one hundred independent stations. (Percy
shrewdly selected the time slot "right after Barnhouse" [5:30–6:30] in order
to pick up a share of his friendly audience.)[10] Various other nondenominational churches were broadcasting their services, including O. R. Palmer's
Berachah Church, where Percy had often preached. Other fundamentalists
would be coming hot on his heels. In the following spring, March 1932,
George Palmer launched his daily *Morning Cheer* broadcast on WRAX.[11]

## THE BROADCAST

Percy's *Young People's Church of the Air* (YPCA) program was different
from other Sunday programs in not being tied to a regular church service
and congregation. This meant that the entire hour-long program was
pitched primarily to the radio audience and not to the four hundred to five
hundred people filling the Barnes auditorium, whose role in the production
was limited to the singing of hymns and choruses.[12]

The program was also distinguished by its heavy emphasis on music.
Nothing even came close to the musical production put on by the 150 young
people who made up the orchestra, chorus, quartet, brass ensemble, and
soloists that Percy and Ruth had assembled for the broadcast. Ruth had
brought with her a fine quartet from her Collingswood church, which soon
stabilized into one of Percy's best ever, consisting of top tenor Horace
Davies, second tenor Charlie Jewitt, baritone Fenton Duvall (Ruth's brother),
and bass Ken Schick. In the first year, baritone Jimmy Blackstone, whom
Percy had encouraged to come from BIOLA to Westminster Seminary, was
the soloist. And Percy and Ruth selected the top instrumentalists from the
various church orchestras that had played at his open-air meetings.

The hymns and songs heard on the broadcast had a brighter, more upbeat
tone. Percy's first songbook, *The Young People's Church of the Air Hymn
Book,* put out in 1932 for use at the broadcasts, was a compilation of older
and more recent hymns and songs from revivalist sources. Percy indicates in
the foreword that he has included in it only "the cream of the songs from the

best song books" and left out the "dead songs." "The result is we have a selection of songs distinctly for young people." The first song in the book,
"Love Wonderful Love," written by the Scottish evangelist and composer
Seth Sykes, became the YPCA signature song and probably best expresses
the larger sentiment of the entire broadcast; the song has a warm and over-
flowing quality, expressing joy and thankfulness for Christ's gift of salvation:

> Love, wonderful love,
> The love of Christ to me.
> Love, wonderful love,
> So rich, so full, so free;
> Wide, wide as the ocean,
> Deep, deep as the sea,
> High, high as the heav'n above,
> His love to me.

Percy tended to view the music on the broadcast as preparatory for his
sermon and as creating the proper mood for the invitation. Because of the
way music could "melt hearts," it was a vital part of his evangelistic service.[13] Although Ruth and the other musicians never lost sight of this utili-
tarian goal, still it can hardly be denied that the gospel music they created
for this purpose had a distinctiveness and an appeal all its own and, I believe, contributed more to the success of Percy's evangelism than he ever
realized. Torrey Johnson once said that Ruth contributed 50 percent to
Percy's ministry. And while this way of putting it does give my mother the
credit she deserves, I prefer to view the relationship between the partners
differently—as contrasting and symbiotic. The melodious, flowing, warm
feeling of the half hour of medleys of music that Ruth composed comple-
mented perfectly Percy's hard-driving, staccato preaching style. Each of
the partners played off the other and would not have had the same effect
without the other.

## RADIO STYLE

It was, however, Percy's unique voice and style that got the YPCA broadcast going and gave it its initial appeal. Mel Larson, writing in 1947 about
the "young men on fire" who inspired the Youth for Christ movement, gives
us an insight into Percy the radio preacher before the advent of television:

Unconsciously many Youth for Christ speakers have patterned their messages
after Crawford's preaching. He speaks the language of youth in a frank, sincere

and fearless way. He wavers not a whit from the old-fashioned Gospel. In a somewhat high-pitched voice, he speaks rapidly, and hammers his points home with plenty of Scripture.[14]

Larson's description of my father's radio personality is on the mark; he presented the plain gospel in no uncertain terms (as he liked to say), and his delivery was high-pitched, piercing, and rapid-fire. Joel Carpenter, writing fifty years after Larson, sees the influence of the radio newscasters on my father's style, claiming that Percy "emulated the urgent, rapid-fire speaking style of the radio news reporter."[15] He spoke directly to the listener in urgent tones: "You there by your radio—look up—I'm talking to you—you have a terrific responsibility on your hands—it's Jesus Christ."[16] His short messages (usually about twenty minutes long on the hour-long radio broadcast and from five to seven minutes on the half-hour programs) had a demanding, insistent quality that could be irritating; it could get under your skin. In this regard, his style contrasted with that of Charles Fuller, who was more laid-back, more comforting. Percy was not interested in making his listeners feel comfortable; he wanted to challenge them, rile them, bring them to a conviction of their sin and their need for a savior, and coax them into making a decision.

He used the language of the common person and the working person (which he felt entitled to because of his own working-class background), with words like "tough," "he-man," "red-blooded," and "backbone" to describe those who "meant business" for Christ and who were willing to stand up to the ridicule of their peers, as opposed to the "weak-kneed" and "spineless" ones who would not. He portrayed Jesus in these strongly masculine terms—as a working man, a carpenter with "calloused" hands and a "great chest," "a two-fisted fighter," and "a real man." Peter, too, was one who was not afraid to stand up for Jesus and say to the Roman soldier, "If you lay a finger on Him I'll take your head off."

He often took a mildly scornful, sarcastic attitude against those who soft-pedaled the gospel, as in this 1937 sermon:

> You go to New York or to Philadelphia and you'll find some lovely churches, with lovely music. You'll find your preacher there too, and he'll say the things that please you, and you'll go out saying, "I was lifted up. Oh, I was exalted. Wasn't the music grand?" It was grand, and your sins are still unforgiven. You can get what you want today, if you want that type of religion you can get it. You'll find it in the most elite and lovely spirals, reaching up to heaven; and you'll not find the blood that can wash away your sins, like you'll find in the lowly man of Galilee.[17]

Larson's description touched on another key element of my father's preaching style, his sincerity. By this, I do not mean simply his candid, straightforward speech, but rather that what he said impressed his listeners as coming from the heart. He conveyed to them a longing, an anguish, that they might listen to him and heed his call—that the only thing that mattered to him was their salvation:

> Jesus . . . died for the sins of the whole world, or else I couldn't stand up here and invite all the ungodly to come to Jesus Christ. . . . I wouldn't exert myself, and go as we did last year, forty thousand miles, that we might win men and women for Christ. I'd sit home by the fireside, and go over the sacred things of the word, and I'd rest.[18]

> What a great salvation God has offered us. I wish sometimes my lips could be dipped in a fountain of eloquence, that I might tell the world of His great love. But that is impossible so I come to you in my own way—earnestly, sincerely, with all my heart. . . .[19]

> (In a closing prayer:) I talked to you like I talked to my brother before he died; I talked to you because I'm interested in you.[20]

So it is not surprising that the YPCA broadcast achieved almost instant popularity in Philadelphia and gave Percy near celebrity status in Christian circles. The invitations to speak at regional churches and tabernacles came pouring in.

### EXPANSION

Even though Percy was eager to take the program to a wider audience, he proceeded cautiously. He did not want to take on any more stations than his new church "members" would support with their gifts. He had witnessed many radio preachers go on the air and then drop off for lack of funds, and he did not want to suffer that sort of setback. He had seen Paul Rader take on ten cities coast-to-coast with CBS in April 1930 (Percy's first summer in Philadelphia), only to crash and burn four months later.

But the gifts for the "radio fund" were sufficient, which clearly indicated to Percy that the Lord was blessing the work, and in the second season (October 1932) the New York City station WMCA was added at the same hour as in Philadelphia. Percy had already extended his ministry into the New York metropolitan area; in the previous year he had been invited to preach and conduct a rally at Will Houghton's historic Calvary Baptist Church—the first of many engagements there. The cost for an hour's program on the Philadelphia and New York stations for the first year was $425/week. Two years later, the YPCA was heard on three stations when WCBM Baltimore was added for about the same total cost. But for the rest of the decade, he limited his coverage to the Northeast region on four metropolitan stations in Philadelphia (WIP), New York (WMCA), Baltimore (WCBM), and Boston (WMEX). By this time he was broadcasting over the summer months from Pinebrook Bible Conference, so that his radio audience could share in the great services and Bible preaching that was going on there.

His goal was to consolidate a constituency in the Northeast that could sustain his other parachurch organizations—the Bible conference and camps, the fishing clubs, the bookstore and book clubs (started in November 1935),[21] and The King's College, which opened its doors in 1938. He was being careful not to overreach. Although the camps and the bookstore were self-supporting, the college was deeply indebted and the radio broadcasts were costing approximately $500/week or about $25,000 annually.[22] Ever since his youth, Percy had prided himself on being able to pay his way, and it was important for him now in his Christian work to be able to pay his bills and pay back loans in a timely fashion and even always to have some cash reserve on hand. So he moved cautiously and deliberately. But he knew all along that the time was coming when he would take his message to a nationwide audience.

## MEETINGS

Meanwhile as radio served to enlarge and solidify his base in the 1930s, Percy was getting more invitations to speak at churches, tabernacles, and missions and to Phi Gamma clubs and other young people's organizations. He also conducted rallies periodically at the Barnes auditorium and other venues in the region. Percy and Ruth spent a good part of their twenty-nine-year ministry together in a car traveling with the quartet to these "meetings" (as we called them), as many as six nights a week, logging forty thousand to fifty thousand miles a year. It was a grueling schedule that certainly took a heavy toll on my father's health.

Ruth and Percy crisscrossed the Northeastern states, conducting single meetings that featured stirring gospel music and spirited preaching. It was a barnstorming operation. Percy and his team would arrive at the church door in time for a prearranged supper or else just before the meeting was to start. He then conducted a fast-paced service with a fifteen- or twenty-minute sermon, but would always take the time to give an invitation and an altar call. As soon as the service ended, he whisked the team out the door into the car and headed for home. He did not spend a lot of time socializing with the pastor and church people; he was there to do the Lord's business, that is, to win souls, and when the business was taken care of, he moved on. This may have ruffled some feathers and impressed some of his hosts as being rude, but the overwhelming response to his services was positive—as evidenced by the number of requests for return visits.

What Percy and the team gave these hundreds of churches was a lively, fun, youth-oriented service that won new converts who would (it was hoped) bring new spiritual energy into the church and its program. He always left it to the churches to follow up on these new converts and nurture them in their new commitment. And what he got from the churches was, first, advertisement for the various YPCA endeavors—the camps, the college, the broadcast—with the expectation that some would want to participate in them; and, second, an offering.

The "terms" for conducting these meetings were that he would receive a freewill offering for the work of the YPCA. This was a policy that he stuck to throughout his ministry. To the best of my knowledge and memory, Percy never asked for more than this. He would sometimes agree to let the church take a second offering to cover their expenses. Or else, at large and attractive venues, he might agree to take something less than the full offering; for example, at Calvary Baptist Church, New York, he took a 60/40 cut of the offering one year. He also insisted that one of his quartet members be present when the offering was counted. Again, some churchmen were put off by this demand, viewing it as mistrustful; but Percy insisted on it, and I believe for good reason: he learned early on in his ministry that if he allowed church officials to deduct their expenses from the offering (his only payment), he could easily end up getting little or nothing for his troubles.

For the most part, the meeting schedule in the 1930s was limited geographically to a range that was more or less commensurate with the coverage of the radio broadcast (extending from Baltimore to Boston). Percy also restricted the schedule to places he could drive to (from Philadelphia) and return home on the same day. The YPCA team rarely lodged overnight at any of their meeting sites—in part because Percy had determined that he could be most effective doing one-night stands and also because the quartet members, who normally were putting themselves through college or seminary, had to be back for classes the next day.

There were, however, frequent evangelistic forays into the Midwest and Far West. Percy had many friends and contacts in the Chicago area and on the West Coast, and he jumped at any chance to visit those regions. But it was not until the 1940s, after Percy took his radio broadcast coast-to-coast on the Mutual network that he began to travel with Ruth and the quartet on major, extended tours across the country, as we will see presently.

## THE MUTUAL NETWORK

In 1940, after nine years of successful broadcasting in the Northeast, Percy finally put the *Young People's Church of the Air* on a coast-to-coast hookup. Though the records are fragmentary, the first big jump in stations seems to have occurred in the 1939–40 season. In various publications in 1940, the YPCA program was advertised as being aired coast to coast on stations numbering from 43 to 66. According to a magazine story published in 1940 by the *Philadelphia Inquirer* that hyped the YPCA as "one of the most phenomenal nationwide ministries of modern times," the broadcast could be heard on 43 radio stations that reach into "every State of the Union and throughout Canada." The article explains that the Sunday program is heard live only on the Philadelphia, New York, Baltimore and Boston stations; and the other 39 stations "receive the services . . . on phonograph discs which Mr. Crawford records and furnishes free."[23] Elsewhere that same year in an advertisement, Percy states, under the headline "55 Stations Coast to Coast," that YPCA was "using the facilities" of the added radio stations (presumably to play his recordings).[24]

Within two year's time—on August 30, 1942—Percy finally signed with the Mutual Broadcasting System and jumped to 207 stations (up from 83). And over the next seven years, through 1949, as Percy juggled Mutual with smaller networks and some independent stations, the total number of stations that he announced being on fluctuated from 250 to 375, but for most of this time held around 275.[25] The cost for thus disseminating the gospel through these years was in the range of $4,500–$5,000/week, which meant that the *Young People's Church of the Air* was paying radio stations and network owners the staggering figure of $250,000 annually, the equivalent of $3,280,000 in current dollars.[26]

\*

The Mutual Broadcasting System (MBS) was formed by a group of independent broadcasters in 1934 at a time when the NBC and CBS networks held sway in the radio world. As indicated above, both NBC and CBS had adopted the policy of not selling time to religious broadcasters, but instead, giving free, "sustaining" programming to each of the three major faiths: Catholic, Jewish, and Protestant. This policy was thought to serve the public interest—which station owners were mandated to do—insofar as it denied a public platform to certain offending sectarian preachers who were making vicious attacks on other religious groups and civic leaders.[27] It was also directed against unscrupulous individuals who were openly getting rich from donations from their radio audiences. NBC worked closely with the Federal Council of Churches of Christ in America in selecting Protestant ministers for these programs, and the council, which represented twenty-five mainline denominations, chose speakers of a decidedly liberal bent. In addition, it sought to promote a message that had "the widest appeal—presenting the broad claims of religion, which not only aid in building up the personal and social life of the individual but also aid in popularizing religion and the Church."[28] CBS also went for moderate representatives from the three major faiths in its Sunday *Church of the Air* program. Thus the fundamentalists felt doubly cheated by this policy: not only were they not allowed to buy time on network radio—thus severely limiting their access to a national audience—but the very churches that they considered to be apostate and deniers of the gospel of Christ were given free access to that same audience. So the Mutual network finally gave fundamentalist broadcasters the opportunity to go national, if they could afford to do it.

Going on the network in 1942 represented a great leap forward for the YPCA. Charles Fuller had gone coast to coast on thirty Mutual stations five years earlier with the *Old Fashioned Revival Hour.*[29] What held Percy back was mainly the enormous cost; and Mutual would not allow its clients to pick and choose among their affiliates, but rather required them to go on all their stations in order to stay in their desired time slots. But Percy found, as Fuller had, that during this time of social upheaval and unrest, when the country was at war, that Americans were willing to sustain the sort of message that spoke to their dis-ease, and gave a sure solution to it. And so he was willing to "launch out" into deeper waters and take on the huge financial burden of network radio.

To be sure, there were significant advantages offered by the networks. In the first place, it meant a live broadcast sent over telephone wires simultaneously to all the network stations throughout the nation. Then too, network stations exceeded the others in power and prestige on the radio dial. Since Congress passed the 1927 and 1934 Radio Acts, the Federal Radio Commission had been given full authority over the granting of licenses and signal strengths. The commission tended to give preferential treatment to the networks by awarding them or their affiliate stations the lion's share of clear-channel frequencies and higher power levels—especially to stations in large metropolitan areas.[30] The rationale for this was that the commercial networks, supported by their national advertisers, were better financed and thus better able to afford the rising costs of technical equipment, trained personnel, and the production of quality programming. Moreover, the networks were viewed as better able to serve the public interest by reaching a larger audience with standardized mass entertainment. The result was that noncommercial and nonprofit stations that served the needs of a particular cultural group or a local community (referred to by the commission as "propaganda" stations) tended to get the short end of the stick.[31] By the end of the 1930s, "NBC and CBS had nearly all of the high-powered stations, accounting for more than 85% of the national nighttime wattage."[32] Mutual had to play catch-up with its competitors, and as one historian observes, even though it grew to include a large number of stations, still it "lag[ged] far behind the leaders in total wattage and audience share."[33]

Percy however was extremely pleased with the hookup he got from Mutual. But even as the network opened new avenues for soul winning, at the same time it was putting severe limitations on him. After only one year on the network, in the fall of 1943, Mutual adopted a policy of allowing religious programming on Sunday mornings only. This meant that if Percy wanted to stay on Mutual, he would have to switch from his accustomed late-afternoon hour to the morning hours when many of his potential listeners would be attending Sunday school and church. (Charles Fuller took his *Old Fashioned Revival Hour* off Mutual, after seven years, because of this change and bought time on a comparable number of independent stations so that he could continue his hour-long Sunday evening program.)[34] Percy decided to stay with Mutual and accommodate his program to the prescribed hours.[35] By shifting the program around to (mostly undesirable) time slots, Mutual was making it very difficult for my father to establish a regular audience who would give on a regular basis.

In the fall of 1944, Mutual put a further restriction on religious broadcasters when it ruled that they could not make any appeals for money on the air. The network was responding to the same pressures that had led to the ban on selling time to religious programs at NBC and CBS. For Percy this was bad news. It meant (as he said in a fund-raising letter that year) that "80% of our stations forbid any announcement concerning our need of funds."[36] He responded in two ways: first, over a period of time he went to the trouble of making (and sending out) two broadcasts—one with an appeal for gifts and one without. Second, he effectively countered the policy by using it as a means to elicit more donations. In the August 1, 1944, newsletter sent to forty-six thousand listeners, he called the new policy "the test of tests for the Y.P.C.A.":

> While many are dropping the Mutual for fear that sufficient funds would not come in, we feel we should at least continue on, as long as the funds come in. . . . I have of late, I confess, been fretting and stewing but I have decided to rest on Him. If funds do not come in, then I will take it we are to back down and drop station after station. Last week when I had to drop some stations, I shed a few tears—it hurt to think the message of salvation through our efforts on that station would be heard no more. I tell you it hurts but I say I will rest in Him.[37]

As we have seen, the funding did come in because he continued on Mutual for the next five years. But even as he was successfully coping with the network's arbitrary decisions, my father must have felt that he was being unfairly manipulated (or as he would have said "kicked around") by the network managers and station owners for their own profit. And what was worse, by holding him back, the companies were preventing him from sending out the gospel—they were tying God's hands. These struggles with the networks and station owners over the years brought home to him the realization that the only way to beat them was to control the media outlets himself. BIOLA and Moody Bible Institute had shown how it could be done. In fact, Percy had had the idea of operating his own radio station since 1937 when he applied for a license for a Philadelphia station. (The Federal Communications Commission had denied the request.[38]) But his interest in becoming an independent broadcaster took on a new urgency as he battled with the networks. He wondered why he could not build his own Christian network of stations, but this visionary idea would have to wait until a more propitious time. Meanwhile, he would work with Mutual, and he would pursue another more attainable goal, taking the radio broadcast onto television.

## RAISING FUNDS

If Percy was going to fulfill his vision of using the mass media to carry the gospel to an entire nation, then he would have to be able to raise the money to pay for it. Taking on a quarter-million dollar financial obligation annually was no small task. And the networks did not issue credit. As he said in one of his newsletters: "Mutual may not put us off the air but if you folks stop giving—automatically we go off."[39] And so he put a great deal of his time and energy into devising ways of getting his radio and television audiences to give.

Percy had no professional fund-raiser or marketing consultant on his staff. He wrote his own copy for all of the advertisements, announcements, calendars, and letters of appeal that went out to his supporters. This was an effective strategy, because it was important that he make these appeals in his own voice in order to capitalize on the personal relationship he had established with his listeners and viewers. His appeals for funds tended to be low-key and moderate; he did not harangue his people for money or throw Scripture at them or promise them God's blessing, but instead explained in frank and realistic terms the urgent need for their support. The message was this: if you have been blessed by these programs and if you want to see them continue on the air, then you should do your part and give something to keep them going.

Percy usually began his pitch by pointing to the consistent results of the broadcasts in reaching lost souls. "Thousands of young men and women have accepted Christ as Saviour because of these broadcasts." "As a result of one broadcast alone, recently, over 150 wrote in saying they had accepted Christ as their Saviour." "At the close of some TV programs as high as 500 wrote in stating they had professed Christ as Saviour." "Some 9000 last year alone professed Christ through the YPCA."

Then he emphasized that "no millionaire or denomination pays our bills; only folk like you, sending one dollar or two or five or ten keep us going." He reminded listeners that every gift counted, no matter how small. In fact, the broadcasts were almost entirely dependent on small contributions over the years, as Percy was never able to get wealthy businessmen to give major sustaining gifts.

Further, all gifts would be used 100 percent for the radio and television broadcasts. He wrote in the 1945 calendar: "For 14 years now we have never used anything from our gifts to pay the preacher, or postage or talent or help in the office. Our means of livelihood comes from Pinebrook. Offerings from meetings pay postage, etc. Your dollar goes farther when sent to Box 1, Phila. 5, Pa." My father was careful to take his annual salary from the camps. Offerings from meetings were sufficient to cover pay for the musical talent and office and mailing expenses.

Percy always had some sort of giveaway or special offer as an inducement to giving. He offered barrel banks (which listeners would send back when full), poems, mottos, pictures of Pinebrook, "twelve-page picture-scripture" calendars, a miniature Bible, dried flowers from the Holy Land, photos of the Crawford family, his book *The Art of Fishing for Men* (for gifts of $1 or more), various recordings of YPCA music, and many others.

By far the most important aspect of his appeals was the idea that the broadcasts were a "faith venture." What this meant to his fundamentalist audience was that even though he had no one underwriting the programs, and going on with them would seem to be foolish or even impossible from a practical standpoint, nevertheless he would go ahead and take on the financial burden, trusting that God would provide. As we have seen, Percy always referred to Philippians 4:19 in this context: "But my God shall supply all your need," preferring a different translation he found in his Greek testament: "My God will make up the deficiency of all your need."[40]

One final aspect of Percy's appeals for funds should be noted: they could not have succeeded if he had not been able to convince his listeners that the broadcasts were "His work, not ours."[41] Here the evangelist meant to convey the idea that the radio and television ministry was the Lord's business and that he was being "used of the Lord" as an instrument to further his purposes. To achieve this, Percy had to project to his audiences a feeling of not exalting self, of subordinating self to God's command. As I have already indicated, I believe my father was genuine in this respect, and this attitude had as much to do with his success in raising funds as his entrepreneurship or his marketing skills. We catch a glimpse of this quality in statements like this: "You know I'm thrilled at the opportunity you folks allow me to have, under God, in standing in front of the microphone telling out the wonderful story of love. Angels would love to do it. But no—God allows us the honor—and what an honor it is."[42]

Whether or not Percy was allowed to ask for money on the air, he always asked for letters: "We depend on your letters." "Let us know you're listening." "Your letters are the life-blood of this work." This was a way of saying: "Send in your contributions." But in addition to bringing in gifts, the letters also provided the only means whereby the evangelist could be in physical contact with his audience. They told him who was listening, on what station, and most importantly, how the broadcast or telecast had changed their lives.

Percy often said that he read all of the letters that were sent in to the YPCA. Indeed he (and my mother) did attempt to read as many of the letters as they had time for, and Percy wrote personal replies to many of them. His responses were usually brief and to the point. He willingly answered questions about how to live the Christian life or enter Christian service and would occasionally pronounce on matters of doctrine, but he tended to steer clear of controversial topics and people's personal problems.

## SHORTWAVE RADIO

It was during the war years, in 1943, that Percy put the Sunday broadcast on eleven shortwave radio stations, which, he stated, were capable of "taking our program completely around the world."[43] (The letterhead he used throughout the 1940s had the logo: "The Young People's Church of the Air —Around the World" surrounding a globe.) He thought of the shortwave as ministering mainly to servicemen and women abroad, as many of the letters he quoted in his newsletters indicate:

> From the Southern Pacific war zone: "Your program has been a constant bless-ing to me Sundays, as I have heard it regularly since being out here on these South Pacific islands."[44]

> From the war zone: "Dear Mr. Crawford: The other day Bob Hope came to our base. Of course he did do a lot to cheer the fellows up but my heart wasn't sat-isfied. I cried out for something spiritual. How we do need your program. When I'm down in the dumps along comes your message and how the Lord does bless my soul."[45]

The shortwave stations were not paying their way. Although the cost was about $10,000 a year, "I doubt if we receive $100 a year direct. I believe you feel with me that we should make this contribution to our service men and those in foreign fields."[46]

But although Percy was now delivering his gospel message to every cor-ner of the world, he did not push this global aspect of his ministry. He kept the shortwave stations going for a couple of years after the war, but then decided to concentrate his efforts and his resources on his "home mission-ary work."

## THE NATIONAL ASSOCIATION OF EVANGELICALS

We have seen how Percy struggled with the radio networks' policies be-ginning in the early 1940s and chafed at Mutual's take-it-or-leave-it re-strictions that unduly limited his access to a national audience, but his attitude toward these restrictive policies was one of reluctant compliance. He played according to the rules that were set by the industry and ultimately by Congress. Perhaps because he was foreign born, he tended to be grate-ful for the opportunities the American free-market system afforded him. In any case, there was very little he could do as an individual to counter the networks' power and dominance over the industry.

He already had reason to believe that the Federal Communication Com-mission (FCC) was not sympathetic to his cause. He reported that the com-mission's decision to deny his application for a license in 1937 was because "we refused to take programs of sects which we felt would be detrimental to the Gospel."[47] It was not that the FCC was prejudiced against religious groups. Although it had opened radio up to commercial interests and national advertisers, it had always tried to reserve a place for noncommercial groups (educational, religious, etc.), both in the awarding of licenses and by requiring that networks and stations offer a balance of public service and commercial programming. But the commission, in awarding and renewing licenses, was wary of stations that promoted the ideas of a single denomination or group and of programs that were controversial or that promoted only private and selfish interests.[48] Percy's problems with the FCC stemmed from the *Young People's Church of the Air* being just a very small minority group within the broad category of religious noncommercial radio that the commission was attempting to accommodate.

But if Percy could not do much as an individual to safeguard the right of evangelicals to buy radio time, we may well wonder why he did not join forces with other evangelicals in trying to resist the networks' exclusionary policies. In 1942 J. Elwin Wright (of the New England Fellowship), Harold Ockenga (pastor of Park Street Church in Boston), and William Ward Ayer (pastor of Calvary Baptist Church in New York) spearheaded a movement to build a united front for evangelicals that became the National Association of Evangelicals (NAE). Wright traveled around the country talking to evangelical leaders, gathering support for the organization; 147 of them joined in signing a letter calling for unity and announcing an organizational meeting of leaders to be held in St. Louis on April 7–9, 1942. Percy was one of the signers, but did not attend the St. Louis meeting at which the NAE was born.[49] The letter formulated guiding principles for the new fellowship and mentioned the "national use of radio" as one of the "fields of cooperative endeavor . . . needed at the present time." Indeed, the threat to gospel broadcasting was the issue that first galvanized the movement.[50]

Two years later (September 1944), the National Religious Broadcasters (NRB) was formed, originally as the "official radio arm of the NAE," with the purpose of being an advocate for evangelical broadcasters. One of the stated objectives of the association was "to secure for its members, and for other persons and organizations engaged in broadcasting such [religious] programs, adequate, fair and regular access to the radio listening public."[51]

Ayer was elected the first president, and Clinton Churchill (pastor of Churchill Tabernacle in Buffalo) was elected vice president. One of Ayer's first tasks was to write a code of ethics for radio evangelism. In a 1943 article in the NAE newsletter, Ayer acknowledged that conservative religious broadcasters had misused their pleas for money and had made their programs a "deplorable racket" in this respect. He continued: "I believe most radio stations, including chains, are amicable to high-type gospel broadcasts; but crackpots, racketeers, fly-by-nights, ranters, and sensationalists bring reproach upon all our programs."[52] His code of ethics called for sponsorship of all programs by a nonprofit organization, full financial accountability, with "annual audits prepared by a qualified independent accounting firm" and prompt acknowledgment of all donations with receipts.[53]

There is no doubt that Percy was well aware of these developments. First, he announced that he was adhering to the NAE's concerns about money even before the NRB's code of ethics was published: "Our Y.P.C.A. books are in the process of being audited by a New York concern and from henceforth will be audited regularly every month."[54] He was also sending receipts for all donations. Further, he had been associated with Ayer, making regular visits to Calvary Baptist Church with his team, while Ayer came to Pinebrook as a speaker in the late 1930s and early 1940s. Also, Churchill was a speaker at Pinebrook in 1945, having just published an article in *United Evangelical Action* in which he called on "every Christian" to support the NAE and the NRB, in their effort to safeguard "the rights and privileges of those engaged in accredited religious broadcasting."[55] But notwithstanding these influences, Percy kept his distance from both organizations, even though he had much at stake in the causes for which they were fighting. Why was this?

The short answer to this question, I believe, is that he was too busy with his own soul-saving work. He did not wish to take time away from his evangelistic endeavors to attend conferences and organizational meetings that, he believed, were not likely to accomplish anything anyway. Further, he was temperamentally ill disposed toward all institutions and bureaucracies, particularly religious organizations that (as he learned from the Presbyterians) tended to put constraints on his way of preaching the gospel. Percy was too much the independent to think of joining in a cooperative effort to meet a common threat, if he thought it might in any way restrict his liberty. Add to this my father being deeply apolitical and uninterested in trying to exert political pressure, and we can understand why he had no inclination to devote time and energy to united action.

In hindsight, we can see that Percy probably underestimated the importance of there being an organized body representing the interests of evangelical churches and independent groups like the YPCA. It might even be thought that he was a free rider, benefiting from the hard negotiating efforts of the NAE and NRB, while refusing to give them his active support. But a close look at the combined efforts of these organizations during this period (1940s and 1950s) reveals that it is doubtful that they made any significant difference to him and his radio and television work. The NRB had succeeded in getting a share of sustaining time for evangelicals on the networks, but Percy had no interest in working with the networks on this basis because he knew there would be strings attached. Nor was he afraid that evangelical broadcasting might be "completely eliminated," as one influential president of the NRB, James DeForest Murch, stated.

Percy was never worried about being kicked off the Mutual network—he had a quality program that was not controversial, he complied with the network's rules, and he paid his bills on time. And even if he were to be thrown off, he could always go to independent stations as Fuller had done. Moreover, as we will see, he was far ahead of the NRB in his efforts to acquire FM stations and a UHF television station.[56]

Finally, in 1951, during his third year of television broadcasting, Percy did speak out publicly on this issue of the rights of religious broadcasters. The occasion for his public statement was an invitation extended to him to speak at a television conference sponsored by the Southern Baptist Convention, November 27, in Washington, D.C. The problem he saw was that the same pattern of limiting access to a national audience that had occurred in radio was now reoccurring in television. NBC and CBS were continuing their policy of giving sustaining time programming to the three major faiths and not selling television time to religious broadcasters, and the third network, American Broadcasting Company (ABC), which began selling time to religious broadcasters in 1949, was under pressure to conform to the standards set by the two leaders. Percy could foresee that he would be forced to accept whatever times ABC made available to him, since he had no other real options. The short address my father gave in response to this situation is worth citing at length since it is the only political statement he ever made in the public square. He opens his remarks with a statement of his thesis that "No station nor network, serving the public interest, has the right to refuse any minority religious group the privilege of buying time on their station or network." This is followed by a brief description of the current situation and how it developed:

When radio first began, most of the networks were anxious for customers and were quite willing to sell time to religious groups. As time became scarce and there were more companies wanting to advertise their product, their policy changed. Suddenly the networks took on a very dignified air, and said, "We are going to set up a policy whereby we give religious time and not sell it." Now, this sounds very philanthropic, but it is certainly not democratic. They throw a crumb of a half hour or an hour a week to three selected groups,—the Roman Catholics, the Jews, and the National Council of Churches. The television networks are starting to operate in the same vicious circle. The networks are now putting on such programs as, "Frontiers of Faith" by National Broadcasting Company; "Lamp Unto My Feet" by the Columbia Broadcasting System, and "Morning Chapel" by DuMont Television Network.

They hire actors, who themselves are not religious, to put on these shows, and request clergymen to come in at the tail end and put their endorsement on the program and give the benediction.

He then offers his critique of the networks' and stations' actions:

The problem before us is this: Since when did the Federal Communications Commission license these networks and stations to go into religion and realms of theology? Where do they get the authority to dictate to one hundred and sixty million people what religion they are to receive? *They* select the speakers; *they* determine the theology.

Unless the networks and stations actually serve the public interest, and at least allow religious minority groups the right to purchase time along with cigarette and beer companies, their licenses should be revoked by the Commission. It is definitely discrimination.

But how about the other groups? The Southern Baptist Convention, the National Association of Evangelicals, the American Council of Churches, the General Association of Regular Baptists, and the independent groups, such as The Young People's Church of the Air, and others, representing millions of Americans?

These three groups, the Roman Catholics, the Jews, and the National Council of Churches, do not approve of Evangelism as presented on a program such as Youth on the March [Percy's program], and as a result, the evangelical message is ruled out. They are not only refused free time, but they are refused the right to buy time.

The Federal Communications Commission should investigate this matter. The policy of giving free time to a few selected groups is no substitute for the open market and the right of religious minority groups to purchase choice time and present a dignified program. Anything short of this is discrimination and is definitely not serving the public interest.

If the Federal Communications Commission cannot do something about this matter, then it's up to these minority groups to organize and petition Congress.

The arguments Percy gives are morally and rationally compelling insofar as they are based on democratic principles embodied in the free enterprise system and on the licensing requirement that the radio airwaves should serve the public interest. The tone of the address is one of moral indignation. The arguments were nothing new, except that the point is driven home forcefully that in allowing the networks to select three religious groups and their representatives to be on the air, the FCC is in effect endorsing some particular religious views and "theologies" and thus violating the principle of the separation of church and state. Percy's arguments and his mild threat that the minority groups he mentions should petition Congress probably had little effect on the network representatives who attended the conference. But he was entering the debate between the networks and the National Association of Evangelicals that had been going on for nine years. Ayer, Ockenga, and Churchill might have thought that Percy was something of a Johnny-come-lately in this struggle. But I think Percy was well aware that he had stayed out of the fray and did not imagine that his statement would have any real effect in the ongoing political struggle. Rather I believe what he wanted to accomplish in giving this address, beyond making public his own view, was simply to weigh in on the issue as one of the leading voices in Christian broadcasting and give his endorsement to the cause and the efforts of his evangelical brethren. It was better late than never.

## PINEBROOK PRAISES

As the Sunday broadcast became more oriented toward a nationwide audience, Percy may have felt a need to shore up his core constituency in the Northeast. In the fall of 1943, he began a daily morning devotional program, *Pinebrook Praises,* similar to the one that George Palmer had been running for a dozen years. The program was on weekdays from 8:00 to 8:30 a.m. and started locally in Philadelphia on WIBG. For the most part, it was limited in coverage to the mid-Atlantic region, providing Percy with a vehicle for keeping in touch with his home audience and promoting his various endeavors and YPCA events. Shortly after it began, Percy moved the program from the WIBG studio to our home in Mt. Airy (on the outskirts of Philadelphia), and it continued to originate live from our living room, both in Philadelphia and after we moved to New York, for the next seventeen years until my father's death.

The daily program was very different from the Sunday broadcast in its mood and its format. It had a more intimate, devotional tone; the pace was slower, and Percy's intonations softer, more soothing. The format consisted of musical selections—by Ruth playing the organ and chimes and singing alone or with a quartet member—a daily poem, a prayer, a "verse for the day," and a short devotional message. Its purpose was to give the listener a brief time of spiritual refreshment and uplift at the start of each day. My father loved doing it; in fact, he seemed to use the program as his own personal devotional time each morning before plunging into his hectic schedule.

The program also had a definite family feeling, as Percy used it to initiate each of his children into the work. We four boys—Don, Dick, Dan, and

Dean—(and later our sister, Donna Lee) were interviewed briefly each day, then recited a Bible verse and sang before heading off to school. (I started singing solos on the morning broadcast at the age of three.) Every year, Percy would broadcast live our Christmas morning with all the bedlam of kids opening presents, followed by some Christmas music and a short message. For us kids, the morning broadcast was a daily ritual that we did without much fuss or complaining; it was just one way in which we were expected to contribute to our parents' great work.

# 12

# The King's College: Wheaton of the East

The King's College will be, as far as it is in our power to make it so, a college with the highest standards of any college in the country. The Lord's hand is in this project, and we're going forward with Him. Although it is a large undertaking we have the assurance of His word that nothing is too great for Him.[1]

IN A LETTER SENT OUT TO "FRIENDS OF THE YOUNG PEOPLE'S CHURCH OF the Air" in October 1936, Percy indicates when he began to think about starting a Christian college: "For some four years now we have been sensing the need and praying about starting a Fundamental Christian College here in the East." Four years earlier, in the fall of 1932, having just completed his studies at Westminster and Penn, Percy had started what he called "The Young People's Bible School," which met one evening a week at the Barnes Mission in Philadelphia. By the second year, two hundred young people had enrolled in the course. Later, he recalled: "This Bible school work was so successful and so blessed of the Lord, and so many young people were coming for this training, that God laid it on my heart to start a regular school."[2]

In a sermon preached on the radio a few months after sending out the letter to friends, "Why Another College?,"[3] Percy laid out his reasons for wanting to establish such a college. He noted that there was a need for an "interdenominational" accredited liberal arts college in the East, "similar to that of Wheaton, Illinois," for the young people seeking such an education. He added that "if we don't provide the proper place for them to attend, nine-tenths of them will go to some school where they will come out agnostics and skeptics."

The main problem with the secular institutions, he noted, was that they "teach a philosophy which is contrary to the Bible." He mentions his own experience at UCLA: "Having gone to a State University myself, I know how difficult it is to believe the Bible and try at the same time to get an education. If one does not swing in with the trend of skepticism and deny the

Bible, accept the theory of evolution, then he is a marked man."[4] He thought that those institutions in which the secular philosophy held sway did all they could to suppress opposing beliefs based on the Bible and undermine their students' faith: "You can find very few books that refute Evolution or other false teachings in any of the supposedly 'open-minded' institutions. You'll find very little if anything in support of the Bible view." The Bible view he referred to gave a very different account of human origins—one that is based on God's creation of humans, the first man's sin against God, God's plan of salvation, and the experience of the new birth. Percy envisioned an academic program like Wheaton's in which all the faculty would accept the biblical view and teach their various disciplines from within it.

Accordingly, the new college would have three essential goals: (1) to provide a thorough training in the liberal arts; (2) to provide a basic grounding in the evangelical, biblical faith; and (3) to so ground the student in this evangelical faith that he or she goes forth with a passion to serve the Lord.[5] The last goal was always paramount in Percy's mind. For him, a liberal arts education had no value unless it was subordinated to the larger purpose of evangelism for the cause of Christ. In his sermon, he notes that Reuben Torrey once said: "I'd rather have a person ignorant as can be and burning up for souls, than the best educated person in the world."

This overarching practical goal was also evident in the way Percy talked to students at the college and counseled them about how they should be planning for their futures, as this excerpt from one of his chapel talks illustrates:

What's the good to living to 70 or 80? Of course right now way up there [in age] just seems an eternity away. It sneaks up on you, and that time comes right along, moves right along, moves right in, whether you like it or not.

You can easily be cut down. I mean, life is short. We should look at life in the light of the ultimate of that which is sure to come which is death. In other words when you are through, when I am through [with] my life, and we look back, what has been the purpose, the motivating power in our lives, that caused us to spend our lives as we did? I think that's the proper perspective; looking ahead and then looking back.

. . . There's nothing wrong with being a teacher or an engineer or a housewife. But my objective is to use these means to ultimately bring men and women to a knowledge of the Son of God. Use every avenue possible, every dollar you can lay your hands on. To me that's life.

. . . And if you're going to be a soldier of the cross of Christ, if you're going to be called and answer His call, you've got to have the equipment down pat, and know the Word of God. . . . Not an armchair critic of it. Not saying I believe that doctrine and this doctrine; this one I'm not quite sure of. But letting these things grip your heart and grip your soul.

. . . We're not sold out. We're not yielded. We haven't got the vision. "Where there's no vision the people perish." And they're perishing by the carload! My prayer is that The King's College will prepare you mentally in all of these various subjects and inoculate you and indoctrinate you with the horrible fact of an everlasting Hell, and that you may make decisions in life in the light of the ultimate of that which is sure to come so that when you're through you can look back and say, "Lord, I loved you, and I failed you so miserably. But I threw down my life. I've thrown it away for you." What an honor! What a privilege! If The King's College fails to do that, and to turn out men and women with that objective, we have failed. We're simply another educational institution.[6]

## The Belmar Campus

Percy's first idea for the college was to locate it in a building in New York or Philadelphia.[7] (Perhaps he had in mind the way Machen had started up Westminster Seminary in a single building in central Philadelphia.) However, by 1935, so many young people and Pinebrookers expressed interest in such a college that he began to look for a property that would be suitable for a larger campus. Within a year he had located the ninety-acre Marconi estate on Shark River Bay in Belmar, New Jersey. The link with Marconi, the inventor of the wireless, made the property seem all the more appropriate for Percy's work. The main building, though in need of repair, was adequate for all the college's main functions, including dormitory rooms for men and women. Another building on the grounds could be converted into science labs.

In the summer of 1936, Percy negotiated a purchase price of $60,000 for the property and buildings. (In his advertisements, he noted that the construction of the main building alone had cost $256,000.) Then in July 1937 he incorporated the Young People's Association for the Propagation of the Gospel and formed a board of trustees, which authorized the purchase of the property and the soliciting of gifts and loans to pay for it. Since there was "no millionaire" to back the endeavor, it was another faith venture, entirely dependent on YPCA supporters for donations. The board initiated a campaign to raise $100,000 by offering bonds for purchase in denominations of $50 to $1,000. Sixty thousand dollars was to pay off the mortgage, and the rest would be used to buy equipment and erect additional buildings—dormitories and gymnasium.

A sign right above "Jesus Saves" in the tabernacle at Pinebrook in the summer of 1937 read: "WON'T YOU HELP US START A FUNDAMENTAL CHRISTIAN COLLEGE HERE IN THE EAST BY 1938?" And in his magazine, he urged: "We know of no finer way for you to invest your money than in this new venture of faith which will not only bring you dividends here while on the earth, but also in eternity."[8] By the time the college opened in 1938, $60,000 had been raised and the board issued "mortgage liquidation bonds" in that amount at 4 percent interest.

Having acquired the property and worked out a way of financing it, Percy now had to find someone to run it. He knew that he could devote only a limited amount of his own time to the college, considering his other enterprises—the radio broadcast, nightly meetings and rallies, and Pinebrook in the summer—and although there was never any question about who would be the president and superintendent of the college, he needed a person to administer the day-to-day operation of the school. For this formidable job, he turned to his brother-in-law, Fenton Duvall, who had been singing in the YPCA quartet from its inception in 1931. During that time Fenton had been able, on his meager quartet salary of $15 a week, to earn his bachelor's degree at Temple University and, like Percy before him, to complete a master's degree at Penn in history. Fenton turned down the offer to be a teaching assistant at Penn and begin a doctoral program in order to take up Percy's challenge of starting a college from scratch. And so, twenty-five-year-old Fenton left the quartet and, with his wife, Hannah, took up residence in a small rented house in Belmar. Fenton's official title was registrar and instructor in history, but throughout the seven years he was at King's he did just about everything administratively that needed to be done to keep a small college running, in addition to teaching a full load of courses in history and the social sciences. Also, he was secretary/treasurer of the board of trustees. His wife Hannah handled the secretarial duties of the college.

On September 19, 1938, The King's College opened its doors with sixty-seven registered students, many of them Pinebrookers, and a skeletal faculty that in the first year hovered around ten in number. Several students in that first class expressed their feeling that the first night at the college was a "never-to-be-forgotten experience." Marion O'Donnell wrote that "Rev. Crawford insisted on a 'get together' in the chapel. Jokes were told, sketches enacted, and hymns sung." Later, they gathered around the fireplace in the main lobby for an informal service. Each student introduced himself or herself to the rest and gave a personal testimony telling why he or she had come to King's, and then Percy gave a brief message, at the close of which "six students made sure of their salvation."[9] Percy was initiating—what would become a tradition at King's—the practice of starting off the first night of Freshman Week with a campfire and a salvation service. His idea was that a student had to know Christ in order to have any chance of achieving the goals that he had set for the college.

The dedication service for the college was held on October 9 with Dr. Oliver Buswell, president of Wheaton College and Pinebrook speaker, giving the address. In it, he emphasized the great need in America for Christian schools. On the same day, the student body participated in the Sunday afternoon radio broadcast with song and testimony—demonstrating the close, synergistic relationship that Percy intended to create between the college and the *Young People's Church of the Air.*

## THE FACULTY

The faculty that Percy and Fenton Duvall assembled in the early years was a mixed lot, with varied backgrounds at both religious and secular institutions. Of the ten or so faculty in the first year, five had master's degrees, and three had doctorates. In the second year, three new members with MAs were added, and one PhD—Louis Allen Higley, whom Percy had rescued over the summer after President Buswell had forced him out of Wheaton. The sixty-eight-year-old Higley was a key addition to the faculty because of the good credentials he brought with him and the solid reputation in the sciences he had built at Wheaton. Percy made him dean of the college, a position he held for eight years.

Higley had been the first PhD hired at Wheaton and had helped to give its science program national recognition by establishing a field laboratory for geological research in the Black Hills, South Dakota. He was also a founder and president of the *Religion and Science Association* (1935–37), one of the first organizations aimed at reconciling the Genesis account of creation and the natural sciences. His magnum opus, *Science and Truth,* published in 1940 just after coming to King's, was the culmination of forty years of thought on this topic.[10] At King's, he taught core courses in the sciences and also two special-interest courses: "Design in the Natural World" and "Evaluation of Scientific Theories." Students described him as a "mild mannered sage" who "finds his chief delight in profound and ponderous thought."[11]

Higley's junior colleague in the sciences (and his former student at Wheaton), Cyril Luckman, came to King's in the same year (1939). Luckman came with a master's degree in biology from the University of Illinois and had also done research at Woods Hole, Massachusetts. His career at King's is telling of the way in which the college administration functioned in its first phase. Luckman quickly earned praise from faculty and students alike for his "smooth" handling of the biology program.[12] He continued at the college until 1947 (with three years out for military service), but was never able to rise above the rank of instructor. In the fall of 1946, he approached the president and (according to the president) "insisted" that the college make good on a promise, made to him by then Registrar James Barkley, that he be appointed dean of men and his salary increased to $2,600. The minutes of the September 2 board meeting indicate the board's unsympathetic response to the situation: it "appreciated Luckman's service, and his capabilities," but "does not approve of the attitude as shown by Luckman." However, the president moved that the two requests be granted, conditional upon his signing the statement (that all faculty signed) "that he will be loyal to the Lord, the College, the Board, including Dr. Crawford, and the student body" and upon the president having a "personal meeting with Luckman" so that the board could reach a better understanding with him and "be sure of his 100% cooperation."[13]

As is so often the case, the students had a very different perception of their professor's attitude: the 1947 graduating class dedicated the yearbook to their teacher and class adviser with these words: "We have found in him an all-round Christian friend: one who joined in our social life, one whom we respect and to whom we look for spiritual guidance."

Toward the end of the school year, however, Luckman turned in his resignation, having accepted a position from Wheaton "under more favorable terms." The board authorized Percy to meet with Luckman "to urge him to reconsider his decision," but unfortunately he could not be persuaded.[14] One wonders where Dean Higley was during these negotiations and why he and the board did not make a greater effort to keep this promising individual on the science faculty for the long term.

Charles Hans Evans was another outstanding teacher who came in the first year. Evans graduated from Juniata College and Princeton Seminary and then studied for two years at Tübingen University in Germany, earning his PhD. His dissertation dealt with the idea of sin in the Qur'an. Evans was mainly responsible for building the philosophy program and the major, introducing courses in logic, a sequence in the history of philosophy, philosophy of religion, theism, and a course he called "Moulders of the Modern Mind." He won the admiration of students for his enthusiastic teaching, his avid chess playing, and his "broad smile."[15] Percy thought highly of him, perhaps because he had returned from studying with the German theologians with his faith intact. Evans left after seven years for full-time pastoring at Coatesville Presbyterian Church, but never severed his ties with King's. He returned in 1953–54 as assistant professor of Bible and theology and then served on the board of trustees for several years. When Percy died in 1960, King's called on him again to be acting president until a successor could be named.

Percy was another notable on the faculty from day one. Students liked him as president and as professor, probably more because of who he was and his charismatic personality than for his competence as a teacher. He was not an intellectual or a scholar, and he knew it, but he felt that it was appropriate for him to be in the classroom, not only because he had earned degrees from Wheaton, Westminster, and Penn, but also so that he could model for the students the "sane, evangelistic zeal" that for him was the more important part of their education.

For the first couple of years, Percy taught the two courses in Bible, Old Testament history and New Testament history, in which he was "assisted by outstanding Bible teachers" (mostly the same Bible teachers the students had heard at Pinebrook). In 1941, Ken Kantzer, (who would become a key figure in the "new evangelicalism" of the 1950s), came on board in education and Bible and taught at King's for two years while finishing his seminary degree at nearby Faith Theological Seminary. The 1942 bulletin lists him as responsible for eleven courses, primarily in education, but also in Bible, Latin, history, and political science. He also taught archeology.[16] By 1942, a full major in Bible was in place with a wide range of thirteen courses.

In 1940 Percy began teaching the two classes for which he was justly famous: "Gospel of John" and "Personal Evangelism." He taught these two one-hour courses, one in each semester, for the rest of his life, and every student who came to King's was required to take them. They were in a sense Percy's answer to the sort of one-credit introductory psychology course that Dr. Moore had taught all the incoming freshmen at UCLA. He loved teaching these classes, and he took them seriously, mainly because of the opportunity it gave him to train up hundreds of young men and women for a life of Christian service and witnessing.

I took the last cycle of these courses in 1959–60 as a freshman at King's. As I remember the Gospel of John course, Percy's interpretation of John outlined the central themes of the gospel and the dominant metaphor used for Christ in each chapter. He stressed memorization and drew from the text the theological motifs that were in line with fundamentalist doctrines. He did very little to reconstruct the historical context of the gospel or the gospel author; nor was there any attempt to compare and contrast the Johannine gospel with the other Synoptic Gospels or with the Pauline writings. The full meaning of each verse, and each chapter, and the entire book was self-contained and ahistorical and could be easily grasped by the untrained mind.

Personal Evangelism was a practically oriented course. Percy used his own book, *The Art of Fishing for Men,* as a text and drew from this manual the methods and techniques and Scripture verses that had proved to be so effective for him in soul winning. One of the requirements of the class was to give out a Gospel of John every week, which meant that local towns-people, tradesmen, delivery men, postal carriers, and so on were bombarded with them. In my years at the Briarcliff Manor campus, it was the toll collectors at the nearby Tappan Zee bridge who were continually peppered with gospels.

Fenton Duvall was a mainstay on the faculty for the first seven years and must have been a master at multitasking. In addition to his administrative duties as registrar and de facto dean, and his teaching responsibilities in history and economics, he also took part in many of the college's outreach activities—singing in a mixed quartet and traveling with the gospel team; and also directing the men's chorus (The King's Singers) on Percy's Sunday radio broadcast.

At the end of the 1944–45 school year, Duvall had a conversation with Percy that, quite unexpectedly, led to his sudden departure. He had been doing some fund-raising for the college and reported to Percy that some people had said they would be more willing to support King's if it was not so closely identified with Percy himself, and he suggested that Percy might therefore want to give over more control to the board of trustees. Percy took offense and charged Duvall with being disloyal. Duvall then offered his resignation, thinking that Percy would never accept it. But he was sadly mistaken, for he soon found that he had been replaced as registrar by James Barkley, a history professor who had just joined the faculty that year. And so Fenton, who had worked for Percy faithfully for fourteen years, and his wife found themselves looking for work.[17]

It is hard to see this action of Percy's as anything but petty and irresponsible. Why would he so easily dismiss someone who was making such a vital contribution to the college in its struggle to become a viable institution? Percy might have thought that in order to do the Lord's work successfully he needed to have people around him who agreed with him and followed his lead; that is what he meant by being "loyal" to him and to the college. But as I see it, this action was just another illustration of the flaw in my father's character that we have already witnessed. What is evident here is, first, an inability to take criticism—even mild and constructive criticism—and profit from it; second, an inability to work with people and try to understand and resolve their problem or difficulty; and, third, a short-sightedness, in that he solved an immediate problem by getting rid of a person, but in the process compromised his own long-range objectives. It was a character fault that had serious repercussions for King's (as we will see) and hampered Percy's entire ministry.

## THE DELAWARE CAMPUS

The first few years of the college's existence were hectic but happy ones, but Percy and the board soon began to face up to their impending inability to meet New Jersey's requirement of a half-million-dollar endowment for four-year institutions. A decision was made to apply to the State Board of Education to be accredited as a two-year junior college, but this door, too, seemed to be closed. The college was working with Robert Morrison of the Department of Public Instruction as its liaison with the State Board, but in a letter to Percy, dated September 13, 1939, Dr. Morrison advised against applying for junior college accreditation. "I am quite sure that the Board would not accredit your junior college," he wrote. The primary reasons were financial: the operating income for the coming year appeared to be insufficient to meet "salaries payable and accounts payable to trade creditors." Further, the college was required to have at least $5,000 per year "stable income from sources other than tuition." The plan that Percy and his board devised to meet the challenge of raising $5,000 annually was to work up a "subscription list" and ask each of the five board members to recruit ten churches that would pledge $10 a month for five years.[18] That there were no businessmen who could be called upon for this relatively small amount of money indicates the extent to which the college was dependent from the outset on its president and his radio constituency for financial support.

The board decided to revert to the original plan for a four-year college course, and it soon became apparent that King's would have to relocate if it wanted to confer degrees on its first graduating class. Other religious leaders might have abandoned ship when faced with the daunting task of starting up again after only three years—especially at a time when the country was on the brink of war, but not Percy. He was getting close to fulfilling his vision of sending college-trained men and women into Christian service and never for a moment thought of giving it up. Board members began to make inquiries and found that the state of Delaware offered the most hopeful prospect, since it did not require an endowment and had less stringent degree-granting requirements. In fact the college would be able to confer degrees in its first year there, on the first graduating class of 1942.

So Percy and the board started looking for a suitable site in Delaware and once again located a fabulous property—the historic Reybold estate, built in 1846, and located on the Delaware River between Delaware City and New Castle, with the stately brick mansion known as "Lexington" as its centerpiece. This forty-room "architectural treasure" stood on sixty-five acres of beautifully landscaped grounds with formal gardens, a nine-hole golf course, and a working farm.[19]

When the students at Belmar learned that the college would be relocating in Delaware, they quickly embraced the idea. One sophomore student, Jane Atno, reported: "With great enthusiasm the entire student body traveled to New Castle on a school holiday to see the new location. We were simply dazzled by what we saw. Nothing could have been more different from the sand dunes and scrub pine of Belmar, than the lovely rolling lawns and the gracious pillars of Lexington."[20] The Belmar campus was sold to the U.S. government, and in the summer of 1941 the moving vans started hauling office furniture, kitchen equipment, and beds and dressers to the new site. Lexington became the main building, housing nearly all the students as well as providing space for the library, dining hall, and recreation hall. Two other more modest structures were remodeled into science labs, classrooms, office space, and a chapel.

The new facilities were ample for the 104 students who attended in the fall of 1941 (with 27 in the entering class). Although the returning students who made the transition to Delaware were enthusiastic and generally had a great love for the college, one member of the first class, Marjorie Absalom (Linton), told me that this was still "a very sad time" for them as they watched "quite a few" of their classmates transfer to Wheaton in order to obtain their degree from an accredited college. The situation was exacerbated by an eight-page promotional booklet touting the new campus, while announcing on the front cover in bold type: "THE KING'S COLLEGE IS NOW ACCREDITED." But when students called the State Board of Education, they were told that the college was not accredited.[21] In fact, it was not, and it would not receive accreditation from the state of Delaware until much later, in 1949. What could be the explanation for this misleading advertisement? It is possible that the State Board was lax in specifying the criteria for accreditation, since there were no other private four-year colleges in Delaware at the time. But the college had access to the same sources of information that the inquiring students did. A more likely explanation is to be found in my father's overenthusiasm for the new campus and his tendency in all his promotional materials to accent the positive and downplay the negative. Although Percy's willingness to hype his literature served him well in all his other endeavors, it was unfortunate in this instance where students' careers were potentially at risk.

Although this false advertising should never have occurred, it should perhaps be noted that Percy's enthusiasm and hopeful vision for King's inspired those who stayed the course with an uncommon loyalty and zeal toward the college that has persisted in those first students to the present day. "We believed in Percy," said Marjorie Linton, and we were persuaded by his "dreams."

More light is shed on my father's approach to publicity in an exchange of letters he had with his chief assistant, Leymon "Deak" Ketcham (in 1955), when the college was about to move for the second time, to New York state. Ketcham had been a member of the first graduating class of 1942. Percy was concerned that representatives of the college were presenting the move to the public in a way that "hurt the college." King's had been granted a provisional charter by the New York State Board of Regents and would have to undergo annual reviews over a five-year period before it could get a permanent charter. Percy impressed upon Ketcham the importance of emphasizing "what we do have and not what we do not have. For they will remember what we do not have and not what we do have." He complained that spokespersons for the college (including Ketcham) were "not coming out rejoicing in the new found 'gain' that we have accomplished in moving to New York." He recommended talking about this new gain in a way that made no reference to the provisional nature of the charter, and added: "This is not misrepresentation at all. I am not in favor of that whatsoever." Ketcham may have thought that a more accurate representation was called for, remembering the situation in Delaware. He replied to Percy: "I think that it is very imperative that we not overstate our position and make claim to any standing that does not really exist. . . . I think it is a mistake to lay claim to equal accreditation to large schools in New York State although we may eventually attain that status. I think we can sincerely and honestly give a good story by simply stating that we do have a charter of the New York Board of Regents." Although it may seem that the two men were not far apart on this matter, Percy, in his reply to Ketcham, was even more emphatic that we would be "better off" if we did not "minimize what we have."[22]

In spite of the confusion at Delaware, twenty-six of the original class of sixty-seven were still enrolled and on course for graduation in the spring. The graduation ceremonies, which took place over a three-day period, were a festive time in which the whole college could rejoice over what had been achieved. One member of the junior class wrote:

We prepared for graduation by having our first Campus Day, when the whole student body doffed their studious attitude, cast away their books, donned their oldest clothes, and armed with brush and pail, scrubbed the house [Lexington] and other buildings until they shone. We will long recall the gatherings on the lawn before the great white pillars of the main building. Dr. MacRae, President of Faith Theological Seminary, preached the Baccalaureate Sermon, and Dr. Edman, President of Wheaton College, gave the graduation address.[23]

It was important to Percy that Wheaton's president should be the one to bless the new college and its first graduates, since The King's College was originally conceived on the Wheaton model.

The war took its toll on the fledgling college over the next four years, as both students and faculty were drawn into the service. Total fall enrollments dropped in 1942 to sixty-seven students; in 1943 there were fifty-nine. Of the sixty-one students who were enrolled in the spring of 1944, only eleven were men. These were hard times for The King's College—with a budget almost entirely dependent on tuition income. In the 1942–43 school year, for example, the tuition fee was $75/semester, and room and board cost $125/semester. Even if all of the sixty-seven students who enrolled that year had lived on campus, finished the school year, and paid the full amount, the college would have taken in a total of $26,800. Percy never took any salary from King's, but there were fifteen full-time faculty and administrators to pay, plus operational expenses.

During these lean years, Percy allowed King's to operate on a shoestring, fully confident that if he had to raise funds to keep the college afloat through appeals for gifts or the sale of bonds, he could always do so. He tried not to drain off any more gifts from the YPCA than was necessary to keep the college running. It was better to invest his limited resources in putting the broadcast on additional shortwave radio stations or in the Victory Center in Atlantic City that he had opened for service men and women.

The Delaware campus flourished in the postwar years with an influx of students, including many returning servicemen, bringing a new vitality to the college. Enrollments shot up to 228 in 1946, 259 in 1950, and 284 by 1953, with some drop-offs in between. This new growth meant increased tuition income; but it also meant additional expenditures—for new dormitory space and capital improvements. Some major renovations were done in Lexington to improve the dining facilities. And a gymnasium was built in 1951 at a cost of $75,000. The college was forced to borrow and sell bonds and went deeper in debt. By 1954, total liabilities amounted to a quarter of a million dollars.

As a result, the college could hardly afford to be more selective in its admissions policies. Throughout the 1940s and early 1950s, King's was accepting just about every applicant who had a high school diploma. This meant that the college had its share of students who were not really prepared for college either academically or socially, and the number of disciplinary cases in some years was alarmingly high. (At the end of the 1951–52 school year, twenty-one students were dropped for disciplinary [including academic] deficiencies.)[24]

Nonetheless, the college always seemed to attract a good number of high-caliber students who were serious about learning.[25] Robert Davies, professor of English at King's, remarked that "the intellectual climate in any class having more than just a few students was always established by the best students in the section, and they were in most cases impressive college students."[26] In addition to good students, King's always had among its faculty a nucleus of bright, stimulating instructors who fostered this sort of intellectual climate—like Davies in English; Duvall in history; Kantzer in Bible and education; Hans Evans, Charles Mason, and Ken Kennard in philosophy; William Ryans in psychology; and Arthur Killian in Greek. This tradition of excellent teaching continued through my two years at King's at the Briarcliff, New York, campus (1959–61).

Student morale was generally good at King's, and the atmosphere approached that quality of congeniality, fellowship, and "sweetness" that Percy wanted so much to create when he first envisioned the college. Part of the explanation for this was the active social life and varied extracurricular life that prevailed at the college. Competitive sports were emphasized from the beginning, largely because Percy believed strongly that young people who opted for Christ were not sissies or social misfits, but red-blooded American men and women. King's fielded intercollegiate teams for men in soccer, basketball, baseball, and touch football and for women in basketball. One milestone in the athletic program was the beginning of a series of basketball games with Wheaton College. Another was when King's basketball star George Dempsey, a 1952 graduate, was signed by the Philadelphia Warriors of the National Basketball Association. (Percy took my older brothers, Don and Dick—both outstanding basketball players—to watch Dempsey play at the Arena in Philadelphia, thus craftily promoting their interest in attending King's.)

Socially, King's students proved (if it needed proof) that Christian young people who chose the "separated life" could still have lots of fun and group activities. The rules governing dating and romance were not overly restrictive, and from the beginning King's was a fertile ground for meeting one's partner in life and getting started with her or him in a life of Christian service. In Belmar and Delaware, the spring formal banquet, held in May, was by far the most important event of the year. Usually held at some hotel or restaurant off campus, it featured YPCA and King's musical talent as entertainment. The writer of the class history for the 1943 *Crown* conveys the feeling of exhilaration surrounding the event:

> Spring at The King's College means one thing—the Spring Banquet. Its influ-
> ence, subtle but pervasive, begins to be felt in February, and by the week of
> the affair itself, the excitement is scarcely bearable. Perhaps the anticipation is
> the best part of it; new dresses, new hairdo's, flowers. Not even the fact that, at
> the last minute, one finds that every girl in the school has a dress of the same
> color as one's own, can take away the magic of that night.[27]

The banquet, however, would not have been complete without a speaker.
The writer adds a postscript: "However, it was not all silk and moonlight
and flowers. In his message, Mr. Rowan Pearce stirred our hearts by his
ringing words telling of the matchless love of Christ for us."

One noteworthy event that took place on the Delaware campus in 1950
was the filming of the promotional film *Lord of All*. The college contracted
with independent film producers Dave McCulley and Hank Ushijima of
Cavalcade Productions to shoot the film on location at King's. For a few
weeks, the camera crew and lights set up in various locations caused quite
a stir on campus, as many students participated in the filming, and many
others looked on. The lead roles were played by hired actors—Noel Rey-
burn and Colleen Townsend (Evans), a Hollywood actress who had given
up a promising film career to go into Christian service.

The main character in the story is an ambitious, good-looking boy, Phil
Sutherland, who comes to King's in order to satisfy his parents, but intends
to stay only a year. Phil plays trumpet and is eagerly anticipating joining
the Jimmy Jackson Dance Orchestra in the coming summer. When Phil enters his room, he notices a plaque on the wall that says: "If Christ is not
Lord of all, He is not Lord at all." This is the lesson Phil will learn at King's.
Later, Phil is overheard practicing in the music building by two brothers
(played by King's students Chuck and Bill Ohman), who are looking for a
third player to join their King's College Trumpet Trio. Phil is reluctant until he meets their lovely sister and piano accompanist, Peg, who very
quickly persuades Phil to give it a try. Phil falls in love with Peg, but Peg
holds back because she realizes that Phil is not a committed Christian. "Is
playing in a jazz band really what God wants you to do?" she asks. She
points out that when he gives his testimony, "it won't be true, unless Christ
is really Lord of your life." She exhorts him: "Let God take over. Let go."
Phil is torn between his love for worldly fame and glory as a big band
soloist and his desire to heed Peg's call to surrender his life and his talent
to the Lord. Alone in his room, he becomes distraught, smashes the accusing plaque to pieces, and then when his roommate enters and sees what is
happening, the two kneel together and Phil yields his life to God. In the fi-

nal scene, Phil and Peg wave good-bye from the back of a convertible, as they drive off with Chuck and Bill on their summer gospel tour.

The film conveys very well the predominant idea, among most students and personnel at King's, of what King's was all about. The message to prospective students is that they should come to King's if they want to prepare for a life of Christian service. Virtually nothing in the film is about the educational goals of the college. I watched the film a couple of dozen times as a youth and never tired of it. It did not occur to me to ask why more emphasis was not placed on the classroom and the faculty and what courses of instruction were available. I did not question these things, because I identified strongly with the ideal of Christian commitment that I saw acted out on the screen. The film hit the right buttons for me. But then again, I may have accepted it because, at age nine, I was madly in love with Colleen Townsend; and I desperately hoped that she would wait for me.

Finally, a large part of the extracurricular life of King's students was taken up by religious activities. There was of course chapel every day with guest speakers and preachers. For their part, the students entered into many different types of Christian service and witness. Those with musical ability sang and played, and those who could preach preached—with the various gospel teams that traveled to churches in the region and (during school breaks) toured all over the East. There was always a strong emphasis on evangelism, fueled by my father's own example and his ministries that intersected in so many ways with King's. Paul Moyer was a budding evangelist in the first graduating class who went on to direct a Saturday night Youth for Christ program in Philadelphia called *Youthcast*. Neil Macauley, a cornetist whom Percy had recruited at Pinebrook by offering him a music scholarship, was another student evangelist who started a series of tent meetings on Saturday nights in Delaware City in 1942. King's students also participated in Percy's radio and television broadcasts and thus had an opportunity to sing and play before a national audience.

Percy could also look with satisfaction at what King's graduates were accomplishing. One survey taken in 1953, after twelve graduating classes, indicated that 50 percent of the more than three hundred graduates were engaged in active religious work as ministers, missionaries, teachers in religious schools, and so on.[28] Fred Hartman and his wife became the first foreign missionaries officially sponsored by the college. And in the late 1950s, Percy arranged to send two King's graduates, Dick Paul and Peter Pak, to Korea to start up The King's Korean Mission (discussed below). My father's vision of training young men and women to go out into the world and save lost souls was coming to fruition.

## THE PRESIDENT

Percy saw his task as president to be that of building the college into a first-rate institution where students would get a sound, Bible-based education. But a difficulty that developed in achieving this goal was that he was spread too thinly over his vast domain of enterprises, and consequently King's was not getting the attention it needed. His normal practice was to come to the college one day a week—to teach his class, conduct a chapel service, take care of urgent business, and generally stir people up. There was no house or apartment or even a room set aside for him at Belmar or Delaware, since he never stayed more than a single day.

Percy put a good part of his limited time and energy at the college into building up the physical plant. He was always thinking about expanding his holdings and acquiring any adjacent or nearby properties that became available. New facilities were constructed. Percy's great love for competitive sports meant that a gymnasium was usually at the top of his priority list. Faculty housing was an ongoing problem. A few administrators who could afford to bought homes or built them on college property; but most faculty (and their families) had to make do with apartment units the college built or purchased, which were often inadequate even as temporary residences. "Faculty row," constructed at the Delaware campus, consisted of ten motel-type units, each having just a single room.

Another major task he took on as president was fund-raising. He never liked being in debt in any of his endeavors, but at King's it was nearly impossible to avoid it. The college soon fell into a pattern of operating with a permanent deficit that ranged from $30,000 to $60,000 each year. Once, when Percy received a letter from the Alumni Association at Wheaton College asking for donations, he answered wryly:

> Thank you for your good letter. I do not know whether you realize the condition of The King's College. We are desperately in need of $60,000 to balance our budget.
>
> Wheaton College is far ahead of us—in the millions—financially. As much as I love Wheaton and appreciate the fine job that they are doing, we are a baby trying to get on our feet. If you have any extra money, I certainly would appreciate your sending it our way.[29]

To meet the financial challenge at King's, Percy adopted several strategies: one was to try to keep down expenditures in whatever way possible. The following excerpts from some letters sent (from Florida) to his executive assistant at the time, Deak Ketcham, are indicative of how he pushed his staff to cut costs:

See that schedule is set up for room and auditorium lights turned out—make teachers responsible. Also students bedrooms. . . . Hold down on everything! . . . Try to find out—Deac—how we can eliminate some help. What can we manage without? . . . Find out from [Harry] Low [the buildings and grounds superintendent] exactly how many men he employs. We'll have to cut down on some. . . . I told Jensen [the chef] not to hire another cook and save $275 a month. . . . Next year (for one year) I'm afraid we'll have to stop paying faculty tuition [$6,000] at Columbia. Then by June if we have it—we'll reimburse those who go.[30]

Percy also sent out frequent heartfelt letters to his large YPCA mailing list and the smaller college list of alumni and friends, soliciting funds for the college—either in the form of gifts or the purchase of bonds. The bonds produced substantial monies, but they were loans that had to be paid back with interest. The amount of gift income gradually increased over the years, but always remained relatively small. Over a fifteen-year period (1942–57), total annual giving ranged from $4,342 to $24,738.[31] In all of his twenty-two years as president, Percy was not able to land a big donor who could enable the college to become solvent. And it was not until the last few years of his presidency that the college finally began to make a serious effort to find new sources of income.

It did not take my father long to realize that the limited financial resources of the college were closely tied to its difficulties in getting accreditation. The point was put succinctly by Robert Davies, professor of English at King's from 1944 to 1950, who later participated in the accreditation process at several colleges including King's:

Accreditation is essentially an economic problem. A college can upgrade its facilities, expand course offerings, and attract better faculty and students only so fast as available funds will allow. If King's had received an infusion of $500,000 in funds in the early years, the college would have made the improvements needed for accreditation more quickly.[32]

King's made its first serious bid for full accreditation from the state of Delaware in 1948, but was turned down. However, a year later when the examiners returned, the college had made enough progress in addressing each of the cited problem areas that accreditation was granted.[33] This victory may have contributed to another growth spurt—over the next four years (1949–53), enrollments increased from 242 to 284.

The college's perennial quest for accreditation brought into relief the many challenges the college faced, most of which stemmed from insufficient funds. In another review of the college—this one by New York state officials (after the college moved to Briarcliff Manor in 1955), the representative sent by the Board of Regents pointed to seven areas in which "marked improvement" was deemed essential. These areas of concern were by then familiar ones:

1. Expansion of the board of trustees to include persons from the state of New York, and possibly one or two women.
2. Increase in faculty salaries: "As you know, the faculty salary scale is exceedingly low particularly with reference to the high economic area in which your faculty reside."
3. Expansion of the library holdings.
4. Raising standards of admission.
5. Stricter grading practices.
6. Better science facilities for advanced courses.
7. Increased financial support: "I cannot overemphasize the importance of the need for increased assistance from business and industry for the enhancement of your educational program. . . . As you know, it is virtually impossible for a higher institution to meet its expenses through income from tuition alone and at the same time offer a program of good quality."[34]

Although these various requirements laid down by the state examiners were onerous for the college, they were useful in goading my pragmatic father into action by giving him concrete objectives to strive for. Whenever he had a specific goal in mind, he usually found a way to achieve it.

The college applied for the much more coveted regional Middle States accreditation in 1951 and again in 1954 and failed in both attempts. It was scheduled to be visited again in the fall of 1960, but Percy requested a deferral until the following January, no doubt because of key changes in personnel (as will be seen). After his death in October of that year, the Middle States visit was put off again. Accreditation was an obstacle to the college's success that my father was never able to overcome. It was left to his successor, Robert Cook, to accomplish that goal as the college finally did achieve it in 1968, seven years after Cook took over the presidency.

*

In 1944 Percy and the trustees, anticipating the postwar growth in enrollments that was coming, finally realized that someone would have to be in the top office on a full-time basis. A promising candidate was on the scene: Vernon Grounds had just come to the college with a bachelor's degree from Rutgers and a seminary degree from Faith; and while at King's he was working on a doctorate at Drew University. He taught classes in Bible and philosophy and in two years' time distinguished himself both in the classroom and in the religious life of the college.[35] The trustees offered him the presidency, but with the proviso that Percy would continue to play a role in overseeing the direction of the college. Grounds declined the offer of what amounted to a shared presidency because he thought it would be unworkable. He told me (in a recent conversation) that he felt "he could not work with [my] dad" and that if there was a disagreement between them, Percy "would still be the dominant figure and he would not be able to countermand him." Percy had no intention of giving up control of the college, and so King's continued to limp along as it had been doing with its part-time leader.[36]

Two years later (1947), William Jelley III came to the college as business manager and a year later was appointed executive vice president, taking over most of the responsibilities of the president in Percy's absence. Calvin Waldron, who spent his entire career at King's as a teacher and administrator, said that Jelley was the "smartest" person (intellectually) he had encountered in his years at the college. Jelley wrote "The President's Annual Report" on the state of the college "on behalf of Dr. Crawford" and delivered it to the alumni at homecoming. These documents were models of good writing and good public relations—always optimistic and yet acknowledging the real challenges the college faced and pinpointing areas in which alumni could help.

Jelley was effective in the area of faculty development and pushed the faculty hard to work toward getting their graduate degrees. Some resented this since Jelley himself did not have an advanced degree. Others praised his academic expertise, gained largely from reading widely. One said that he "had rarely met anyone who is as well versed in so many fields as he."[37] However, when math professor John Ries, who had been on the faculty for thirteen years, resigned because of "a basic lack of confidence in the leadership of Mr. Jelley not only in academic matters, but also in spiritual and faculty relationships," the board decided (at Jelley's suggestion) to make a wider survey of the entire staff's sentiments in each of the areas mentioned by Ries. Interviews were conducted, and the outcome was that Jelley was let go in 1956, one year after the college moved to New York, while facing a host of new challenges. Jelley left just as Percy was coming on board full-time at the Briarcliff campus. My guess is that my father allowed Jelley to be purged from office by this somewhat coarse evaluation process either because he did not think he could work comfortably with this man or felt that his office as executive vice president had become redundant or both. Whatever the reason, another good administrator was let go at a time of great need.

The area of the college that was most neglected by Percy as president and that he was least prepared to deal with was that of setting educational goals and building a strong faculty to achieve them. Over the twenty-two years of his presidency, as we have seen, King's was able to attract its fair share of outstanding individual faculty members in various fields, who made vital contributions to the life of the college. But a serious problem that emerged for the college was that these dedicated teachers did not stay long enough to build strong departments and a solid program. In reviewing the evolution of the faculty at King's during my father's lifetime, one notices a lack of key individuals teaching key courses, who are there to stay and around whom departments or even a division of the college might coalesce. One looks in vain for individuals who made long-term contributions to the curriculum.[38] Because of this lack of stability and continuity, there were few, if any, departments or programs at King's that were consistently strong or productive. This was true even of the Bible program, which never produced any outstanding teachers or scholars. After Hans Evans left in 1945, finding suitable people to teach philosophy proved to be a real stumbling block for the college and for Percy (as we will see). The same was true in psychology, starting with the first full-time hire, Willard Harley, a graduate of Wheaton with a master's degree from Penn, who clashed with Percy over his absentee presidency and called for him to resign.[39] In both fields (philosophy and psychology), there were periods in which there were no instructors and the programs languished. The only program that maintained a strong reputation over the years was music, and that was because it managed to attract a succession of exceptional people, largely in voice and choral music.[40]

A pattern developed of hiring either senior professors who had higher degrees but lacked the motivation and commitment necessary to build a cohesive curriculum or junior people brought in at the instructor level, often with only a bachelor's degree and working on a master's, or with a master's degree working on the doctorate. These younger professors were usually dedicated teachers and up-and-coming scholars. But invariably they left the college before they had a chance to establish themselves at King's or in their professional fields.

This problem of retention of faculty can be seen in the way faculty members were distributed along the scale of faculty rank—from instructor to assistant professor to associate professor to full professor. What is remarkable is how thin the college was in the middle ranks where one usually finds the leaders and core strength of a department. By the fourth year of the college (1942), Crawford and Higley were full professors and all of the other fifteen faculty were instructors.[41] Five years later (1947), even with the expansion that occurred after the war, there were four professors (Crawford, Higley, Barkley in history, and Schofield in classics) and all the rest (fifteen) were instructors. It was not until 1948, as the college entered its second decade, that two professors were elevated to the rank of associate professor—Arlene Barnes in music in her eighth year, and Robert Davies in English in his sixth year. This lack of continuity and stability in the faculty at King's led to a curriculum that was constantly in flux and a lowering of the overall quality of the academic program.[42]

What explains this high volatility among The King's faculty? One factor undoubtedly was the "very low" faculty salaries[43]—even for a Christian college. As an example, Ken Kennard, a Wheaton graduate, taught philosophy at King's from 1951 to 1953 and made $2,500 both years. Two years later, he received a full-time position at Wheaton at $3,500.[44] The 1954 Middle States review committee noted that "full-time faculty members holding a master's or doctor's degree receive $2700 for a nine month school year"; while "faculty members with a bachelor's degree and some teaching experience receive $2600." By comparison, public school teachers in New Castle, Delaware, with a bachelor's degree earned from $2,800 to $4,400, with a master's degree from $3,000 to $4,600, and with a doctorate from $3,400 to $5,000.[45] As a consequence, faculty had to supplement their income with part-time jobs—usually ministerial work of some kind—and work during the summers, making it difficult for them to continue their graduate programs.

Another factor that contributed to the high rate of turnover was overloaded teaching schedules. A 1951 report noted that the average teaching load was seventeen hours per week (approximately five to six courses). It noted that "one man teaches twenty-seven hours [nine courses], another, twenty-one [seven courses]."[46] And in addition to normal teaching duties, faculty were often called on to take on extra courses or administrative duties or fill in for someone who left the college.

But while these adverse material conditions may have contributed to the problem of retention, I doubt if they were decisive in most cases, because most of these dedicated teachers (and their families) were willing to take on extra work and make large personal sacrifices as part of their commitment to serve the Lord.

The main problem, as I see it, had to do with the lack of clear-cut criteria for job continuation and promotion and a system of governance that put the final authority for the hiring and firing of all personnel almost exclusively in the hands of the president. Faculty members would be likely to stay at King's only if they had the sense of security that comes with knowing what was required of them for continuation and advancement, but these requirements were not clearly specified. There was of course the statement of doctrine and the statement of practice (of Christian living) that all faculty signed as a condition of employment.[47] A further condition, written into their contracts, was a pledge "in all my acts and words to be loyal to the College and its President, Dr. Percy B. Crawford."[48] But they were left in the dark as to what constituted acts and words of disloyalty to the president.

Further conditions were that faculty members should "produce in their field" and also carry out the purposes of the college, which, as stated (vaguely) in the catalogue, meant that they should "correlate" their field of knowledge with "the evangelical tenets of faith which have characterized historic Protestantism."

It added to the problem that the dean of the faculty lacked any real authority over matters of retention. Admittedly, in this era before the tenure system was established in higher education, presidents of colleges and universities had much freer rein over the hiring and firing of personnel. But at King's, Percy kept his hand too much in these matters and did not delegate primary responsibility for them to the dean (and the Faculty Membership Committee) as most presidents did. The fact is that contracts were renewed or not renewed at his pleasure. If he was dissatisfied with anyone's performance, beliefs, or attitude, he would simply tell the dean not to renew their contracts, and the faculty member had no recourse. This absolute power, which Percy insisted on retaining, created a climate of insecurity and uneasiness among faculty (and administrators), who never knew when they might cross the president, and it naturally caused many of them to go looking for a more secure situation.

Percy seemed oblivious to the effects of his autocratic style on faculty morale and on the long-term prosperity of the college. He ran King's the way he ran the YPCA, with him at the top and everybody else underneath him, without any delegated chain of command. He treated the college staff as his employees and had no sense of the college—its faculty and administrators—as a self-governing body. He thought that replacing a dean or filling a slot on the faculty was as simple as finding a new tenor for the quartet. But the old problem that plagued the YPCA—of letting good people go who might have strengthened the organization—was recurring at the college, where it was even more critical to retain qualified personnel. Percy's insistence on maintaining total control over the college was defeating his stated purpose of creating a high-quality and enduring institution of higher learning. And he did not face up to this situation and acknowledge that there had to be a change in leadership until the last year of his life.

# 13

## The Fundamentals of His Faith

PERCY WAS NOT A THEOLOGIAN OR A DISTINGUISHED WRITER. HIS ONLY published books were a collection of sermons and his handbook for personal evangelism, *The Art of Fishing for Men*. The latter book was intended to be a manual for dealing with unsaved men and women in personal face-to-face encounters. It contains strategies for meeting nine different types of problem cases or categories of individuals that the personal worker might confront, such as "the indifferent," "those who have difficulties," "those who lack assurance," "backsliders," "skeptics and infidels," and so on. The chapters are arranged in outline form, with subtopics supported by one or a few passages of Scripture supplemented by brief commentary; there is very little continuous prose in the book.[1] But the types of objections and difficulties he considers open a window on what Percy thought were the most serious challenges to his faith, and the types of responses he gives to these problems reveal his theological perspective and the ways in which he defended his beliefs.

My aim in this chapter is to draw out from this book and his sermons some of the main theological beliefs and commitments that made up his fundamentalist creed. The doctrine of regeneration or the new birth was at the center of his theology, and all other doctrines flowed to it or from it. Other doctrines that were fundamental for him were the belief that the Bible is the inerrant word of God and the belief in a literal hell. A third important tenet was his acceptance of the standard of conduct known as "the separated life"; this rule for Christian living was for him a crucial test of whether someone was truly born again. In the following sections, I will discuss these three core elements of my father's theology and how each of them is related to the central theme of regeneration.

### THE BIBLE IS THE WORD OF GOD

The belief that the Bible is God's spoken word was, and is, the cornerstone of fundamentalist belief. In *The Art of Fishing for Men* and various sermons, Percy lays out a series of reasons or evidences establishing that the

Bible "can be relied upon to be the Word of God in truth." Indeed he thought that the Christian believer could be completely certain about this. I want to consider in some detail the reasons my father gives in support of this central doctrine in order to understand his general view about the reasonableness of faith and the role that reasoning and argument can play in the defense of and propagation of the gospel. In this regard, it is noteworthy that Percy was convinced that the Christian worldview is more rational and makes better sense of the world and the place of humans in it than any alternative view, and consequently he thought that good reasons were always available to the Christian to meet any objections that might be coming from the nonbeliever. Hence the personal worker should "be ready always to give an answer to every man that asketh you a reason of the hope that is in you" (1 Peter 3:15).[2]

Percy had formed his beliefs about the Bible under Torrey's instruction at BIOLA and then refined them in his studies at Westminster under Bible professors J. Gresham Machen in New Testament and Robert Dick Wilson and O. T. Allis in Old Testament. All three of these professors had been part of the long-standing theological tradition at Princeton Seminary maintaining the inerrancy of Scripture that reached back to the great biblical scholars Benjamin Warfield and Alexander Hodge and the latter's renowned father, Charles Hodge. In a seminal paper entitled "Inspiration," coauthored in 1881, the younger Hodge and Warfield had written:

> The historical faith of the Church has always been, that all the affirmations of Scripture of all kinds, whether of spiritual doctrine or duty, or of physical or historical fact, or of psychological or philosophical principle, are without any error when the *ipsissima verba* of the original autographs are ascertained and interpreted in their natural and intended sense.[3]

The particular form of the doctrine of inerrancy that my father adhered to did not differ in essentials from this Princeton position; it included the following points (as he expressed them):

1. The Bible (spoken of always as one single book) is "the very word of God." "Even though man wrote it, it was inspired by the Holy Spirit, . . . and we have God using these men as a means that He might give to you and to me in this day and age a message from on High."[4]
2. The "original autographs" (in the Hebrew and Greek languages) are infallibly true. Admittedly, some errors have been introduced into our current editions by translators, copyists, and printers. However, "we have hundreds of copies of the original which, when carefully compared, indicate exactly what the originals contained."[5]

3. The Bible is wholly God's Word. No part of it can be separated from the rest and judged to be inauthentic, false, or of merely human authorship.
4. The Bible is literally true (in those passages in which it intends to be so).
5. The Bible is historically accurate in every detail.
6. The meaning of Scripture is revealed in plain language that is accessible to all; "for God has made salvation so plain and simple that we can take it today and adapt it, to the world of our time."[6]

Nine reasons given by Percy for believing that the Bible is God's word are summarized below. They point to general characteristics of the Bible as a written document that are presumed to be recognizable by any unbiased observer and to have argumentative force for anyone who doubts its supernatural origin. For the most part, he presents these reasons without a lot of commentary or backing. His purpose, it should be remembered, is not to construct rigorous arguments, but to provide reasons that could be useful in answering "skeptical" objections and clearing away intellectual doubts that may be preventing a person from opening his or her heart to Christ.

1. *The Bible has proved to be a reliable historical record.* The accumulating empirical (archeological) evidence either confirms the Biblical record or at least is "consistent" with it: "Instead of digging up missing links, scientists are digging up missing evidence which has coincided [with] and thrown light, in every detail, on the Bible. . . . There have been many excavations at Jerusalem, Jericho, Gaza, Gezer, Ashkelon, Capernaum and other sites in the Holy Land and never has there been any evidence unearthed which would contradict the Bible."[7]

Percy was so convinced of the Bible's truth that he tended always to overestimate the evidential value of archeological finds; for example, he pointed to some writing on "fragments of tablets" that referred to "Adapa, or Adam," which he argued confirmed "the story of Adam and Eve" and the fall of the human race—though this was certainly claiming too much for these discoveries.[8] (It must be said, however, that the archeologists working in Palestine at this time, of whom W. F. Albright of Johns Hopkins University was the leading light, approached their fieldwork with the same assumption about the Bible's historical truth and the same predisposition to find confirmatory evidence.)

2. *The popularity and wide circulation of the Bible.* It has survived repeated efforts to suppress it and destroy it and in fact "is more widely read, and more revered than any other book in the world."[9]
3. *The overall beneficial effects the Bible has had on individuals and nations.* "All who read this book are influenced for good, and not for evil, showing that God must be in it."[10] Nations that have rejected the Bible have tended to be "back-

ward": "God was ruled out of them, the Bible was ruled out and they are in darkness."[11]

4. *The book contains the highest ethical teachings of all*—even greater than the teachings of the Qur'an and other religious traditions.[12]

5. *If man wrote the Bible, man could write a better book* (this is the argument that Percy recites most often). Advances have been made in every other area and genre of literature, but no one has been able to improve on the Bible.

6. *The unity and coherence of the Bible taken as a whole.* "How wonderfully they dove-tail. Written as they were under God by over 35 different authors covering a period of some 1500 years, the first man not seeing the last, yet when all these 66 books are brought together, all agree perfectly, not one conflicting with the other."[13]

7. *The Bible's prophecies have been fulfilled*—especially those prophecies concerning Jesus.

8. *The Bible itself claims to be God's spoken word.*

9. *Jesus recognized the authority of the Old Testament* when it is said of him (in Luke 24:27): "And beginning at Moses and all the prophets he expounded unto them in all the scriptures the things concerning himself."[14]

The first five reasons are *external* reasons in that they refer to effects the Bible has had in human history and its relations to other human endeavors. The last four are *internal* reasons, referring to characteristics the Bible has as a self-contained unit. All of them together are clearly intended to make a cumulative argument supporting the conclusion that God is the author of the biblical texts.

But how strong is Percy's argument? Each of the nine reasons he gives offers a piece of evidence that merits further discussion. We can easily imagine how further debate on some of the points might go. Can we infer from the greater popularity of the Bible to its truth? Is it the most influential of all sacred books? Does it contain higher ethical teachings than other religions? Has the Bible always influenced individuals and nations for good and not for evil? Can we appeal to the Bible itself, and what it claims, as a witness to its own authority?

A careful examination of each of these points would carry us into a lengthy, and probably inconclusive, discussion. It may suffice for our purposes to point out that philosophers and theologians—even evangelical theologians—have come to see the difficulties in moving from premises about finite, earthly things to conclusions about supernatural causes. If Percy's nine reasons seem convincing, it is probably because they presuppose what they are trying to establish, namely, that God is "in" the Bible. Even if it is granted that he has given some good reasons for his thesis that God intervened miraculously in the historical process, the most that he could hope to show is that this hypothesis is more probable than other possible explanations. Natural reason has its place, but it cannot certify the Bible's authority with the degree of certainty that Percy expected from it.

This is not meant to be a criticism, however, because Percy fully realized that the Christian's belief (and certainty) that the Bible is God's word is not based solely on what reason can demonstrate. In other passages, he states emphatically that our confidence in the Bible is based on trust: "Our assurance comes only as we trust the character and integrity of God to keep His word of promise to the believer."[15] Passages like this reveal a certain tension in my father's thinking about what reason can accomplish; on the one hand, he believes that his Christian faith is thoroughly rational and justifiable; on the other, he embraces Paul's doctrine that spiritual truths are not "discernible" to "the natural man" and natural reason: "But the natural man receiveth not the things of the Spirit of God: for they are foolishness unto him: neither can he know them, because they are spiritually discerned" (1 Corinthians 2:14).[16] So Percy is prepared to admit that some of his basic commitments and beliefs are ultimately grounded in faith.

Another tension in Percy's thought should be mentioned. Although he recognized the value of reasoning when put in the service of the truth, at the same time he was deeply suspicious of reason and rational inquiry when it was used to examine and question the Bible and its teaching. He believed that critical inquiry, on its own, tends to work against faith and lead to skepticism and atheism. Some of his most scornful and negative criticism is reserved for the atheistic university professors whom he saw as attacking religion and undermining their students' faith. Some remarks seem to be directed toward the "biblical criticism" of modern scholarship, but others are broadside attacks on all of (secular) higher education. Referring to a current movement to develop a "shorter Bible," he writes: "Yes, they delight to tear the Word of God apart and to shorten it and take out what they don't want. Thank you, you can have it. I prefer the Bible as we have it today."[17] Percy lashes out at these "Christ-rejecting professors" who "under the guise of education . . . feel they have the license to criticize the Bible."[18] He even went so far as to brand their methods and criticisms as sacrilegious and as "trifling" with God's holy word, and he warned that God would judge them.

It may seem from these comments that Percy is rejecting scholarship altogether; but in fact he praised those Christian scholars who used their knowledge and their expertise to defend the Bible and argue against its critics. He singles out Old Testament scholar Robert Dick Wilson as a model of how scholars should use critical methods: "Robert Dick Wilson, one of my professors and one of the greatest linguists who ever lived, . . . a man who knew forty different languages, said that no one word of the Bible could be questioned by man, and he was a giant among linguists. Oh yes, it's reliable!"[19] "True science," Percy declared, "never conflicts with the Bible."[20] And the same holds for good critical scholarship. How could it, if the Bible is God's own words?

Percy followed Torrey in thinking dualistically that only two extreme views of the Bible are possible. Percy wrote: "The Bible either *is* or it *isn't* the Word of God," that is, either it is the infallible product of the divine mind, or it is the doubtful product of human thinking. Indeed he takes this point even further, pronouncing that if the Bible is not wholly God's word, then it is "a fraud and a farce."[21] He could not allow any human element to enter into the texts (except for differences in style); hence the "contribution" of the thirty-five different authors of the sixty-six books of the Bible to its essential meaning is nil.

We may well wonder why Percy was so committed to this principle of the total divine authorship of the Bible? Why would he not entertain the possibility that the Bible is partly contributed to by its human authors and partly by God? There are several interrelated reasons why he had to hold this all-or-nothing principle. First, he thought that if he compromised on this point, he would be losing his grip on the simple and clear message that he found stated in Scripture—namely, salvation through Christ's atoning death on the cross. Once it is allowed that some aspects of what the Bible teaches are tainted by their human authors' thought processes and their particular circumstances, then it may become cloudy just what part of the message is from God.

Second, if we give up the total divine authorship of the Bible, we lose the element of certainty and the assurance of our salvation. If the Bible comes from a human source to any degree, then it is corruptible and prone to error and can no longer be relied upon as an infallible guide to truth. As Torrey put it in one of his popular sermons, it would be "the mere product of man's thinking, speculating, and guessing, . . . [and] then we are all 'at sea,' not knowing whither we are drifting."[22] Percy believed too that unless we believe that God is "in" every single word of the Bible, we will end up in a state of doubt and despair. In contemplating this possibility, he reveals an existential dread when he asks: "If the Bible is not really the Word of God, where are we to turn?"[23]

Specifically, and most importantly, the certainty of the Bible's authorship is a guarantee of the believer's "full assurance" of eternal life in heaven (and deliverance from hell). Without that certainty, we could no longer be sure of God's promise (in John 3:16) that whoever believes in Christ will not perish but have everlasting life. Percy could not afford to allow the slightest doubt to creep in concerning this fundamental doctrine of that "blessed assurance," which is "a foretaste of glory divine."

But a serious question arises regarding this interpretation of inerrancy—that there can be no *human* contribution to the biblical texts. In his determination to safeguard the "God-breathed" and God-inspired character of the Bible against any human element or interpretation, Percy tends to forget completely that he (and his mentors) are humans who are interpreting Scripture. That is, he overlooks that he comes to the Bible from the perspective of a particular theological and exegetical tradition. The evangelical tradition that Percy imbibed mainly from Torrey reached back to the Protestant reformers—Luther and Calvin—who in turn were strongly influenced by Augustine and the letters of Paul. In this tradition, the central doctrines were original sin and divine grace, justification by faith, and belief in the Bible as the only means of knowing God's purposes (*sola scriptura*). Further, a strong Arminian doctrine of the individual's role in achieving salvation infused the particular strand of the tradition Percy inherited. Also, Percy followed T. C. Horton and Torrey in putting the greatest weight on the highly theological gospel of John and particularly those passages that stressed the divinity of Jesus and his blood-sacrificial death.

But in thus focusing the meaning of the New Testament gospel story on Jesus' divinity and sacrificial death, this interpretation loses sight of the human side of Jesus' nature and his life on earth—especially as it is presented in the Synoptic Gospels: Matthew, Mark, and Luke. The events of Jesus' life that were of greatest importance for Percy are the calling of his disciples to follow him, his efforts to get people to believe that he is God's Son, and his "great commission" to his disciples to go and preach the gospel to all nations. But the concentration of Jesus' life and mission into these few events downplays or completely ignores whole sections of the Gospels. For example, it misses that Jesus was a rabbi who had much to say to his followers about how they should live and act toward their fellows. When Jesus instructed the rich young ruler to go and "sell whatsoever thou hast, and give to the poor" (Mark 10:21), did he mean this literally? How significant are the ethical prescriptions Jesus set forth?

The image of Jesus that Percy constructed in his sermons was of someone masculine and tough, a "real man" with strong, "calloused" carpenter's hands, and willing to stand up to his enemies. In one sermon, he described Jesus as "a perfect specimen of an athlete."[24] But this picture of Jesus seems artificial and is hard to square with any of the gospel accounts.

Once it is realized that different portrayals of Jesus' life and its significance are possible and that the New Testament is always seen through an interpretive lens, then we must admit that a human factor comes into the equation whenever anyone decides which passages, books, and authors are most important and which episodes in Jesus' life reveal the deepest meaning of that life and its mission. And with this human element, there comes inevitably the possibility of error, misinterpretation, and putting the emphasis in the wrong place.

And yes, Percy is right that an element of uncertainty and risk creeps in at this point. But are we thereby forfeiting the assurance of our faith and our salvation as he feared? The answer depends on how one views faith. We have already seen that we cannot presume, as Percy did, that our faith is grounded in rational certainty. But there is a conception of faith that views it as compatible with risk and uncertainty, indeed as an affirmation of the truth of the Bible in the face of this uncertainty. This view of faith was expressed by Machen in a passage quoted above from his book *What Is Faith?*, which Percy was drawn to, but could not finally accept: "Though we have attained no rigidly mathematical proof, we have attained at least certitude enough to cause us to risk our lives . . . we must act in accordance with the best light that is given us and doing so we have decided for our part to distrust our doubts and base our lives, despite all, upon Christ."

## HELL

From the beginning of his Christian life, Percy subscribed fully to the doctrine of hell as it was formulated in BIOLA's statement of faith—"All those who persistently reject Jesus Christ in the present life shall be raised from the dead, and throughout eternity exist in a state of conscious, unutterable endless torment and anguish."[25] He never wavered in this belief about hell or softened his view. It was a pivotal doctrine in his theology and a theme he consistently brought into his sermons.

Torrey (who authored BIOLA's statement of faith) had impressed upon Percy the centrality of the doctrine of hell from the pulpit of the Church of the Open Door and in numerous books that Percy read and absorbed.[26] He also drove home the important link between this doctrine and soul winning. In order to be a successful soul winner, Torrey wrote, one "must have a love for souls, i.e. a longing for the salvation of the lost." And in order to generate a love for lost souls, one should think about their plight:

> Do not believe this doctrine in a cold, intellectual, merely argumentative way. If you do, and try to teach it, you will repel men from it. But meditate upon it in its practical, personal bearings, until your heart is burdened by the awful peril of the wicked and you rush out to spend the last dollar, if need be, and the last

ounce of strength you have, in saving those imperiled men from the certain, awful hell of conscious agony and shame to which they are fast hurrying."[27]

Percy was one who dwelled intently on the thought of the imminent peril
of those who were without Christ, and this image was indeed one of the
chief causes and motives of his lifelong passion to save the lost.

In a similar vein, my father was drawn to missionary Amy Wilson Carmichael's apocalyptic vision of lost souls falling into a bottomless chasm,
and he later cited her entire narrative, "Daisy Chain," in various sermons
and publications. Unable to sleep one dark night, and hearing the drums
and wild cries of native dancers, she envisioned lines of blind people pouring over "a precipice [that] broke sheer down into infinite space" while
Christians sat under trees "with their backs turned toward the gulf" making daisy chains. "There were shrieks as they suddenly found themselves
falling, and a tossing up of helpless arms, catching, clutching at empty air."
She also saw that "along the edge there were sentries set at intervals, but
. . . there were wide unguarded gaps between, and over these gaps the people fell in their blindness quite unwarned."[28]

Percy was haunted by this vision (in his words) of "thousands and millions" of lost humanity headed for death and destruction. He described
himself as one of the sentinels whose job it was "to stand on the brink of
the precipice and wave men and women back from the pit toward which
they are bound."[29] It was this strong desire—to rescue as many of the unsaved as he could from the terrible fate that awaited them—that stood behind his evangelistic fervor.

Percy took pride in being willing to stand up for the doctrine of hell,
however unpopular or unsophisticated it might be in the eyes of the world.
He tells us that he went to seminary so that he could study the Bible in its
original languages and obtain proof that what the Bible said about hell was
true. In working through the Greek New Testament, he "found to [his] horror" that when Jesus uses the Greek word *pyr* to describe hell, it "always
has reference to fire with flames as we know fire."[30] The doctrine of a literal hell was manifestly in the Bible, and that gave him solid ground on
which to stand. To ignore hell or interpret what the Bible says about it fig-
uratively would be to start down the path of selecting what one wanted from
the Bible rather than taking it as it is. "We ought to take what God said and
not what our rational minds tell us—good or bad," he proclaimed.[31]

What do our rational minds tell us about hell? The passage just cited is
from *The Art of Fishing for Men,* where Percy is responding to an objec-
tion or difficulty that an unbeliever might have, namely, why a loving God
would allow any of his creatures to suffer endless physical and mental tor-

218 A THIRST FOR SOULS

ment in hell. Percy evidently took the problem seriously because it is discussed in several places in the book: "My rational mind won't believe a loving God . . . would send a person to Hell." "Such a God as you present is unjust and cruel." "God is too good to damn anyone."[32] The objector is pointing to an apparent inconsistency in the Christian's position between God's nature (loving, good) and God's actions (judging, condemning to hell). The task of the personal worker who is charged with meeting every honest difficulty is the same as that of the theologian—to resolve the apparent contradiction by giving a coherent account of God's nature and a rationale for God's actions.

Percy takes on the formidable challenge of making God's actions intelligible. His strategy (again, following Torrey) is to try to show that God is both loving and just; God does not want any of his creatures to go to hell, but the crime of rejecting Christ is so horrendous to God that God is fully justified in dispensing an equally horrible penalty upon the sinner.

We must start then with God's great gift of love to us in sending his Son to die on Calvary as propitiation for our sin. We humans have to decide what we will do with Christ—whether to repent of our sin and receive him into our lives; or reject him and by so doing "trample on Him" and "spit in His face." Rejecting Christ is "the most serious sin man can commit." God will forgive murder, adultery, theft, "but you can never, never disbelieve, refuse to believe, in Jesus Christ as your Saviour and hope for a ray of mercy at the judgment day."[33] We sinners have rejected God's "love gift," and for this terrible act God (and Christ) will punish us in the day of judgment and cast us into outer darkness:

Now the time will come for you my friend, I'm talking to you, I say the time will come . . . that death will open up before you and you'll shudder. You'll cry out and your cries will only echo through the caverns of hell. You'll call for God but He knows what you did to his Son and the bell will toll—it will toll and out you'll go and your soul will go weeping and wailing along the sides of the pit crying My God, My God where art thou? Mercy followed you to the very edge of the precipice but you wouldn't listen.[34]

It is a terrifying picture. Percy raised the awful specter of hell in practically every sermon he preached—usually at the end, along with an illustration of someone who had died without Christ. Undoubtedly he was trying to evoke fear in the hearts and minds of his listening audience in order to get a response. But from his perspective, this was perfectly justifiable because of the enormity of what was at stake in their decision and because hell was a real consequence of their refusing to accept Christ. Percy would have said that as long as the convert had a minimal understanding of what it meant to say that "Christ died for our sins," that was sufficient, and it did not matter if the decision was made out of fear.

But on this point, it seems to me, there could well be room for a doubt to enter into the minds of new converts about whether their motives for conversion were acceptable to God and sufficient for their salvation. I can use the case of my own conversion to illustrate this difficulty. As a boy I used to lie awake at night for hours imagining the horrors of hell and worrying that I might end up there. I tormented myself by imagining what it would be like for the suffering and the burning to go on forever and ever and ever. I had not had a datable conversion experience, and I just was not sure that I was definitely saved. I kept these anguished thoughts to myself, until finally one evening while I was doing my homework at the dining room table, I told my father that I wanted to make sure I was saved. It was April 11, 1955, and I was thirteen years old. He prayed with me in the same way I had heard him pray with thousands of other converts. The whole process took about two minutes, and I went back to my homework, somewhat relieved that I had finally "clinched it with the Lord." There was no great change in my character or conduct after that evening. I had been a good Christian boy before the experience, and I continued to be after it. But in hindsight, I have to wonder if my decision, motivated as it was by fear and the desire to escape hell, made any difference as far as my eternal salvation is concerned. I was not acting from any sense of being a sinner before God and of my sin being atoned for by Jesus' sacrifice. These ideas always seemed too abstract and theological and did not mean much to me. I certainly doubt now whether my eternal destiny was significantly altered by that boyish act. But at the time I felt reassured, and I did stop having nightmares about hell.

I am afraid that what I have said about my father's use of the doctrine of hell makes him out to be the stereotypical hellfire and brimstone preacher. But in actuality he does not fit that description. It is true that he hammered his audience with the imminent prospect of hell, but there was another aspect of his preaching—a tone that came through in his invitations—that tempered these dire warnings. Alongside the doomsaying, there was an element of pathos, of deeply caring, of yearning for the sinner to accept God's loving gift. The following passage, at the close of one sermon on hell, is typical:

And you know that's your trouble as you listen to me, you're trying to argue with God. . . . [Y]ou're charging God as a brute, and you forget the cross. You forget the price He paid that you might not go to hell. You forget the agonies of Calvary. You forget Jesus said, "greater love hath no man than this, that a man lay down His life for His friends." That's what he did. He showed the greatest manifestation of love possible and died for you to save you from the caverns of hell, and all you do is to try and justify yourself in *not* accepting Christ. . . . No, God doesn't want you to die, for He said, "Turn ye, turn ye, for why will ye die?"[35]

The dual nature of God—God's love and God's wrath—so effectively conveyed in Percy's sermons, was a part of his theology that was mirrored in his own personality. We have seen that Percy could be harsh and judgmental in punishing those who rejected his authority or who were not steadfast in their loyalty to him. He was often insensitive to the pain he inflicted on the people around him—even those who were closest to him. But he also had a tender and giving side that was manifested in the way he took a personal interest in the lives of many individuals connected with his work —usually by way of a handwritten note or a small act of kindness, but which came out primarily in the genuine affection he showed to Ruth and his five children (as we will see presently).

The very idea of hell and of sinners bound for hell never ceased to wrench him. He grieved over those who refused to accept Christ and were therefore doomed to destruction. This was especially true for members of his own family: "Oh yes, it makes my heart heavy and tears come to my own eyes as I think of many of my own loved ones who refuse to receive Jesus and trust Him as Saviour. I say I shudder at the thought of hell and flames reserved for them throughout eternity."[36]

His two older brothers, Willoughby and Alph, whom he was never able to convert, were often cited as tragic examples of individuals who died without Christ. When Willoughby visited us in Philadelphia shortly before he died of multiple sclerosis, he also refused to take my father's hand to receive Christ, saying, "Perc, I can take your hand, but I can't take your Savior's." As Percy told this story so often at the close of his sermons, he had to face squarely the existential consequences of his theological beliefs, and he bore them with deep anguish. Even when it was his own loved ones— who were not bad people and had many admirable qualities—going to hell, he still submitted to the inexorable logic of his beliefs rather than yield to the cries of his heart. Once he had formulated his solution to the charge that God is a "brute," he never questioned the morality of God's condemnation of sinners. God "is not obligated to do one blessed thing for a man outside of Christ," he said.[37] But he, Percy, did all that he could to alleviate the miserable plight of his fellow human beings—he devoted his life and his whole being to saving as many souls as he could from perdition.

## THE SEPARATED LIFE

My father fully endorsed the social code that defined the "separated life" for fundamentalist Christians. Although not itself a doctrine, it was a standard that he thought followed from other doctrines and accordingly, it came to be used as a test of whether a person was truly fundamental.

One of Percy's strongest convictions was that born again Christians should be different from nonbelievers in the way they live. He used to drill into us five children the precept "you're not better, you're different"—trying to dispel from our minds the idea of moral superiority, while strongly impressing upon us the importance of being readily distinguishable from our peers. The prohibited activities in our realm included drinking alcoholic beverages, smoking, swearing, card-playing, and going to the theater, movies, and dances; physical contact with members of the opposite sex was not forbidden.

Except for the fact that all four of us boys had a rebellious streak in us (like our father's) that occasionally surfaced, we pretty much willingly embraced this behavioral code without complaint. I had no difficulty accepting it; all of my high school friends knew that I did not participate in these activities for religious reasons, and I at least felt that I was respected for my moral stand and my "witness." I was socially active in other ways, with a steady girlfriend (who was Jewish). However, since I did believe that the activities I was abjuring were morally wrong, I probably did feel some of that moral superiority that my father warned me against.

In the early 1930s, the young people who gathered around Percy and who were saved through his ministry for the most part adopted this strict code of living as a matter of course. They assumed that they needed to make some sort of personal sacrifice in order to show in their lives that their decision to accept Christ was genuine. But apparently a question arose for a number of these new Christians about the morality of dancing, and whether it was consistent or inconsistent with their commitment to Christ. And this prompted my father, who was directing his entire ministry to young people, to give serious thought to this question.

Percy may also have been motivated to address this topic because he himself had been an avid dancer before he was converted, and since he was athletic and well coordinated, he was probably a very good dancer. It is surprising how often dancing crops up in the brief accounts he gives of his rebellious youth. Dancing was one of the ways (along with smoking and going to pool halls) he willfully disobeyed his parents: "My parents said, 'Don't ever let us catch you in a dance hall,' so I took dancing lessons."[38] "As regular as clockwork Saturday nights I was at the dance hall."[39] Further, he tells us he danced with "two young women" on the boat that brought him to Los Angeles; and on two of the next three evenings before his conversion at the Church of the Open Door, he went to dance halls. Dancing was for him emblematic of the unsaved life and the pleasure that the world offered. And so he takes up the challenge of the dance, knowing full well that "this question demands sympathy for the young man and woman of the twentieth century. . . . Recreation for a Christian is a real problem."[40]

The question, as he formulated it, was: "Can a person dance and be a Christian?" Percy had preached a sermon with this title at the Rhawnhurst Church in the summer of 1930, while still in seminary. He later reworked the sermon and published it as a two-part article in *Young People Today*.[41] Dancing was the only part of the social code that Percy dealt with in a serious and substantive way. This article is important then because it formulates Percy's considered view of the separated life in this one aspect and how it links up with other basic doctrines, and also because it reveals the manner in which he dealt with young people in these important matters of social conduct.

If only the Bible had something definite to say about modern dancing, that would be the end of the story; but Percy recognizes, after looking up all of the twenty-seven passages in the Bible that refer to dancing, that "the Bible nowhere says 'Thou shalt not dance.'" In fact, he says, "it is clear that dancing was both a form of worship and an expression of joy."[42] But Percy also recognized that "the dancing mentioned in the Bible was a different kind of dance." "Not once in the Bible is dancing described as taking place between the opposite sexes." Dancing, like smoking, card-playing, and the movies, is an activity about which the Bible does not speak, so whatever it has to say about dancing must be inferred from its other teachings.

However Percy is wary of those preachers who make pronouncements about these extrabiblical matters: "I have heard some men who are supposedly Evangelistic, harangue and lambaste people for playing cards, going to movies and dances and say, 'if you do so, you are bound for Hell.'" He goes on to repudiate these tactics: "I do not believe that there is any man living who has the authority, or the right, [or] the power to stand up before any group of young people and say, 'Do this,' or 'Do not do this,' except as it coincides with the Word of God."

Since no one is authoritative about these social matters, then (he concludes) the question of whether dancing is right or wrong is "an individual one," by which he means that each Christian must judge for himself or herself whether the act in question is right or wrong. He cites Scripture as follows: "So then every one of us shall give account of himself to God," and "Let us not therefore judge one another any more." This view, which sounds relativistic, does not mean that when each of us asks the question (about dancing) that there is no objectively right or wrong answer; but it means that we must find the answer for ourselves; others can give us their advice and testify to their own reasons for giving up (or not giving up) the activity, but we must ultimately decide if the activity is consistent with our commitment to Christ.

These initial comments strongly indicate that Percy, in this article, is reacting to one of John R. Rice's widely circulated (printed) sermons, "What's Wrong with the Dance?" delivered a year earlier, June 1935, in the Baptist Tabernacle in Dallas. In it, Rice browbeats and bullies his audience with comments like these: "Multitudes are going to hell on that road, the dance road, because they won't listen to the gospel and turn to Jesus Christ and be saved." "Murder goes with the modern dance, and all kinds of devilment. The curse of God is on it! The devil is in it! There is terrible danger in it! God help you to leave it alone!"[43]

Percy's entire article seems to be constructed as a more moderate and noncoercive approach to dancing than Rice's harangue. He is saying to the young person in effect: I recognize the struggle you are going through, and I am not going to pronounce judgment on you if you dance. I am going to tell you why *I* gave up dancing after I received Christ and give you the best reasons I can muster based on our common Christian beliefs, in the hope that I can persuade you to do the same. But ultimately you will have to decide whether dancing is in keeping with your Christian commitment.

Percy begins to formulate his answer to the question whether a Christian can dance by pointing out that what usually happens when someone is converted is that they find that they no longer want to dance. This happens because "if any man be in Christ Jesus he is a new creature; old things are passed away, behold, all things are become new" (2 Corinthians 5:17). The new life in Christ brings with it "a new desire and a new mode of living different from that previously lived." But, as if realizing that this answer will not satisfy the young inquirer who still feels the desire to dance and still feels that she or he has to make a decision about it, Percy restates their predicament: "I asked you, Can a person dance and be a Christian?" and then surprisingly he answers: "If you must have it, I answer 'Yes.'"

What is he admitting here? I interpret him to be saying, first, that the activity of modern dancing is not in itself wrong or sinful or "of the devil," and so dancing cannot be used as a litmus test to determine whether one is saved or lost. A person can dance and still be a regenerated Christian. But in making this concession, Percy is not condoning dancing; nor is he opening the door (very wide) for allowing individuals to decide that dancing in certain contexts is acceptable for them. Even if the dance is not inherently wrong, it may still be wrong for individual Christians to dance once they take into account the possible harmful effects of dancing on others and on their own spiritual lives.

He then sets out several reasons why the decision to dance would be harmful in most or all of the contexts that Christians might be in, and although he presents them as reasons for *his* giving up dancing, he clearly intends that these reasons have normative significance for other Christians as well:

1. Dancing "has a tendency to lead to sinning"—primarily sexual misconduct. "It sets a fire going that is not easily quenched."
2. The setting of the dance is not "conducive to holiness"; it is not one that the Lord himself would want to go to.
3. Dancing does not satisfy. "It is momentary satisfaction of the flesh, and that only in a very small degree." When Jesus comes into our lives, we experience a joy and a peace that is "far better" than the things of this world.
4. Dancing can be a "stumbling block" to other Christians, causing them to be lax in their commitment to Christ. Or it may stand in the way of others coming to Christ; dancing "tends to hurt soul-winning."

Each of these reasons gives support to Percy's conclusion that the Christian should not dance only when taken in conjunction with other ethical and theological beliefs and commitments—ones that Percy could readily assume the Christians he was addressing would hold. His first reason assumes that certain other sorts of conduct are sins, and so dancing should be avoided because it usually occurs in a setting in which those other things are easily obtainable. The other reasons rely on theological premises and particularly on the doctrine of the new birth. The main thrust of Percy's argument is to put the whole question of the dance in the context of a person's salvation. If the dance is a problem for the Christian, the solution to it should come as a consequence of the individual's prior act of accepting Christ: "I honestly believe, my friend, it is not a question of your *giving up* the dance, it is a question of your *giving in* to the Lord, accepting Him as your personal sin bearer. Then I believe He will show you what to do with regards to the dance."

The question whether to dance or not to dance will take care of itself once a person genuinely gives his or her life to Christ. When this happens, there is "a natural change within the heart, and the Spirit of God comes in to abide and change the life." Percy called the new birth "a mysterious work of God in the hearts of men and women," accomplished only when they believe in Jesus Christ.[44] He is putting all the emphasis on the miraculous transformation that takes place in a person's life when he or she is born again. His assumption is that the Holy Spirit will take away the Christian's

desire for the dance and substitute new desires. He is convinced that dancing "does not satisfy"; it gives only a transitory happiness that is not fulfilling. He recalls an experience he had as a youth "coming home from a
dance on the last or early car" that signaled a deep dissatisfaction with his
life: "I . . . caught myself saying 'If this is all there is in life there isn't much
in it.'" But he had found something "far better"—and with it a joy that is
more lasting and satisfying.

What are the new desires that come into the life of a person who is born
again? Percy thought of them as new loves or passions. The ones he stressed
were, of course, the love for lost souls and the desire to save them, a yearning for knowledge of God's word as found in the Bible, and a desire for fellowship with other Christians. Further, the saved person will want to live
a holy life. Holiness or piety, on this view of the Christian life, meant living a clean, moral life, which in turn meant (primarily) the separated life—
not smoking, drinking, or dancing. "Modern dancing is not conducive to
holiness—the atmosphere, the company, the conversation, the smoking and
drinking."[45] So then, whether or not someone dances becomes a sign or a
criterion for whether they are wholly committed to Christ. In the end, Percy
does not leave much room for the individual to decide that he or she can
dance and still be a Christian.

It is significant that holiness, on this view, does *not* include a desire for
moral goodness, understood in terms of the virtues of justice toward the
poor and the oppressed, beneficence toward one's fellow humans, or char-
ity of the kind exemplified by the good Samaritan. Clearly, Percy's rejection of the social gospel is coming into play in the way he understands the
new life in Christ. Once again, we can see how the fundamentalism he espoused that establishes the rather narrow standard of Christian piety and
Christian living—centering on the separated life and a small set of soul-
winning activities—depends on giving a highly selective interpretation of
the Bible and its ethical teachings.

Percy was sure that the promised "joy and peace" that would be experienced by the convert was real and could be spelled out in terms of tangible
enjoyments and fun living. Accordingly, he concludes the article by setting
out a practical social "program for the born again Christian." It includes attending parties "that can be made lively and yet not questionable . . . they
could always be wound up with a five-minutes devotional period"; sports—
"I think everyone should specialize in some kind of sport"; and elsewhere
he mentions other activities and games, such as symphony concerts, mu-
seums, zoo, walks, car rides, hymn sings, picnics, carams, checkers, television.[46] The final activity he suggests is to "get busy in His service": "I
know of no better way to be occupied and to be kept out of trouble than to

be busy trying to win someone for Christ. Take a Sunday school class. Take one night a week at some down and out mission. Start a Phi Gamma Fishing Club. Start a gospel team. Get Gospels of John and canvas the neighborhood giving [them] out."

Percy tried to make good on these recommendations, first, by implementing this sort of wholesome, fun atmosphere at his camps and at The King's College. He also incorporated these values and priorities into his own life. He was a fun-loving person with a fondness for jokes and humor, and he enjoyed a variety of recreational activities, especially the game of tennis. Above all, he got tremendous satisfaction from winning someone to Christ. Once after winning the soul of a soldier who thanked him for his time, he said: "You didn't waste my time, I'd go a long way for this." "I *could* dance, but I don't want to," he said; "I do not have time to think of the dance." God had given him a thirst for souls, and in its powerful grip, the things of earth had grown "strangely dim" and faded from sight.[47]

# 14

# U.S. Tours and Mass Evangelism

Pᴇʀᴄʏ'ѕ ᴇxᴘᴀɴѕɪᴏɴ ᴏꜰ ᴛʜᴇ ʀᴀᴅɪᴏ ʙʀᴏᴀᴅᴄᴀѕᴛ ᴛᴏ ᴀ ɴᴀᴛɪᴏɴᴡɪᴅᴇ ᴀᴜᴅɪ-
ence in the early 1940s opened up a new horizon for evangelistic enterprise. What distinguished his ministry from that of other prominent national
broadcasters of that era—Walter Maier, Charles Fuller, Paul Myers, M. R.
DeHaan, Theodore Epp—was the extent to which he took his evangelistic
team on the road to gather the harvest of souls that the broadcast had made
possible. Thousands had already turned to Christ through the broadcast.
But many more souls would respond if they could meet the evangelist and
his team face to face. Percy had been schooled in the methods of personal
evangelism by T. C. Horton and Reuben Torrey, and he never lost his appetite for taking the gospel directly to lost souls and meeting them on a personal basis.

And so in 1941 he began a series of extended tours with Ruth and the
quartet that would take them the length and breadth of the country. The
quartet through most of the decade was possibly the finest that Percy and
Ruth ever assembled with first tenor Alan Forbes, lead tenor Ray Pritz, baritone Ken Brown, and bass Joe Springer.

Of course, Percy was already experienced at traveling with a gospel team
across the nation. He had done it at BIOLA and Wheaton. Later, he traveled often with his team to Chicago from Philadelphia, where longtime
friend Wendell Loveless would put him on the Moody station WMBI, and
where he would return to Wheaton College to speak at a chapel service.
And in 1939 and 1940 he expanded the Chicago link to include additional
meetings in Illinois and at good friend Bob Ketcham's churches first in
Gary, Indiana and then Waterloo, Iowa.[1]

It was not until June 1941 that Percy took the YPCA team on its first ex-
tended tour of the Midwest. For twelve straight days they held meetings in
Cleveland, Detroit, Chicago, Wheaton, Cicero, Waterloo, Cedar Rapids,
Kansas City, St. Louis, Indianapolis, and Cincinnati.

But Percy always had it in mind to get back to the West Coast, where he
still had many contacts, and finally in January 1943 he and the team headed

west. With fuel rationed, they traveled by train, first to Chicago for a radio stop and then directly to Washington State, whereupon they toured the entire coast for twelve days from Vancouver, British Columbia, to Long Beach, California. It was on this trip that Percy first spoke at the Church of the Open Door in Los Angeles, where he had accepted Christ nineteen years earlier. Pastor Louis Talbot turned over to him the Sunday afternoon and evening services, and 3,500 and 4,000 people attended, with 10 and 100 souls won at the two meetings.

The trip must have buoyed my father and convinced him that he could draw large crowds anywhere in the country. Nine months later, the team hit the westward trail again, this time on a route that took them through the Southwest for the first (and only) time. The evangelistic party for this trip consisted of seven: Percy, Ruth, the quartet, and Al Zahlout with his "singing violin."[2] Percy had arranged a torturous schedule of seventy meetings in fifty-four days. He announced the trip in his newsletter:

WESTWARD HO . . . !
My, how we would love to meet you all on this trip, and we hope to meet 75,000 of you!
We are anticipating between two and three thousand professions of Christ en route. Will you all pray that the Holy Spirit will use us mightily?
It will be a hard old grind, night after night, but we must work, for the night is coming.[3]

And what a grind it was! Traveling again by train for the first leg of the journey, their first stop was in Indianapolis and the next day in Memphis at Robert G. Lee's Bellevue Baptist Church; then to New Orleans, Houston, Dallas, Amarillo, Phoenix, reaching California on the ninth day. There they rented a car for the trip up the coast along with an open trailer to haul the luggage. Travel conditions were less than ideal with seven in the car—except when the boys took turns riding in the open trailer (at speeds of 60 mph). In California they held twenty-seven meetings in eighteen days, with audiences frequently in the thousands. (The broadcast was done every Sunday en route and sent out live over the network.) Then eight days of meetings in Oregon; nine in Washington; and finally the long twelve-day trip home with stops in Salt Lake City, Denver, Omaha, Waterloo, Minneapolis, Duluth, Milwaukee, Kenosha, Chicago, and Detroit.

The tour was a great success by the measure that counted most. Ray Pritz had started keeping a log of the number of persons attending the meetings and the number who made decisions. Percy's predictions had been remarkably accurate: there were 77,575 in attendance, and 3,316 decisions.

There would be more of these grueling trips—four to the West Coast, by car in 1946 (eight weeks) and 1948 (six weeks) and by plane and car in 1952 (three weeks) and again in 1956. And in between these were shorter tours to Florida, Oklahoma, Chicago, and Detroit. But by far the most adventuresome trip was the five-month world tour that was coming up in 1953–54 (as we will soon see).

The tours took a heavy toll on Percy, Ruth, and the different quartets that took part in them. Now in his forties, my father knew that he was putting a severe strain on his heart—weakened by the rheumatic fever he had had as a child. Instead of slowing down, he seemed to pick up the pace in the latter part of his life. My mother was making good on her vow to subordinate her life to Percy's work. And the quartet members, some of them married and attending college or seminary were making a huge personal sacrifice. One wonders how they managed to endure the rigors of these long travels—the endless hours in the car, often driving all night, the cramped quarters, getting "up" for singing at meeting after meeting, and all the time maintaining a positive and cheerful attitude. Ruth certainly helped with her pleasant and sympathetic disposition, as did Percy with his good humor. But the overall goodwill that characterized these trips in spite of the hardships, I believe, is indicative of the dedication and loyalty the quartets had to Percy and Ruth and their work. As one quartet member, Shorty Yeaworth, said: "We believed in [Percy's] ministry."[4] Ray Pritz wrote: "You must remember it was an honor to be a member of the YPCA male quartet and Percy was an important person in Christian circles. So you always functioned in the light of this fact."[5]

Pritz and Springer kept a diary of the 1946 West Coast tour (later published in booklet form), and some excerpts from it will give us a window on what the quartet members themselves thought about what they were doing on these tours. The cast of characters for this eight-week trip, all by car, consisted of Percy, Ruth, Ray and Joe, Ken Brown, and Don Schultz (substituting for Alan Forbes). Don had been in combat in Africa and Italy with the Fourth Ranger Battalion, and was one of the few from that unit to survive the Anzio Beach invasion. The trip got off to a rocky start:

**Sunday, January 27**
California sounded plenty good to us as we left the studio [after the Sunday broadcast] and rushed through the sub-freezing weather to our car. The problem of packing enough luggage in the trunk for six confronted us, but after much struggling and grunting, we jammed the trunk lid shut, bid our well-wishers good-bye, and headed West. With five new tires, no wonder we thought over thirty-five was a safe speed. As a matter of fact, it wasn't till Lancaster that we had our first blow-out, and that's a good 65 miles! Dr. Crawford does most of the driving, and seems to find a relaxation in it.

It had been our plan to drive until about midnight, then stop for lodging, but we could find no vacancies and we had no alternative but to drive on through the long night [to Columbus, Ohio].

### Sunday, February 3
[The morning after a Youth for Christ rally in Bellflower, California.] Three A.M. came all too quickly, but our Six A.M. broadcast was to be in San Diego, 125 miles distant and we had no other alternative but to roll out and ride. We were none too early either for it wasn't until 5:45 that we entered the studios of KGB in San Diego for our first broadcast of the trip.

### Thursday, February 7
Biola, alma mater of Percy Crawford in 1926, invited us for their morning chapel service, and one thousand vibrant Christian youths eagerly awaited our program. In this place so dear to his heart, Percy Crawford stood up and told how years before, he had found Christ in this same auditorium. Then he related how he had come into the auditorium a few days ago all alone, and rededicated his life at the very spot where he found the Lord twenty-two years before. As he knelt there he prayed that the Lord would use him even more in the forthcoming twenty-two years. Dry eyes were few as the brief message was ended.

### Saturday, February 9
Youth for Christ is held every Saturday in the Church of the Open Door [at BIOLA] and it was our privilege to be featured this night. With the meeting starting at 7 P.M., the main auditorium was already filled, and many were filing in downstairs. Announcements were made that the main floor was for young people only, and everywhere, older people got up to give their seats to youth. . . . One of the church officials told us that it was probably the largest crowd in the rich history of the Church-of-the-Open-Door. . . . Preaching the same type of message as the one under which he was saved—the wrath of God—Percy Crawford, through the Spirit of God, made many realize their lost condition without Christ.

### Tuesday, March 5
Twelve hundred miles ahead and only two days to make it. We, of necessity, left that night [from Spokane], heading for Denver, Colorado, and driving, driving, driving! This section of the West is famous for its heavy snows, and believe it or not, some of the drifts covered the telephone poles! Even though the roads were cleared, we were forced to travel slowly because of the treacherous holes in the road, and despite our caution, the two rear tires blew out from the punishment. And it was a hundred miles to the next town that might have a spare for us. We realized again that the Lord was with us, for upon arriving in town, we located a store that had just been allotted a tire our size, one that would have been gone in another ten minutes!

**Saturday, March 9**
Minneapolis and a great Youth for Christ meeting was our program for this evening. Here was our largest meeting of the trip, for 7,500 came to the huge hall for this thrilling Saturday night rally. What a testimony to see so many interested in things eternal.

**Saturday, March 24**
Dawn was pushing back the night as we approached Philadelphia, after driving all night. As we sat at breakfast together in a home-town restaurant this morning, we looked back over the past eight weeks. Almost 100,000 people had heard the Gospel through us in that time, and nearly 3,000 had answered Dr. Crawford's invitations to accept Christ as Lord and Saviour. Truly this tour was planned *by* God, filled *with* God, and used *of* God to draw souls from all over the country into the fold in these the last days.

The remarkable quartet of Ray and Joe, Ken Brown, and Alan Forbes sang together for about eight years (1940–47) during the time when my father was at the peak of his ministry. All four of them were working their way through college and seminary while singing with Percy and Ruth. They understood Percy's great gift of evangelism and their effectiveness in working with the YPCA. As they were coming to the end of their seminary training, they thought about the possibility of continuing with Percy. Pritz recalled:

> We as a quartet talked together seriously about [postgraduation plans] and felt we would like to stay together if we could find some key positions in the YPCA ministry. We had been with the Haven of Rest Quartet in California on one of our trips and this was the arrangement they had and it seemed to work very well. We then got together with Percy and proposed something like that to him but he was not willing to do that. We assumed that he wanted his sons to become an integral part of his ministry. At various times he intimated this in group conversations.[6]

In 1947 Alan, Ray, and Joe all left the quartet and went on to different lines of full-time Christian service. (Ken had left a year earlier.) Joe went with station HCJB in Quito, Ecuador; Alan went into youth work in Buffalo; Ken and Ray took churches for several years, and then Ken joined Charles Fuller's *Old Fashioned Revival Hour* quartet, and Ray became a career air force chaplain. Percy was fond of all of them and in later years invited Alan, Ray, and Joe to be speakers at Pinebrook. His response to their proposal, however, reveals an important aspect of his ministry and his thinking about it. Organizationally, there was no place in his ministry for these talented, committed young men—no hierarchy or distributed power within the organization. Brown said of my father: "He was a one-man band; he would do everything."[7] Percy was unwilling to give these individuals (or any of his quartet members over the years) a permanent role in his evangelism and was quite prepared to see them move on to other forms of Christian service, having used his ministry as a training ground. My father's response also brings out that the only ones who, in his mind, could take his place were his children. He wanted his boys—the oldest of whom at this time was ten—to carry on his work.

## THE ATLANTIC CITY VICTORY CENTER

Percy responded to the war effort with fervent patriotism and an action program. He saw the opportunity to reach the thousands of service men and women who were stationed at, or passing through, Atlantic City, New Jersey, and opened a service center, the Atlantic City Victory Center, in April 1943, at Steel Pier on the boardwalk. The main room of the center was a long, elegant lounge (175 × 65 feet), lined with plants, and hundreds of comfortable chairs and lamps, where servicemen and servicewomen could read, listen to the phonograph or radio, play board games, and have coffee and doughnuts.[8] (Percy wrote to his supporters: "In faith we've purchased three large shiny coffee urns, hoping you folks will keep us supplied with coffee, as the ration board will not supply us.")[9] At the end of the lounge was a partitioned recreation room with ping-pong and shuffleboard tables, which doubled as a meeting room for daily Bible classes. On the wall of the rec room was a large print of *Washington Crossing the Delaware* flanked by mottos that read: "The Bible Says Ye Must Be Born Again," and "The Bible Says Christ Died For Our Sins." In another letter to friends, Percy wrote: "Literally thousands of men visit our Center each day and each day souls have accepted Christ. It is the largest Center of its kind in the United States."[10] Later, in a newsletter he reported: "A large group of WAC's have come in, and now some 10,000 more shell-shocked boys, having seen action, are coming to recuperate. We're determined through prayer to reach these boys and I am sure now, more than ever, they will be thinking of things eternal."

In a newsletter appealing for funds, he noted that the cost of running the Centre was $2,000 a month for rent, utilities, staff, and supplies, but that "this past month we have not received enough to pay for the rent." The extra cost was justified, however, by the results they were getting: the same newsletter included a letter "from a soldier: I am one of the soldier boys that was saved at your Victory Center in Atlantic City and I thank God for leading me to Him."[11]

## YOUTH FOR CHRIST AND MASS RALLIES

Percy's youth ministry was not the only one experiencing phenomenal growth during the war years; there were signs of revival all over the country. In the spring of 1944, Percy watched as Jack Wyrtzen launched a series of meetings at New York's Madison Square Garden that took mass evangelism to a new level. On April 1, in what was billed as a "Youth for Christ Victory Rally," Wyrtzen filled Madison Square Garden—and then did it again six months later in September. Percy accepted Wyrtzen's invitation to give a testimony along with other "prominent speakers" at the September rally. He had been the guest speaker for Wyrtzen at one of his New York City Saturday night rallies as recently as April 29 of that year, but now he was taking a backseat as his junior colleague took the lead before a packed house of twenty thousand.

The four-hour service started with a one-hour band and choir concert featuring the New York Salvation Army Band and a 3,500-voice all-girl choir. Gil Dodds, the indoor mile record holder, was the main attraction—his name appearing on the Madison Square Garden marquee along with that of Wyrtzen and Carlton Booth, the soloist and organist. Beverly Shea would also sing at these rallies.

It is well known that Wyrtzen's Madison Square Garden rallies served as a stimulus for Chicagoland Youth for Christ's huge victory rallies in October 1944 and May 1945. It is not so well known that they also prompted Percy to conduct a similar rally at Convention Hall, in Philadelphia, seven months after the one he attended. Not to be outdone, Percy drew nearly twelve thousand to the April 28 rally with a stepped-up program that shamelessly imitated Wyrtzen's. Fenton Duvall, director of The King's Singers, led the audience in the singing of the national anthem to start the service. The program featured Peter Slack at the organ, the vocal quartet, brass quartet, and entire musical ensemble, plus Gil Dodds giving testimony, a thousand-voice white-clad all-girl choir, and (would you believe?) the New York Salvation Army Staff Band.[12] My father certainly had to acknowledge that Wyrtzen had raised the bar as far as numbers attending his rallies, but this did not stop him from trying to regain the edge back on his home turf in Philadelphia. From this point on, the relationship between Wyrtzen and my father became more competitive, but respectful, as their ministries overlapped more and more. Wyrtzen continued to invite Percy to be the main speaker at his New York rallies and boat rides, and Percy promptly put Wyrtzen on the speakers list at Pinebrook. When Wyrtzen opened his summer camps in 1947, Percy is rumored to have said "This is war!" but the two directors were still on good terms and even arranged to exchange visits (with their families) to each other's camps over several years.

Meanwhile, in Chicago, at about the same time that Wyrtzen was filling Madison Square Garden, evangelist Torrey Johnson and Chicagoland Youth for Christ were also moving into larger quarters. After drawing large crowds at Orchestra Hall all summer, Johnson and his team planned a huge victory rally in Chicago Stadium for October 1944. Thirty thousand people attended the rally with evangelist Merv Rosell the principal speaker, as well as some familiar faces—Gil Dodds testifying, and Bev Shea singing.

Spurred on by this success, Johnson and the Youth for Christ team planned a Memorial Day Victory rally that would be the "biggest youth rally yet."[13] And it was. He rented mammoth Soldiers Field and put on a spectacular show of shows. Johnson invited my father to be the main speaker. He had looked up to Percy ever since his student days at Wheaton when he was a freshman and Percy a senior and had invited him to speak at his church the year before on one of his tours.[14] So Percy was probably not surprised to get the call.

He set out by overnight rail to Chicago, arriving Wednesday morning, May 30, with eager anticipation, but not knowing quite what was coming. At 6:30 p.m., seventy thousand people gathered in the stadium under clear skies. Chuck Templeton of Toronto Youth for Christ was master of ceremonies. Music was provided by a three-hundred-piece Salvation Army band, a five-thousand-voice choir, and soloists Pruth McFarlin ("America's greatest Negro tenor") and Bev Shea. One medley of gospel numbers, directed by Merrill Dunlop, featured eight grand pianos, vibraharp, organ, and chimes. Early in the program, five hundred white-uniformed nurses in the formation of a cross marched down the field honoring the war dead. A missionary pageant representing six different countries featured men and women in native costumes forming a star in the center of the field, while representatives of those countries spoke on stage. (Billy Graham spoke for the United States.) Gil Dodds ran two spotlighted laps around the stadium and gave a testimony. Percy preached, and hundreds responded to his invitation by turning in cards indicating that they had accepted Christ. At the close, the lights were turned out and the choir sang "We Shall Shine as the Stars in the Morning" as a spotlight from a beacon in the center of the field revolved around the vast audience.[15]

I have often wondered what my father felt as he stepped to the podium to address seventy thousand people. There is no record of his sermon or even his sermon topic. I doubt very much if he wrote anything new for this service or even made lengthy notes. Relying on the Lord for strength and speaking extemporaneously from a simple outline, he did what he had done on thousands of other occasions—he brought his audience to the realization that they were sinners in need of a Savior and he asked them to accept Christ into their lives. Percy may have felt that his role as messenger, as soul winner, was diminished somewhat by all the hoopla and pageantry surrounding his message. He would have liked to have had an altar call and may have wondered why this was not possible even in the huge stadium. What, after all, was the purpose of all this if not to win more lost souls to Christ?

Years later, when Johnson was talking about the Soldiers Field rally in an interview, he remembered something that Percy had done when the entire team gathered the next morning to assess the rally and its results. The mood was euphoric, for the rally had gotten favorable coverage in the local papers and the national wire services. Johnson recalled that Percy's reaction was to challenge them all by taking from his pocket a "Horton's Gospel of John" (which he always carried with him) and reminding them of the importance of winning individual souls to Christ through personal evangelism. Percy was certainly not opposed to mass evangelism, but I imagine he felt that the rally organizers were getting too caught up in the numbers game and in putting on a spectacular show. Apparently Johnson got the message.[16]

A year later in 1946, Percy delivered the sermon at another huge Saturday Youth for Christ rally at the Hollywood Bowl that drew twenty thousand, in which two thousand came forward (to the stage) to accept Christ. And back in Philadelphia, Percy continued to hold rallies in May at Convention Hall for the next two years (1946–47), attracting a crowd of about seven thousand at each. The next year, May 1948, he moved from Convention Hall to the smaller Academy of Music for a Friday night rally that drew twenty-eight hundred, and then two weeks later took the program to Carnegie Hall in New York for a Sunday afternoon rally that attracted about the same number. The following year, 1949, he repeated the same cycle at the Academy of Music and Carnegie Hall. At all of these rallies, Percy stayed with his own ensemble of musicians, instead of importing huge choirs and outside talent. This meant cutting back on the scale of the rallies—the optimum number was about three thousand—but it also meant a more intimate and distinctive YPCA sound.

It was during these years that Ruth began to build an orchestra for the Sunday broadcast, collaborating with a talented young singer and arranger, Alfred Black.[17] Al Black was a Philadelphia boy who auditioned for The King's Singers at age thirteen. At sixteen he was singing with Ruth on the

morning broadcast and subbing in the quartet and then sang for two years
with the regular quartet. Ruth and Al recruited additional instrumentalists
and gradually built a full orchestra.

At the Carnegie Hall rally in 1948, Percy and Ruth put on a program that
was quintessentially the *Young People's Church of the Air,* full of the distinctive brand of soft gospel music my mother had cultivated over the
years—on the broadcast and at Pinebrook. The twenty-six-piece orchestra
conducted by Black opened the service with a "prelude" of five numbers,
old and new: "Have Thine Own Way Lord," "'Tis So Sweet to Trust in
Jesus," "Near the Cross," Norman Clayton's "Now I Belong to Jesus," and
"Marvelous Grace." Later in the program they played another Clayton favorite, "We Shall See His Lovely Face." The song service, led by Larry
McGuill, opened with the YPCA signature song "Love Wonderful Love."
Then we four children, billed as the "4 D's, Don, Dick, Dan, and Dean,"
sang. (We boys were ten, nine, six, and three and had just started that year
singing at meetings.) There followed a series of medleys performed by the
vocal quartet, the brass quartet, the twelve-voice King's Singers, and orchestra. Solos were done by soprano Hilda Schmeiser ("Yes, There Is Comfort"), tenor Mel Peterkin ("Saviour Like a Shepherd Lead Us"), and bass
Danny Bartkow ("A Great Calm"), all of whom had a remarkable ability
to express the warm, heartfelt quality of Ruth's selections. Interspersed
were testimonies and four numbers by The King's College Choir under the
direction of Gordon Curtis.

This superb cast and musical format developed by Ruth and her associates was by now a proven quantity and was making the YPCA broadcast
and these spin-off rallies in Philadelphia and New York into first-rate productions with wide popular appeal. It was at this time that a new horizon
for evangelism was opening up with the coming of television, and Percy
soon realized that the program he and Ruth had formed could readily be
adapted to this new medium. He saw the possibilities that television afforded for reaching another audience with the gospel, and he moved
quickly to convert his existing program to a television format.

# 15

## The Move to Television: Youth on the March

PERCY WENT ON THE ABC TELEVISION NETWORK ON SUNDAY EVENING AT 10:30, October 9, 1949, with the first broadcast of *Youth on the March* from the WFIL-TV studio at 46th and Market Streets, Philadelphia. The advertising card announcing the program proclaimed:

**ON TELEVISION!**
The Young People's Church of the Air Presents
**"Youth on the March"**
Pioneering Again on THE FIRST GOSPEL PROGRAM
Televised Coast-to-Coast.
Look and listen Every Sunday

In the fall of 1949, television was just taking off. The previous year had been the year that television began its explosive growth. At the beginning of that year seventeen television stations were on the air serving eight cities, and by the end of the year forty-eight stations were serving twenty-three cities.[1] By June 30, 1949, three months before *Youth on the March* started, seventy stations were on the air. In 1948 coaxial cables for network relays between cities became available in the Midwest, as it had been on the East Coast for two years, and regular network service began. Between 1948 and 1952 the number of television sets in use rose from a quarter-million to over seventeen million.[2]

As it was with radio, so with television, ABC was the number three network and usually had to take the third station licensed in the major cities for its affiliate. But ABC was Percy's obvious choice, for it was the only one of the big three networks willing to sell time to religious broadcasters; NBC and CBS continued their policies of giving sustaining time programming to each of the three major faiths. A fourth network—Dumont—operated from 1946 until 1955 and was hardly in a position not to do business with religious clients. (Percy did eventually move to Dumont in the fourth year of his program.) But he was delighted to begin broadcasting on the ABC network, which took his program into eleven major cities and served his purpose of taking the gospel to a wider audience. In the first year, *Youth on the March* was seen in four cities in the Northeast (Philadelphia, New York, Baltimore, Washington, D.C.), six in the Midwest (Chicago, Detroit, Grand Rapids, Columbus, Indianapolis, Minneapolis), and one on the West Coast (Los Angeles). The program was live on only five stations in the East and Midwest and shown on film (kinescope) in the other cities.

In the next year with ABC, Percy jumped to twenty-two stations, adding Lancaster, Atlanta, Ft. Worth, Rock Island, San Francisco, San Diego, and others. In the third year, dropping to eighteen stations, he could now claim that *Youth on the March* was "the first religious program to be aired coast-to-coast on the new $40,000,000 microwave relay. Simultaneously with the program's production in Philadelphia at 11 o'clock it was seen in Chicago at 10 o'clock, and on the West Coast at 8 o'clock."[3] And in the fourth year, switching to the Dumont network, the program was again viewed in eighteen cities.

During these four years, he continued to air the Sunday radio broadcast on hundreds of stations where television did not go, but replaced the program with the soundtrack of the telecast, in effect bringing to an end the eighteen-year career of the *Young People's Church of the Air* Sunday radio program. When he shifted to television, Percy was moving forward with a new program on a new medium, and he was not looking back.

Since the television industry was just getting off the ground, the production facilities at the WFIL studio were minimal. ABC provided technicians in the booth, but offered virtually no assistance on the studio floor beyond camera and microphone crew. Percy had to come up with his own production staff. To get the ball rolling, he called on a former quartet member, twenty-three-year-old Irwin "Shorty" Yeaworth. Shorty was both musically gifted and experienced on the technical end of broadcasting. He had put on his own broadcast in Philadelphia in 1943, *Good News,* at age seventeen. In that year too, he worked at Pinebrook, sang with The King's Singers, and went on Percy's eight-week West Coast tour. When Percy contacted him about producing the television program, Shorty jumped at the chance. (In a phone interview I had with him shortly before his untimely death in 2004, he quipped that he had started out his career in television as a "network producer.")[4] My father's keen eye for talent was vindicated once again as Shorty proved to be the man for the job. Working fifty hours a week, he wrote script, designed sets, arranged music, directed The King's Singers, and floor managed the entire show. He was paid $10 a week for his efforts (later raised to $15), but he said that he was learning so much on the job that *he* would have paid $100 to do what he was doing.

Shorty worked closely with Percy in what he described as the "best partnership." Every Monday morning, after the Sunday telecast, they would sit down together and brainstorm. Shorty proposed things that were technically feasible, and Percy would act on them. The suggestion was made that they take the show on the road to Detroit and Chicago (since ABC had a microwave loop from Pittsburgh to Detroit). Within a week, Percy had scheduled a two-week trip with a Saturday night rally at the Masonic Temple in Detroit (five thousand attending), followed by a Sunday public telecast (three thousand attending), and a Youth for Christ rally followed by a live telecast from Moody Church in Chicago the next Sunday, before an overflow audience. Shorty recalled that lights had to be installed in the Moody Church, and the whole operation was so disruptive that the board decided they would never again allow another live telecast in the church.[5]

Shorty was the invisible hand behind the whole production of the first one and a half years of the telecast.[6] His success with the program got the attention of other evangelists: Billy Graham asked him to do his *Hour of Decision* television broadcast, but Shorty turned down the offer because he "couldn't leave Percy."[7]

But he did leave Percy, and his leaving was unfortunate, not only because of the synergistic relationship the two men had together, but because Shorty was the most creative person in the visual media field that Percy would ever know. Shorty later started his own film production studio, Valley Forge Films, in Chester Springs, Pennsylvania, and produced more than four hundred films—some for Warner Brothers and Universal Pictures. The film that won him fame was the 1958 science-fiction cult classic *The Blob,* starring Steve McQueen.[8]

The parting with Percy occurred in December 1950, after a disagreement over whether Shorty's wife, Jean (who had been singing with the girls' trio), would now help Shorty in the booth as a go-between with the ABC producers. Shorty claimed that he needed her there and when Percy balked, he took offense and said, in effect, if you don't want her, then you don't want me; and when Percy refused to allow it, he quit. One wonders why Percy would let such a valuable person go over such a small matter. It may be simply that he lost his temper when Shorty bucked him, but I suspect it was more than that. My hunch is that after more than a year of producing the program, Shorty began to think of himself as the one in charge. And Percy was threatened whenever any of his staff attempted to take the reins of any of his enterprises. His instinctive reaction was to fire such persons and replace them with someone else who would take orders from the man at the top. This defensive posture of my father is evidenced in one of the contracts that he had his quartet members sign when they came on board;

it included this clause: "I will be loyal 100%. Willing in every respect and do my job thoroughly, having been told once so to do."

Percy turned to Al Black to take over The King's Singers and direct the music, and the show continued without noticeable effect. But I cannot help wondering how my father's work would have been different—perhaps stronger and more far-reaching—if he had been able to build it around talented individuals like Shorty Yeaworth. Shorty went on to work for Jack Wyrtzen and produced his television program, which came on the year after Percy's. Shorty told me this amusing (but revealing) anecdote: when Percy visited Jack in his television studio in New York City and saw all the expensive, state-of-the-art equipment Jack was using, he commented: "We just slop along, and the Lord blesses."

## THE PROGRAM

*Youth on the March* appealed to a wide spectrum of the viewing public. As Ben Armstrong notes in his 1979 book *The Electric Church:* "With secular variety shows making the TV screen the equivalent of the old vaudeville stage, there was a demand for programs that featured musical productions. Percy Crawford had just that type of program."[9] Indeed he did. We have seen that Ruth's musical cast was entirely in place and ready to go. The lineup for each telecast consisted of about fifty musicians drawn from the Philadelphia area and The King's College in Delaware, including the quartet, The King's Chorus (sixteen men), an orchestra of about twenty-five, a trumpet trio, a girls' trio, and the Crawford children. The format was a carryover from the radio program, with the addition of The King's College Trumpet Trio (replacing the brass quartet), and the four D's: Don, Dick, Dan, and Dean.

The trumpet trio, consisting of Chuck, Bill, and George Ohman, accompanied on the piano by sister Ruth Ohman, brought a distinctively contemporary sound to the program with their own jazzy arrangements of old and new gospel songs, such as "Sound the Battle Cry," "Love Lifted Me," "Power in the Blood," and "He Lives." The girls' trio, made up of Hilda Schmeiser, "Dink" Bullock, and Jean Yeaworth, added close harmony arrangements not unlike their popular secular counterparts. And the 4 D's singing in three-part harmony added a light, bouncy touch to the program, with songs such as "Give Me Oil in My Lamp," "On My Journey Home," and "Hide You in the Shadow of the Rock." We four boys, ages twelve, ten, eight, and five, had bright faces and clear voices that blended well. We memorized all our songs easily and performed them heartily. The children also added some levity to the broadcast: Dean delighted viewers with his antics and one-liners; and our cute "baby" sister, Donna Lee, who came on in 1951 at age two, amused everyone by pulling her brothers' hair and generally distracting us.

As it had been with the radio program, the predominant tone of the music—instrumental and vocal—was soft and sentimental, melodious and rich in harmony, clearly bearing the mark of my mother's brand of what music historian Don Wyrtzen calls the *romantic* style of gospel music prevalent at this time.[10] Ruth would organize the medleys and individual songs around a theme such as Christ's love, the cross, the name of Jesus, hands, garden, sea, harvest, yoke, and so on. There were occasionally dramatic presentations and elaborate props to go with these themes—a ship, a western scene, a Thanksgiving feast, or a family Christmas eve.

The success of Percy and Ruth's television program was recognized by another television evangelist who had ventured into this new terrain in 1950, but found it to be tough going. Billy Graham wrote this to my father in a letter dated November 1, 1951, while conducting his Greater Greensboro Crusade:

> I want to tell you how I rejoice in your thrilling television program. It is absolutely out of this world. I am afraid we have made a miserable flop thus far on our program. I had no idea that television demanded so much time, thought and energy. With our radio program and our evangelistic campaigns, I am afraid TV is going to be absolutely impossible for us. I am thinking seriously of going off altogether January 1st. The money is coming in quite well for its support . . . , but we do not have the time nor the know-how to put on the right type of a production. . . .
>
> If we do go off TV, I shall ask the people to stand behind you. . . . We must get religion on TV. It is definitely the greatest medium for reaching people today. God has given you the ability and know-how. His hand is on you and it thrills me every time I hear you preach the Gospel.[11]

As we have seen, the radio broadcast was successful because of the mix of the musical production and Percy's preaching. The telecast, in turn, was a success because both of these elements were enhanced by the camera. Armstrong remarks that "the visual dimension [of the program] made the attractive young musicians and speakers even more appealing and their testimony of the Christian life more compelling than could be achieved through radio alone."[12] A television columnist writing for the Allentown *Beacon* pointed to the "sincerity" and "unrehearsed warmth" conveyed by the singers, without the "stuffiness" of most religious presentations.[13]

What the writer was getting at, but did not fully grasp, was that the unaffected sincerity and fervor of the singers was an expression of their feeling of devotion and thankfulness to God. They were willing to put in a whole day's work for a few dollars, because they had committed their lives and their talents to him. Their singing and playing was pleasing and even entertaining, but it was also a form of testimony; it was from the heart and it touched the heart. One could hardly hear Hilda Schmeiser sing "Follow I Will Follow Thee," or Mel Peterkin, "In His Presence," or Jerry Harrison, "If You Know the Lord," or Bob Straton, "Rose of Sharon," without being moved.

We kids too contributed to this feeling of piety and devotion. One magazine article said of the 4 D's: "They sing praises to the Lord with grins on their faces and fervor in their hearts . . . their shining faces, telling of their joy in the Lord, preach as eloquently as their father's sermons."[14]

My mother has to be included among the "attractive young musicians" of whom Armstrong spoke. A young thirty-three, Ruth's graceful manner and appearance, whether singing or playing the piano or organ, was one of the distinctive visual attractions of the entire program. Quartet member Sam Seymour, who regularly sang duets with my mother, said of her: "We all thought she was beautiful, and she got more beautiful as she got older."

My father was physically attractive and comfortable in front of the television camera. As emcee of the program, he had a natural, spontaneous, and upbeat style that put the viewer at ease, but also kept the program moving at a quick pace. In his preaching, the message was the same, but he was now able to speak more directly to the individual viewer than on radio. He did this through expressive body language—his body swaying, eyebrows dancing, and mouth articulating, with that bony index finger pointing right into the camera. His short, crisp, seven-minute sermons (the same recycled ones he had been giving for twenty years) moved quickly to the invitation to the viewers, right there by their television sets, to give their hearts to Christ.

Of course, whether the program was successful or not had everything to do with whether it was reaching souls. And on this score the letters poured in from viewers whose lives had been transformed through the broadcast. A sampling of letters from viewers was read each week on the "Mailbag" segment of the show. In an article featuring the telecast, the *Sunday School Times* reported: "During the first fifteen weeks, more than 100,000 letters came in from all parts of the land and from all types of listeners. . . . After one program, during which an offer of a New Testament was made to all who, that night, would accept Christ as Saviour, more than 500 letters came in, each saying that the writer had found the One who is able to save to the uttermost."[15] The article went on to cite excerpts "from actual letters that have been taken from the files of 'Youth on the March'" (like the following):

> When I saw your telecast my heart was heavy because in the last three months I have lost just about everything in life. I was going to take my own life. When I heard your program I felt like crying out loud, so decided I would watch it again the next Sunday. . . . Sir, that night after the telecast I went to my room and prayed and this week I have felt as though I were a new person. God began to open things up for me.

Without asking explicitly for funds Percy made the viewing audience aware that unless they sent in their gifts, the program would go off the air. "Your letters are the life-blood of this work." We are broadcasting "in the hope that you will feel led to assist." Initially the cost of the television and radio broadcasts was not significantly more than radio had been at its highest—about $4,000–$5,000 per week.[16] Production costs were high, with one program—probably one of the public telecasts—costing $20,000.[17] In the second year, with twice as many television stations, he advertised that he needed $7,000 a week for the television network plus an additional $1,500 for the radio ministry.[18] When he switched to Dumont in the fourth year, he did so in order to realize a "real saving" in cost. That year he needed $7,800 a week for all radio and television time—making a total of $275,000 for the thirty-five weeks he was on Dumont. "It's an all-out, life-or-death appeal to keep Youth on the March on TV," he wrote to his thirty-five thousand magazine subscribers. "Will you help in this modern Home Missionary Work?"[19] They did help. Week after week, the contributions came in to sustain the broadcasts. As before, Percy did not overreach or incur significant debt, purchasing only as much television and radio time as his listeners were willing to support.[20]

## WORLD TOUR

At the end of his fourth year on national television, Percy began to think seriously about another missionary endeavor—taking his evangelistic team into the foreign fields. The YPCA broadcast had been heard around the world on shortwave radio during and after the war and had laid the ground for a world missionary tour. The time had come to carry the gospel to every nation. Percy was also riding a wave of increased missionary activity on the part of conservative evangelical mission boards following the war. Joel Carpenter notes this "surge" in growth and points out that "by 1952 fully half of the 18,500 North American Protestant missionaries were sent by evangelical agencies."[21]

In announcing the tour in his magazine, *Christian Newsette,* Percy gave two reasons for going—first, that he had had some difficulty securing a "satisfactory television spot for this fall," and, second, that he was "yielding to the invitations of Army chaplains and missionaries around the world." He hastened to add that he "has not abandoned his radio and television work. He will still maintain some television broadcasts and [will] continue his daily Pinebrook Praises program over six east-coast stations," and he would broadcast "tape recordings from the foreign fields" on these and other stations. Finally he revealed his high hopes that the trip would "become the highlight of his already fruitful evangelistic ministry."[22]

The eighteen-week tour overseas (November 1953–April 1954) would take the team first to the Far East (ten weeks), the Holy Land and Mediterranean countries (three weeks), and finally through Western Europe to the British Isles (four weeks). The evangelistic party consisted of Percy and Ruth, and the three members of the quartet: Bob Straton, Sam Seymour, and Steve Musto—all King's students at the time—who had been together for a couple of years and made their reputation singing on the television program.

Percy and the team began their trip with a ten-day minitour across the United States, with stops for meetings in Pittsburgh, St. Louis, and Denver, before coming into California, where they held their last meeting stateside for "thousands of servicemen" at Camp Stoneman near San Francisco.[23] This meeting set the stage for the entire tour, a great part of which would be conducted at military bases and outposts around the world, particularly in Korea where an armistice had just been signed with communist China after three years of fighting.

As they were setting out, my mother had the best one-liner; when Sam Seymour admitted he had forgotten to pack his Bible, she commented wryly: "You're going on this tour to save the world, and you forgot your Bible?"

The first stop was Honolulu, Hawaii, where Youth for Christ director David Hansen had arranged three days of meetings. In the first letter he wrote to us on the third day overseas, Percy left no doubt about his priorities for the tour: "Having fine trip so far. Had 22 decisions for Christ the other night—Hawaiians."[24] Ruth was also enjoying the first leg of the trip: "It's all Arthur Godfrey says it is: Hawaiian singers and guitars—the palm trees and warm tropical air and the moonlight shining on the waves at Waikiki Beach really get into your blood."[25]

The long flight to New Zealand required two stops for refueling at Canton Island and Nandi (Fiji Islands), and at each place Percy got right to work and led one of the "native boys" to make a decision. He was acting on his firm belief that the simple gospel message he preached could be understood and received by anyone regardless of their cultural differences; and nothing that would happen on this tour would cause him to change his mind about this.[26]

In another letter, Percy described the flights to New Zealand and Australia: "On all the flights—in each plane we sang for all the people & I gave a little message"[27]—apparently in-flight rules were more relaxed in those days. There was more good weather for a week of services in these countries down under. In Auckland, they encountered a choral group made up of forty-four Maori-Christian people who sang and testified for the taped broadcast that Percy sent home.

Then things got a little tougher as the team headed north on a twenty-hour, 4,500-mile nonstop flight to Manila, Philippines. Hosted there by Ellsworth Culver of Orient Crusades, they conducted three days of meetings and had "over 200 decisions for Christ."[28]

Next was Taipeh, Formosa, meeting up with former Pinebrook speaker James Graham for two meetings. Speaking to the Chinese through an interpreter (which the team referred to as an "interrupter"), Percy continued to be pleased with the results: "We had an opportunity to speak to Chiang Kai Shek's hand-picked officers and 1700 of his soldiers. Scores of them responded to the invitation, and the General and his officers were thrilled at the presentation of the Gospel."[29] Wanting to avail himself of every opportunity to carry the gospel to every nation, Percy jumped at the chance to minister to the "head-hunting" Aborigine tribes and asked Graham to take the team up into their villages in the mountains where (as he wrote to us) "I gave them the gospel and the boys sang for them."[30]

In Tokyo, hosted by Glenn Wagner of Pocket Testament League, they conducted two big rallies with 350 decisions[31] and Sunday services at GI chapels. Percy wrote: "Truly Japan is wide open and needs more missionaries."[32] Ruth reported enjoying the Wagners' home where they had the luxuries of an electric blanket and a hot shower each day. After arriving at the next stop (Korea), she wrote: "You don't know how wonderful it is to be able to take a hot bath every day, or a shower, when you get away from home, and don't have the accommodations lots of places. I don't expect to get a hot bath for three weeks in Korea. . . . The poor boys stayed at a mission in Japan and haven't had a bath for over a week now. . . . So they'll be good and dirty in a month's time."[33]

As the team headed into Korea for "three solid weeks," Percy geared up for what he clearly expected would be the high point of the tour. He asked his supporters back home to pray that God would give them "health and strength, as we have a very heavy schedule and we are anticipating His rich blessing among the GI's as well as the Korean People."[34]

In Pusan, Percy and the team were based for a week at the Koryo Presbyterian Mission and Seminary, founded by the Orthodox Presbyterian Church. On the first full day there, December 24, with Pocket Testament League's Don Robertson as their guide, they held meetings all day—at schools and hospitals (singing in each ward) and at two GI chapels on the eve of Christmas. Robertson would be with them for the entire three weeks and would write the final report that appeared as "Operation Korea" in *Christian Newsette*. Christmas day started with services for hundreds of wounded Korean soldiers lying in hospital wards, two meetings at the local prison for 100 women and 1,700 men (Ruth wrote: "Practically all of them responded"),[35] a turkey dinner at the officers' mess hall, and a "Baptist Hour" service for 600 Koreans and soldiers.[36]

There were six services in all in Pusan for American troops—the largest at the Thirty-fourth Infantry regiment, where 450 soldiers packed the chapel, and 40 accepted Christ. Five hundred soldiers filled a theater on the nearby island of Koje and (Robertson reported): "75 moved out boldly as the invitation to accept Christ was given." In Taigu, Percy spoke to 5,000 Koreans in four meetings and to 1,200 prisoners at the local jail. In the same city, 65 airmen came forward at two Air Strip chapels. And there, too, Percy was able to do a live broadcast over radio station KILROY of the Armed Forces Korean Network to servicemen over the entire sector.

A long train trip brought the party to Seoul and near the front lines, where Vic Springer, a Pocket Testament League worker on loan from TEAM Mission and brother of former quartet member, Joe Springer, had set up "an intense itinerary." In Seoul, the team was stationed at the compound of the Presbyterian Church in the U.S.A. Their party of seven had the use of a sound truck (courtesy of Pocket Testament League) that took them "over bumpy, dusty, and frozen roads from the capital right up to the front." On the first day out of Seoul, the party moved up to an outpost, where (as Robertson told it) "the Crawfords and boys sang and preached from the stage of an open theater. Dr. Crawford, coatless and cold, urged the men to face the reality of death and judgment, and to place their trust in Christ who took their judgment." Later that day, as they were driving back to Seoul, they made an impromptu stop at the First Marine Division Headquarters, where Percy was given permission to hold a service in the mess hall after a movie. "What an atmosphere for a Gospel meeting. Smoking, oaths, and complaints filled the air as the movie ended and Percy stepped forward. . . . In a matter of minutes the whole atmosphere changed. Seventy of these hard fighting marines took PTL Gospels from Percy and promised him to read it and trust Christ for salvation."

Later in the week, the head Protestant chaplain of the Second Division invited the team back to the front lines to conduct services for his men. Again, Robertson captured the mood:

> I wish you could have seen these young, rugged, hardened soldiers crowd into a mess hall, Chapel dugout, and a dugout made of sandbags, to hear the program. With guns in hand, they listened and grasped every word, they applauded as the boys sang, and they responded to the invitation. . . . A rough wooden mess hall table was the pulpit, hard old benches were the pews, and there were no curtains on the clear glass windows that faced north to Korea.

On the same day, the team was able to view through a telescope "Communist front-line guards" at their positions. Returning to Seoul late, the weary team held an evening service for seventeen hundred Koreans at the beautiful Yongnok Presbyterian Church; and the next day, they visited the hospital ship *Repose,* anchored in the port of Inchon, ministering to the wounded and over one hundred sailors, who packed the mess hall.

There was a sense of adventure and physical danger in all of this—and my father loved it. He loved being out there, near the front lines, with the fighting troops; and he thrived on these opportunities to be a real soldier of the cross and to offer these men what they needed more than anything in their perilous circumstances—a chance for eternal life.

Operation Korea had been exhausting and exhilarating. My mother reported the results in a letter to her sister: "We spoke to 10,000 Koreans—with several thousand decisions, and 3800 GI's—450 professed Christ as Saviour."[37] I spoke recently with Dr. Sam Moffett, who spent twenty-six years in Korea as a Presbyterian missionary and teacher, and asked him about the significance of winning several thousand Korean converts. "That was not unusual," he said, for the Korean people were "open to American evangelism." And they were not simply trying to assimilate Western culture and values, but were doing it as Koreans. When I asked him if these mass conversions would have had a real impact on the Christian missionary endeavors there, he responded unhesitatingly that they would have strengthened the churches and their outreach.[38]

When the team returned to Tokyo for a few days of rest and relaxation (they were all nursing colds), Percy expressed his gratitude for their sacrifice and endurance by opening his wallet and putting them up in a first-class hotel. The gesture was greatly appreciated by Ruth and the uncomplaining boys.

The tour would last twelve more weeks and take them to twenty more countries in the Middle East, Asia Minor, and Europe. It ended in London, where the team linked up with Billy Graham's London crusade at Harringay arena, and Billy warmly invited Percy to give a prayer and the boys sang (with Cliff Barrows and Beverly Shea). After Korea, the tapes kept coming back for the broadcast, but the letters were sparse and tended to include less news about the tour and more instructions about what everyone should do to get ready for their return.

Percy returned from this world tour with a new fervor for missions and a strong desire to do something for the Korean people. He had said in an interview, as he was leaving that country: "Korea is in a miserable condition. It is sad, sick, and suffering. It needs the power of Christ and His resurrection."[39] But the way he hoped to remedy this sad situation was not by backing any of the existing missions he had visited, but by starting his own mission and staffing it with King's graduates. And so he conceived of The King's Korean Mission. The project signaled a slight, but important, shift in my father's thinking (and theology) about the social gospel. He had gone into Korea believing steadfastly that the only thing that mattered for the people of this country was the salvation of their souls and having "a hope beyond the grave." But he came away with a burden to do something that would raise their hopes for a better life this side of the grave. Later, in a letter of appeal for funds to support The King's Korean Mission, he wrote: "During my world tour, some years back, the land of Korea made a deep impression on my heart, even a deeper impression than any other country in the world. The Lord laid upon my heart the spiritual needs of the people of Korea, and He has given me a vision to help meet these needs through orphanages, education, and medicine."[40]

Percy went to great lengths to get The King's Mission established, but unfortunately he died before he could bring the plan to fruition. He came closest to achieving his goal in 1956 when he worked out an arrangement with The Evangelical Alliance Mission (TEAM) whereby a King's graduate, Dick Paul, and his wife and children would go to Korea "as missionaries under TEAM . . . [and] be assigned to the project you [Percy] have in mind for them." In the meantime, Percy was setting up his own mission board—The King's Colony Foreign Missionary Fellowship—which would take over sponsorship of the Pauls as soon as it became functional.[41] Unfortunately, the plan never materialized. In a letter to a contributor who inquired about The King's Mission a year and a half later, Percy responded: "We have tried to get two of our college students into Korea but without success. There is some underlying force preventing us."[42] In the last year of his life, my father did finally send a King's alumnus, Dr. Peter Pak, and his family to Korea. Pak was eminently qualified, having received his PhD in agricultural economics from the University of Illinois. He returned to his homeland to begin work on the mission, but never received sufficient funding to accomplish anything. (In his letter of appeal, Percy set a goal of only $200 a month to support Pak and his family.) When my father died, Dr. Pak was forced to abandon the project.

*

After Percy returned from the world tour (April 1954), he had to make some critical decisions about how to restart his nationwide ministry and, specifically, what to do about television for the coming season (1954–55). It was a difficult situation: having advanced to television and done it successfully, he wanted to maintain his image as a national television broadcaster. On the other hand, he needed to continue to reach the loyal supporters in smaller cities and rural areas that he had cultivated on the Mutual network. In 1951 and 1952 he had put *Youth on the March* on Mutual's powerful New York WOR radio station that covered a seventeen-state area. This was the sort of wide coverage he wanted most.

Then, too, television was expensive. As his weekly radio and television bill crept toward $10,000, he balked. There were limits to how much he could expect his constituency to give, since virtually all of his contributions were in small amounts of $1, $2, $5, and $10. (It took a lot of these gifts to make $350,000.) He thought he could get more for his money from radio, where the rates (and revenues) had dropped markedly because of competition with television. As he said later in one of his newsletters: "Our objective in the YPCA has been to reach the most people with the least."[43]

Further, the television networks and stations were making the same sort of arbitrary rulings about religious programming that the radio networks and stations had done in their heyday. For instance, in the 1952–53 season, one of Dumont's choicest stations, WGN-TV in Chicago had put *Youth on the March* off the air after only three months. Percy wrote in his magazine: "[The station] received thousands of complaints and people wrote the FCC complaining"—to no avail. But there was an upside: "As a result of losing WGN-TV—for the same money—time was purchased on about 68 [radio] stations" for the audio part of the telecast.[44] No doubt Percy would have preferred to be on live television in Chicago, but he was learning the hard way that radio was more reliable and more cost effective. If radio could efficiently serve his goal of getting the gospel out to unsaved and unchurched souls, then he would let national television go.

In the end, he found a way to keep both television and radio going. In the fall of 1954, he signed a contract with the ABC network to put *Youth on the March* on two hundred radio stations, beginning October 4. And in the following spring (May 1, 1955), he started a live television program locally on WDEL, channel 12, in Wilmington (which adequately covered Philadelphia) and aired the soundtrack of the telecast on the national radio hookup.[45] The scaled-down cast for the new television program featured Ruth and the quartet (which then consisted of the veteran trio that had accompanied Ruth and Percy on the world tour—now joined by baritone Don Crawford), as well as the 4 D's, with Don doing double duty, and Donna Lee, age five, who became a television celebrity in her own right in this series.

After only one year of this arrangement, Percy decided to take on more. It seems he could not resist the lure of a full-production television show, and so in the 1956–57 season he signed on with ABC-TV in New York, channel 7, for a 1:00 p.m. Sunday program. Once again Ruth let out all the stops and brought together her entire musical ensemble, including a full orchestra, The King's Singers, trumpet trio, girls' trio, and the five D's with Donna Lee doing regular solos. The program ran for twenty-six weeks and reached the same high standard of performance as the original national program.

Amazingly, Percy and Ruth did the New York program without interrupting the channel 12 (Wilmington-Philadelphia) program, which was on at 10:00 p.m. on the same day. This meant that they were producing two live television broadcasts in one day—the second one a more modest version of the first, with Ruth, the quartet, the five D's, and organist Clayton Erb repeating most of the musical numbers done on the earlier show. The double performance meant some hard traveling for us kids, from Briarcliff Manor, New York (where we lived at the time), to New York City, to Wilmington, and back to Briarcliff on the same day. And school the next morning. We children continued to take in stride the heavy demands placed on us by our active service to the Lord.

The live New York telecast on ABC lasted only one season. However Percy did put "films" of the channel 12 program on the New York station in other years. A clear pattern emerged: the telecast was being shown in Philadelphia and New York City, but in the rest of the country *Youth on the March* was going out almost entirely on radio.[46] The channel 12 program continued until March 1958 when Percy finally canceled it in anticipation of putting *Youth on the March* on his own television station.[47]

## HEALTH

It was in the mid-1950s that my father was forced to think about his health and about his own mortality. His first heart attack occurred in the summer of 1955 at Pinebrook at age fifty-two and gave everyone a good scare. The sequence of events that occurred after that first episode set a pattern that would be repeated five more times over the next five years before he suffered his final fatal attack. He lost consciousness and was rushed to the hospital. As soon as he was revived, he sent back word to everyone that he was okay and that they should carry on with the scheduled events. To be sure, within a day or two he was back on his feet and resuming his regular activities. As it happened, the great flood that occurred that summer at Pinebrook gave Percy the occasion to swing back into action. On the second morning after the flood, he conducted live interviews on the *Pinebrook Praises* broadcast with the quartet (whose house with all their belongings in it had been swept away by the flood waters), Ruth, us kids, and some survivors from the stricken Camp Davis across the creek whose lives had been spared because they attended the evening service at Pinebrook. When my mother finished her report, she unexpectedly broke into tears, thanking the audience for their prayers for "my husband" after his recent heart attack. Percy paused briefly to acknowledge his wife's loving gesture and then quickly returned to the more urgent business at hand.

My father had always known that he had a weak heart because of the rheumatic fever he had as a boy. So these reckonings with his heart were not surprising. However he very deliberately tried to hide them from the public. As one of the nation's foremost youth evangelists, Percy always tried to project a youthful image and consequently wanted to avoid giving the impression that he was sick or aging.

I remember vividly another of my father's heart attacks that happened after the evening meal at Pinebrook. I was about fifteen and was playing an intense set of tennis with my older brother Dick, but I was no match for him that day. As Percy watched, he became more and more frustrated by my inability to play at Dick's level and finally walked onto the court and took my racket from me. I had not seen him play tennis in years. It took only a few of his hard, driving forehand shots before his lights went out, and the onlookers were carrying him over to his car and sliding him into the backseat. Leaning through the open window of the back door, I helped position his limp body so that both doors would close. As before, he instructed us from the hospital to carry on with the Saturday night schedule, but no one was in a mood for stunt night and we had a fervent prayer meet-

ing in the tabernacle instead. The Lord answered our prayers, and Percy
was back on the job in a couple of days, ready to greet the next week's incoming guests.

After 1955 Percy did cut back on his traveling some. He reduced his
schedule of meetings to three or four nights a week. And he only took one
more West Coast trip (in 1956), traveling by plane. Also he and Ruth started
taking more vacation time—driving twice a year to their favorite spots in
Miami, Fort Lauderdale, and Key Biscayne, Florida. But for the other
forty-nine weeks of the year, Percy kept pushing. He realized that his body
was giving out, and he was determined to accomplish as much as he could
for the Lord in the time that remained.


## YOUTHARAMA

In the spring of 1956, my father was swinging into what was to be the most
active period of his life. He had just put into effect a major rebuilding project at Pinebrook, after the 1955 flood; he was moving his family from
Philadelphia to the new campus of The King's College in Briarcliff Manor,
New York, so that he could devote more time to being president there; and
(as we have seen) he and Ruth were preparing to take *Youth on the March*
on ABC-TV in New York in the fall. But, as if this was not enough, Percy
was also planning a new evangelistic effort for Philadelphia. He wanted to
devise some new and different form of evangelism that would attract young
people. He imagined a type of program that would be large scale, but also
fun and entertaining. As in the past, music would be the main attraction,
and so he discussed the idea with Chuck Pugh, a gifted musician who had
worked with Percy and Ruth as a teenager at Pinebrook twelve years earlier. Pugh was a trombonist who had studied at Julliard and was at that time
Minister of Music at Grace Chapel in nearby Havertown, Pennsylvania.
When Percy suggested to him that he take on the challenge of producing
such a Saturday night program, Pugh was wary, recalling that the first time
he had worked for my father at Pinebrook, he had gotten into a nasty quar-
rel with him and Percy had sent him packing. Although he was invited back
to the camp later that summer, he still had a bad feeling about it because he
thought that he never should have been forced to leave. But when Percy
said to him: "You're the one I want," Pugh yielded and gladly accepted the
invitation to become production director of the new spectacular show that
Percy called Youtharama.

Youtharama was to be held the first and third Saturday of each month in
Philadelphia's Town Hall, which seated about two thousand. All three

Philadelphia papers published the news release announcing that "Philadelphia area teenagers are expected to jam Town Hall auditorium" for the first Saturday night program on October 6, 1956. Percy did not mention himself or Ruth in the advertisement, wanting to make the program sound as if it was semi-independent of the YPCA, which it was not. The announcement went on to say that Youtharama had been "in the planning stages for two years with businessmen and youth leaders." "Highlighting the affair will be the appearance of famed Boston disc jockey John DeBrine." Also scheduled for the first night were the "Starlighters"—a forty-voice chorale, a nineteen-piece string ensemble, a brass ensemble, quartet, and "TV personality Steve Musto." Featured on the second show (October 20) would be "Walter Haman, former Harry S. Truman body guard and ace pistol shot [who would] demonstrate pistol use and talk to the teenagers."

Pugh's musical productions for orchestra and chorus over a four-year period were impressive in their scale and richness. His arrangements of gospel hymns old and new were upbeat and expansive—making heavy use of brass and tympani. This style was conducive to the patriotic themes that were often introduced. Also prominent were medleys of Negro spirituals, which always included several numbers by the superb African American baritone soloist Jimmy McDonald, a regular on the show. Pugh added a new dimension to the musical side of Percy's ministry; although the repertoire of gospel songs was the same, it sounded different. Ruth's warm, smooth, legato sound was transposed into one that was more up-tempo and marcato, louder and fuller. Ruth of course participated in Youtharama, but primarily as accompanist for the quartet. The 4 D's were not on the program. Percy wanted this to be a more modern format, distinct from the family-oriented television program. And Pugh was able to do something different and original with Youtharama because Percy let him run with it. He wrote to me: "I have always been able to accomplish more if given the freedom to do so. In Youtharama, your father gave me that freedom—to design a program, to recruit some 200 volunteers, to write the music and to direct and produce programs."[48]

Percy used guest speakers at Youtharama, selecting from his stable of Pinebrook speakers the ones he thought would appeal most to youth, including, in addition to DeBrine and Haman, Don Lonie, Jim Vaus, Alan Forbes, Anton Marco, Gil Dodds, Alex Dunlap, Larry McGuill, and musical artists Beverly Shea and Neil and Pat Macauley. College athletes, such as Dave Burnham, little All American football player from Wheaton College, and other celebrities gave their testimonies. And the usual procedure was for Percy, with Ruth and the quartet, to step in after the speaker's "talk to teeners" and close the service with an invitation.

In addition to the showy musical productions, guest speakers, and demonstrations, the Youtharama program included an entertaining skit in which my father had a chance to ham it up. In one, "The Lighthouse Keeper's Daughter," Percy gets stabbed. In another, "The $64,000,000 Question," the host of the quiz program, Mal Harch, introduces contestant Percival P. Pennypincher Crawford, whose category is Historic Personalities. Prunella escorts him into the booth, and the first question he is asked, worth $1.28, is: "What was the first name your mother gave you when you were born?" After getting out his glasses and looking in his wallet, Percy answers correctly. But then he elects not to continue with the $2.56 question, but to take his winnings and run.

*Mal:*　What, you don't mean you're done already?
*Percy:*　Yes, it's been a pretty strenuous evening. My brain can't stand the pain. I think I'll go home now.
*Mal:*　But you can't stop now . . . you've just begun.
*Percy:*　The rules say I can quit anytime at all.
　　　　(Escorted Off)

Like all good comedy, there was a kernel of truth in this.

Financially, Youtharama was a losing proposition. It never got the financial backing from the "Christian businessmen" that Percy so often spoke of. A 1957 financial statement of income and expenses showed that the enterprise had broken even the first year, but then began to lose ground; midway through the second season there were $3,000 in unpaid bills. Executive director Bill Drury remembers that the debt reached $7,000. At one point, he recalled, the manager of Town Hall refused to open the doors for the evening's show until three weeks of back rent was paid. Drury had to scramble to raise some quick cash.[49] He also claimed that he went for "10 solid weeks" without getting his salary. The reason Percy did not pay off these relatively small amounts of money with YPCA funds was that he needed all of YPCA's income and cash reserves to finance the Philadelphia FM radio and television stations that he was in the process of obtaining.[50] In addition, he probably wanted Drury and the Youtharama board of directors to do more to keep the operation running on its own steam.

In any case, he did keep Youtharama going because it was proving to be a successful experiment. Young people and church delegations were coming out in large numbers; attendance ranged from one thousand to two thousand each night. And souls were being saved. In a 1958 letter to DeBrine, Percy reported exuberantly that at the last meeting at which Don Lonie spoke, 1,600 attended, "with 57 for salvation." Moreover Percy thought that Youtharama was another first. He wrote in a newsletter: "Youtharama is resetting the pattern all over the nation. It's a model for Youth meetings."[51] Percy was willing to invest his precious time and resources into Youtharama because it served his purpose of putting on a high-profile, pacesetting evangelistic rally in his home territory of Philadelphia.


## Family

I have described the ways in which Percy and Ruth brought us five children into their evangelistic ministry, but not the effect this had on our family life. What was it like to be reared in this fundamentalist home? What were Percy's aims and hopes for his children, and how did he foster the sort of atmosphere at home that would enable him (and us) to realize those goals?

Our parents did not try to insulate us from the surrounding secular world; we were encouraged to participate in it fully—except when it came into conflict with our Christian witness. We were supposed to be "*in* the world, but not *of* it." Accordingly, Percy's plan for our primary and secondary education was that we should attend secular (not religious) schools, and since he wanted us to have the best education—something that his own parents had denied him—he sent us four boys to a reputable private boys school, Germantown Academy, to obtain it. Donna Lee was only six when our family moved from Philadelphia to Briarcliff Manor, New York, but she too was sent to a private girls' school for part of her first year in school. Putting five children in private schools was costly then, as it is now—even with the discount for clergy that Percy always claimed—but he never stinted when it came to paying for good schooling.

He expected us to do well in our studies and in sports and pushed us hard to be achievers. Fortunately it came easily for me and my older brothers, Don and Dick. We got good grades, were elected officers of our class, and received prizes for being all-around Germantown Academy boys. I began to distinguish myself as the student in the family, bringing home mostly A's on my report card. Dean, on the other hand, who suffered from an (undiagnosed) learning disability, was not doing well and was constantly in danger of being held back a grade. Percy tried to remedy the situation by transferring Dean to a Christian day school in the fifth grade. But the little boy who was such a big hit singing solos and clowning on television did not live up to Percy's high expectations in school, and for this he had to pay the heavy price of his father's disapproval and censure.

Percy delighted in all four of his sons being athletic and playing team sports in school. He wrote under our picture in the 1951 calendar: "They are real American boys, full of life and fun. Three of them are on the school

football team, and seek to bear a testimony for their Saviour whether at play
or at work." (The three of us who were playing football were thirteen, eleven,
and nine at the time.) Percy fully endorsed the competitive structures that
were built into the American school system and fostered these tendencies in
us. There was plenty of sibling rivalry in our family—especially between my
older brothers, who did their share of fighting in their teen years and who
mercilessly picked on their younger brothers. Percy was thrilled over Don's
and Dick's success as all-star basketball players in high school and college.[52]
Our successes in sports and other school activities were important to him
because they validated the argument he made over and over again in his sermons that the young people who followed Christ were vigorous, "red-
blooded" American types and not social dropouts or misfits.

Along with these traditional American values, our parents fostered in us
the essential Christian values of living the separated life and serving the
Lord. This aspect of our lives was crucial to Percy's understanding of conversion and its transformative effects. If we were truly born again, we had
to show it in our daily living. For the most part, we children lived this different life and did so cheerfully. What this came down to in practical terms
was that we did not go to movies or attend school dances. But in all other
respects, we were fully integrated into the school program and had close
friends. We did not try to win our classmates to Christ, but we did seek to
make our lives a testimony to our avowed Christian beliefs.

In our family, serving the Lord meant that we had to make far greater
sacrifices than other Christians. We children were called upon to participate in hundreds of services and broadcasts, perform on cue before audiences large and small, and spend endless hours in the car going to and from
meetings. We forfeited good sleep, good health, and a normal school day
with our peers at Percy's bidding. In one of his newsletters, he posed this
question: "How do you account for the fact the Crawford children all love
the Lord?" and then tried to explain what he and Ruth had done to bring
this about. He pointed out that "they have seen Christ is a reality to us. They
know that we have denied ourselves in serving Him." His idea was that
when we saw the extent of his and my mother's personal sacrifice, we
would naturally want to deny ourselves to the same degree. It is true that
we all sensed the importance and urgency of our parents' mission. Although
I did not see it this way at the time, I now realize that we were fortunate to
have had parents who devoted their entire lives, unselfishly, to bringing
others to a new life. But we were children then, and we cooperated in their
great work mainly because they expected us to.

One of the quartet members from the 1950s, Sam Seymour, told me recently that after seeing firsthand what Percy and Ruth put us kids through

by making us part of his evangelistic work, he and his wife vowed that they would never do that to their children. I can recall driving home from meetings with the quartet, sleeping on Sam's shoulder or on the floor of the backseat under his feet. But I do not fault my parents for putting us before the public in the way they did. Though we were not in a position to decide for ourselves, we embraced what we were doing and enjoyed the perks and privileges that came with being minor celebrities. As for the long hours spent traveling, we were learning the important lesson of what it means to live a life of service.

Another related criticism that has been made of my parents is that their rigorous schedule meant that they had to forgo any meaningful family life. It is undeniable that they were away from home four or five evenings each week and sometimes for weeks and months at a time. But on many days and evenings we did have a "normal" family life. In the 1940s, Percy would sometimes join us as we boys sat around the radio listening to our favorite programs—among them *The Lone Ranger, The Shadow, Amos 'n Andy,* and *Jack Benny.* By 1949 we had a television set and, with all of us gathered in the living room, watched such shows as *Red Skelton, The Milton Berle Show,* Ed Sullivan's *Toast of the Town,* and *Fireside Theater* (as long as they did not conflict with our own television program). Percy did not put any restrictions on what we could watch, even allowing us to view the old Hollywood movies that came on. (Later on, when we were living in New York, Percy used to find it relaxing to watch his favorite program on television— Monday night boxing from Madison Square Garden.)[53] And there were regular rituals in our family: on Saturday mornings after the broadcast, Percy would cook pancakes on the griddle for all of us and whichever quartet members were there. On Sunday afternoons we had a home-cooked family dinner with Percy at the head of the table and Ruth at the other end. And there were seasonal outings such as going to nearby Willow Grove amusement park for an evening of rides and fun.

We had a succession of babysitters and caretakers to look after us when my parents were away, but often we were left alone with no one to cook the evening meal. And when we complained, our father had no sympathy for us—reminding us that there were cases of canned fruit and other foodstuffs in the pantry in the basement. (How do you make a meal out of canned peaches and tomatoes?) Luckily, during the 1950s, there was another possibility for a decent dinner. Percy owned a diner that was a couple of miles from our house, so we could ride our bikes there for a free meal. We learned how to fend for ourselves in our parents' absence.

My favorite caregiver by far was my grandmother, Ruth's mother, Nancy Duvall, who stayed with us most often. It was common in that era for grandparents to live with their children and to help in rearing grandchildren. In fact, it is probably fair to say that she raised us. I adored my grandmother, "Nan," who cooked for me, read me bedtime stories, and protected me from my older brothers.

My least favorite caretaker was Aunt Margaret (not a real aunt), the short stocky Pinebrook night watchwoman who took care of us only once, when Percy and Ruth went on their five-month evangelistic world tour. Aunt Margaret was selected for her toughness, with the idea that she could handle the older boys. Don had just turned sixteen that year and had a driver's license and a car; fourteen-year-old Dick had a steady girlfriend; and the two boys liked spending their weekends doing what "fun-loving, red-blooded" American boys do on weekends. Alas, poor Aunt Margaret proved to be no match for them as the boys ran right over her when she tried to enforce weekend rules. I was glad when Aunt Margaret did finally leave when she hurt her back in a tussle with Dick, and Nan came to take her place.

Speaking from my experience, I feel that there was enough love in our household—coming from my parents and from Nan—for me to be contented with my lot as a child. My mother's love was expressed in a warm, affectionate, caring way. She worried over her children and tried to do as much mothering and nurturing as time and work would permit. In looking through her datebooks, I found in one of them a surprising entry in which she acknowledges committing an offense that I did not think she was capable of—missing a meeting. On October 30, 1953—my twelfth birthday—she wrote: "St. Albans, N.Y. I didn't go—stayed home with Dan on his birthday."

Percy did not express affection easily, but his love for us came through in other ways—in generous acts of giving; in being supportive of our various interests, hobbies, and activities; and generally in taking delight in us and in our being his children. These qualities were perhaps most evident on Christmas mornings when we kids would file into the living room where each of us would have his or her own individual pile of presents stretching halfway across the room.

Percy would on occasion take one of us with him to his office on Chestnut Street above the Pinebrook Book Store. We would ride into the city with him on the train and then spend a fun day roaming the premises and the store and sometimes doing small jobs. When I went with him, an added bonus for me was stopping at Gimbels Department Store on the way back to the train station to shop for stamps for my stamp collection. I remember one day we were running late, but he waited patiently for me as I carefully picked out the stamps I wanted to buy. It was one happy little boy running alongside his dad (out in the gutter of the street in order to get around the throng of pedestrians) to catch our train. His dad did not seem concerned about his heart condition or begrudge his son the time he had spent with him. It was an act of pure kindness.

Percy's tender side can also be seen in the following excerpts from some of the letters that he sent back to us from abroad during his world tour; the letters were usually dashed off in a hotel room or on a plane en route to his next destination:

Dear Boys and Baby:

Merry Christmas to you all. Don your Christmas present in cash you'll get on my return. Dick we feel good that you & Don are there and handling things and helping the younger ones & baby have a nice Christmas. We'll be thinking of you all! We'll miss you five more than anything. I hope Don is at the head of the table & baby [Donna Lee] at the other end.

Enclosed are stamps for Dan. If any of the rest want stamps say so & I'll get more. (December 16, 1953, Taipei, Taiwan)

Dear Boys and Babe:

Greetings to you all!

Don—congratulations on your mark in Geometry—Great—I knew you'd get it. Your other grades good too!

Dick—you pulled all your grades up—fine—I'm delighted—you can even do better.

Dan—it goes without saying you couldn't have done any better—swell boy!!

Dean—your marks were much better—splendid!

Baby—you are fine & perfect without even going to school. But soon you'll be going. Mama & I bought you a swell present. (March 14, 1954, Paris)

Love to the four finest boys on earth & the best baby of all.

Dad (January 27, 1954, Singapore)

*

My father had very definite ideas about the direction we children should be going in and the way in which we should serve the Lord. In a 1944 newsletter (under a family photo of Percy, Ruth, and three boys), he wrote: "We want the three of them to be good soldiers of Jesus Christ. I'll be disappointed if they become Presidents of Banks or even President of the U.S. I want them to be soul winners and do the will of God."[54] He was grooming all of us to step into some part of his work. He pegged Don and Dick as the ones most likely to be preachers and to take over the evangelistic ministry on radio and television and at Pinebrook. Since I was recognized as academically inclined, Percy hoped that I might someday step into the presidency of The King's College. He even had a place for our little sister. In the 1951 calendar (when she was one, going on two), after describing the four boys and their singing on television, he added: "Isn't it wonderful that the Lord has provided a baby sister to some day be their pianist and soloist."

Don started preaching on the broadcasts (to a national audience) when he was still a junior in high school—and Percy proudly reported the results in his magazine for youth:

> When my 15 year old son, Don, gave the invitation on television and on the radio, a drunken father, for whom many had been praying for years broke down and by the television set, gave his heart to Christ. It was cause of great rejoicing in the family and through his tears of repentance, he came to the Son of God. Four hours later that man was killed!
>
> At the close of my son's message, many teen agers as well as others gave their heart to Christ and wrote to tell us about it.[55]

A few years later, in a newsletter, he wrote: "Both Don and Dick have been pinch-hitting for me on the radio and TV. [Eighteen-year-old] Dick was quite thrilled in preaching to 500 people the other night and 8 young people gave their hearts to Christ."[56]

By and large, as we boys were coming of age, we were marching in step with the grand plan. Don, Dick, and I all chose to attend King's. Percy had just moved the college to the Briarcliff Manor campus, and the prospect of going there was appealing to each of us. Dick had some misgivings about turning down the basketball scholarships he was offered at twelve colleges and universities, some at schools with highly competitive programs. And Don and I would probably have gotten into more prestigious colleges if we had tried. But there was real pressure on us to attend King's. It was hard not to want to do what our father wanted us to do; but none of us openly resisted.

Donna Lee was stepping comfortably into the vacuum left by her brothers as one by one we outgrew being interviewed on the morning broadcast and singing on television and at meetings. Percy was extremely affectionate toward his "little girl," and she loved her daddy. They enjoyed each other's company at various events at the college and around town. Once he took her along with him to a doctor's appointment and had her sing for the people in the waiting room. She was a sheer delight to him for the entire eleven years they had together. Their relationship was made easier no doubt because she was female and therefore did not have to be trained up to take a leading role in evangelism—only a supportive one, like her mother's.

But there were some difficulties and tensions mounting between father and sons, which must have indicated to him that things were not going quite as planned. Don was one of the few people on the earth bold enough to criticize my father. He complained to Percy about the way he treated his employees: "If you did nine things right and one thing wrong, he would get you for the one thing."[57] Don graduated from King's with distinction and decided to go on to graduate school, entering the master's program in history at Columbia University. But by this time Percy's health, and his future, were uncertain after his several heart episodes, and he became apprehensive that he might not live long enough to see his eldest son take over part of the work. So he went to New York City and pleaded with Don to drop his program and come to work for him as manager of his new television station, WPCA in Philadelphia. The dilemma of either staying with the course of life he had chosen or becoming the chief assistant of his ailing father's organization was not an easy one for the twenty-two-year-old. "That was the saddest day of my life," he said, when he had to make that decision—knowing full well that he could not refuse his father's request.

Dick was drawn into studying philosophy at King's with the inspiring new philosophy professor, Alfred Black, and then moved on to Philadelphia to pursue a master's degree in philosophy of religion at Temple University, studying with the renowned Kant scholar, Richard Kroner. This must have worried Percy who always feared that philosophy would engender doubt and disbelief. But Dick had not abandoned his faith and seemed willing to take on a greater role in the organization, motivated in part, no doubt, by his need to support his growing family.

I too had gotten interested in philosophy while in high school and declared a philosophy major at King's with Al Black in my first year. It was during that year, however, that I learned that there was a movement afoot to get rid of Professor Black for unorthodox beliefs and that Percy was considering firing him. This was deeply troubling to me, and I recall saying to my father that if Al Black left King's, I would follow him. Black was not fired, and I did not have to make good on my threat, but the whole incident over whether to purge several individuals from the faculty at King's caused my father considerable pain, as we will see, and led to his taking a strong stand against philosophy and academic freedom at the college. But I did not think that philosophy was weakening my faith, and I stood by my announced intention of going on to seminary and graduate school after King's.

At about the same time, my younger brother, Dean, was having some emotional problems and actually ran away from home for a time, sleeping in an unused dorm room at the college. Some of us thought that Dean should get psychological counseling, but Percy would not hear of that; he stayed with the sterner methods of discipline to bring Dean into line. Although these methods were successful in the short run, there were some serious frustrations that were building up in Dean that would have to be faced sooner or later.

These fractured relations with his sons weighed heavily on Percy. He seemed to think that he was losing us. What he feared most was that some of us might stray from the fold—especially Dick and I, under the influence of philosophy. Another disappointment for him was that none of us quite measured up to the high standard that he held up for us. We did not have the same burning passion for souls that he had; and none of us seemed to have his gift of evangelism. But the real problem was that the image he had in his mind for each of us was tailored too closely to fit his own form. If he had only given us a little more leeway to move in different directions, he could have spared himself a lot of grief. He was asking too much of us; by depending so heavily on his children to carry on his work, he had placed too great a burden on us, and one that we could not possibly bear.

Although Percy was deeply concerned about the course in life his sons were taking, he was not one given to resignation or despair over these things, important as they were. He always maintained a positive outlook and seemed to be able to find a way to hold things together and move forward. He was not about to give up on any of us, and he would continue to do what he could to keep us from falling away from him, knowing, however, that there was always the chance that he might fail. And I believe it was some consolation to him in the last years of his life that he did not fail and that he did manage to keep at least a tenuous hold on the four of us right to the end.

A misleading brochure put out after the The King's College moved from Belmar, NJ to Delaware in 1941. The college was not officially accredited by the state of Delaware until 1949.

This YPCA quartet (left to right: Alan Forbes, Ray Pritz, Joe Springer, and Ken Brown) stayed together through the 1940s and epitomized the high-quality music of the Sunday broadcasts on the Mutual network.

**Evangelist Percy Crawford in the early 1940s.**

**Percy opened the Victory Center in April, 1943 at Steel Pier, Atlantic City—a place of respite for service men and women. Percy and Ruth standing at left.**

Percy and Ruth with Charles Fuller on one of their Western tours in the mid-1940s.

Percy with two loyal members of his team, Dan and younger brother Dean.

"You there in front of your television set, I'm talking to you."

Percy's television program, *Youth on the March*, featured a full orchestra assembled by Ruth (at piano) and Al Black (conducting).

The Crawford family (clockwise) Ruth, Don, Dick, Percy, Dan, Donna Lee, and Dean. Percy's *Youth on the March* program was televised coast-to-coast on the ABC network from 1949–1952 and on the Dumont network, 1952–53.

"The Four D's" (clockwise from top left): Don, Dick, Dan, and Dean.

Ruth Duvall Crawford contributed more to Percy's ministry than even he realized.

Percy and Ruth's last quartet, (left to right) the Crawford brothers: Dick, Dan, Don, and Neil Fichthorn.

World Tour, Percy with microphone and quartet member Steve Musto near the front lines in Korea, January 1954.

Percy's novel type of youth rally, *Youtharama,* began in Philadelphia in 1956, with musical director Chuck Pugh conducting the "Starlighters" and orchestra. Ruth Crawford at piano in foreground.

# 16
## The King's College: The Briarcliff Years

IN THE SUMMER OF 1954, EVEN AS THE KING'S COLLEGE WAS STEADILY PRO-
gressing at the Delaware campus, it became apparent that Tidewater Associated Oil Company was buying up the land surrounding King's as the site
for its proposed oil refinery and shipping facilities. The new $100 million
plant would make the Delaware Valley area the nation's second largest oil-
refining center, exceeded only by the Texas Gulf coast.[1] Percy orchestrated
a vigorous campaign among all his constituents opposing the plan and the
rezoning requested by the company. At a hearing before the New Castle
County Zoning Commission, he asked: "Why should 'big money' move in
here and force out another institution, already established and based on the
Bible?"[2] But in the end, the state opted for economic development over
Christian education. The rezoning was approved and King's was forced to
relocate once again, to avoid the prospect of being completely surrounded
by the refinery. The property was sold to Tidewater for $1,250,000, and all
the buildings, including lovely old Lexington, were razed by the oil company soon after commencement exercises in June 1955.

A new property was located in New York State, where the Board of Regents was willing to grant King's a provisional charter and degree-granting
status. The new campus would be situated in Briarcliff Manor, Westchester
County, thirty miles north of New York City. The fifty-two-acre site was
originally a resort hotel built in 1901 and then a junior college for women
and had facilities in place that could accommodate five hundred students.
As Percy contemplated the move to Briarcliff, he realized that it would
open up the possibility of significant growth for the college. At the close of
the final year in Delaware, he wrote:

> The Lord has, in a wonderful way, given us this larger campus, with increased
> facilities and equipment, so that we can better serve a larger group of young
> people. As we move to New York State, . . . we have attained to a stature which
> possibl[y] would have taken years to accomplish at our present location. . . . As
> we close out our operation in Delaware, . . . there is opening to us a new door

of increased opportunity and a new horizon toward which we must resolutely press.[3]

There were serious challenges ahead. Renovating the existing physical plant and converting it to fit the college's needs would prove to be extremely costly. The entire heating system and electrical system needed to be modernized. Additional properties, adjacent to the college, were acquired. At the end of the first year, the college launched a $125,000 capital campaign to fund these projects, and bonds were issued. A chapel-auditorium-classroom building and a new gymnasium were envisioned for the second phase of development, as the college made plans for an expected increase in student enrollment from three hundred to between eight hundred and nine hundred over the next decade.

It very soon became apparent that the reserve funds from the sale of the Delaware campus would have to be used for the development and maintenance of the new property and that the college would need to find new sources of revenue. It could not continue to be wholly dependent on tuition and such limited giving as Percy could muster from his YPCA supporters, if it was going to meet its operating budget and begin to build the endowment required for New York State and Middle States accreditation.

At the same time, my father recognized that King's could not meet these challenges unless there was strong leadership at the top and consequently that he could not continue his attenuated status as a one-day-a-week president. He either had to take on the challenge himself or turn the responsibility over to someone else. A strong reason for wanting to continue as president was to be assured that his vision for the college would be sustained—that every graduate would be "a devoted follower of Christ" and go into the world with a passion to serve the Lord. Also, he cherished the hope that he could keep going long enough that one of his sons could step into his shoes, and he was quite open about this with the board. Since I was considered the "brain" in the family, I was the chosen one.

For these reasons, in the spring of 1956, Percy and Ruth left Philadelphia where they had started their ministry almost twenty-five years earlier, put their lovely home on the market, and moved to Briarcliff Manor with the three of us children who were still living at home—Dean, Donna Lee, and myself. (Don was a freshman at King's, and Dick was about to enter King's in the fall.) Our family moved into a grand house on a ten-acre estate called "Braeview" adjacent to the college. Percy loaned the college the $25,000 our house had sold for toward the purchase of the property with the stipulation that he could live in it as long as he was president.

### RETHINKING CHRISTIAN EDUCATION

Part of my father's commitment to move the college forward and meet the challenges that confronted it required that he give more careful considera- tion to the objectives of the college and to the idea of a Christian educa- tion. The stock phrases that had served the college well for so many years, written mainly for publicity purposes, about "combining a curriculum em- bodying the highest academic standards and a faculty who maintain a firm belief in the fundamentals of Protestant Christianity" would no longer suf- fice in attracting new students and donors or in satisfying evaluators. Percy began to give serious thought to such questions as the following:

- What is distinctive about a Christian education?
- How does our product (our graduate) differ from that of secular institutions?
- How do you put together the liberal arts (the sciences and humanities), with its emphasis on open inquiry, with Christian belief in the authority of the Bible?

He tried to give some answers to these questions in several articles he wrote over the next few years and published in *King's Life*. For help in these deliberations, Percy turned to one of the newer faculty members, Alfred Black, who had just come to the faculty in Bible and philosophy that year (1956). Al Black had joined the YPCA team in 1940 at age thirteen, as a member of The King's Singers. Later, in 1948, he was given a spot in the quartet and then became the director of the orchestra and King's Singers for the television broadcast. He graduated from King's and Reformed Epis- copal Seminary in the same year (1951) and then left the YPCA to take a small church in New Jersey while working on his doctorate at Temple Uni- versity's School of Theology. He said (in correspondence with me) that when Percy invited him to join the faculty at King's, he was "ecstatic." Percy also asked Black to teach the introductory course in Bible with him, which gave them both an opportunity to enter into a dialogue about the educational goals of the college. Percy needed Black as a conversation partner in order to work out his own educational philosophy. The two fre- quently had lunch together in the president's dining room, and Black rode with Percy when he made his weekly trip to the Philadelphia office. His re- lationship to Percy was that of close colleague and academic adviser, as my father tried to deepen his thoughts and assume more the role of an educa- tor. For his part, Black felt that because of their long association, Percy "ac- cepted and trusted" him. "Likely I was the only academician who was close to your dad," he said. Black thought he was close enough to my father that he could count on his protection from conservative critics at the college, but he also realized that Percy was the "consummate pragmatist" and that if you did not "share his passion," he would not hesitate to let you go.

In an article written for *King's Life* in the fall of 1957, Percy addressed the question of how the liberal arts fit into the larger ideal of a Christian education. He approached the question by laying out seven qualities he held up as "the aims and hopes we have" for a King's alumnus. He or she should be one who

1. Is genuinely saved; one whose Christianity is a part of his whole life;
2. Has a broad cultural training;
3. Is interested in the salvation of souls and seeks to win them to Christ;
4. Is missionary-minded;
5. Has strong loyalties—to the Lord, country, alma mater, family, job or calling, friends;
6. Has developed his intellectual capacities to the fullest extent;
7. Keeps on learning and growing throughout his life.

The article as a whole gives every indication of being a joint effort putting together Al Black's emphasis on liberal learning (#2, 6, 7) and Percy's emphasis on saving souls (#1, 3, 4, 5). What it lacks is any attempt to integrate these two concerns. For example, in the commentary given for #6, one hears Percy's academic adviser speaking: "To develop the spirit of inquiry, careful analysis, critical judgment, and cautious conclusions is our aim." And immediately following that statement, we hear Percy's voice (which practically takes back what was just said): "We desire that every King's graduate be a person who brings all of his knowledge and understanding into submission to Christ and the revelation of God in the Word of God."[4]

During these last four years of his presidency, my father wrestled intently with the question of the place of the liberal arts, with its method of rational inquiry, in Christian education. He came to think that it did have its proper place in several respects. First, he conceded that it contributed to a person's personal development and led to good citizenship. If one is acquainted with the various areas of human endeavor and knowledge, this will "give him a good basis for a richer and fuller life, . . . [and] make him a better citizen, more capable of playing an effective role in his society."[5]

Second, the study of secular philosophies can be an aid in soul winning, for the Christian has to know about these views in order to be able to respond to them adequately in leading men and women to Christ. "We study such men as Descartes, Spinoza, Leibnitz, Schleiermacher, Hume, Russell, etc., and thus acquaint ourselves with their views of life. . . . Thus, we can better deal with the minds of men in presenting the Gospel to them."[6]

Third, a believer should be able to give a rational defense of his Christian beliefs, and in order to do this, he must develop his intellectual capacities and broaden his knowledge.

> When one goes forth from a Bible school and knows only the one side and then comes face to face with these other philosophies, one may be knocked off his feet and flounder in the faith. Certainly, we do not want fellows and girls to be graduated from The King's College and just have answers memorized and go forth as puppets. We want them to think. . . . We want them to understand all the issues of life and to be able to defend their position with all their mental powers. True, we have a heart experience when Christ transforms our lives, but we also must be able "to give a reason for the hope that is within us." . . . Our faith can be defended from an intellectual standpoint. . . . This is where we maintain that the liberal arts and the sciences can bolster our faith instead of destroy it.[7]

But in spite of these honest efforts to achieve an integration of secular and Bible-based knowledge, occasionally a far more extreme view would surface in him that discredited rational thinking and repudiated all secular philosophies. This happened at a chapel talk that Percy gave in the last year of his presidency (December 10, 1959), when King's was embroiled in a bitter controversy having to do with academic freedom and the teaching of philosophy. In strongly emotional tones, Percy bared his soul regarding the issues that were confronting the college, and as he talked, some of the old negative attitudes and fears of philosophy came spilling out: "We don't have to go to Socrates or Plato or Aristotle for their beliefs so far as our faith is concerned. . . . We don't go to [skeptical philosophers] to eat the food and the bread of life. . . . So they'll throw in their questions; we throw them out —after you know what they are, and you should know them." He scoffed at the notion of academic freedom, which he clearly saw as hostile to religious belief:

> [You say] we're thinking, creative men; we want the liberty to think for ourselves. When that spirit creeps into The King's College whereby we must have academic liberty at the expense of our objective in life, we might as well close our doors. . . .
> [You say] this infringes on my academic liberty; well that's too bad. If my study of philosophy infringes on the foundation and the basis of my sole salvation then the vain philosophy must go. . . . If [academic liberty] takes away my faith, it is of the devil. . . . My rule of faith is the Bible; all else is wrong when it fails to match up with the dictates of this doctrine of faith which we believe.

I was at this chapel talk, finishing my first semester at King's, and I well remember the chilling effect it had on the students and faculty who were present. One chemistry professor left the meeting in tears. The new dean of the college—Fenton Duvall, who had just returned to King's that year—apologized to the faculty for Percy's remarks later that day at a faculty meeting. But Percy never reproached himself or made any apologies for what he had said. Even though his harsh criticisms of philosophic inquiry were not in keeping with his official published statements, I believe they did reflect his deepest beliefs and strongest sentiments on these matters. He had said what he thought it was necessary to say to keep the college on the right course.

## DECLINE AND FALL OF ACADEMIC FREEDOM AT KING'S

The same sort of struggle that was going on internally in my father's mind at this time was also occurring externally within the college community, as tensions mounted between two groups that I will refer to as conservatives and progressives. Black emerged as the reluctant leader of the progressive forces. He had reinvigorated the philosophy program, which had been moribund for half a decade, formed an active Philosophy Club, and was re-instituting the philosophy major. In some articles in *King's Life* and some "tractates" circulated among the faculty, he pressed for higher intellectual standards and a more meaningful definition of Christian education. In one article, he stressed what he called the "discipline of doubt"—that faith needs to be "refined in the fire" of critical questioning.[8] It was also contro-versial that Black had chosen the Revised Standard Version of the Bible (RSV) as a textbook in his (and Percy's) Bible class.[9]

Fenton Duvall, whom Percy had asked to return to the college to be dean of the faculty, after a fourteen-year absence, had left his position at Whit-worth College in Washington State to take on the deanship at King's in the fall of 1959, just as the battle was heating up. Because of Duvall's strong academic credentials (he was just completing his PhD at Penn that year), his appreciation of the place of the liberal arts in Christian education, and his willingness to defend the faculty's interests before Percy and the board, some saw him as a reformer and the leader of the progressive forces. One faculty member told me that he was one of seventeen faculty who sup-ported Duvall's "liberal" vision (although Duvall himself does not recall that he had any such vision). Black described Duvall as "a believer, but not closed-minded."

Meanwhile, another opposing group was mounting a counteroffensive. This group consisted of a conservative wing of the faculty and some influ-ential members of the board of trustees, led by archfundamentalist Alex

Dunlap, a realtor from the Philadelphia area who had been on the board since the mid-1940s and was one of Percy's closest friends and confidants. This group was quick to interpret the progressive forces as modernists who were compromising the basic doctrines of the faith. Dunlap focused his attack on the use of the RSV and on the question of whether liberal professors accepted a literal, historical interpretation of the Bible in all respects —particularly with regard to Adam and Eve in the Genesis account of creation.

The controversy was becoming a hot issue on the campus in the fall of 1959 when I arrived as a freshman. The conservatives were focusing their attack on two professors, Al Black in philosophy and Bill Willey in the English department. Both were being charged with holding "neoorthodox" beliefs—Black, because he happened to be writing his doctoral thesis at Temple on neoorthodox theologian Reinhold Niebuhr, and Willey, because he seemed to be espousing the neoorthodox ideas of Paul Tillich.[10] Black was also being accused of causing students in his Bible class to question their faith, and both were blamed for a spiritual malaise that some thought was prevalent on the campus.

A battle was shaping up. Percy was very much involved in it, but was having a difficult time settling it because a part of him was sympathetic to Black and the progressives and a part of him was drawn to Dunlap and the conservatives. The situation was complicated for him by his two sons, Dick and myself, being philosophy majors who admired their teacher and seeming to be more interested in philosophy than in saving lost souls. It must have given my father pause when I said to him in the midst of this episode that if he fired Al Black I would "follow him." His reply to me was: "I thought you might do that." I knew when I made this remark that I was challenging my father on a matter that was very important to him, but I had no idea at the time how deeply I was wounding him. Be that as it may, this whole episode over the two professors was one of the few times in my father's life in which he was torn by conflicting impulses and did not know how to act.

The issue before him was whether Black and Willey had forsaken the statement of doctrine they had signed and more generally whether they were furthering the college's mission or hindering it. All members of the faculty were required to sign the statement of doctrine annually, consenting to the following five points (condensed): (1) that the Scriptures are "verbally inspired by God and without error in the original writings"; (2) the doctrine of the Trinity; (3) "that God created man in his image; that man sinned and thereby brought upon himself death"; and that "all human beings . . . inherit this sin-nature from the first Adam"; (4) regeneration through the "shed blood" of Christ, his bodily resurrection and premillennial return; (5) the bodily resurrection of the dead and the "everlasting punishment" of the unjust in hell.[11] The relevant doctrines were the first and third: did the reference to "the first Adam" in the doctrine of original sin (together with the infallibility of Scripture) imply that the Genesis account of creation should be interpreted as referring to a literal six-day creation and a historical Adam and Eve? Although the statement, in its simplified form, did not exactly say so, this is what most fundamentalists believed, and Percy would have concurred. However, whether a faculty member espoused all the correct doctrines was not nearly as important to Percy as whether he or she was endeavoring to strengthen faith in their students and was encouraging them to go out into the world and promote the gospel. Unorthodox belief was for him just a sign that a person was straying from his faith and commitment to the Lord.

Dunlap was eager to conduct an inquiry or trial to test the beliefs of the errant professors. Percy was not so eager to hold a trial; he had had enough conversation with Black to know how he would respond to questions. But he did not trust himself on the question of the RSV and on Black's Niebuhrian theology, and thus felt that he had to rely on outside "experts" to help in making a final judgment. However, the expert brought in to expose the RSV's "fallacies and misinterpretations" in a series of lectures and chapel talks—a Lutheran pastor-theologian, Rev. Charles Bauer—succeeded only in generating a campus-wide debate in which Black held open forums and was allowed by Percy to use a chapel service to rebut the clergyman.[12] It was free inquiry in action, but it did not result in the sort of clear-cut answer that Percy was looking for. In fact, the discussion seemed to satisfy his qualms about the RSV; he subsequently wrote in *King's Life:*

> We believe in the infallibility of the scriptures in the original languages. Error comes when one translates it into our English language. Frankly, I do not think any version or translation is perfect. . . . However, this does not mean that these [various translations] cannot be consulted as reference books. Because there are errors in The King James Version does not mean that I am modern [i.e., a modernist] because I read from the King James Version. Because there are errors in the Revised Standard Version and I refer to it in my study, does not mean that I have gone modern. Let us not get into a class where we label everybody as modern because they happen to read the Revised Version or disagree with us in nonessential matters. . . . One can strain at a gnat and swallow a camel.[13]

The question of Black's and Willey's neoorthodoxy was more difficult. Percy rejected neoorthodoxy out of hand, because he rejected any viewpoint that attempted to reinterpret or revise in any way what for him was the clear and simple meaning of the gospel. He knew, however, that he was not competent to judge these theological matters, and again he relied on an outside person. But once again, the evaluator in this case, Walter Martin, a self-proclaimed expert on cults, lacked the credentials to be authoritative on neoorthodox theology, and it is doubtful that the negative judgment he delivered to the board against Black had any effect on my father's decision.[14]

By April 1, 1960, Percy had instructed Dean Duvall to withhold the contracts of Black and Willey. In doing so, he must have thought he was upholding a promise he made to his constituency in a *King's Life* article written at this time in which he said: "There has never been, and never will be so long as I am connected with the college, any sign of modernism at The Kings' College. I, for one, will be the first to root it out."[15] Duvall was shocked and deeply troubled by Percy's action and the reasons given for it. In a bold letter, responding to Percy, he strongly protested the action and, in so doing, clearly aligned himself with the progressive forces at the college (and against the Dunlap forces). Referring to the charges of neoorthodox beliefs, he broached the question of academic freedom:

> I was sorry to withhold the contracts of Al Black and Bill Willey because they are recognized by all to be among the very few good teachers we have at Kings. . . .
> The basic issues here hinge on our statement of doctrine and on our attitude towards our faculty members. We have defined the area of agreement we insist upon in our statement of doctrine which every faculty member signs each year. Is this area of agreement to be constantly and arbitrarily expanded? Cannot a faculty member voice his opinions freely, confidently, and without fear of punishment, on matters other than those covered by the statement of doctrine?

Concerning the charge that Black was responsible for some students losing their faith, he continued:

> Just a couple of weeks ago in the President's Cabinet meeting you mentioned that you had talked with Al Black about getting students "back in the boat" and that your confidence in him was fully restored. I cannot understand how that confidence could be so thoroughly dissipated by a vague rumor, which may have been unfounded or distorted, and which on the face of it does not merit withholding contracts.

He concluded by recommending a policy of tolerance and fidelity toward the faculty:

> These spasmodic flare-ups bring nothing but discredit to the administration of the college in the eyes of the faculty and students. . . . And when future criticisms come, as they surely will, let us meet them unitedly with statements to

the effect that our faculty is agreed upon our statement of doctrine and on basic objectives; on other matters we are willing to allow for disagreement.

Such loyalty to the faculty on the part of the administration would be rewarded with far more genuine loyalty from the faculty than can possibly be secured by demand. . . . It should also help to displace the suspicion and distrust which are so marked on the campus of Kings, and which are so completely antithetical to genuine Christianity, with some of the love of the brethren which Jesus seems to have indicated was to be the first fundamental for His followers.[16]

The letter must have come as a surprise to Percy. He was used to his subordinates following his orders, not protesting them. The contents of the letter could certainly have been construed as "disloyal" as Percy understood that term. But, as it happened, my father seemed to take Duvall's letter in stride and in fact withdrew his order to withhold Black's and Willey's contracts. But for Duvall, the die was cast. He had challenged my father on matters that he knew Percy deemed essential. He had urged him to be more tolerant of diverse opinions. He had suggested that administrators needed to show loyalty to their faculty. He had accused Percy and the conservatives behind him of missing the fundamental teaching of the gospel. When he signed off on that letter with these words: "Such a letter is not easy to write. There is very much more I should like to say; I hope I have not said too much. And I trust it will be received in the spirit of constructive helpfulness in which it is written," he knew that he was effectively turning in his resignation.

I have puzzled for a long time over why my father reversed himself on this matter of the contracts of these two professors. It was uncharacteristic of him to change his mind about anything, especially when it meant acting against his conservative tendencies and on the side of his more progressive leanings. We can only guess at his motives. My best guess is that the factors that weighed most heavily were, first, that he was listening to the voices of some of the progressives around him. Duvall's scorching letter may have influenced him since he acted so soon after receiving it. But that letter was in fact reinforcing other moderate voices that Percy would have taken seriously. For, example, Leymon "Deak" Ketcham, a cabinet member who had been assistant to the president for the previous four years and who had been a staunch defender of academic learning at the college, once proclaimed in voicing opposition to Dunlap, "We are a college, not a Bible school!"[17]

Another voice of moderation was board member Charles Phillips, a businessman from nearby White Plains who had just been asked to join the board in September 1958. Phillips, whose son was attending King's, had distinguished himself in active service to the college as chairman of the

Parents' Auxiliary. He had a keen appreciation of the difficulties and challenges facing King's and was not afraid to voice them. His poignant questions and probings (in letters to board members) were usually accompanied by constructive proposals.

In a thoughtful letter sent February 6, 1960, only to Percy, anticipating some of Duvall's points, Phillips expressed concern about "some on the Board" who wanted "to add doctrinal points to those now in our corporate charter, which doctrinal points are to be conditions for hiring and tenure in the Faculty."[18] The doctrines in question were "a repudiation of the RSV" and a "specific interpretation of Genesis 1–3." Phillips had done his homework on both of these topics and argued persuasively against taking a dogmatic stance on either of them. Regarding the interpretation of Genesis and human origins, he cited an authority whom Percy would have respected, Frank Gaebelein, a Harvard-educated fundamentalist and headmaster of Stony Brook School for Boys, who wrote:

> Our human understanding of the book of nature must not be made the norm of acceptance of the other book, The Bible. . . . Christian education must recognize the fragmentary state of our knowledge of the vast book of the created universe. The attitude of an Einstein who compares the universe to a watch, the case of which is forever locked, and likens the scientist to a man, who from the outside, must find out its intricate workings, holds a lesson for us. A great deal of humility is needed to avoid the rash assurance with which some Christians who know next to nothing about the spacious realm of science dogmatize regarding the book of creation.[19]

But Phillips also brought up another point that surely would have grabbed Percy's attention, namely the "real danger" that the action of dismissing faculty members over such doctrinal matters could pose for the college's accreditation. Pointing to King's having been granted only a "temporary and provisional charter," he comments: "I believe that we will be under rather close examination and supervision for the next year or two by the Board of Regents. Should there occur any significant exodus of Faculty or students during this probationary period on the issue of academic freedom a permanent charter might be jeopardized." The lack of full accreditation by New York and by the Middle States Association had been a serious handicap for the college in the recruitment of students and faculty, and Percy might well have been influenced by this possible effect of his action on the college's future.

Another consideration that loomed large in my father's thoughts was the strong emotional bond he had to his children, closely bound up with his deep desire that we would take over his work after he died. Percy had built a good relationship with Black for over eighteen years, and theirs was a friendship that could not easily be discarded. But he was deeply suspicious of Black the philosopher, and that suspicion took on immense proportions when his own sons' souls were at stake. My father despised philosophy insofar as it tended to erode faith, and he was convinced that it did indeed have that tendency.

I only recently learned how deeply troubled my father was about the possibility that my brother and I might lose our faith under the influence of philosophy and Black's teaching. In a conversation with Calvin Waldron, the former professor of education at King's who had been acting dean before Duvall arrived, I was asked the question: "Did you ever see your father cry?" When I answered that I had not, he said that he had. He recounted that Percy had come to his office and said that he wanted to talk to him in private. Visibly upset, my father proceeded to lament Black's influence on my brother and me, and as "tears came to his eyes," he said that he was afraid he was losing us. Percy expressed a similar thought to his close associate, John DeBrine, that summer at Pinebrook when he said to him: "I have lost my entire family and I really don't know how to get them back," and even counseled DeBrine not to marry and have children in order not to suffer the same deep disappointment.[20]

What did he mean that he was "losing" us? Why was he trying so desperately to hold on to us? I believe that what it meant to him was that his sons might not be there to continue his work when he passed away, and as a consequence, the whole edifice that he had labored over for twenty-nine years might collapse. But far worse, it meant for him that his sons might be losing their faith entirely and thus be headed for damnation. These were the thoughts that were breaking his heart.

I did not think that I was losing my faith. As an eighteen-year-old about to enter my sophomore year at King's, I was a philosophical novice, with no thought of doubting my basic beliefs. I had known since my senior year in high school, when I wrote a term paper on Descartes's search for knowledge, that I wanted to study philosophy above all else. I was fascinated by the ideas and systems of the great philosophers—Descartes, Spinoza, Leibniz, Schleiermacher—that list of names that Percy had rattled off and dismissed so often in his sermons—only I thought there was knowledge and profit to be gotten from reading them. I wholeheartedly embraced the idea that I was hearing from Black that my Christian beliefs were rationally defensible and that any knowledge that I acquired from my study in philosophy and science was fully compatible with the revealed truths of Scripture.

But Percy could see the dangers that lurked when one stepped into the world of rational inquiry, where all of one's beliefs stand before the bar of reason and none of them are unchallengeable. He could see, better than I, that this commitment to open inquiry would eventually lead me away from those fundamentalist doctrines that he had tried so hard, by instruction and by example, to instill in me. His despairing attitude indicates to me that he had come to the realization that I would not succeed him as president of the college. His strategy now was to do what he could to limit the damage and keep each of his sons in the Christian fold. All was not lost. He had persuaded Don to drop out of graduate school at Columbia and come to Philadelphia to manage the new television station that YPCA had just acquired. Dick graduated from King's that year (1960) and was off to study philosophy and theology at Temple University, but there was still the hope that he would take a more active role at Pinebrook. And he dealt with the third, straying son by renewing Black's contract for another year so that he could at least keep a watchful eye on the errant professor and his devoted student.

*

As it happened, the victory for the moderates gained by the renewal of Black's and Willey's contracts was short-lived. By June, Duvall had resigned as dean, and suddenly the progressive movement was without its spiritual leader and its voice in the administration. What triggered Duvall's resignation was the departure of another key administrator, Deak Ketcham, who had been a loyal devotee of the college (and of Percy) ever since its inception in 1938. Ketcham was in the first graduating class at King's (1942), excelled in athletics, and traveled and preached with The King's Messengers. He went on to Faith Seminary and then took a church for eleven years while teaching Bible part-time at King's. In 1953 he returned to the college on a full-time basis as director of public relations; then in 1956 he moved into the spot vacated by William Jelley, assistant to the president, taking on the multiple jobs of public relations, promotional activities, alumni relations, publications, liaison with the local community, chapel program, and myriad other duties—all this on top of taking care of a constant flow of instructions and projects coming from the president. Ketcham handled Percy's demands and bold ideas with patience and grace. One example is telling of their relationship: encouraged by the intercollegiate successes of the basketball and touch football teams in the mid-1950s, Percy proposed a way in which the college might field a full-fledged football team. Ketcham's tactful response in a letter to Percy gave five good reasons against the idea, any one of which should have been sufficient. He ended the letter with this mild criticism of Percy's absentee governance:

I do not wish this to be construed as a personal criticism, nor as opposition to starting football at King's. I am reporting and stating questions which have already been asked of me. I think they are questions we must ask ourselves and answer before we go too far. . . . I bring these things to your attention knowing your interest in the progress of the College in every area and in order to acquaint you with the climate of thought as it appears to be here on campus.[21]

Ketcham embodied probably more than anyone else the sorts of qualities that my father envisioned for The King's alumnus, and Percy's confidence in Ketcham was shown by his inviting him to be a speaker at Pinebrook. In January 1960 Percy persuaded him to take on the challenge of fund-raising for the college on a much larger scale, as vice president in charge of development. He was just getting going in this new capacity when his time at King's came to an abrupt and unexpected end.

It is not known what caused the falling out between Percy and Ketcham. The minutes of the May board meeting indicate that "Dr. Crawford reported Ketcham's resignation." Lengthy discussion followed, in which Ketcham's many contributions were recited; however Percy made it clear that "Deak made the statement that he [Deak] couldn't work with him." A motion was made to accept the resignation, but it did not carry. Instead, a committee was formed to meet with Ketcham to see if it was possible to "reconcile Dr. Crawford and Mr. Ketcham." Duvall, who was at the meeting, recalls that every board member, including Dunlap, disagreed with Percy over Ketcham's leaving, but Percy insisted that he should go. Duvall told me that he realized in that meeting that if he ever crossed Percy he too would be gone and decided then that he had made a mistake in returning to King's and that he would begin to look for a new job.[22]

This whole episode was yet another instance in which Percy lost a proficient member of his staff because of his obstinacy and inability to work with people. Many felt, as I did, that The King's College in 1960, with Duvall as dean, was on its way to becoming a first-rate Christian college, on a par with Wheaton.[23] A core of well-qualified, devoted faculty and administrators could have moved King's toward academic excellence and enabled the school to capitalize to a greater extent on the opportunities afforded by its new location. But this was not to be. The progressives on the faculty were dispirited and disunited, while the conservatives kept pushing. And since my father's support for the progressives had been halfhearted, he was increasingly susceptible to Dunlap's leadings. He began to swing more toward his conservative constituency.

The tumultuous year at King's (1959–60) had taken a toll on my father. He had done his best to resolve the situation, but it had not been a good outcome. The criticism he had gotten from within the college, though not new, had shaken him, as evidenced by the defensive tone of his December 10 chapel talk. The controversy over Black and Willey had been stressful. Ketcham was gone and had left a huge hole in the administration. Percy had to ask himself whether he should step down.

Sometime in the spring of 1960, Percy decided that he would vacate the office of president, find a suitable replacement, and move back to Philadelphia. He announced his intentions to the board at the June 4 meeting, saying (according to the minutes): "All I want is the good of the school. I do not want to be a drag." He said that he felt that his health was good and that "he had hoped at one time that someday one of his sons might be available for the Presidency," but did not think he could "wait for this possibility." He praised Duvall (who had not yet resigned and was at the meeting) for his having "hold of the faculty and know[ing] where we are going better than any man we have ever had."

In saying all this, my father was trying to wrap up his twenty-two-year presidency, and he needed to think that the college he was handing over to someone else was in good shape. Also, it was important that there be someone there to carry on the enterprise and its mission, and Duvall was the only one left who could do it. Percy respected him; he was an in-law; and he had helped establish the college in the early days. But Duvall would be gone within the month. And the fact was, the college was not in good shape—in terms of its personnel, its finances (it continued to operate with a large permanent deficit), and its prospects for accreditation.

To make matters worse, Percy wanted to set up a situation in which he would still maintain ultimate control over the college, even while he turned over the duties and responsibilities of the president to someone else. His proposal was that he "take the position of Chancellor," retain his place on the board, and continue to teach his class and direct the radio program. Moreover his successor would be one in whom he and the board "would have complete confidence." The college must keep its thoroughly evangelical position. The new president must have "no taint of neo-orthodoxy or 'New-Evangelicalism.'"[24]

But the problem with this arrangement was that Percy was offering to step down from the office of president, but without giving up his final authority over the college and its future. He and the board should have known the plan was unworkable; they had tried the very same thing once before, when Vernon Grounds had been offered the presidency in 1945 and had turned it down because he did not want any part of a shared presidency.

Percy had done what he could at King's, but he had come to see that the problems facing the college were either intractable or would require long-

term solutions, and he did not have much more time to give. He was leaving King's because he wanted to devote his remaining time to another venture. During the previous three years, he had acquired several FM radio
stations and a television station in Philadelphia, and he was rapidly becoming absorbed by the prospect of building a Christian broadcasting network. He had not been candid when he told the board he was in good health.
He had had six heart attacks over the last five years, and his doctors were
warning him that the next one could be his last and that he probably had no
more than two years to live. He realized that if he wanted to accomplish his
vision of building a Christian communications network, he would have to
devote the better part of whatever time, energy, and resources were left to
him to that visionary project.

# 17

## A Christian Broadcasting Network

Percy must have envisioned having his own radio station ever since his student days when he appeared on BIOLA's station KTBI and Moody Bible Institute's WMBI with his gospel teams. In the spring of 1937, a year before he opened the doors of his own educational institution, he announced: "The Board of Trustees for our new 'King's College' has made application to erect a radio station at the college [in Belmar, New Jersey] strong enough to reach through Philadelphia and New York and up and down the coast."[1] When the application was denied, Percy responded: "We know this is the Lord's will in the matter, and so must wait until a later time when He will see fit to open the way."[2] He waited almost two decades. Tired of paying exorbitant fees for radio and television time and tired of being "kicked around" by station owners and managers, Percy resurrected the idea of owning and operating his own station. In 1956 he started looking to purchase an AM station in a major market in the Northeast. He discussed with eldest son Don, then a sophomore at King's, the possibility of buying a New York station for $300,000 under the auspices of The King's College. Percy knew that he needed to have substantial financial backing in order to buy into the AM market. As usual, he looked to Christian businessmen to invest in it, either on a gift or loan basis, or even a limited ownership basis, but he could not generate any interest. He may have wanted The King's College to be the applicant for the station because of its location in New York and also because King's had just set aside a half million dollars in reserve from the sale of the Delaware campus to Tidewater Oil. Possibly, Percy thought he could use that vast sum of money as security in such a venture, although there is no record that he ever approached the board about using the college's funds for this purpose.[3] But even if Percy could not make this plan work, he was now committed to the goal of acquiring a radio station.

In 1957 he discussed with Don the possibility of the *Young People's Church of the Air* buying a station. At this time, YPCA was taking in more in contributions than it was paying out for radio and television time and even had some cash reserves. They both felt, however, that there were insufficient assets to take on such a large expenditure.

A third possibility was that he could put up his own money to pay for a station and personally own it. This option had the advantage that it would give him complete control of the station and its operation and of what happened to it after his death. However, one difficulty was that my father did not have a lot of money. He had begun to build up a personal estate with the intent of "caring for" Ruth and his children after his death. His financial records indicate to me that his net worth at that time was somewhere in the range of $150,000; this might have been enough to finance adequately a single station.

Another potential problem with personal ownership was that he would be blurring the line between his own personal finances and the YPCA's. Percy had always been careful to keep these two spheres distinct so that he could honestly say that every dollar that was contributed would be used to purchase radio and television time. He made his living from his annual salary from Pinebrook and from the proceeds of the Pinebrook Book Store and book clubs, which he owned in partnership with manager Norm Kellow. If the stations were owned by him personally, then he would not be able to use gifts sent in to the YPCA to support them.

In spite of these risks, Percy began to think in terms of private ownership, and eventually he used his own money to finance all six of the radio stations he acquired in his lifetime. He solved the problem of appealing for funds by asking his constituents to support specifically the Philadelphia FM and television stations that he was applying for, both of which were to be owned by YPCA.

As Percy struggled with the difficulties of raising sufficient funds to buy into radio, it occurred to him that there was a much easier—and cheaper—way of gaining access to the radio market, and that was through FM radio. It was possible in the late 1950s to purchase FM stations dirt cheap (compared to AM stations), and it was also relatively easy to obtain new licenses because the FCC was encouraging commercial development of the FM spectrum. And as he began to think in terms of FM, suddenly the possibility of acquiring multiple stations—a network of stations—was no longer just a dream. He now saw an opportunity (as he would later put it) "to gain control of communications" by starting a Christian broadcasting network.

At that time, FCC regulations allowed an individual or company to own no more than seven AM stations, seven FM stations, and seven television stations (VHF or UHF). Percy moved quickly to obtain his quota of FM stations and also began to look into UHF television. In the next three years, before his death in 1960, he was able to obtain five FM stations (Detroit,

Hammond, Lancaster, Des Moines, and Fort Lauderdale) with two applications pending (Philadelphia and Buffalo), one AM station (Forest Grove, Oregon), and one UHF television station (Philadelphia).

Nineteen fifty-seven was a very good year for my father to have chosen to go into FM radio. After 1945, when the FCC assigned a new and wider spectrum to FM, there was a significant increase in applications granted. The number of FM stations owned and operated rose from 88 commercial (and 9 educational) stations in 1946 to 733 commercial (and 48 educational) stations in 1950. But FM was not commercially viable even in these boom years. A few big independent stations with loyal audiences did fairly well, but almost all operated at a loss. Hundreds of stations folded after 1950, and by 1957 the number of stations had shrunk to 530. But it was in that year that the industry picked up, and the number of new applications finally exceeded the number of stations going off the air. Percy was among the applicants in this new wave.

There were several reasons why commercial FM lagged behind AM. First, profitable AM stations often acquired an FM companion in their locality as a hedge against competition and were willing to operate it at a loss. Second, AM stations ran duplicate programming on their sibling FM stations, and so advertisers saw no reason to buy time on both. Third, manufacturers were not building FM receivers into AM radios or car radios, which meant that listeners had to buy a second radio or an adaptor. Finally, FM radio was identified in the public mind with classical music and educational formats, with minimal or no advertising, and thus appealed mainly to special interest groups.

In 1957, when Percy started looking to acquire a television station, UHF television was in a situation similar to that of FM radio vis-à-vis its stronger sister service (VHF). The VHF band (channels 2–13) had been authorized in 1941 with UHF and noncommercial educational television (channels 14–83) appearing first in 1952. Adopting a policy of "intermixture," the Federal Communications Commission assigned VHF and UHF channels to almost all cities. Although the commission tried to promote the equivalence of the two bands, in actuality the 108 VHF stations that were in operation prior to 1952 and were already established in the major markets had a significant economic edge over UHF stations. After a two-year period of initial growth, UHF began to decline sharply. Of the 165 new UHF stations started between 1952 and 1959, over half would later go off the air. When Percy's Philadelphia station went on the air in July 1960, there were 80 UHF stations, down from the high point of 127 in 1954. The main reason UHF lagged behind VHF was that the latter stations were well entrenched in the major cities when UHF came on the scene. But there were other problems. VHF had better reception and a greater range of transmission: its reliable coverage was sixty to seventy miles as against thirty to forty miles for UHF.[4] In addition, the limited number of UHF capable receivers in television sets meant smaller audiences. All pre-1952 sets could receive only VHF channels, and for the next decade only one in six new televisions had all-channel capability.[5] By the end of the 1950s, approximately 10 percent of homes had UHF capability.[6] Most viewers who wanted to tune in to his station on channel 17 had to buy an adaptor that could be attached to the antenna terminals (which the station was able to sell to them for the low price of $14.95).

Percy was able to see the advantages that FM radio (and to a lesser extent UHF television) afforded him as a Christian broadcaster. The features of FM that drove away capital investors and national advertisers did not affect him. At the time he entered the market he already had a faithful following that would be willing to go out and buy FM receivers and UHF adaptors in order to listen to *Pinebrook Praises* and watch *Youth on the March*. In fact, he was able to use some of the distinctive features of FM, such as better sound reproduction, good music, and limited advertising, to his advantage. In a promotional brochure for his Lancaster station WDAC, he announced that the station would "capture the Christian audience" in the area by offering "well-balanced, static-free programs of news, hi-fi, semi-classical music, and evangelical religious programs." "People are tired of the beer, jazz, and multitudinous commercials so predominate on radio and TV stations."

His plan was to invite local evangelical churches, national programmers, and "reputable advertisers" to purchase time. Using this simple formula, he would be able to build a network of commercial religious stations that would be self-sustaining.

Although the network of seven radio stations that eventually materialized was distributed across the country, with three stations in the East (WDAC in Lancaster, WMFP in Fort Lauderdale, with Buffalo pending), three in the Midwest (WMUZ in Detroit, WYCA in Hammond/Chicago, and KDMI in Des Moines), and one in the West (KWAY in Forest Grove/Portland),[7] Percy always gave the highest priority to the Philadelphia station—the only application that was denied. It was to be the flagship station of the entire network. Since YPCA was running a large surplus in radio and television gifts,[8] Percy had ready cash available to invest in the Philadelphia radio and television stations. He got the ball rolling by applying for an FM license early in 1958, but the application was rejected and the frequency given to an applicant whom Percy always identified pejoratively with "the Catholics." He decided to appeal the FCC decision, perhaps because he had already invested considerable time and resources into the application process. Or it may have been that he just wanted to do battle with his Catholic opponents. In a letter to a contributor, dictated just before he died, Percy spoke of the "obstacles" that he faced in getting the station and added: "But we are fighting it on through, and we believe God is going to bless and lead us."

Another reason my father may have been willing to fight it through was that another FM license was readily obtainable. Station owner David Kurtz was selling a Philadelphia construction permit for $25,000.[9] No doubt my father wanted to avoid putting up another $25,000 if he did not have to, but he might have chosen to take the riskier route of appealing his case because there were other options open to him if the appeal failed. Whatever his motives, the unfortunate result was that the case was delayed and had not been decided by the time he died. And so, ironically, he never did get the station he coveted most. Nevertheless, he was so sure that he would somehow obtain the Philadelphia FM station that he began to line up clients and even spoke on the radio as if he already had it in hand. On the last *Pinebrook Praises* tape he made before he died (which was to be aired November 12, 1960), he stated: "We are erecting" an FM station in Philadelphia that will be "Christian-owned" and one of the "strongest" stations in the city.

While the Philadelphia application dragged on, Percy was busy getting his other satellite stations in place. WMUZ-FM in Detroit was the first station Percy acquired, and it will serve to illustrate the process he went through in making his stations operational. He purchased the station and its tower and equipment from Michigan Music Company for $25,000. In the application to the FCC for the transfer of the license, Michigan Music Company claimed that it had lost $100,000 in operational costs. The document also listed Percy's personal assets, totaling approximately $183,000. In addition, lines of credit for $10,000 or $15,000 were pledged by three businessmen.[10] Percy signed the bill of sale for WMUZ on October 21, 1958, and immediately began broadcasting. This was the beginning of a frenzy of media acquisition over the next two years.

Finding capable Christian people to run his stations was a daunting task, since Percy had virtually no experience in the operational end of radio or television. He took chances on people whom he hoped could learn on the job, but given his high expectations and his lack of patience with anyone who was not "producing," there were bound to be casualties. As in the past, he called on some people who were at that time, or had previously been, a part of his own organization. Chuck Pugh, music director of Youtharama, took on the formidable challenge of starting up the television station, and Bob Brooks, a recent quartet member whom Don replaced, became manager of the Fort Lauderdale station.

Percy found the first manager of his Lancaster station WDAC through Bill Ohman of The King's College Trumpet Trio, who was then manager of a Christian station in Montrose, Pennsylvania. Bill recommended his chief engineer, Dick Gage, who agreed to move to Lancaster and build a station from scratch. Percy signed over a $10,000 loan to Gage and gave him carte blanche to get the station going. Gage managed to get the studio and tower in place in a record three months and then bring on board some of the national programmers that Percy wanted, such as Theodore Epp (*Back to the Bible*) and Wilbur Nelson (*Morning Chapel Hour*). He even managed to turn a small profit for Percy over the ten-month period that my father lived to see the station in operation. Gage said that he had had a good relationship with Percy and came to "love him like a brother."[11]

The hiring of WDAC's first salesman was a more haphazard affair. Percy was visiting the area several months before the station went on the air and stopped for gas. He started talking to the attendant about the new station and learned that the fellow was a graduate of Lancaster Bible College and pastor of Smithville Church of God and was pumping gas to make extra money. Before he had left, Percy had extended an offer to Jim Weaver to be WDAC's first sales manager.

But there were serious difficulties with personnel at the other stations. As I see it, the problem was that Percy was starting up seven new media outlets in a very short time and was putting people in charge of them who, in many cases, had little or no experience in the broadcasting field. It would take time for them to learn the ropes and build a stable operation that could attract the religious programmers and advertisers that Percy wanted. Further, it did not help that Percy was not giving his managers the capital they needed to do this; as usual, everything had to be done as cheaply as possible. And yet, he wanted immediate results. The notes he had signed to pay for these facilities were coming due, and he expected each station to be able to operate in the black and begin paying off its debt. Not surprisingly, this was not happening. And Percy could not afford to take the time away from his other endeavors to travel all over the country and give direction to each station. It must have been frustrating to him that the stations were not meeting his financial goals, and yet he could not go to each one of them himself to assess the situation and straighten things out.

The situation finally came to a head at the Detroit station. Percy had hired Lynn Wheaton, a recent King's graduate, to manage the fledgling station, but he was dissatisfied with the whole operation and decided to clean house. Unable to go to Detroit himself, he sent his twenty-year-old son, Dick, a junior at King's, to do the hatchet work. It was not a happy scene for either the son or the Detroit staff. Dick identified one of the staff whom he thought had the right attitude and commitment, Bob Anderson, made him the new manager and fired the rest.

Anderson found favor in Percy's eyes and within six months (by October 1959) he was made general manager of the whole radio operation. Percy liked him because of his optimistic attitude and because he made my father believe that the station was meeting all his goals, even if it was not. Most impressively, he sent his boss a monthly check, without fail, thus assuring him that the station was making a profit. In his communications with Percy, Anderson pushed all the right buttons. In one early letter he described the program he and his wife put on—the Bob and Bea program—a variety show with music, news, household and cooking hints, church announcements ("a great public relations boost"), and spot commercials ("the clients are happy because of the great response in buying their products"). He listed the "new religious accounts," including Barnhouse, Revivaltime, and Bob Pierce,[12] and then explained his (deceptive) strategy for getting new clients: "My theory is [a] simple approach to get them on—boost our average by announcing we carry ALL the national programs. This fills our Sunday programming. . . . The reaction is great. This helps to quell the so called gossip that we are ready to fold up. We are headed for better things." Anderson went on to describe some of his policies and style of leadership:

> My salary budget is kept within the limit. I work 48 hours as well as keep track of the other matters in Hammond and Lancaster. This is the least I can do. If I work hard then I can expect others to do so—and they do. We must all work as a team. . . . We don't waste money. What we need we get. What we don't need we don't get. . . .
>
> I want you to know that DETROIT has just begun. The future is great. The path is hard work and consistent pressing on. I pledge you my best. . . . In summary—the prophets of gloom are dispelled. WMUZ-FM is still on the air—the signal is better than ever—and our hearts are strangely warmed.[13]

Percy did not mind hearing this puffy prose about his stations. He wanted his employees to always stress the positives, not the negatives. He appreciated Anderson's enthusiasm and his dedication. But in his reply, he was restrained and kept pushing for better results: "I liked the review and the report on [the station]—sounds good! I think it's pretty good that we get Barnhouse on there and the others. We must sell further time to get it as on a productive basis as possible."[14]

*

Back in Philadelphia, Percy was becoming dissatisfied with what was happening at the new television station, WPCA-TV. The *Young People's Church of the Air* had applied for a UHF license and had purchased a building and tower in West Philadelphia that had been used as a transmitter site for a VHF station. Station manager Chuck Pugh and his chief engineer, John Adison, were hard at work building the station practically from scratch. Their immediate task was to construct new studios at the site and convert the facility to UHF transmission. Adison had impressive credentials in television, having worked with NBC for four years as chief engineer and then with CBS for another four years before being let go when CBS sold off its UHF television station in Milwaukee. After a series of interviews with Percy and other engineers who advised him, Adison accepted the job at half the salary he had been making with the networks.[15]

To begin equipping the station, Pugh recalls that he was able to work a deal through a Christian executive at RCA to purchase used equipment worth $150,000 for only $11,000. Three truckloads of equipment arrived at the station and was unloaded and installed with the help of a volunteer force of about one hundred RCA employees from RCA's Camden plant, who came over in the evenings and lent their services and their expertise to help get Percy on the air.

By the end of the first year, after Pugh had filled the key positions on his staff, his relationship with Percy began to sour. The two men were not fully comfortable with each other. Pugh did not take orders well and chafed under Percy's supervision. He was not being given the same degree of freedom that he had as director of Youtharama. Percy had given Pugh a free hand over most matters, but always reserved the right to step in and give direction. Sometimes the owner and the manager openly disagreed about relatively minor things, as when Percy wanted Pugh to schedule back-to-back programming in the main studio, but Pugh thought that programmers should be allotted studio time for setup and rehearsal before going on the air. This was just one way in which the manager tended to be in favor of higher quality in program production, whereas Percy was "always looking for a cheaper way to do it."[16]

The circumstances surrounding Pugh's leaving the station are hazy. He remembers that Percy asked him to "interview someone named Anderson" for a high-level job at the station. (Was it WMUZ's Bob Anderson?) Apparently the candidate had told Percy that he could "run the station for half of what you are now paying." When Pugh told my father that he did not see how this person could help the team, Percy insisted on hiring him, and when Pugh said: "Well then, count me out," Percy responded: "Have it your way."

Was this a setup or a real disagreement over the qualifications of a job candidate? My suspicion is that it was the former and that Percy wanted to get rid of Pugh, mainly because of a difference in style and personality. Of course, my father must have known that in dismissing his station manager, he was also losing a creative musician and one of the main attractions of his Youtharama rallies. Pugh left WPCA in December 1959, finished the 1959–60 season at Youtharama, and then continued with his ministry of music at Grace Chapel and at George Palmer's Sandy Cove conference. Percy then turned to quartet member and King's faculty member, Neil Fichthorn, another capable musician, to take his place at Youtharama.

There is another reason that Percy may have been willing to let Pugh leave. It is quite possible that he saw the need to bring his eldest son Don into the organization before it was too late and that the television station was the logical place for him to occupy. We saw above that in December 1959 Don was finishing his first semester's work on his master's degree in history at Columbia. He had just turned twenty-two—the same age that Percy was when he committed his life to the Lord. He had wrangled with his father over his management style and other matters and at this time in his life wanted more than anything to continue his education. When Percy went to New York and pleaded with his son to take on the television station, saying that he probably only had two years to live, Don could hardly say no. Although Don remembers that day as the "saddest" in his life, it was one of the happiest for my father; he now had a manager at the television station in whom he had complete confidence, and he had successfully drawn his eldest son, and likely successor, into a key position in the organization. The grand plan for his succession was coming together.

When Don took over as manager of WPCA, the station was ready to begin broadcasting from an engineering standpoint, but a whole new schedule of programming for television had to be worked up, and an audience generated from Percy's constituents. It would take time to attract paying customers and advertisers, and there were no national programs to solicit. To meet these challenges, Don brought on board the inexperienced team of former YPCA quartet members, Bob Straton, Sam Seymour, and Steve Musto, and within six months, these neophyte broadcasters put WPCA-TV on the air. On July 17, 1960, Percy Crawford and the Young People's Church of the Air began operating the first religious television station in the nation (and the world). It was a critical turning point in the history of evangelicalism that opened a whole new horizon in the use of the media for the cause of evangelism.

There was an interesting subplot that took place alongside this historic event. Attending the dedicatory service Percy held for the opening of the station was a young Christian minister whom some participants remember being very vocal about his vision of building a whole fleet of television stations. Pat Robertson had contacted my father to inquire about his new venture and came to the station to see it in operation. At the opening ceremony, Percy asked him to give a prayer.[17]

## TRIALS, THE FOOD OF FAITH

The last two years of my father's life were anxious ones as he worked to bring into existence his great vision of a Christian broadcasting network, while struggling to maintain financial equilibrium in his own personal accounts. He had to draw on all of his considerable entrepreneurial skills in bringing off this, his most ambitious project.

The challenge he faced was that all of the financing for the stations he acquired (except the television station) was coming from his own personal funds. No one else was putting up hard cash. The immediate task was to make each new application credible to the FCC. He had to demonstrate that he had sufficient funds (and credit lines) to make the station operational and cover costs if it failed. Each station would require a significant outlay of start-up money, and thus his financial position got progressively weaker with each new acquisition. In addition, he had to sink large amounts of money into improving his facilities and equipment, and upgrading the stations' power.[18] By the end of 1959, when three of the six radio stations were operating, he had already accumulated the enormous personal debt of $300,000 (equivalent to $2,200,000 in current dollars), and on the horizon were the costs of starting up three more stations including the heavily indebted AM station in Forest Grove, Oregon.[19]

Against this mounting debt, Percy had real assets worth approximately $150,000, with only about a third of this readily available to him. This included a 50–50 partnership (with Norm Kellow) in the Pinebrook Book Store and book clubs valued at $67,000; a small farm near Pinebrook in which he had about $12,000 of equity; and a note for $25,000 from King's that he had loaned the college toward the purchase of the president's home. In addition, Percy always kept a cash reserve in bank accounts usually totaling $35,000–$40,000.[20] To bolster his assets, he was not above asking anyone with whom he had a good business relationship to back him with a letter of credit in the amount of $5,000 or $10,000.

He was constantly figuring and refiguring his net worth—sketching out assets and liabilities in hard-to-decipher rounded numbers on blank sheets of paper. He calculated that he would need to make $5,000 monthly from six stations to pay off his notes. But WMUZ Detroit and WDAC Lancaster were the only stations operating in the black, and the small profits they were generating were not nearly enough to cover debt plus losses at the other stations. He had a serious cash flow problem, and the unpaid bills started piling up at all the stations (with the exception of Lancaster).

It is a surprising fact that the asset column of my father's balance sheet remained fairly stable throughout the entire acquisition process. Since most of the start-up money for the stations was borrowed, the liability side of the ledger grew steadily, but he never had to sell off any of his holdings or use up his cash reserves in order to raise capital. As a result, he could put up essentially the same money for each new station. It always looked as if he had a substantial base—which he did not—when all of his liabilities were figured in. I think, too, that his inflated column of assets gave him a false sense of security. He thought there was money there to fall back on. But if the bubble had burst and he had been forced to sell everything, he probably could not have realized more than $100,000.

To make matters worse, Percy could not count on YPCA's finances to relieve in any way his financial problems. Getting the television station and the impending FM station established would tie up YPCA funds indefinitely.[21] So instead of reducing his financial burden, YPCA was adding to it. One could sense this in his appeals for funds on the radio, which were usually low-key and self-assured, but began to take on a more insistent tone. On one broadcast, he beseeched his listeners: "How can we get you to realize how great our need is, and to help with it?" Percy would even allow business considerations to take precedence over spiritual concerns. On one occasion, he shocked one of the employees at the television station who was working long hours to get it on the air by telling him he did not want the staff to be conducting its daily prayer meeting for the success of the station on company time.

But Percy did not, and perhaps could not, see that he was dangerously overextended—and indeed remained remarkably calm about his finances right to the end of his life. He did put the brakes on any further acquisitions, resigning himself to the fact that he would not obtain his full quota of stations in his lifetime. But not entirely. Even at the end, he was on the lookout for additional AM stations. In a letter (dictated just before he died, but not sent), to an associate who had advised him of a station that was for sale, he wrote: "I regret at the present time to say that I am afraid we could not handle this station. I am on the market, however, for an AM station in some of the major cities such as St. Louis or Kansas City or Denver or Los Angeles. I imagine with the finances we have it would have to be a distress case or a real good buy."

What explains this determination to push on, and this seeming blindness to the possibility of financial collapse? I think the explanation lies in his vision of what a Christian broadcasting network could achieve for evangelism and his utter assurance that the Lord was in this venture and would bless it. In the same batch of final letters, there was one to Bea Anderson, who with her husband Bob at WMUZ was taking on the critical task of centralizing all the stations, in which he wrote:

> I think you have a fantastic opportunity there now with that great station. I have perfect ease and rest knowing it is handled by you and Bob so capably. . . . If I did not feel that the Lord is in all of this I would be exhausted long ago, but I have faith to believe that this is going to be a great instrument in his hands in the years ahead after you and I are gone.

What kept my father marching on was an irrepressible faith that the Lord would bless and that each station would in due time be able to pay its own way. God had opened up the way for him to accomplish this great work, and now God would "make up the deficiency" to enable it to continue (Philippians 4:19). I do not believe that Percy ever really entertained the possibility that the whole enterprise might sink. At least he was confident that through his own diligence and business acumen, with the Lord's blessing, he could keep it afloat.

Another factor that eased my father's anxiety about his financial situation was his realization that the stations themselves were his chief asset. FM stations could be had cheaply in 1959, but he had the foresight to see that FM radio was going to contend with AM and that the stations would greatly increase in value. He knew that they belonged to him personally and noted this on the financial statements he left for Ruth. In these statements, he began to put a value on them as soon as he acquired them. In one, he estimated the market value of five stations at $100,000; in another, he projected a figure of $375,000.[22] In a letter to Ruth listing his assets, he counseled his wife: "Please don't sell anything, but leave all to our five children equally."[23]

But why was the road to success in building a Christian network proving to be so difficult, especially since it was so clear in Percy's mind that this was the way forward in accomplishing the larger mission of carrying the gospel to a lost world? It was not just that he was encountering obstacles along the way; he viewed his entire ministry as one of overcoming challenges coming from a hostile world. But the problems he was encountering in this venture seemed more intractable, and they were not bending to his will. He began to think differently about these difficulties; instead of viewing them as hurdles to be jumped, he saw them more as hardships to be endured, trials that God had placed before him in order to test his faith—but always with the purpose of achieving some greater triumph. He expresses this theme in his last publication—a giveaway booklet containing selected poems, lessons, aphorisms, and jokes. In a section entitled "Precious Thoughts," there are a surprising number that touch on the theme of how to cope with adversity:

The hardships of today prepare us for the demands of tomorrow.

Trials are the food of faith.

Our disappointments should not reduce us to spiritual weaklings.

God gets his greatest victories out of apparent defeats.[24]

The difficulties he faced were opportunities for greater faith and renewed effort. Percy pressed on and never wavered in his belief that all of his efforts and his struggles would have a fruitful outcome.

But was he pressing too hard? The danger was that in working so strenuously to realize his vision of a Christian network, he was allowing his own personal ambitions to take precedence over the greater mission of serving the constituency he had built up over the years. By using all of his resources to acquire more stations, rather than making the ones he had operate smoothly and effectively, it seems to me that this is what was happening. Many years earlier, when Percy was a student and just beginning his career, his sister-in-law, Willoughby's wife Dorothy, sent him a note after his highly successful first evangelistic tour from Los Angeles to Vancouver, that included a warning: "May He bless you in His work [she wrote] and Percy don't be too anxious, leave a little for Him." In his eagerness to "gain control of communications," Percy made the acquisition of stations too much his own project, and did not leave enough of the work for Him.

*

In the end, it did turn out—almost—as Percy had hoped. After his death, the three weakest stations (Des Moines, Ft. Lauderdale, and Forest Grove) could not be maintained and were sold. Don continued to manage the television station until 1964, when he was forced to sell it. At that time (he wrote), the station was operating "at break-even, but the bills and debt we had accumulated were so significant we had no choice but to sell to liqui-date debt, especially with no bank financing available. . . . The station could have succeeded if we had been able to endure financially for 12–18 months more."[25]

But WMUZ Detroit and WYCA Hammond were retained and are cur-rently operating as Christian stations, fifty years after his death, within the Crawford Broadcasting Company that Don owns and manages. And the Lancaster station WDAC, owned and operated by my brother Richard Crawford and myself along with retired station manager Paul Hollinger, has been one of the most successful commercial Christian stations in the nation since its inception in 1959.[26]

## FINAL DAYS

On a crisp, fall Saturday morning, October 29, 1960, I got in my 1953 Wind-sor Chrysler and drove from the main building at King's about a quarter of a mile to the president's estate, Braeview, which had been my home for three years before I moved into the dormitory at the college. It was the day before my nineteenth birthday, and I was making the short trek home to col-lect my present from my father before he left for a meeting that afternoon. In keeping with my growing intellectual interests, I was asking for money to buy a book at the local bookstore—Vernon Louis Parrington's *Main Cur-rents in American Thought*. My father wrote me a check for $15, apparently pleased with my interest in serious reading. I, of course, had no idea that even a check for that small amount of money was taxing his already strained bank accounts. It must have pained him a little, but he did not show it.[27]

Percy and Ruth had just finished making the next batch of *Pinebrook Praises* tapes that would go out on their stations over the next two weeks. The last one of these programs (which was to be aired two weeks later) still survives, and there is deep irony in Percy informing his listeners that his longtime colleague, Donald Gray Barnhouse, was in critical condition in a Philadelphia hospital with a brain tumor. He asked them to pray for him and send a card. "His passing, if it should take place, would be a great loss to the church," he said, acknowledging with respect Barnhouse's lifelong commitment to the Presbyterian Church. Within the week, however, both of these fundamentalist leaders would be dead.[28]

I found my father in good spirits that Saturday morning—even more so than usual. He was getting ready to go to a Youth for Christ meeting in Lan-caster, Pennsylvania, about a three-hour drive from Briarcliff. This rally was special for him because he would be able to talk up his new FM station WDAC, which had been on the air for ten months. He talked about the stations, which by then totally preoccupied him, and he said to me: "If I can only have five more years." Usually he asked for two years, but on that day, perhaps because, by then, he could see the time when the stations would be self-sustaining, he hoped for more. In hindsight, I think my father was happy that morning because he could finally see his hard work on the stations coming to fruition.

He left with Ruth and ten-year-old Donna Lee, intending to visit the station and meet up with the quartet in Lancaster. On the way, he planned to stop at a Howard Johnson's rest stop on the New Jersey turnpike, where he had left his topcoat on his last trip home. He pulled over on the opposite side of the road and trotted across the turnpike to the restaurant on the other side. Ruth and Donna waited for what seemed a long time, and then when my mother saw a man across the way waving to her, she knew what had happened. She rushed across the highway, with a frightened Donna Lee following a little later, and both watched as the medics pounded on Percy's chest—much too hard, Ruth thought.[29]

He was taken to the nearest hospital, which happened to be the Catholic St. Vincent's Hospital near Trenton. Ruth could see that this attack was much more serious than the previous six, but throughout the whole ordeal she believed that he would pull through as he had always done. After he regained consciousness she recalled him saying: "Air, air, can't get air," and gasping and coughing. His lungs were unable to deliver the life-giving oxygen his damaged heart needed. Then Ruth saw that her husband was crying—something she had never seen before in their twenty-seven years of marriage. He was taken to his room, placed in an oxygen tent, and given fluids intravenously.

He coughed blood throughout the night, but the next day, Sunday, he seemed better. Don visited with him for a couple of hours, and he talked to Dick on the phone. Donna Lee went back to Briarcliff that evening. On Monday, he managed to keep down some breakfast and, later, some soup. Ruth thought he "looked good" and teased him about his bright red face. She thought all along he was going to make it. He died that evening, October 31, 1960, at 6:00 p.m. He had asked for a doctor, and when an intern arrived, they cleared everyone out of the room while they worked on him. Ruth remembered that he had a long coughing spell, and then the attendants came out of the room "with long looks on their faces, and said 'the doctor will tell you.'"

Phone calls started going out from the hospital. I was called out of an evening physics class and told of my father's death by my Aunt Esther,

Ruth's sister, who had been with her at the hospital. I immediately carried the sad news to Dean and Donna Lee at the house and comforted Donna in her tears.

One humorous incident occurred in communicating word of Percy's death to his many associates when quartet member Bob Straton, who had a reputation for mixing up his words, sadly informed one colleague that "Passy perced away."

Percy had had only a few visitors in his final three days, since we all believed he would recover. On Sunday, he had spent time with Donna Lee and talked to her affectionately about growing up to be a fine woman. In addition to Don, Percy's associates, Bill Drury and Alex Dunlap, were there, and we can know from their reports some of what was going through my father's mind at the end.

Drury told an amusing anecdote. While talking to Percy, he remembers that something was said about his "getting ready to go home to heaven." The nurse who was attending to him heard this and commented innocently: "I hope so." Percy got a little annoyed by her comment and replied, "This isn't something we *hope* for; it is something we *know*," and asked Bill to take her into the hall and explain to her how they could have assurance of their eternal salvation. Percy also told Bill to go ahead with the plans for Youtharama the following Saturday. "I'll be there," he said confidently.

But my father was having serious thoughts about the work and how it would continue. He wanted so much to die knowing that it would be carried on and that his children would have their part in it. He had said to Ruth that the Philadelphia FM station was "a must." His conversation with Don was (as Don later put it) "testamentary," although the son did not quite see it at the time. Don remembers that he was "deeply concerned about The King's College, for he felt there was no successor in the ready." He spoke about Pinebrook. And "he hoped that Channel 17 would survive and that the radio ministry would go on with mother and me at the helm." "As I left, [Don recounted] I will never forget his last words to me: 'Everything is in good hands!'"[30]

These were my father's final thoughts. He died thinking not about his approaching death or even his imminent being with the Lord, but about the work to which he had given his all for thirty years and that had finally consumed him. He had said to the Lord when he was converted in Los Angeles: "I'll give you every drop of blood I have," and he kept that promise. He had said that he wanted to die "with his boots on"—serving the Lord, and he did. And it was fitting that this youth leader died at a young age, fifty-eight years and eleven days, so that he himself—and all of us—never had to think of him as old. And finally, he died in peace, convinced that he had done everything in his power to ensure that his work would go on, with the same goals and the same mission that he had lived and died for.

The memorial service was held at Town Hall in Philadelphia on the following Sunday. More than two thousand people filled the auditorium, with many more outside who could not get in. Don gave an eloquent eulogy in which he depicted his father as "no ordinary man." Billy Graham was the main speaker. He gave a warm and generous speech in which he acknowledged that Percy's evangelism had paved the way for his own and that Percy had made it easier for him to win converts. He closed with the words: "I loved that man, I respected him," and then fittingly gave an invitation, at which hands went up and people came forward.[31]

Fundamentalist leaders and many hundreds whose lives had been touched by Percy sent my mother letters of condolence. Carl Henry, editor of *Christianity Today,* spoke of "Percy's long-standing devotion to evangelism, his more recent interest in education, and the trail of conversions he has left to carry on."[32]

Harold Ockenga, fellow seminarian at Westminster and pastor of Park Street Church in Boston, pointed to some aspects of my father's personality and ministry that he admired, even though the two men were a study in contrasts. He wrote to Ruth:

> I admired him greatly from the first days when I knew him back in theological seminary.
>
> Percy was a rugged individualist, a spiritual pioneer, . . . [who] could not be confined to the restrictions of any denominational hierarchy but took his orders direct from God. As such, he was always an inspiration to others who wished that they could emulate his faith and energy but who were apt to follow more conventional channels.
>
> The indefatigable labors in which Percy engaged wore him out. . . . Perhaps you remember when he and you had dinner with several of us at the Wayside Inn some years ago. I had not seen Percy for several years and the effect of his labors was evident. I warned him at that time but you know Percy's attitude of disregard of self.[33]

My mother's immediate reaction at the hospital after Percy died, and repeated on several occasions on which she spoke publicly about him, revealed her deep devotion to his soul-winning mission: "Oh, think of the souls that will never be saved now—that only he could have reached."

Percy's work did continue, and Ruth and we children did attempt to fill the large void that he left behind. Don and I and our mother continued the morning broadcast, *Pinebrook Praises,* for the rest of the 1960–61 year,[34] and then Don and Ruth did a fifteen-minute program through 1967. Don earned his law degree from Temple University and then took the three gems that were left in Percy's estate—Detroit, Lancaster, and Hammond—and built them into the much larger Crawford Broadcasting Company—a network of Christian stations that Percy could not have imagined.

As we have seen, Dick took charge of the camps and directed them himself for a few years, then leased them to evangelist Ross Rhoads for several years before selling Pinebrook to the Bible Fellowship Church in 1968. It continues to be a summer Bible conference and retreat center to the present day. Later Dick became president of the Lancaster station WDAC and took an active role in the running of that station.

As soon as my father died, I began moving in my own direction toward a career in college teaching. I spent the rest of my sophomore year at King's, fighting with the new administration and board of trustees—whom I did not trust—to try to keep them from terminating the contracts of the teachers I admired most at King's, Al Black and Bill Willey; but the board forced both of them out that year, claiming that this is what Percy had wanted to do.[35] Dissatisfied with these developments, and knowing that my mother was planning to move to Philadelphia at the end of the year, I began looking at some schools in the Philadelphia area that had good philosophy programs and was accepted at Haverford College—my first choice. After finishing at Haverford, I went on to get a Master's degree in religion at Princeton University and a PhD in philosophy at the University of Pittsburgh and have been teaching philosophy ever since.

# 18

## A Life Fulfilled

IN THE DECEMBER 1926 ISSUE OF *THE KING'S BUSINESS*, T. C. HORTON CON-
tributed his last editorial before stepping down as editor. In it, he gave a
brief sketch of his fifty years of dedicated, full-time service, which began
in 1875 when he was invited to become secretary of the Indianapolis YMCA:

> In those good old days every "Y" secretary laid out his own program. . . . Soul
> saving was the appeal and purpose of the services. Meetings were held day and
> night, in the rooms, on the streets, in the parks, jails, hospitals and churches.
> Pastors were in happy accord. The old Gospel and the whole Gospel was given
> out, and a refreshing atmosphere of real revival prevailed. We believed men
> were lost. Men themselves believed they were lost, and many of them broke
> down, bowed the knee and confessed Christ as Saviour and Lord.

But all this had changed over the intervening years: "The devil . . . was
aroused to action and step by step, we have been able to watch his influence in the steady decline in schools and churches."

> So-called "intellectuality" took the place of spirituality. A chill was wafted in,
> . . . and icicles began to hang around the church walls. The Y.M.C.A. and
> Y.W.C.A. were unable to withstand the tide and, as a result, millions of conse-
> crated gifts to these institutions, intended for soul-saving work, are now being
> used for merely social service and the betterment of the body, but one listens in
> vain for the ringing of the joy bells over souls newborn.[1]

But Horton's young protégé, Percy Crawford, who had just graduated
from the Institute, saw things differently. At that time, Percy was making
plans for his summer cross-country tour with the BIOLA gospel team. He
was not disposed to see the "old Gospel" as fading; and he was prepared to
take up Horton's call to evangelize and to restore the "atmosphere of real
revival."

Percy's commitment to evangelism and his clear sense of purpose were
already evidenced in the speech he had given at graduation representing

the "men graduates" of BIOLA's class of 1926. In it, he suggests that the mission to which these men are called is somehow new, that a new horizon is opening:

> We have no desire, as the apostle Peter had, to go back to the old nets, nor have we merely a desire to be hewers of wood and drawers of water, as the Midianites of old. Ours is a great calling, namely to "Go into all the world and preach the gospel" pointing lost men and women to the Lamb of God that taketh away the sin of the world.

It was the same gospel message and the same evangelistic mission, but it would be carried to the world in a wholly new way. The torch was being passed to a new generation.

## CONTRIBUTION TO FUNDAMENTALISM

However much the Bible Institute of Los Angeles may have been charged with religious fervor, Percy was representing a movement that had become increasingly isolated and marginalized from the larger culture. In the period following the Scopes debacle in 1925, fundamentalists were in retreat— separated not only from the surrounding secular world, but also from the Protestant churches that, in their view, had drawn too close to the world. And to make the situation even worse, fundamentalists were engaged in bitter internal disputes—drawing sharp lines, accusing one another of heresy, and separating themselves from their impure brethren.

Moreover, Protestantism generally was in decline in the decade 1925– 35, undergoing what one historian has called a "religious depression" paralleling the great economic depression.[2] Percy was well aware of this decline in the Protestant churches, attributing it to the fact that many of the denominational churches had "gone modern" and compromised the fundamental tenets of the faith. For him, these churches were moribund. He was especially concerned about the younger generation who were turning away from the church and their Christian upbringing and falling into a life of sin and worldly pleasures.

Percy realized that the internal strife and external wars with the modernist churches had weakened the movement and diminished its effectiveness in communicating the gospel. He was determined to strike a more upbeat and moderate tone, and deliberately refrained from making negative attacks against other fundamentalists and churchmen with whom he may have disagreed. He stayed clear of doctrinal controversies and resisted lashing out at groups the fundamentalists opposed. He avoided harangues against what he saw to be the social evils of his time—Hollywood movies, divorce, smoking and drinking, dancing and dance music. In these ways, he helped to change the public face of fundamentalism over the next two decades, and repair its damaged reputation.

Percy was a maverick who never lost the rebellious quality he exhibited as a youth. After fully embracing the guidance and authority of Daddy Horton and Reuben Torrey at BIOLA, he found himself, over the next ten years, resisting the authority of his teachers at UCLA, Westminster, and Penn, and church officials in the Philadelphia Presbytery. He repeatedly said that he would never let any board or committee tell him how he should preach the gospel. When the Presbytery refused to support his radio broadcast, he quietly left the church, thus freeing himself from any human authority or censure and becoming fully independent. Percy wanted to be bound only to the authority of Scripture and to the Lord's will as he was able to discern it.

We have seen that this absolute independence that Percy enjoyed was an asset in building his organization, but also a threat to it because there was no significant oversight from any board or institutional authority that could restrain him when he made unfair or unwise decisions. Percy was never good at delegating authority or trusting others to manage his business. He had to be the one in charge, the one who made all the decisions. But this inability to share power and to retain some of the talented individuals that passed through his organization in meaningful positions proved harmful to him and weakened his overall ministry. Also, the absence of any second tier administrators or associates meant that there was no one capable of continuing his work after his death. His great hope was that his sons would take over different parts of his work, but since all of his enterprises were so centered on and dependent upon his individual person, this hope was bound to be unrealized.

He was criticized for attempting to do too many things and not doing any of them well. There is some truth to this criticism; toward the end of his life there was simply too much on his plate and not enough of him to go around. But it must be admitted that his main enterprises—Pinebrook, YPCA, and The King's College—were run well enough and achieved solid results. The charge that he should have concentrated his energies on fewer ministries underestimates his abilities. Percy had to be juggling five balls at once. If he had focused his energy and talent on one thing, such as the radio or television broadcast, the Lord's work would have been deprived of all the others.

Percy was ambitious and adventurous, always trying something new. He was a restless soul who had difficulty settling into one thing. When he got tired of something or bored with it, he would move on to something new.[3]

He liked to brag about being the first to venture into some new territory whether it was something as small as a new advertising gimmick or as large as a new format for youth rallies. Many people who are familiar with my father's ministry think of him as a pioneer who initiated many new works and enterprises. Percy undoubtedly viewed himself in this way, probably because he built up his entire organization from scratch. As I survey his many accomplishments, the ones that seem to me to be real firsts were his taking the radio broadcast onto network television in 1949, and at the end of his life, his putting in place a Christian broadcasting network, (which included the first religious television station in the nation).

However, to my mind, Percy's most original and important contribution to the evangelical movement in the 1930s and 1940s was the unique package of music and preaching that he and Ruth put together for their rallies and for radio and television. Over the years, Ruth assembled a succession of fine quartets, vocalists, and instrumentalists, and created a distinctive musical sound that set a new standard in gospel music for more than a decade; while Percy crafted his own rapid-fire voice and hard-hitting message that captured his listeners and brought them to a moment of decision. Their complementary styles resulted in a fresh formula, intended to bring a new vitality to the gospel message and a joyful exuberance to the Christian life. Percy was out to prove to young people that living for Jesus was more attractive and fun than anything the world had to offer. As evangelist Torrey Johnson said of Percy (in a letter written for his This Is Your Life dinner): "you gave the enlarged and fresh approach to the ministry of youth across the country";[4] in so doing, Percy (and Ruth) helped to reenergize the fundamentalist movement in the 1930s and into the 1940s, when it was languishing and in need of a new stimulus.

In his letter, Johnson went on to point to another aspect of Percy's work, his perpetuation of mass evangelism:

> God raised you up at a time when mass evangelism was in the doldrums and it was thought that the day of great crowds was past. It was you, together with a few others, who held high the torch, and dared to believe God to see us through the thin days of the early 30s to the thrilling days of the 40s and 50s.

The old style of tent-and-tabernacle revivalism was on its way out. In part this was the result of the excessive tactics and theatrics of Billy-Sunday-type evangelism that had spoiled the image of revivalism. Another factor was the rise of new forms of entertainment—on radio and later television—which people could now enjoy in the comfort of their homes and private establishments. Since the churches were not drawing large numbers, the revivalists turned to the radio to reach the people where they were. And to capture an audience, they had to make their show as appealing as the variety shows of their secular rivals. This is what Ruth and Percy did with their radio and television broadcasts, thus helping to keep the spirit of revivalism alive. Percy then followed up his broadcasts with rallies and meetings across the nation so that he could meet with his listeners face to face, and bring more of them to Christ.

Torrey Johnson himself would be among the evangelists who would attract "great crowds" in the mid-1940s at Youth for Christ rallies. But in the previous decade, mass evangelism was taking place over the air waves, and mass conversions were happening not as people walked down the aisle and stood at the altar, but as they bowed their heads and kneeled in front of their radio sets. Percy was among that small band of national radio broadcasters who kept revivalism going forward until the next generation of evangelists—Jack Wyrtzen, Billy Graham, Merv Rosell and others—reverted to citywide campaigns. Instead of joining that group, Percy stayed with his strength—radio and television; and then in the last phase of his life, drawing on his entrepreneurial skills, he moved to develop new communication channels for the gospel by building a Christian broadcasting network.

## SALVATION FULL AND FREE

Percy's evangelistic mission of saving souls was couched in a theology that was historically linked to the Reformed tradition as it came down to him through the teachings of Reuben Torrey at BIOLA. It was a theology that was focused on the twin doctrines of universal sin and salvation through Christ's atoning death. Salvation was a "love gift" from God offered "full and free" to every individual; one only had to will to believe in God's Son in order to have eternal life (John 3:16).[5] Percy rejected Calvin's doctrine of divine election and substituted a decidedly Arminian view that allowed the individual's choice to play a decisive role in determining his or her destiny. His whole theology centered on conversion and the individual's act of accepting or rejecting Christ.[6] Percy believed that everyone at some time in their life made the choice whether to receive Christ. And thus as an evangelist, he bore the awful responsibility of bringing the gospel message before the mind and will of the sinner so that he or she might have the chance to be saved from certain death.

Those who accepted Christ into their life then experienced the new birth. Percy had witnessed scores of individuals throughout his ministry whose lives were radically transformed by the gospel message, and for him these changed lives constituted the most convincing argument for the truth of his message.

Coupled with these doctrines of God's great gift and the sinner's ultimate choice was the corresponding belief that God would judge those who rejected him. God hates sin and has "declared war" on those sinners who "spit in the face" of his Son. He viewed the act of rejecting Christ as tantamount to the unpardonable sin. God punishes sinners by casting them into a "real hell of fire and brimstone," and Percy did not shrink from depicting the horrors of hell in graphic terms. He preached on hell more than any other subject. Although he agonized over the thought of hell and flames reserved for sinners—especially his own loved ones—he never softened his view of hell. For him, eternal suffering was a perfectly logical consequence of a just God meting out punishment to those who rejected the gift of his Son.

Part of the reason for Percy's success in evangelism was that he presented his audience with strict dualities and clear-cut alternatives—heaven or hell, saved or lost, eternal life or everlasting punishment, full assurance or doubt, sin-sick or filled with joy and peace, going 100 percent for Christ or for the devil. There were no gray areas, no compromises, and no room for doubt or indecision in his system of belief. Percy's own character and temperament reflected these theological dualisms: he was decisive in action and disdained fence-sitting and half-heartedness. Had he been more cautious and reflective and more sensitive to the ambiguities and uncertainties that pervade our lives, he would not have been the great soul winner that he was.

*

Percy stuck to the unadulterated gospel message and tried always to keep it from being weakened or contaminated by extraneous elements. As a preacher and as an educator at The King's College, he fought against the idea that Christian beliefs had to be reinterpreted in order to accommodate the intellectual trends or cultural conditions of a particular period in history. Specifically, he resisted the attempts of modernists to integrate fundamental beliefs with the modern worldview of science and philosophy. Indeed, Percy's own view was countercultural in as much as he rejected modern thought and scholarship in a package—one that included science and evolutionary theory, biblical criticism, rationalist philosophy, and any sort of social progressivism. He rejected the popular idea of progress as it was being realized in the growth of business and industry, science and technology, and in the attempts to achieve a just social order. Instead, he adopted the more pessimistic view that because of man's sinful nature and rejection of

God, all of these human efforts were ultimately bound to fail. The Christian's only hope for the redemption of society lay in Christ's return.

He was opposed to modern science because he thought it was based on the premise of atheistic naturalism—the belief that everything in nature can be explained in terms of natural causes—thus ruling out God. Evolutionary theory was the prime example of a naturalistic theory. Against this, he believed that God's supernatural acts are revealed in scripture, and that the course of nature and of human history can only be explained in terms of these divine acts.

But the assumption Percy was making in this regard was that his conservative theology and interpretation of scripture could not be reconciled with modern science and evolution. There were however a few thoughtful fundamentalist voices around him that were trying to find ways of reconciling modern scientific ideas with their biblical theology. There was the dean at The King's College, Louis Allen Higley, who tried to reconcile an old earth and the fossil record with the Genesis account of creation by means of his "gap theory." And John MacInnis and John Gresham Machen both held that it did not make any difference for their theological beliefs if evolution was true. But Percy was not listening to what these scholars were saying, and even if he had heard them, he would not have condoned their views.

He distrusted philosophy because he thought its method of questioning and inquiring about the grounds of any belief engendered doubt and disbelief, and therefore led to atheism. But again, Percy ignored the fact that many who questioned their faith did come to find a valid reason for believing in the Christian God, and that faith could be reasonable even if there were doubts that could not be resolved (as Machen had argued). Percy might have acknowledged this point, but nevertheless thought there was too much at stake to allow any room for doubt. If one begins to question his faith, he is more than likely to lose it.

Over and against these modern ideas Percy proclaimed the old-fashioned Bible view. Ignoring his reliance upon the Reformed interpretive tradition, he was utterly convinced that the simple gospel message he preached was the word of God—spoken once and for all in the Bible, in language that anyone can understand, and applicable to all times and places. At the same time, he thought that the evangelist needed to take these timeless truths and apply them to the special needs of his time, (which is not the same thing as modifying those truths in order to accommodate the ideas and trends of the time). Percy was beginning his full-time ministry just as the country was moving into the worst phase of the Great Depression. Accordingly he crafted a message and a style that addressed the particular demands of that time. He was speaking to many who felt helpless in the face of large, impersonal social and economic forces they could not control, and told them that it was in their power to make a decision that would change their lives and determine their eternal destiny. He brought consolation to suffering souls by telling them about someone who "loved them and died for them." Although he had nothing to give them that would relieve their immediate physical needs, he offered them a "hope beyond the grave." He threw them a lifeline, and they took it. Souls were saved. Lives were transformed. Percy proved Daddy Horton wrong: men and women were still ready to acknowledge they were sinners and in need of God's saving grace, and willing to confess Christ as Lord and give their lives over to him.

Percy continued to preach the message of sin and salvation and a new life in Christ for the rest of his career. Even as he devised new avenues and strategies for communicating the gospel—the television program, Youtharama, a broadcasting network, a foreign mission—the content of the message and its delivery did not change. Percy's own effectiveness diminished in these later years as his recycled sermons became ever more condensed and simplified, and more theologically thin. But he never lost his ability to win converts. He moved quickly in his sermons to the invitation to accept Christ and the altar call, and his listeners and viewers continued to respond in great numbers.

## Meeting Adversity

From the beginning of his active ministry, Percy saw himself as engaged in a constant battle with hostile forces that worked against him and his efforts to preach the gospel. After leaving the congenial and supportive environment of BIOLA, he soon came up against the world's resistances —first in his UCLA professors who denied truth and fostered doubt; in his Calvinist professors at Westminster who discouraged his evangelism; in the liberal faction of the Philadelphia Presbytery that wanted to drive out the conservatives; in the uncooperative Federal Communications Commission; and in the networks whose high costs and arbitrary restrictions severely limited his reach across the nation. In fact, he conceived of his entire career as a series of struggles against opposing forces. To a certain extent, this opposition was imagined and a reflection of the general feeling among fundamentalists of being alienated from, and at war with, secular society. Percy also tended to exaggerate the opposing forces in order to show that faith could surmount great obstacles. But the resistances he encountered were real enough, especially toward the end of his life.

Percy met with adversity on several different fronts in the last five years of his life. At his beloved King's College, the goals he had originally set for the college were being challenged. He could not get the college operating in the black. And there was a growing movement to push him out of the presidency. Although he did finally decide to step down, he could not find a way to do it and still retain ultimate control.

But worse than this, there was the problem of his own sons, who seemed to be deserting him. "I have lost my entire family, and I don't know how to get them back," he confided to his friend John DeBrine. This was the difficulty that brought real sorrow and disappointment into his life for the first time.

The most exhausting struggle for him, however, was his attempt to build a Christian broadcasting network in order to "gain control of communications." This endeavor was a bold stroke that challenged the secular power brokers who were holding back evangelical broadcasters from full and equal access to the air waves. Percy put everything he possessed on the line in order to make this vision a reality. He spent his last years frantically trying to build up a network of stations that would be minimally operational and self-sustaining before he died. But once he got going in this process, he was so determined to win the prize in the time that remained to him, and so sure that the Lord would bless this work, that he overreached, made some poor business decisions, and nearly brought the whole venture to ruin. Percy was on a precipice with no one to wave him back. Now more than ever he needed the perspective of a high-level associate or a board that could restrain him; but he had long ago precluded that from ever happening. If Percy had lived longer, I believe he would have been able to obtain the Philadelphia FM station he so desired and sustain the other eight stations he had acquired; but I am less confident that he would have been able to slow his pace and curb what seems to have been an insatiable appetite for more acquisitions. His death was timely in as much as it forestalled an implosion in his organization that was almost certain to come.

Percy did not shrink from his problems, but faced them and tried to find ways to resolve them. With his stations, he just kept pushing, scurrying to find personnel, funding, and the right formula for success. At the college, he searched for a successor and did finally settle on someone who would be acceptable to him.[7] And with his four boys, he realized he had to have patience; he did not attempt to force or harangue us back onto safe ground, but instead gave us some room to follow our own path, confident that in the end he could gently lead us back home. What I admire most about my father is the attitude with which he faced these difficulties—through it all he maintained his faith and his sanity, his courage and his cheerful optimism.

*

Percy Crawford was one of the "young men on fire," who, with his lifetime partner, Ruth, created a unique ministry of music and preaching that reinvigorated the fundamentalist movement in the 1930s and 1940s, and helped to give it a more moderate and credible public image. Also, during this period, he was one of a small group of national radio broadcasters who kept revivalism moving forward by taking the gospel to a mass audience on the radio until the mid-1940s and 1950s when revivalism reverted to citywide campaigns and crusades. And in the 1950s he put into operation the first viable Christian broadcasting network that opened up new channels of communication for evangelism and showed evangelicals how it was possible for them to compete successfully in the world of commercial broadcasting.

Percy was first and foremost a preacher, whose gift of evangelism encompassed other gifts—a singular vision, an entrepreneurial spirit, and an uncanny ability to invent new strategies and new avenues for spreading the gospel. "Attempt great things for God; expect great things from God" was the motto he lived by. Through it all, he was driven by a passion to save lost souls, and this burning thirst for souls dominated everything he did. In his multifaceted ministry extending over thirty-four years, Percy Crawford brought tens of thousands of people throughout the nation and the world to a new life. And he never ceased ringing the joy bells for souls newborn.

# Notes

## PREFACE

1. Joel A. Carpenter, *Revive Us Again: The Reawakening of American Fundamentalism* (New York: Oxford University Press, 1997), xi–xii.

2. Bob Bahr, *Man with a Vision: The Story of Percy Crawford* (Chicago: Moody, n.d.). At the time of Percy's death (1960), Bahr was a student at The King's College (the college Percy founded), graduating in 1964.

3. *Young People Today* ran from 1934 to 1942. I found the last few years of it (catalogued) at Dallas Theological Seminary. *Christian Newsette* ran from 1951 to 1954.

## CHAPTER 1. INTRODUCTION

1. In this introduction and in chapter 3 ("The Roots of Fundamentalism"), I am relying heavily on Martin Marty's account of this split within the Protestant churches in *Righteous Empire: The Protestant Experience in America* (New York: The Dial Press, 1970), esp. part 2, sections 5, 6. For other very helpful accounts of the fifty-year period leading up to fundamentalism, see George M. Marsden, *Fundamentalism and American Culture: The Shaping of Twentieth-Century Evangelicalism: 1870–1925* (New York: Oxford University Press, 1980), esp. chs. 1–3, 8–11; Ernest R. Sandeen, *The Roots of Fundamentalism: British and American Millenarianism: 1800–1930* (Chicago: University of Chicago Press, 1970), esp. ch. 7; and Martin E. Marty, *Modern American Religion,* vol. 1, *The Irony of It All: 1893–1919* (Chicago: University of Chicago Press, 1986).

2. Percy Crawford, *The Art of Fishing for Men* (Chicago: Moody, 1950, 1935), 14. All quotations are from the 1950 revised version of the original 1935 edition.

3. The phrase was used by Mel Larson in his firsthand account of the young evangelists and youth workers of this period in his 1947 book chronicling the Youth for Christ movement: *Youth for Christ* (Grand Rapids: Zondervan, 1947), 41. Percy wrote the brief introduction to the book.

## CHAPTER 2. CONVERSION IN LOS ANGELES

1. Percy Crawford, "My Testimony," in *Salvation Full and Free: A Series of Radio Messages* (Philadelphia: Westbrook, 1943), 7–10.

2. Percy Crawford letter in response to Nancy Keller, dictated shortly before Percy's death, but not sent.

3. Barr Crawford, at Percy's This Is Your Life dinner, April 24, 1953.

4. Crawford, "My Testimony," 8.

5. In one of his sermons, Percy states that he had never touched a drop of whiskey.

6. "'Y' Will Graduate 67," May 27, 1923 (clipping from unknown newspaper). A letter from his brother Alph (November 1, 1922) was addressed: "Percy B. Crawford Esq., YMCA, Portland, Oregon."

7. Family archives.

8. In his November 1, 1922, letter to Percy Crawford, Alph reminds Percy that in choosing his own profession, he should not forget his "financial obligation" to him (Alph) and adds: "This need not concern you greatly in making your choice, for at present my prospects are fairly bright."

9. Percy had acquired a letter of recommendation (May 18, 1923), from one Mr. A. Whittaker, Inspector, The British Columbia Permanent Loan Company, which said that the young man was "upright, able, and honest . . . and that he will apply himself thoroughly, in any position which he may be appointed to fill." The recommender concluded: it is "my belief that he will prove successful in any career he may pursue."

10. Percy Crawford sermon entitled "Tragedy with Triumph" preached January 12, 1936 (in collection of three sermons), 8.

11. Message delivered at Percy Crawford memorial service at Town Hall in Philadelphia on November 6, 1960.

12. Crawford, "My Testimony," 9.

13. Bible Institute of Los Angeles Bulletin (January 1923): 86.

14. Robert Williams and Marilyn Miller, Chartered for His Glory: Biola University, 1908–1983 (Marceline, Mo.: Herff Jones, 1983), 19. It was Horton's success with the Sunday school program that engendered the idea of a Bible training school that became the Bible Institute of Los Angeles, founded by Horton in 1908.

15. "Pioneer for God: The Biography of Percy B. Crawford" (1954), ch. 2. A copy of this typed draft of a biography (by an unknown author, no pagination but fifty-two pages long), which was authorized by Percy but never completed or published, is in the Billy Graham Center Archives. One of the boys in the Sunday school class, Herb Cassel, later enrolled at the Bible Institute while Percy was still a student there and wrote the following in Percy's graduation autograph book: "Dear Percy: I remember when I first met you—when you attempted to teach the s.s. class I was in. You had only been saved a few months. . . . I'll never forget the fellowship we had in those early days."

16. "Worth While Work," editorial in The King's Business (December 1926): 702.

17. T. C. Horton, Personal and Practical Christian Work (Los Angeles: BIOLA Book Room, Bible Institute of Los Angeles, 1922). At this time, Horton was superintendent of the Bible Institute and listed on the faculty as teaching in the areas of "Practical Methods of Work and Pastoral Theology."

18. Ibid., 59 (emphasis original). He goes even further in the following passage: "If soul saving is the business of the Church, and it is, and you are not saving souls, you are hindering rather than helping the cause of Christ" (65).

19. Ibid.

20. Percy Crawford, The Art of Fishing for Men (Chicago: Moody, 1950), 15. All quotations are from the 1950 revised edition unless otherwise specified.

21. Advertisement in one of the 1926 issues of The King's Business.

22. "The Gospel of John the Apostle," arranged by T. C. Horton (Chicago: Moody, 1950), 5–6.

23. "Pioneer for God," ch. 2.

24. Crawford, *Art of Fishing for Men,* 16.

25. "Pioneer for God," ch. 2.


## Chapter 3. The Roots of Fundamentalism

1. Martin E. Marty, *Righteous Empire: The Protestant Experience in America* (New York: The Dial Press, 1970), 151–54.

2. Walter Rauschenbusch, *Christianity and the Social Crisis in the 21st Century: The Classic That Woke Up the Church* (New York: HarperCollins, 2007), 287.

3. Ibid., 57–58.

4. Ibid., 171.

5. See George M. Marsden, *Fundamentalism and American Culture: The Shaping of Twentieth-Century Evangelicalism, 1870–1925* (New York: Oxford University Press, 1980), 80–85, 88–92.

6. H. Richard Niebuhr, Wilhelm Pauck, and Francis P. Miller, *The Church Against the World* (Chicago: Willett, Clark & Co., 1935), 1–2; cited in Robert T. Handy, "The American Religious Depression, 1925–1935" (Fortress Press, 1968), 19; Handy's article originally published in *Church History,* 29 (1960): 3–16.

7. R. A. Torrey, *Why God Used D. L. Moody* (New York: Revell, 1923), 51–59.

8. Ernest R. Sandeen, *The Roots of Fundamentalism: British and American Millenarianism, 1800–1930* (Chicago: University of Chicago Press, 1970), 246.

9. George M. Marsden, *Fundamentalism and American Culture,* 33.

10. See William G. McLoughlin, *Modern Revivalism: Charles Grandison Finney to Billy Graham* (New York: Ronald, 1959), 233–38 for a vivid description of Sankey's success as a song leader.

11. Bruce J. Evensen, *God's Man for the Gilded Age* (New York: Oxford University Press, 2003), 173, 179–80.

12. Marty, *Righteous Empire,* 162.

13. Ibid., 163, 180.

14. "The Second Coming of Christ," *The Best of D. L. Moody,* ed. Wilbur M. Smith, (Chicago: Moody Press, 1971), 193–95; cited in Marsden, *Fundamentalism and American Culture,* 38).

15. Marsden, *Fundamentalism and American Culture,* 35.

16. Ibid., 33.

17. Cited in McLoughlin, *Modern Revivalism,* 272.

18. McLoughlin, *Modern Revivalism,* 380–81.

19. Ibid., 384–85.

20. Ibid., 426.

21. Ibid., 427.

22. Ibid., 421.

23. Ibid., 415. McLoughlin argues that this figure is probably accurate. In his twenty most successful revivals between 1912 and 1921, Sunday recorded 593,004 converts. (415–16)

24. Percy Crawford radio sermon entitled "The Blood" (preached November 24, 1935), 13.

25. McLoughlin, *Modern Revivalism,* 451.

26. Ibid., 415, 452.

## CHAPTER 4. REUBEN TORREY'S BIBLE INSTITUTE

1. Robert Harkness, *Reuben Archer Torrey: The Man, His Message* (Chicago: Bible Institute Colportage, 1929), 68.

2. For revealing sketches of Torrey and his song leader, Charles M. Alexander, see William G. McLoughlin, *Modern Revivalism: Charles Grandison Finney to Billy Graham* (New York: Ronald, 1959), 366–77.

3. Ernest R. Sandeen, *The Roots of Fundamentalism: British and American Millenarianism, 1800–1930* (Chicago: University of Chicago Press, 1970), 182–83.

4. Torrey's contributions were "The Personality and Deity of the Holy Spirit" (vol. 1), "The Certainty and Importance of the Bodily Resurrection of Jesus Christ from the Dead" (vol. 5), and "The Place of Prayer in Evangelism" (vol. 12). See George M. Marsden, *Fundamentalism and American Culture* (New York: Oxford University Press, 1980), 118–23, for a valuable discussion of *The Fundamentals* and their significance.

5. Ernest R. Sandeen, *The Roots of Fundamentalism: British and American Millenarianism, 1800–1930* (Chicago: University of Chicago Press, 1970), xiv.

6. Proceedings and addresses of the conference published as *God Hath Spoken* (Philadelphia: Bible Conference Committee, 1919), 11–12.

7. Torrey's response to Mathews is reprinted in *The Fundamentalist-Modernist Conflict: Opposing Views on Three Major Issues,* ed. Joel A. Carpenter (New York: Garland, 1988), 10, 32; see also Joel A. Carpenter, *Revive Us Again: The Reawakening of American Fundamentalism* (New York: Oxford University Press, 1997), 39.

8. Martin E. Marty, *Modern American Religion,* vol. 1 (Chicago: University of Chicago Press, 1986), 244–45. See also Matthew A. Sutton, *Aimee Semple McPherson and the Resurrection of Christian America* (Cambridge: Harvard University Press, 2007), 39.

9. The Bible school was later renamed "Lighthouse of International Foursquare Evangelism" (LIFE). The Foursquare Gospel stood for Jesus Christ, savior, healer, baptizer with the Holy Spirit, and coming king.

10. "A Continuous and Ever-Increasing Revival," *The Bridal Call* (April 1923): 3. Cited in Gloria Lothrop, "West of Eden: Pioneer Media Evangelist Aimee Semple McPherson in Los Angeles," *Journal of the West* 27 (April 1988): 55.

One of McPherson's admirers was Percy's mother, Margaret, who moved to Los Angeles after Percy had left, and for a time lived on Echo Park Avenue.

11. McPherson herself had had an ecstatic experience as a teenager in which she spoke in tongues, but downplayed it in her church in an effort to make Pentecostalism more acceptable to the mainline churches. For her own detailed account of the experience see *This is That: Personal Experiences, Sermons, and Writings* (Los Angeles: Echo Park Evangelistic Association), 43–47.

12. *The King's Business* (January 1922): 17–18.

13. Not all fundamentalists repudiated Aimee Semple McPherson. Paul Rader visited Angelus Temple; William Jennings Bryan spoke there frequently; and Methodist revivalist and preacher, L. W. Munhall preached there in 1924, praising McPherson's loyalty "to the Bible as the word of God, and all the fundamental doctrines of historic Christianity." Matthew A. Sutton, *Aimee Semple McPherson and the Resurrection of Christian America* (Cambridge: Harvard University Press, 2007), 51.

I could find only one instance of a link with BIOLA. In 1921, McPherson approached Lyman Stewart, who had financed the Institute and its related publishing house, and asked if he would help her publish a collection of messages entitled *Divine Healing Sermons* which included accounts of both divine healing and speaking in tongues. Stewart decided to overlook his differences with the evangelist and printed the book. Matthew A. Sutton, "Between the Refrigerator and the Wildfire: Aimee Semple McPherson, Pentecostalism, and the Fundamentalist Modernist Controversy," *Church History* 72.1 (March 2003): 159–88.

14. Cited in McLoughlin, *Modern Revivalism,* 372.

15. R. A. Torrey, *How to Bring Men to Christ* (7th ed.; New York: Revell, 1933 [1893]), 7. A decade later, Percy would model his own 1935 handbook, *The Art of Fishing for Men,* on this work even more than on Horton's *Personal and Practical Christian Work.*

16. *Why God Used D. L. Moody* (New York: Revell, 1923), 7.

17. Advertisement in *The King's Business* (March 1926): 176.

18. Bible Institute of Los Angeles Bulletin 8.1 (January 1923). Torrey's hand is easily recognizable in this text. The goals reflect recurring themes from his writings and probably give an accurate portrayal of his own self-image.

19. Ibid., 13.

20. Ibid., 43.

21. Percy Crawford, *The Art of Fishing for Men* (Chicago: Moody, 1950), 28–29.

22. Torrey, *How to Bring Men to Christ,* 114.

23. Percy must have been deeply impressed by the life of this missionary to Africa, for he named his third son (the author of this work) after him.

24. Cited in "Pioneer for God: The Biography of Percy B. Crawford" (unpublished, 1954), ch. 2.

25. The call letters, originally KJS (King Jesus Saves), were changed to KTBI (The Bible Institute) in September 1925. It is not known what program the gospel team appeared on; it was most likely the daily *Devotional Service* (8:30–9:00 a.m.) or *Inspirational Service* (2:00–3:00 p.m.); see *The King's Business* (January 1927): 44. Percy mentions in a magazine article written six years later that he had "had previous experience in preaching over the radio on stations KTBI in Los Angeles and WMBI of the Moody Bible Institute and others" ("A Modern Revival," *Revelation* [August 1932]: 349).

26. Apparently KTBI was the second religious station in the United States, not the first. A researcher of Los Angeles radio history found that the first religious station on the air was WDM radio, owned and operated by Church of the Covenant in Washington, D.C. WDM was licensed on December 22, 1921, and had its first broadcast on January 1, 1922. The station operated a little more than three years. Jim Hilliker, "History of KSFG: Pioneer L.A. Christian Station Stops Broadcasting After 79 Years" (written for Web site LARADIO.com, 2003).

27. Report from M. E. Carrier, manager of Radio department, with letters from listeners in New Hampshire, Oregon, Hawaii, and Mexico (*Biola Alumni Annual* [1923]: 28–29).

28. *The Bridal Call* (December 1923/January 1924): 24. At the time McPherson was constructing her station (1923), there were 200,000 radio sets within a hundred-mile radius of Los Angeles.

29. *The Bridal Call* (July 1923): 18.

30. Ibid., 15.

31. In one sermon, McPherson declared: "Who cares about Hell, friends? Why, we all know what hell is. We've heard about it all our lives. A terrible place, where nobody wants to go. I think the less we hear about Hell the better, don't you? Let's forget about Hell. Lite up your hearts. What we are interested [in], yes Lord, is Heaven and how to get there!" (Cited in David Clark, "Miracles for a Dime: from Chatauqua Tent to Radio Station," *California History* 57 (Winter 1978/79): 357.

32.  Percy wrote in, by hand, on his original typed copy a revision of the last five words of this paragraph, substituting the overused phrase "to preach the unsearchable riches of Christ."

33.  B. Chadwick letter to Percy Crawford, July 20, 1926. Percy also received a letter a few days later from his sister-in-law, Dorothy Crawford, married to Earl Willoughby Crawford, whom he (along with Harlan Fischer) had just visited in Vancouver, that says in closing: "May He bless you both in His work and Percy don't be too anxious leave a little for Him." Is his sister referring perhaps to an overreaction by the ardent evangelist to the results the team was getting?

34.  The November 1926 issue of *The King's Business* reported on the summer tours of two gospel teams of BIOLA students (the other team represented the Fishermen's Club) as follows: "Both teams returned in time for school, to recount, as did the disciples of old, the wonderful way in which the Lord had used them. Many, many souls were graciously saved through their efforts, and scores of names were added to the student prospect list. We praise God for the way in which He has used these talented young men" (650).

## CHAPTER 5. UCLA: "ATHEISM WAS RAMPANT"

1.  Percy Crawford radio sermon entitled "Why Another College?" (preached December 6, 1936). Dr. Lewis Sperry Chafer was president of Dallas Seminary.

2.  Percy Crawford sermon entitled "A Place of Consciousness," in Percy Crawford, *Whither Goest Thou? A Series of Radio Messages Preached on 250 Stations over the Mutual Network* (East Stroudsburg, Penn.: Pinebrook Book Club, 1946), 46.

3.  Crawford, "Why Another College?"

4.  Percy Crawford sermon entitled "The Bible" (preached January 26, 1936), 14.

5.  It was in that very year that the University of California, Southern Branch became the University of California at Los Angeles (UCLA).

6.  Harlan Fischer's admiration of, and liking for, Percy is revealed in the note he put in Percy's autograph book on graduating from BIOLA (1926): "Dear Perc: I will never cease praising God enough for bringing me in contact with you. Its great to have some one to go to who understands and cares a little when the clouds seem dark. Your life and zeal at B.I. has meant more to me than any other thing I know of. What I am today has been brought about by God thru your life. Though years may separate us, lets never forget one another in prayer. Fifty years from now if He tarries, after God has used you mightily and I know He will, just try to look back at your old B.I. days and remember this poor old sinner saved by His grace. Love In Him." He adds (on the side): "Remember when I first met you Perc— mid night mission, Sept. 14, 1924, 9:30 o'clock."

7.  Percy Crawford sermon entitled "Did the University Make Me an Atheist?" (original typed copy, undated but signed with seminary address: "1528 Pine St., Phila. Pa.").

8.  Ibid.

9.  This same point is made by philosopher William James in his famous essay "The Will to Believe" (1896). Percy probably got this idea from John MacInnis's classes, where James's pragmatist philosophy would certainly have been discussed.

10.  Percy discloses this fact in "Esau," a sermon included in *Highlights of Pinebrook: Twenty-Four Inspiring Messages Delivered at the Pinebrook Bible Conference,* ed. Percy Crawford (Philadelphia: Pinebrook Book Club, 1938), 254.

11. *Alpha Gamma Omega: The Christ-Centered Fraternity,* part D: "A Challenge for the 90s," a speech presented by E. Harlan Fischer at the 63rd Founders' Day Banquet held at the Castaways Restaurant in Burbank, California, on February 24, 1990.

12. My thanks to Adam Blauert, the current historian of Alpha Gamma Omega, who sent me the official histories of the organization and other helpful material. A recent graduate of UCLA, he wrote that Alpha Gamma Omega "was the single most important part of my time in college and I'm sure that I would have found UCLA as cold, secular and unfriendly as your father found it if I had not found AGO" (letter to author, December 20, 2004).

13. Fischer, "Challenge for the 90s."

14. Percy Crawford sermon entitled "How the Treasurer of Ethiopia Found Christ" (November 3, 1935).

15. Percy Crawford sermon entitled "A New Creation" (preached January 5, 1936).

16. Bill Hoffman, "Historical Notes, Alpha Gamma Omega" (unpublished May 2002 paper, revised February 25, 2004), 2.

17. Ibid., 3.

18. Mark Ward, *Air of Salvation: The Story of Christian Broadcasting* (Grand Rapids: Baker, 1994), 30–31.

19. Percy Crawford sermon entitled "Lot's Escape," in *Whither Goest Thou?* 80.

## CHAPTER 6. TRAINING AT WHEATON

1. Wheaton College 1927–28 catalog, 9.

2. See Paul M. Bechtel, *Wheaton College: A Heritage Remembered, 1860–1984* (Wheaton, Ill.: Shaw, 1984), chs. 8–9.

3. This is not surprising since the doctrinal statement was drafted at a meeting of the World Christian Fundamentals Association in Philadelphia in 1920 and Reuben Torrey was one of the chief contributors, as was Wheaton's previous president, Charles A. Blanchard.

4. Bechtel, *Wheaton College,* 104.

5. Ibid., 105.

6. Allen Higley and a colleague, John W. Leedy, opened Wheaton's well-known summer science station in Black Hills, South Dakota, in 1935, Higley directing field work in geology, and Leedy in biology.

7. Dan Higley (L. Allen Higley's son) phone interview, August 6, 2004.

8. Percy roomed off campus at Professor Moule's house on College Avenue.

9. *Tower* (1929 [yearbook]): 88–89; (1930): 105, 106, 109.

10. Condolence letter after Percy's death from Stephen Paine to Ruth Crawford (November 2, 1960).

11. What Joel Carpenter said of Bible institutes was also true of the Christian colleges.

12. Anne T. Howard letter to Ruth Crawford (November 13, 1960).

13. Stephen Paine letter to Ruth Crawford (November 2, 1960).

14. The student newspaper, *The Wheaton Record,* gives a partial breakdown of how Percy arrived at this large total: thirteen hundred attended one service in Minneapolis, and five hundred men showed up at the Minnesota State Reformatory; "Student-Evangelists Heard by Thousands," *Wheaton Record* 41.11 (April 25, 1928).

15. *Tower* (1930): 166.

16. Ibid., 167.

17. In his monthly column reporting on station WMBI in the *Moody Monthly,* Wendell Loveless thanks the Wheaton College Quintet (along with many other individuals and groups) for appearing on the Moody station (July 1929). It is not known which program the team appeared on, but two of them are described as having short gospel messages followed by a gospel invitation (*Moody Bible Institute Monthly* [January 1928]).

18. Contributed by Dr. Clarence B. Wyngarden to "Stones of Remembrance" (Wheaton, Ill.: Wheaton College, 1995), 5. This same story was reported in the student paper (*Wheaton Record* [September 25, 1929]).

19. "New Dean for Bible Institute," *Los Angeles Times,* April 7, 1925, II, 1.

20. *The King's Business* (April, May, and June issues, 1927). Quotation from "More About the Christian Philosopher" (May 1927): 281.

21. John M. MacInnis, "The Editor's Statement to the King's Business Family," *The King's Business* 1 (January 1927): frontis.

22. Much of the factual information I am using comes from an unpublished essay by Kelly Damon Barton, "Fundamentalism and Higher Fundamentalism: The MacInnis Controversy at BIOLA" (July 22, 1988), which I uncovered in the Church of the Open Door archives.

23. "Pioneer for God: The Biography of Percy B. Crawford" (1954), ch. 2 (Billy Graham Center Archives).

## CHAPTER 7. A WESTMINSTER MAN

1. The only nondenominational seminary that might have attracted Percy was Dallas Theological Seminary, as Dallas recruited heavily from BIOLA and Wheaton. As we have seen, Percy had some acquaintance with its president, Lewis Sperry Chafer, whom he credited with having impressed upon him the need for higher education. I can only speculate about this, but Percy may have rejected Dallas because Chafer had openly criticized revivalism as a method of evangelism in his 1919 book *True Evangelism; or, Winning Souls by Prayer.* Chafer sparked a debate with Reuben Torrey on this issue in which Torrey championed revivalism as the God-appointed method of winning converts. See Vernon Eugene Mattson's *The Fundamentalist Mind: An Intellectual History of Religious Fundamentalism in the United States* (PhD diss., University of Kansas, 1971) for a useful account of the Chafer-Torrey exchange.

2. Ernest R. Sandeen, *The Roots of Fundamentalism: British and American Millenarianism, 1800–1930* (Chicago: University of Chicago Press, 1970), xiv, 251–52.

3. The General Assembly was considering a recommendation to combine the board of directors and the board of trustees into one board of control, which would be constituted by members who were sympathetic to Stevenson's liberal agenda. See Ned B. Stonehouse, *J. Gresham Machen: A Biographical Memoir* (Grand Rapids: Eerdmans, 1954), chs. 21–22; see 409–45 for a full account of the controversy leading to Machen's departure from Princeton.

4. *Moody Bible Institute Monthly* (September 1927).

5. Stonehouse, *Machen,* 443–44.

6. The unpublished biography states simply: "When Percy Crawford left Princeton, New Jersey in 1930 [*sic*] to enter the new Westminster Theological Seminary he could never have conceived what God had in store for him" ("Pioneer for God: The Biography of Percy B. Crawford" [1954], ch. 3 [Billy Graham Center Archives]).

7. The catalogue for 1929–30, too, announced that "while [Westminster] will welcome to its student body candidates for the ministry from non-Presbyterian churches, and while

it rejoices greatly in the presence of such students during this its first academic year, yet its faculty and its governing board will be unreservedly committed to the Westminster Confession of Faith and the Presbyterian form of church government, and the character of its teaching will be determined accordingly" (17).

8. Excerpts from "Westminster Theological Seminary: Its Plan and Purpose" taken from *J. Gresham Machen: Selected Shorter Writings,* ed. D. G. Hart (Phillipsburg, N.J.: P&R, 2004), 187–94.

9. This is how Van Til explained the grade thirty-one years later in an interview with Don Crawford on his television program *Nitewatch,* aired on Percy's Philadelphia television station, WPCA, on May 3, 1961 (Billy Graham Center Archives).

10. "Pioneer for God," ch. 3.

11. "Our History" Rhawnhurst Presbyterian Church (unpublished).

12. Percy Crawford, *The Art of Fishing for Men* (Chicago: Moody, 1950), 35.

13. D. G. Hart, *Defending the Faith: J. Gresham Machen and the Crisis of Conservative Protestantism in Modern America* (Baltimore: Johns Hopkins University Press, 1994), 131. As a graduate student, Machen was a member of Princeton University's Benham Club, where he "gained a reputation as one of the greatest 'stunters,' " which meant, according to Hart, "relating a humorous tale in an exaggerated and boisterous manner" (14). Clarence Macartney reports that as a stunter at student gatherings Machen "would get off an amusing recitation about 'Old Bill' and Napoleon"; *The Making of a Minister* (Great Neck, N.Y.: Channel, 1961), 187.

14. Percy Crawford letter to Machen, dated only "Wednesday," with a note written on it: "Check fwd(?) to Mr. Crawford March 21, 1931" (Machen archives).

15. He managed a 2 (= B) in only one of his major courses: Elements of Hebrew with Allan MacRae.

16. Percy Crawford sermon entitled "Esau," in *Highlights of Pinebrook: Twenty-Four Inspiring Messages Delivered at the Pinebrook Bible Conference,* ed. Percy Crawford (Philadelphia: Pinebrook Book Club, 1938), 252.

17. See the next chapter for more about Percy's work at the Barnes Center.

18. Stonehouse, *Machen,* 222–24.

19. Ibid., 222–28.

20. J. Gresham Machen, *Christianity and Liberalism* (repr. Grand Rapids: Eerdmans, 1972), 48–49.

21. *Young People Today* (May 1937): 18.

22. J. Gresham Machen, *What is Faith?* (New York: Macmillan, 1925), 180.

23. "What Is Original Sin?" one of a series of radio addresses collected in the volume *The Christian View of Man* (Grand Rapids: Eerdmans, 1947 [orig. 1937]), 267–70.

24. J. Gresham Machen, "The Sermon on the Mount," in *The Christian Faith in the Modern World* (New York: Macmillan, 1936), 171–72.

25. Machen, *Christianity and Liberalism,* 158.

26. Correspondence in Machen archives, Westminster library. Machen's talk was given on November 25, 1932.

27. *Young People Today* (December 1936): 18.

28. About a decade later, Percy refused to allow Gordon Clark to give a guest lecture at The King's College because of his conservative Reformed theology, even though Clark was by this time one of the foremost Christian philosophers (thanks to Gerald Vaughn for this information).

29. *Young People Today* (May 1937): 15. After leaving Westminster, MacRae went on to join Carl McIntire in the formation of a new seminary, Faith Theological Seminary, which

opened its doors in the fall of 1937, and became its first president. Percy consented to be listed on the board of the new seminary and directed many King's College graduates to Faith.

30. MacRae's letter of resignation (addressed to Harold Laird, who was at that time chairman of the board) and Kuiper's reply were reprinted in *The Christian Beacon,* April 29, 1937.

31. Nor did Percy have any interest in joining forces with Carl McIntire and Oliver Buswell in trying to change Westminster. Buswell submitted a letter to Machen shortly before the latter's death in January 1937 in which he made an extensive critique of the seminary. The charges (as delineated by Machen's colleague and biographer Ned Stonehouse) included "the issue of dispensationalism, . . . [the seminary's] view of Apologetics, its conception of evangelism, and its attitude toward 'the separated life.' " Percy certainly would have concurred with these criticisms and no doubt, during the previous summer when Buswell was a speaker at Pinebrook, conveyed to him *his* dissatisfaction with Westminster's attitude toward his evangelism (Stonehouse, *Machen,* 504–5).

## CHAPTER 8. EARLY MINISTRY IN PHILADELPHIA

1. Percy Crawford, "A Modern Revival," *Revelation* (August 1932): 325, 349–50. Unreferenced quotations in this chapter are from this article.

2. Donald Roth Kocher, *The Mother of Us All: First Presbyterian Church in Philadelphia, 1698–1998* (Philadelphia: First Presbyterian Church in Philadelphia, 1998), 107.

3. Percy used this case as a sermon illustration many times throughout the years, adding a touch of humor. He describes himself as not being afraid, but walking a little faster as the man approached him from behind. And when he caught up to him he said, "Reverend, will you pray for me when you come into your kingdom?"—to which he added: "I didn't know what *kingdom* I was coming into."

4. Annual report of the Summer Evangelistic Committee, 1928.

5. Annual report of the Summer Evangelistic Committee of Philadelphia for 1931, 9. The other fixed station meetings were conducted by Rev. Francis Di Simone (in Italian) at the Second Italian Church at Callowhill and Simpson Streets.

6. It is not clear why the sound-equipped car was needed since Percy apparently had his own amplifying equipment. Pictures of the meetings show three speakers mounted between the pillars above the platform and podium. But it is not known whether these pictures were taken in the first year of the meetings or in subsequent years. It is difficult to see how the audience across the street would have been able to hear the service without amplification. The report estimates that 1,600 people attended these three meetings and that a total of 3,624 were in attendance at the two-week series. This is in accord with Percy's calculations of 500 at some meetings and 3,875 overall for the two-week campaign.

7. The report came from members Fulton, Lynn, and Frame and was summarized in the 1931 annual report.

8. It is noteworthy that in subsequent years the committee continued to support the Washington Square open-air meetings: in 1932 it sponsored two weeks of meetings at a cost of $90, which were conducted in part by Percy (ten days) and in part by his close friend, Harlan Fischer (five days), who was then attending Westminster. In 1933, the year Percy opened his summer Bible conference, he was one of four evangelists who together conducted twenty-three Washington Square meetings. In 1934, although Percy requested two

weeks of meetings, he did not take part in any of them that summer, probably because he was so absorbed at his conference. In 1935 First Church refused permission to use the porch because of "property damages incurred in past series" (annual reports of the Summer Evangelistic Committee, 1932, 1933, 1934, 1935).

9. Presbytery Minutes, November 3, 1930.

10. Thirty-third annual report, Summer Evangelistic Committee, Summer of 1931, 8.

11. In his August 5 letter to Machen requesting financial support for the broadcast, Percy explained the situation a little differently. He writes that he had agreed to continue at the Barnes "on condition he [Fulton] assist me in installing a radio for an hour's broadcast" and adds that "he has decided to assist me in a very small way." The very small assistance that Fulton gave was probably just his giving permission to use the auditorium and perhaps paying some share of the installation costs.

12. Percy Crawford letter to Machen, August 5, 1931. The phrase "over the ether waves" is taken from an article in the *Philadelphia Record* (April 4, 1936), with a supertitle over a picture of the radio team: "THEY PREACH OVER THE ETHER WAVES."

13. Irene Campbell would later marry evangelist Harry Vom Bruch, who came as a speaker to Pinebrook for several years, where the friendship between the Crawfords and the Vom Bruchs grew.

14. Ruth Crawford interview by William Drury, 1981 (Billy Graham Center Archives).

15. Ruth remembers that she may have had to miss the very first broadcast due to illness—unusual for her (interview with William Drury).

16. "Pioneer for God: The Biography of Percy B. Crawford" (1954), ch. 4 (Billy Graham Center Archives).

17. *Revelation* (May 1932): 214.

18. Donald Barnhouse, "When Winter Comes," *Revelation* (April 1935): 139.

19. Both men received honorary doctorates at about the same age (thirty-nine), Percy from Bob Jones College in 1940, and Barnhouse from Dallas Theological Seminary in 1933. Barnhouse was also awarded the Master of Theology degree from Eastern Baptist Theological Seminary in 1927; and another doctoral degree was given to him in 1952 by Aix-en-Provence seminary, which Barnhouse had supported. See C. Allyn Russell, "Donald Grey Barnhouse: Fundamentalist Who Changed," *Journal of Presbyterian History* 59 (Spring 1981): 36.

20. Full-page advertisement in *Revelation* (May 1932).

21. Allen Guelzo reports that one of the stock letters Barnhouse sent out in reply to thousands of letters he received began with the sentence: "I am so happy to know that you received Christ as your Saviour during my recent meetings in ———." Allen C. Guelzo, "Barnhouse," in *Making God's Word Plain: One Hundred and Fifty Years in the History of Tenth Presbyterian Church of Philadelphia,* ed. James M. Boice (Philadelphia: Tenth Presbyterian Church, 1979), 80.

22. John DeBrine interview, July 12, 2003. DeBrine (who also worked with Percy as a youth minister in Boston) recalls that Barnhouse gave only one invitation for salvation in all the many times that he spoke at his "Songtime" rallies.

23. Paul A. Hopkins, "What Made the Man?" *Eternity* (March 1961): 38.

24. Barnhouse wrote "Men Whom God Struck Dead" for the November 1936 *Young People Today.*

25. Percy wanted to bring Barnhouse back to speak at Pinebrook in the 1950s, but (to the best of my knowledge) was unable to work it out with him.

26. Paula Shumard (Alexander Pantellas's daughter) letter to Don Crawford, April 9, 2005.

27. "Fishing Clubs," *Young People Today* (August 1934): 10. All the quotations in this section are from this article or another, "How to Start a Phi Gamma Fishing Club," *Young People Today* (September 1936), unless otherwise specified.

28. This statement of doctrine is significant because it is the only one that I am confident my father composed himself. It is a highly abbreviated version of the doctrinal statements adopted by BIOLA and Wheaton. I quote it in full: "We accept: 1. The Virgin birth of Christ. 2. The Deity of Jesus Christ, He is God. 3. Redemption through His shed Blood. 4. The Resurrection of the Body of Christ. 5. His Bodily Ascension into Heaven. 6. His Personal, Visible, and Premillennial return. 7. Regeneration as the only entrance into the Kingdom of God. 8. The Bible, as Verbally inspired of God and the only infallible guide" (*Young People Today* [September 1934]: 18; restated in the September 1936 issue, p. 18).

29. *Young People Today* (September 1934): 18.

30. Ibid. Percy used this 1934 edition of the Gospel of John throughout his entire ministry. They sold originally for 2 cents each (and as cheaply as 1.2 cents in bulk). Even later editions continued at this inexpensive price.

31. This question pin was no doubt the type of pin Percy was wearing in many photographs of him during his BIOLA and Wheaton days.

32. *Young People Today* (June 1941).

33. "Facts about Tracts," *Young People Today* (May/June 1940).

34. In the first year of the banquets, February 1936, approximately seventeen hundred club members attended, but many hundreds who sent in for reservations could not be accommodated. "Pinebrook for 1936 Greater Than Ever," *Young People Today* (March 1936).

35. The last reference to the Phi Gamma clubs in Percy's literature that I am aware of is in the 1943 calendar, where one of the photos shows Brandt Reed speaking to a group of young people in a school setting, with their Bibles open and several of them holding musical instruments. The caption clearly gives the lie to the Bornagainers Clubs: "Phi Gamma Clubs are Fishing Clubs for young people and the Born-Againer Clubs are soul-winning groups in High Schools. Brandt Reed now has some 300 of these scattered over the nation in connection with the Y.P.C.A."

## CHAPTER 9. THE PRESBYTERIANS

1. "Can a Person Dance and Be a Christian?" *Young People Today* (August 1936): 17.

2. Quoted in C. Allyn Russell, "Donald Grey Barnhouse: Fundamentalist Who Changed," *Journal of Presbyterian History* 59 (Spring 1981): 47. The initial charge brought against Barnhouse (in November 1929) was that he was violating the spirit of Christian comity by holding meetings outside his church (Tenth Presbyterian) at various missions around the city. The particular complaint had to do with the regular Sunday evening meetings he conducted at his "mission" at the Tower Theater on Sixty-ninth and Ludlow Streets, which drew an average of two thousand people, much to the chagrin of other ministers in the neighborhood who were holding their own services at the same time. The trial ended in March 1932 with Barnhouse being ordered to cease holding meetings at the Tower Theater.

3. *Constitution of the Presbyterian Church in the US of A, 1805–1930* (Philadelphia: Publication Department of the Presbyterian Board of Christian Education, 1930).

4. The typed letter, dated April 8, 1932, appears to be a carbon copy and has "sample" handwritten in the margin. Whether this was the final letter Percy sent to Fulton is not

known, but in any case it gives us a good indication of his unfriendly attitude toward the church official.

5. In one of his statements, Laird speaks of his "suspension" from the church. I can find no evidence that he was formally suspended and can only infer that he took the rebuke as if it were a suspension.

6. It later became Faith Independent Church and aligned itself with the Carl McIntire–led Bible Presbyterian Church.

7. The statement is cited in full in the *Christian Beacon* (April 9, 1936).

8. From Laird's initial statement upon being brought to trial, cited in "New Castle Presbytery Votes to Try Harold S. Laird," *Presbyterian Guardian* 1 (October 21, 1935): 32.

9. The others were Rev. H. McAllister Griffiths, Rev. Edwin H. Rian, Rev. Paul Woolley, and Rev. Charles J. Woodbridge.

10. Minutes of the Philadelphia Presbytery, June 8, 1936.

11. Laird had made the same claim in his August 5, 1936, rebuttal: "Indeed the time has now come, I believe, when no man can be absolutely faithful to his ordination vows and remain in the Church, for, in order to be true to his ordination vows, he must . . . be zealous to maintain the truths of the Gospel and the purity of the church. . . . But the powers that be demand that there shall be no such criticism. . . . It is perfectly proper for one to be disloyal to Christ, whom the constitution recognizes as the only Head of the Church, but he must not show disloyalty to the boards and agencies of the Church" (*Christian Beacon* [August 13, 1936]: 2).

12. Laird published seven sermons in *Young People Today* (between 1934 and 1940), and MacPherson three. Also, they were both represented in two volumes of sermons that Percy edited, given by Pinebrook speakers: *Mountaintop Messages* (Philadelphia: Pinebrook Book Club, 1939) and *Echoes of Pinebrook* (Philadelphia: Young People's Church of the Air, 1941).

13. Barnhouse struck a similar note in a statement in which he explained why he decided to remain in the church after being admonished: "I believe that God needs missionaries in the midst of our church today as much as he needs them in Africa. We believe that some of us who hold to the full doctrine of the Reformed faith as the expression of the truth taught in the Scriptures constitute the true Presbyterian Church in the U.S.A. denomination. . . . As the church is in the world but not of the world, I can truly say before God that we, though in the church organization, are not of it in spirit as it is at present organized and believe that what we are seeing is a part of the prophetic tendency so clearly pictured in the Word of God that shows us all church organization running into the confusion of Babylon the Great, the Mother of Harlots" (February 6, 1937, letter to Carl McIntire, cited in Guelzo, "Barnhouse," 77–78).

14. In one of Percy's very few references to the apostasy of the church, he wrote in a sermon on the popular theme of the "Signs of the Times" (preached December 16, 1934): "God also tells us there will be a church apostasy. . . . God is shelving many visible churches today because of their infidelity and lukewarmness. In I Tim. 4:1 we are told, 'In the latter times some shall depart from the faith.' In II Thes. 2:3 we are told there shall be a falling away" (reprinted in *Young People Today* [January 1935]: 5–6).

15. Other Pinebrook speakers in the years 1935 and 1936 who were involved in this dispute with the Presbyterians were Oliver Buswell, James Bennet, Wilbur Smith, Roy Brumbaugh, and Charles Woodbridge.

16. "Percy Crawford Denied Church," *Christian Beacon* (September 24, 1936): 1.

17. *Young People Today* (April 1937): 15.

## CHAPTER 10. PINEBROOK BIBLE CONFERENCE:
## A MOUNTAINTOP EXPERIENCE

1. "Sweeter Than the Day Before," by Wendell P. Loveless, words by Robert C. Loveless, in *New Pinebrook Songs* (Philadelphia: n.p., 1936).

2. "The Origin of Pine Brook Bible Conference," *Young People Today* (February 1934).

3. This figure is equivalent to approximately $350,000 in current dollars.

4. "Percy Crawford: Ever on the March," *Power for Teens* (October 22, 1961), part 4.

5. 1933 Pinebrook brochure.

6. A week at Pinebrook was always a bargain. In 1950 the cost was only $15 per week (a reduced price); and in the last year Percy ran it (1960), it was $28.

7. *Young People Today* (May 1935): 7.

8. Quotes are from an advertisement in *Young People Today* (Spring 1939), no page number.

9. *Youth, the Christian Newsette* (July 10 and July 31, 1952).

10. Toward the end of his life, as we will see, Percy responded to the social needs of the Korean people in attempting to establish a Korean mission.

11. From an advertisement in *Young People Today* (Spring 1936), no page number.

12. Advertisement in *Young People Today* (Spring 1935), no page number.

13. "Pinebrook for 1936 Greater Than Ever," *Young People Today* (Spring 1936), no page number.

14. 1941 Pinebrook brochure.

15. 1954 Pinebrook brochure.

16. Isabelle Van Buskirk interview, February 3, 2003.

17. Advertisement in *Young People Today* (Spring 1936).

18. "YPCA Bible Conference," *Young People Today* (April 1936): 7.

19. Rowan Pearce was an itinerant Methodist minister who had a daily radio program in Philadelphia called *Christian Voices*. He had been a four-letter athlete at Dickinson College.

20. "Memorial Service for Dr. Percy Crawford" (printed address), November 6, 1960, Philadelphia Town Hall, 3.

21. Tape recording of *Pinebrook Praises* broadcast (approx. September 1959); Percy's handwritten title on this tape recording is "What I Think of Billy Graham" in family archives.

22. In addition to the banquets for Phi Gamma clubs, in the early years Percy held annual banquets for Pinebrookers during the off-season in Philadelphia and New York City and invited Pinebrook speakers and musicians to conduct the program.

23. George Beverly Shea, *Then Sings My Soul* (Old Tappan, N.J.: Revell, 1968), 60–61.

24. This, no doubt, is why Percy did *not* invite G. Campbell Morgan to Pinebrook, a pastor in Philadelphia, whom Percy greatly admired as a Bible teacher. My father would never have tolerated anyone's smoking at Pinebrook, and Morgan made no apologies for his enjoyment of cigars. On this question of smoking cigars, Fenton Duvall relates that Campbell used to say about his critics: "They don't seem to understand that I only smoke *good* cigars." Another obstacle to inviting Morgan may have been that when John MacInnis, Percy's teacher at BIOLA, had been forced to resign as dean in 1928 because of alleged modernist tendencies, Campbell had protested the firing and resigned his post on the faculty because of it, whereas Percy was fraternizing with the hardliners such as William Bell Riley, who had a hand in forcing MacInnis out.

25. Percy and McIntire were not unfriendly toward each other; the latter would occasionally come to Pinebrook to try to persuade Percy to join him in support of (or opposition to) some cause.

26. Percy Crawford, "America's Greatest Men of God," promotional article, *Young People Today* (March 1936): 5.

27. Percy had recorded (in his notebook) eight hundred in attendance and twenty-five professions at this meeting.

28. See C. Allyn Russell, *Voices of American Fundamentalism* (Philadelphia: Westminster, 1976), 79–106 (ch. 4: "William Bell Riley: Organizational Fundamentalist").

29. The theory was supposedly advanced in the *Protocols of the Learned Elders of Zion,* first published in Russia in 1905, but later shown to be a forgery. For Riley's views, see William V. Trollinger, *God's Empire: William Bell Riley and Midwestern Fundamentalism* (Madison: University of Wisconsin Press, 1990), 68–81.

30. *The Lamb of God* (Grand Rapids, Mich.: Zondervan, 1937).

31. Booklet entitled "Facts for Baptists to Face" (Waterloo, Ia.: Walnut St. Baptist Church, 1936 [2nd ed. in 1942]), introduction.

32. In a progress report after ten years of his leadership, Ketcham reported that 370 churches had entered the GARBC. J. Murray Murdoch, *Portrait of Obedience: The Biography of Robert T. Ketcham* (Schaumburg, Ill.: Regular Baptist Press, 1979), 256.

33. "Facts for Baptists to Face," 19.

34. The actual title of this song is "Contentment."

35. Blanche D. Osborn wrote musical settings for words written by Ruth's sister, Esther Eden. The duo contributed seventeen songs to the last of Percy and Ruth's songbooks, *Songs of Heaven* (1959), including "Consider" and "Wait on the Lord" (in addition to "How Wonderful") and many more to the next two songbooks that Ruth published alone: *Sing My Heart* (1962) and *Singing thru the Years* (1967).

36. After her single in the *Young People Church of the Air Hymn Book,* "The Nail-Pierced Hand," Ruth did not publish any new songs until after Percy's death, when she composed two books worth of songs to words written by her sister, Esther Eden: *Hearts in Harmony* (1973) and *Singing and Making Melodies* (1982).

37. McDonald also sang in the winter months at Percy's Youtharama rallies in Philadelphia, which started in 1956.

38. Douglas Yeo, "An Interview with Bill Pearce" (online).

39. Jack Wyrtzen oral history interview, October 5, 1991 (Billy Graham Center Archives, audio tape, transcript #1).

40. Camp Davis was operated by conservative Baptist minister Rev. Leon Davis of Nanuet, New York; its campers would regularly attend services at Pinebrook. In a moving account of the flood, one survivor, Mrs. Irene Weber, told the story of the thirty-four campers who retreated to the only year-round bungalow on the campgrounds. As darkness fell and the water rose around them, children and adults moved up to the candle-lit "attic." She wrote: "We were now quite alarmed, but tried not to say anything to the children that would reveal how serious the situation was. No children were crying. Rather several led in prayer in the last half hour between the singing of choruses. One chorus they sang over and over was 'I've Got a Mansion over the Hilltop.'" And then a wall of water broke the house into pieces. Weber survived but her two children, ages five and nine, were lost in the torrential waters. See Irene Weber and Leslie Flynn, "Survived the Camp Davis Tragedy," *Power* newsletter (Chicago: Scripture Press) 14.3.8 (July–September 1956): 1–3, 6–7. "Mansions

over the Hilltop" by Ira Stanphill was the first chorus in the songbook used that summer in the meetings at Pinebrook: *Youth on the March Songs* (1954).

41. 1937 brochure.

42. Don Crawford letter to author, June 25, 2004.

43. C. H. Brudenell composed the words and music of "Salvation Time," published in *Songs of Heaven* (1959). Norman Johnson wrote words and music of "Day and Night," published in *Mountainbrook Melodies* (1956).

44. Jesus explicitly condemns divorce, except for the reason of unchastity. In the YPCA newsletter (March 1, 1947) Percy gave his answer to the question "Should a Christian get a divorce?": "How blessed it is to get the right mate. There is nothing sweeter on this earth than to have one's own wife or husband. . . . Incompat[i]bility, however, is no cause for divorce. Scripturally, the only cause for divorce is adultery—Matt. 5:32 and Matt. 19:9. . . . Marriage should never be an experiment. It is a sacred move."

45. Betty Johnson, "Echoes of Pinebrook," *Young People Today* (September 1937): 18.

46. *Young People's Church of the Air News* (September 1, 1944).

47. "Sylvia Visits Pinebrook," *Young People's Church of the Air News* (March 1, 1947): 4.

48. Peggy Craven phone interview, December 10, 2003.

49. Jack Wyrtzen oral history interview, October 5, 1991 (Billy Graham Center Archives, audio tape, transcript #1). Other accounts of Marge's conversion are in Forrest Forbes, *God Hath Chosen: The Story of Jack Wyrtzen and the Word of Life Hour* (Grand Rapids: Zondervan, 1948), 18–20; and Harry Bollback, *The House That Jack (God) Built* (Schroon Lake, N.Y.: Word of Life Fellowship, 1972), 11–16.

50. Ockenga went on to say: "As such, he was always an inspiration to others who wished that they could emulate his faith and energy but who were apt to follow more conventional channels" (Harold J. Ockenga letter to Ruth Crawford, December 5, 1960 [after Percy's death]; family archives).

51. *Young People's Church of the Air News* (September 1, 1944).

52. In the *Pinebrook Praises* broadcast referenced above, "What I Think of Billy Graham" (approx. date, 1959), Percy praised Billy Graham for being "humble as an old stick."

53. The Pinebrook grounds were sold to Bible Fellowship Church, and it continues as Pinebrook Bible Conference to the present day.

54. Percy Crawford sermon entitled "Lot's Escape," in *Whither Goest Thou?* 80–81.

## CHAPTER 11. RADIO: THE YOUNG PEOPLE'S CHURCH OF THE AIR

1. This is apparently an allusion to the Great Depression—the only reference to it that I have found in all of Percy's writings—he seems to view it as a sign of the general decline of society and as accentuating the need for revival.

2. *Revelation* (August 1932): 350.

3. Paul Starr, *The Creation of the Media: Political Origins of Modern Communications* (New York: Basic Books, 2004), 379.

4. Percy Crawford radio sermon entitled "God's Method of Drawing Men" (preached January 19, 1936), in "Sermons preached by Rev. Percy Crawford, Sundays in January, 1936" (pamphlet), 11.

5. Percy Crawford radio sermon entitled "A New Creation" (preached January 5, 1936), in "Sermons preached by Rev. Percy Crawford, Sundays in January, 1936" (pamphlet), 2.

6. Joel A. Carpenter, *Revive Us Again: The Reawakening of American Fundamentalism* (New York: Oxford University Press, 1997), 130. Percy figures in this statistic—"bought radio" is entered in his calendar book on June 28, 1930, his first year in seminary.

7. Starr, *Creation of the Media,* 354.

8. Advertisement in *Young People Today* (Summer 1934).

9. It may have been to avoid confusion with this program that Percy did not list his own program as *Young People's Church of the Air* until it had established its own identity. The program was initially listed (in the *Philadelphia Inquirer*) as *Albert Barnes Memorial Young People's Hour with Orchestra and Chorus, Rev. Percy Crawford.*

10. Percy Crawford letter to Machen, August 5, 1931.

11. Booklet entitled "Morning Cheer, Pastor George A. Palmer, 1935" (n.p.). This autobiographical piece states that the morning broadcast continued on WRAX until March 1934. In the first year, Jimmy Blackstone of Westminster Seminary, who had been singing with Percy, was also Palmer's soloist. By 1935 the *Morning Cheer* broadcast was on stations WIP and WMCA (New York) from 7:00 to 8:00 a.m.

12. Although the message and invitation was directed to the mass audience he could not see, Percy would never have missed the opportunity to give a (second?) invitation to those individuals and church delegations who were gathered before him. When he moved the broadcast to the WIP studios after being denied permission to use the Barnes (September 1936), the live audience was reduced to about twenty to thirty, who had to view the program through a glass window.

13. He writes this in a column entitled "Chorus Conscious," *Young People Today* (February 1934): 18.

14, Mel Larson, *Youth for Christ* (Grand Rapids: Zondervan, 1947), 35, 41 ("young men on fire").

15. Carpenter, *Revive Us Again,* 130. Of course, Carpenter is speaking of an unacknowledged influence. On a slightly different note, I remember that my father used to be fascinated by auctioneers, presumably by their ability to use rapid speech to mesmerize their hearers (and get a bid from them).

16. Percy Crawford sermon entitled "Hands," in *Sermons Preached over 275 Stations Coast to Coast on the Mutual Network* (undated pamphlet [approx. 1945]).

17. Percy Crawford sermon entitled "The Lamb of God," *Young People Today* (October 1937): 16.

18. Crawford, "Lamb of God," 16.

19. Percy Crawford sermon entitled "Great Things in the Bible," in *Whither Goest Thou?* 24.

20. Telecast, invitation.

21. The Pinebrook Book Store opened at 42 North Eighth Street in Philadelphia on November 22, 1935. By April 1936 Percy had started a "Book-a-Month Club." In February 1937 Percy moved the bookstore to its permanent location, 730 Chestnut Street, and set up his headquarters there.

22. This figure squares with a balance sheet that survives for September 30, 1935, to September 30, 1936, which shows that "Donations from Radio" were $25,628.39, and the money "Paid Radio" was $25,537.52. The balance of $90.87, added to the previous year's balance of $1,746.50 made a total "in Bank, Oct. 1, 1936" of $1,837.37 (unpublished YPCA records).

23. "From Pulpit on a Plank," *Everybody's Weekly—The Philadelphia Inquirer* (May 19, 1940): 5. The article continues: "The country is divided into circuits and a set of records arrives at a studio in time for the Sunday hour. On Monday the records are taken by the ex-

332    NOTES TO PAGES 174–76

press company at no expense to the station and sent on to the next station." Percy continued to make these transcriptions on 16″ discs and use them on the air, at least through 1947.
Many good recordings exist of programs from 1946 and 1947.

24. The existing records of this increase in stations are scanty and confusing. In one advertisement (*Young People Today* [May/June 1940]), Percy lists fifty-five stations in twenty-
seven states, Alaska, and Canada, but in another ad that appeared earlier (February 1940),
he lists sixty-six stations in twenty-nine states, Alaska, and Canada, with thirty of these stations overlapping. (In both ads, he states that listeners can sponsor a program on any of these
added stations for just $3 each week.)

25. In later publications, after starting the television program in 1949, Percy stated frequently that he had "formerly" broadcasted on 450 stations. I have not been able to correlate this figure with any published statements from the earlier period, but the surviving
records are sparse. Given that the number of outlets fluctuated so dramatically, he could well
have reached that number at some point. His son Don remembers Percy telling him that he
had finally gone over the 400 mark. Being on over 400 stations seems to have had a special
significance for him—perhaps signifying that he had pushed radio to its upper boundary
and so could move on to a new horizon (television); or perhaps, as Don suggests, 400 was
just the figure that gave him "bragging rights" in the evangelical arena. It is worth noting
that Charles Fuller's *Old Fashioned Revival Hour* had reached 456 stations by the fall of
1942, and was on as many as 1,000 stations; see Daniel P. Fuller, *Give the Winds a Mighty
Voice* (Waco: Word, 1972), 83, 139.

26. This figure tallies with the balance sheet for the fiscal year ending August 31, 1946,
which shows that total "Radio Expenses" were $276,305.22, while "Radio Gifts" totaled
$284,145.94. The balance sheet was prepared by the firm Arthur Collins of Clementon, New
Jersey, and is the only one surviving from this 1942–48 period.

27. One of the worst offenders in this regard was the provocative "radio priest," Father
Charles Coughlin, who was kicked off the CBS network in 1933 for refusing to allow his
volatile sermons to be censored. Fr. Coughlin started his radio program on a Detroit station
in 1930 and three months later was broadcasting over seventeen CBS stations (reportedly)
to ten million listeners, and receiving fifty thousand letters per week. See Wallace Stenger,
"The Radio Priest and His Flock," in *The Aspirin Age, 1919–1941* (New York: Simon and
Schuster, 1949), 232–57.

28. Cited in Tona J. Hangen, *Redeeming the Dial: Radio, Religion, and Popular Culture
in America* (Chapel Hill: University of North Carolina Press, 2002), 25.

29. Fuller, *Give the Winds a Mighty Voice,* 120–22.

30. A clear-channel frequency was one that was assigned to a single broadcaster.

31. Starr, *Creation of the Media,* 349–53, 367. See also Hangen, *Redeeming the Dial,*
22–30, for a concise review of these developments and their effect on fundamentalist broadcasters.

32. Starr, *Creation of the Media,* 367.

33. Ibid., 367. Another problem faced by Mutual was the difficulty in gaining access to
key cities when all the existing stations were controlled by NBC and CBS. By the end of
the 1930s, only about half of the ninety-two cities with more than one hundred thousand
people had three or more stations operating full-time (Starr, *Creation of the Media,* 368).

34. See Fuller, *Give the Winds a Mighty Voice,* 156–57.

35. During these years, the broadcast could be heard locally in Philadelphia on the independent WPEN at 4:30–5:00.

36. Percy Crawford letter, March 15, 1945.

37. In the next month's newsletter (September 1, 1944), Percy explained further that when he had tried to drop "over 100 stations" that fall, "the company . . . refused to let us out saying we had to complete our six month contract. This means we must continue with the 375 stations we now have. On top of this, comes the Mutual shut down on money appeals so we will be hit hard." Apparently Mutual's ban on appeals was not a new policy. Fuller, *Give the Winds a Mighty Voice*, 116–17, mentions that Charles Fuller had to deal with the same restrictions when he first went on Mutual in 1937 with what was then the *Radio Revival Hour*. And like Percy, he responded by making a plea to his listeners for gifts "when the obstacles in the way of the 'Radio Revival Hour' seem almost insurmountable."

38. The Communications Act of 1934 created the seven-member Federal Communications Commission that replaced the Federal Radio Commission.

39. *Young People's Church of the Air News* (December 1, 1944).

40. "A Modern Revival," *Revelation* (August 1932): 349. Elsewhere, in further commentary on this verse, he points out that what is meant is that God will provide for our "actual" needs: "Thank God He has never failed and never will to supply that which we actually need. Many times He has not given us all we want. We want many more stations and many more things but He knows best. He does all things well" (*Young People's Church of the Air News* [December 1, 1944]).

41. *Young People's Church of the Air News* (September 1, 1944).

42. *Young People's Church of the Air News* (December 1, 1944).

43. "We are now broadcasting from four stations in Quito, Ecuador, two stations in Panama, Puerto Rico, Cuba, British Guiana, Alaska, and Hawaii" (*Young People's Church of the Air News* [September 1, 1943]). Station HCJB in Quito had four transmitters, each of which could be considered a separate station. Their signal could be heard all over the world when conditions were right (email from Joe Springer to author, June 2005).

44. *Young People's Church of the Air News* (September 1, 1944).

45. *Young People's Church of the Air News* (December 1, 1944).

46. *Young People's Church of the Air News* (September 1, 1943).

47. *Young People Today* (March 1938): 17.

48. For a helpful discussion of FCC policies, see Hangen, *Redeeming the Dial*, 24–27.

49. Others who signed the letter with whom Percy would have felt some affinity, besides Ockenga and Ayer, were Roy L. Brown, Schuyler English, Charles Fuller, Frank Gaebelein, Will Houghton, Harry Ironside, Bob Jones, Robert G. Lee, Oscar Lowry, Robert McQuilkin, Stephen Paine, George Palmer, Roland Philips, Harry Rimmer, Paul Rood, and Charles Woodbridge. Others who attended the St. Louis meeting were Oliver Buswell, Robert Ketcham, Charles Lampman (representing "religious magazines"), Cornelius Van Til, and Carl McIntire. McIntire was present in an antagonistic role, having just formed a competing organization of evangelicals, the American Council of Churches.

50. Mark Ward Sr., *Air of Salvation* (Grand Rapids: Baker, 1994), 64.

51. "Gospel Broadcasters of Nation Organize," *United Evangelical Action* (October 1, 1944): 5.

52. "Broadcasting Gospel Is Evangelical Duty," *United Evangelical Action* (July 1943): 7.

53. "NRB Code of Ethics," in Ben Armstrong, *The Electric Church* (New York: Nelson, 1979), 178–84.

54. *Young People's Church of the Air News* (September 1, 1944).

55. "Is Religious Broadcasting in the Public Interest?" *United Evangelical Action* (July 2, 1945): 3.

56. A very different view of the role of the NRB in the 1940s and 1950s is voiced by James DeForest Murch, president of the NRB from 1956 to 1957. In his 1956 history of the NAE, *Cooperation without Compromise* (Grand Rapids: Eerdmans, 1956), 79, in a chapter entitled "The Rescue of Evangelical Broadcasting," he writes: "After many months of correspondence and conference, understandings were reached which fully protected the rights of all accredited religious broadcasters at national and local levels. The distinctively evangelical testimony was assured of a voice on the air. Means had been provided whereby the airlines would be kept perpetually available for the preaching of the Gospel. The National Association of Evangelicals was given its proportionate share of sustaining time on all the national networks and evangelicals were recognized as having a valid claim to considerations at the local levels." Writing about this same period in a later work, he repeats the above paragraph verbatim and adds: "I am very definitely of the opinion that if it had not been for the National Religious Broadcasters the National Council of Churches would have taken over all Protestant time on the airwaves at the national level and that evangelical broadcasting would have been completely eliminated" (*Adventuring for Christ in Changing Times: An Autobiography* [Louisville: Restoration Press, 1973], 177). But Murch fails to make his case that the policies regarding the sale of commercial time to religious broadcasters would have been any different had it not been for the NRB's actions. Lowell Saunders reaches this skeptical conclusion in his careful study *The National Religious Broadcasters and the Availability of Commercial Radio Time* (PhD diss., University of Illinois, 1968), 208–14. Saunders points to several factors that affected the networks' decisions (other than the influence of the National Council of Churches on the networks), namely, that some religious broadcasters were racketeers; that many religious programs were of poor quality in regard to content and technical production; and that the availability of time to conservatives tended to reflect the "economic health" of the broadcast industry: "When the networks needed money, they sold time" (214).

## CHAPTER 12. THE KING'S COLLEGE: WHEATON OF THE EAST

1. Percy Crawford, "The Editor Chats," *Young People Today* (August 1937): 9.

2. *King's Life* 7.4 (April 1960).

3. Percy Crawford radio sermon entitled "Why Another College?" (preached December 6, 1936). All quotations in this section are from this sermon unless otherwise indicated. The sermon strikes some of the same themes as Percy's earlier sermon "Did the University Make Me an Atheist?" written while he was still in seminary.

4. Percy Crawford letter to friends of *Young People's Church of the Air,* October 1936.

5. These three goals were encapsulated in a single statement, repeated in the college bulletin for the first eleven years: "The purpose of this school is to combine a sane, evangelistic zeal with the highest standards of sound scholarship." The formulation of the three goals in the text is taken (almost verbatim) from an unpublished document entitled "Proposed: Purposes of The King's College" with "Revisions by Percy B. Crawford," signed and dated January 15, 1960.

6. The entire chapel talk is quoted in Bob Bahr, *Man with a Vision: The Story of Percy Crawford* (Chicago: Moody, n.d.), 56–62. This eighty-nine-page booklet was published within a year or two after Percy's death in 1960. The source of the chapel talk is not given, but I am confident, based on its style and content, that it is an authentic transcription of the talk.

7. *Young People Today* (February 1935).

8. *Young People Today* (January 1938).

9. Marion O'Donnell (Briggs), "Impressions of The King's College," *Young People Today* (November 1938): 7–8. "Never-to-be-forgotten experience" from Marjorie Absalom. See also Percy Crawford, "Around a Campfire," *King's Life* 3.8 (October 1956).

10. Gerald F. Vaughn, "Evangelist Percy Crawford and The King's College in Delaware, 1941–55," *Delaware History* 27.1–2 (Spring 1996–Winter 1997): 22. Convinced by the geological evidence that the earth was much older than the six thousand years allowed by the literal six-day interpretation of Genesis (and Bishop Ussher's dating based on the genealogies of the Old Testament), Higley argued that an "old earth" is compatible with the Genesis account, which, he maintained, affirms two creations (in Genesis 1:1 and 1:2) with a long gap between them.

11. *Crown* (1942 yearbook).

12. Fenton Duvall interview; Vaughn, "Evangelist Percy Crawford," 26; *Crown* (1942).

13. Minutes, "Meeting of the Trustees of The King's College, September 2, 1946." Members present were Dr. Percy Crawford, C. Grey Watson, and Alex O. Dunlap, which at that time, with William Miller, was the entire board.

14. Minutes, "Special Meeting of the Board of Trustees of The King's College, February 26, 1947."

15. *Crown* (1945).

16. *Crown* (1942, 1943).

17. Fenton Duvall interviews, April 27, 30, 2001.

18. Minutes of October 6 board meeting, held in Dr. Morrison's office in Trenton, New Jersey. The five board members at the time were Percy, Fenton Duvall, Erling Olsen, James Bennet, and lawyer Weidner Titzck.

19. Vaughn, "Evangelist Percy Crawford," 24. In 1946 ten King's students took over the farm, which was losing money, and formed The King's Farm Association. They turned the operation into a profitable enterprise, providing the college with its produce, fruit, dairy products, poultry, and meat at wholesale market prices (*Crown* [1947]: 44).

20. Jane Atno (Ries) in *The King's College 10th Anniversary: 1938–1948 Alumni Memoirs*, 7; cited in Vaughn, "Evangelist Percy Crawford," 24.

21. Marjorie Absalom Linton letter to author, August 3, 2005. The rest of the brochure said nothing about accreditation.

22. Percy Crawford letter to Deak Ketcham, April 27, 1955; Deak Ketcham letter to Percy Crawford, May 13, 1955; Percy Crawford letter to Deak Ketcham, May 18, 1955.

23. *Crown* (1943): 22.

24. In his 1952 annual report, Vice President William Jelley described the year as "a year of 'growing up' in that for the first time we dealt very carefully with students who were called up for discipline, and we . . . had only one major disciplinary problem. It was a year of 'growing up' in that our students seemed to acquire a new maturity and a greater respect was engendered for the faculty and administration." This was shown, he said, "by the fact that of the twenty-one students who were dropped over the summer for academic deficiencies only one requested a review of his case and a reconsideration."

25. The entering class of 104 freshmen in 1953 included 49 percent (50 students) in the top two-fifths of their high school class, 22 percent in the middle one-fifth, 22 percent in the bottom two-fifths, and 7 percent unreported (1954 Middle States Report, 16).

26. Robert Davies letter to Gerald Vaughn, May 16, 1995; Vaughn, "Evangelist Percy Crawford," 34.

27. "Tale-Lights," *Crown* (1943): 21.

28. Middle States 1954 report, 1. See also *Crown* (1950): 74.

29. Percy Crawford letter to Obed Kay, August 23, 1960 (Percy Crawford file at Wheaton College).

30. These handwritten letters were sent to "Deac" (Percy's own spelling) Ketcham from Florida, where Percy and Ruth were vacationing, in September 1957 and February/March 1958.

31. In fiscal year 1957–58, it leaped to $38,513, which was still less than 8 percent of the college's total expenditures of $489,752 (Summary Financial Report, March 1960).

32. Conversation between Robert Davies and Gerald Vaughn, 1995; cited in Vaughn, "Evangelist Percy Crawford," 38.

33. See Vaughn's detailed account of the improvements that were noted by the board of education's 1949 report ("Evangelist Percy Crawford," 29–33). Vaughn indicated to me in conversation that James Barkley, King's registrar and professor of history, may have used his considerable influence among state education officials to obtain the committee's favorable review. Barkley taught in the field of education at the University of Delaware for twenty years before coming to King's in 1944. Percy may have had this in the back of his mind when he let Duvall go and promoted Barkley to registrar.

34. The original letter to the college sent by the official, Margaret Kelly, has not survived. A summary with quotations from the letter was given in a memorandum from Deak Ketcham to the board of trustees, May 29, 1958.

35. The 1945 *Crown* was dedicated to "our beloved Philosophy teacher, Mr. Grounds, a man of careful scholarship, profound erudition, and genuine spirituality."

36. Vernon Grounds phone interview, September 6, 2006. See also Vaughn, "Evangelist Percy Crawford," 27. I first learned about the 1944 offer of the presidency to Grounds in Vaughn's well-documented article. Vernon Grounds was offered the presidency of King's a second time, in 1961 after Percy's death, but he declined again, saying that he had unfinished business as president of Conservative Baptist Seminary (now Denver Seminary) (minutes of The King's College board of trustees, January 6, 1962).

37. This comment is taken from an August 1955 report to the board of trustees by L. W. Ketcham, director of public relations, on the answers given in interviews conducted with staff members about Jelley's performance.

38. The closest the college came to achieving this was in the science program under Louis Higley, who was a stabilizing force for twelve years. Higley failed, however, in his capacity as head of the science program and dean of the college, even to groom a successor.

39. Marie Shober, a graduate of the first class of 1942 recalled that some of Harley's students working in the area of political science circulated a petition calling for Percy's resignation. Percy called a general assembly to discuss the matter. By some means he determined that 98% of the students did not want him to resign, and said that he had no intention of resigning anyway. Harley left King's after two years, in 1942 (Marie Shober phone interview, July 31, 2005).

40. Some of these able practitioners who stand out were Arlene Barnes, Gordon Curtis, Donald Butterworth, Dean Arlton, and opera singer Norman Curtis.

41. That the whole operation of the college was greatly reduced during the war and several faculty members were called into the armed services explains to some degree this lopsidedness.

42. The 1951 report of the Middle States Review Committee indicated the problem of faculty retention, noting that "of the twenty-six names listed in the 1946–47 catalogue," only five were still actively teaching four years later when they visited the college. They

commented: "This large turnover creates instability and seriously interferes with educational efficiency. A student may have as many as three or four different teachers in his field of concentration before he graduates" (Report to the Commission on Higher Institutions of the Middle States Association of Colleges and Secondary Schools on The King's College, April 1951).

43. Middle States Report, April 1951, 11.

44. Ken Kennard phone interview, September 12, 2005. Kennard told me that while at King's his doubts about his own salary were allayed somewhat when he learned that Dorothy Braun, who had been teaching Christian Education for eight years, was making only $2,150.

45. Report to the Commission on Higher Institutions of the Middle States Association of Colleges and Secondary Schools on The King's College, March 1954, 11.

46. Middle States Report, April 1951, 11. In the 1960–61 school year, every faculty member was teaching at least fifteen hours and seventy-five students (letter from Dean Fenton Duvall to Percy Crawford, April 15, 1960).

47. The statement of doctrine will be discussed in a later chapter. In signing the statement of practice, the faculty member vowed that he or she was "living a surrendered, prayerful Christian life" regarding "loyal obedience to the moral precepts taught in the Word of God for believers," in these three respects: (1) "I am separated from the world and worldly amusements, such as dancing, card-playing, theatre-going, etc."; (2) "I am free from membership in an oath-bound secret society" and from "entangling alliances with unbelievers," defined as any "voluntary affiliation with an organization, ecclesiastical or otherwise, based upon principles which are opposed to the fundamentals of the Christian faith as outlined in the Statement of Doctrine of The King's College"; and (3) I agree to conduct myself beyond reproach, being free from carnal indulgence, such as the use of intoxicating liquors, tobacco, in all its forms, and narcotic drugs, all of which are harmful, a stumbling block and out of harmony with a dedicated life" (this wording taken from the contract signed in the Briarcliff years).

48. This specific wording is taken from a 1956 "Contract of Employment of Teachers."

## CHAPTER 13. THE FUNDAMENTALS OF HIS FAITH

1. Percy Crawford, *The Art of Fishing for Men* (Philadelphia: Mutual Press, 1935); citations are from the revised paperback edition (Chicago: Moody, 1950). The dust jacket on the first edition states: "These lectures were given by Dr. Crawford to young people's groups in and around Philadelphia," and indeed the overlapping points and repetition of Scripture strongly suggest that the book is a compilation of outlines for talks or sermonettes given to various groups—probably many of them delivered to the Phi Gamma fishing clubs that were forming all over Philadelphia. The book borrows heavily from Reuben Torrey's *How to Work for Christ* in its division of categories of problem cases, the heuristic points proposed in dealing with them, and the scriptural verses offered as relevant to each type. As noted, Percy acknowledges, in a small way, Torrey's influence on his work in his preface: "The writer is deeply indebted to the teachings of Dr. R. A. Torrey. . . . The influence of this great man of God on the writer's life was tremendous" (12).

2. Crawford, *Art of Fishing for Men,* 15.

3. A. A. Hodge and B. B. Warfield, "Inspiration," *Presbyterian Review* 2 (April 1881): 225–60 at 260; cited in Mark A. Noll, *Between Faith and Criticism: Evangelicals, Scholarship, and the Bible in America* (San Francisco: Harper & Row, 1986), 19.

4. Percy Crawford sermon entitled "The Bible Reveals" (preached November 22, 1936).

5. Percy Crawford sermon entitled "The Bible, the Word of God" in *Whither Goest Thou?* 18. Percy thought that it was probably a "very good thing" that we do not possess today any of the original manuscripts, because if we did "we would have churches using them as a racket, pretending that they had some healing or supernatural powers" (17–18).

6. Crawford, "The Bible Reveals."

7. Crawford, "The Bible, the Word of God," 16–17.

8. Ibid., 16. Adapa is a semidivine character in a Mesopotamian myth that gives an account of human mortality. There are interesting parallels between Adapa and Adam (in the Hebrew Bible), but they are different characters from different cultures.

9. Crawford, *Art of Fishing for Men,* 24.

10. Ibid., 24.

11. Crawford, "The Bible, the Word of God," 13.

12. Crawford, *Art of Fishing for Men,* 23.

13. Percy Crawford sermon entitled "Is the Bible the Word of God?" in *Sermons Preached over 250 Stations on the Mutual Network* (undated pamphlet [approx. 1943]), 7.

14. Ibid., 4.

15. Crawford, *Art of Fishing for Men,* 49.

16. The verse is cited twice in *Art of Fishing for Men,* 76, 88.

17. Crawford, "The Bible," 14.

18. Crawford, "The Bible, the Word of God," 14.

19. Crawford, "The Bible," 15–16. Noll points out that Robert Dick Wilson and O. T. Allis (Percy's professors at Westminster Seminary), in their Old Testament studies, used critical methods to authenticate the Bible and uphold the traditional view of inerrancy. But, Noll notes, both scholars were disengaged from the academic, professional study of the Old Testament and did not have a significant impact on American academic life. "Academic essays [by these scholars] appeared regularly in the *Princeton Theological Review,* but rarely in professional journals" (*Between Faith and Criticism,* 52–53).

20. Crawford, "The Bible, the Word of God," 16.

21. Crawford, "The Bible," 14–15.

22. Reuben Torrey sermon entitled "Some Reasons Why I Believe the Bible to Be the Word of God" (Billy Graham Center Archives).

23. Ibid., 15.

24. Sermon in audio collection of John DeBrine (approx. 1944).

25. Bible Institute of Los Angeles Bulletin 8.1 (January 1923): 21.

26. Reuben Torrey, *What the Bible Teaches* (New York: Revell, 1898), 303–14 (a chapter entitled "The Future Destiny of Those Who Reject the Redemption That Is in Jesus Christ"); *How to Bring Men to Christ* (New York: Revell, 1893), passim; and Torrey's published address on "Future Punishment" at the World Conference on Christian Fundamentals in Philadelphia in 1919, published in the volume *God Hath Spoken: Twenty-five Addresses Delivered at the World Conference on Christian Fundamentals, May 25–June 1, 1919* (Philadelphia: Bible Conference Committee, 1919).

27. Torrey, *What the Bible Teaches,* 313–14. Torrey makes the same point in *How to Bring Men to Christ:* "If any saved person will dwell long enough upon the peril and wretchedness of any man out of Christ and the worth of his soul in God's sight as seen in the death of God's Son to save him, a feeling of intense desire for that man's salvation is almost certain to follow (9–10; see also 8).

28. Quoted in Percy Crawford, "I See in My Scrapbook" (1958), 57–61.

29. Percy Crawford, "Some Reasons Why I Believe in a Real Hell of Fire and Brimstone," *Young People Today* (April 1939): 5, 17 at 17.

30. Percy Crawford sermon entitled "Hell," in "Sermons Preached over 250 Stations on the Mutual Network," 10.

31. Crawford, *Art of Fishing for Men,* 75.

32. Ibid., 75, 82, 94.

33. Percy Crawford sermon entitled "Life and Death," in *Whither Goest Thou?* 99.

34. Crawford, "Hell," 11.

35. Percy Crawford sermon entitled "Some Delicate Questions Regarding Hell," *Young People Today* (June 1939): 7.

36. Crawford, "Hell," 10. Torrey tends to be far more legalistic and uncaring regarding how God would deal with "our impenitent friends and loved ones": "If, after men have sinned and God still offers them mercy, and makes the tremendous sacrifice of His Son to save them—if they still despise that mercy and trample God's Son under foot, if then they are consigned to everlasting torment, I say: 'Amen! Hallelujah! True and righteous are thy judgments, O Lord!'" (*What the Bible Teaches,* 312). Percy would never have been this triumphant in his attitude toward God's condemnation of unbelievers. Admittedly, in the next paragraph, Torrey backtracks some and admits that his reasoning might not be entirely sufficient and that some may not find it convincing. Perhaps we cannot "defend [God's wrathful judgment] on philosophic grounds" alone. Nevertheless, since "the doctrine of conscious, eternal torment for impenitent men is clearly revealed in the Word of God, [we should] leave it to the clearer light of Eternity to explain what we cannot now understand, realizing that God may have infinitely wise reasons for doing things for which we in our ignorance can see no sufficient reason at all" (312). I cannot find any passages in which Percy qualifies our knowledge of God's intentions even to this extent.

37. Percy Crawford sermon entitled "Thanksgiving for God's Gift," in *Whither Goest Thou?* 113.

38. Percy Crawford, "My Testimony," in *Salvation Full and Free: A Series of Radio Messages* (Philadelphia: Westbrook, 1943), 8.

39. Percy Crawford, "Can a Person Dance and Be a Christian?" (part 2), *Young People Today* (August 1936): 4.

40. Percy Crawford, "Can a Person Dance and Be a Christian? (part 1), *Young People Today* (July 1936): 6.

41. *Young People Today* (July 1936): 6, 17; (August 1936): 4, 18. All quotations in this section are from this article unless otherwise indicated.

42. From an undated tract entitled "Dance?," a very condensed version of the *Young People Today* article.

43. John R. Rice, *What's Wrong with the Dance?* (Grand Rapids: Zondervan, n.d.), 23, 28. I first learned of this sermon in Joel Carpenter's treatment of Rice's uses of rhetorical devices to bully and intimidate his audiences (*Revive Us Again,* 66–67).

44. Percy Crawford radio sermon entitled "Regeneration" (preached November 29, 1936).

45. "Dance?" Percy does make reference to the "fruit of the Spirit" described by Paul in Galatians 5:22–23, but almost as an afterthought. In his sermon on regeneration he says that after the Holy Spirit comes to abide in the believer's heart, "then there comes the fruit of righteousness and the fruit of the Spirit which is love, joy, peace, and long suffering and so on." But except for "joy and peace," the Christian virtues mentioned by Paul—love, patience,

kindness, goodness, faithfulness, gentleness, and self-control—do not figure at all in Percy's description of the new life in Christ.

46. Percy Crawford, "Teenage Questions Answered" (undated tract [approx. 1959]).

47. Percy cites the text of this old hymn, "The Heavenly Vision," which had just been published in his chorus book *New Pinebrook Songs* (1936), 112: "Turn your eyes upon Jesus, / Look full in His wonderful face; / And the things of earth will grow strangely dim, / In the Light of His glory and grace."

## CHAPTER 14. U.S. TOURS AND MASS EVANGELISM

1. Bob Ketcham's Walnut Street Baptist Church in Waterloo would become a regular way-station for Percy and his team on future tours. One of the quartet members, Ray Pritz, became associate pastor there for a year when he left the quartet in 1947.

2. On this tour, the quartet consisted of regulars Ray Pritz and Joe Springer and re-placements Irwin "Shorty" Yeaworth, and Bob Miller. Miller was drafted into the service shortly after this trip. Al Zahlout was a regular instrumentalist on the Sunday broadcast.

3. *Young People's Church of the Air News* (September 1, 1943).

4. Shorty Yeaworth phone interview April 3, 2004.

5. E-mail correspondence from Pritz to author, August 16, 2001.

6. Ibid.

7. Ken Brown phone interview, November 13, 2002.

8. Percy Crawford letter of appeal to friends, May 2, 1943.

9. Ibid.

10. Percy Crawford letter to Harold Ockenga, June 3, 1943 (thanks to Garth Rosell for passing this letter on to me).

11. *Young People's Church of the Air News* (September 1, 1943): 3.

12. This information about the two rallies was taken from two similar-looking flyers: Jack's was printed after his April rally and advertised the coming September rally, with a picture on the front of the full house at the Madison Square Garden. Percy's brochure was printed after his April rally and had on the front a picture of the (almost) full Convention Hall.

13. James Hefley, *God Goes to High School* (Waco: Word, 1975), 25.

14. Another connection was that Bob Cook, Torrey's brother-in-law and close associate, had worked with Percy in the 1930s in Philadelphia as the managing editor of his magazine *Young People Today.*

15. "70,000 Attend Chicago Youth for Christ Rally Held on Memorial Day," *United Evangelical Action* (June 15, 1945): 1, 8; see also Joel A. Carpenter, *Revive Us Again: The Reawakening of American Fundamentalism* (New York: Oxford University Press, 1997), 166.

16. Torrey Johnson interview by Paul Hollinger (manager of WDAC-FM radio station, Lancaster, Pennsylvania), April 29, 1993 (Billy Graham Center Archives).

17. The idea was quite original in the East; the only other Christian orchestra at the time was Ralph Carmichael's on the West Coast.

## CHAPTER 15. THE MOVE TO TELEVISION:
## YOUTH ON THE MARCH

1. Sydney W. Head and Christopher H. Sterling, *Broadcasting in America,* 4th ed. (Boston: Houghton Mifflin, 1982, 1956), 187.

2. Ibid.

3. "Crawford Makes History Again," *Youth on the March: The Christian Newsette* (November 15, 1951), 24. This biweekly magazine ran from October 4, 1951, to February 4, 1954 (forty-nine issues); its name was shortened to *Christian Newsette* on March 12, 1953 (hereafter referenced as *Christian Newsette*). See also "First Religious Program on Coast-to-Coast TV," *Radio Daily* (57.22): 1.

4. April 3, 2004.

5. The tour was from March 24 to April 8, 1950. It started after a Friday night meeting in Long Island. My mother's datebook for March 24 says: "Left after meeting. Drove all night. Arrived in Detroit at 4:00 P.M. Four D's came on train with Shorty."

6. In viewing most of the kinescopes of these broadcasts, I saw Shorty's image only once, superimposed on The King's Singers as he artfully conducted them.

7. Shorty Yeaworth phone interview, April 3, 2004.

8. Shorty told me that he had always wanted to do a biographical film of my father's life, with Jimmy Stewart cast as Percy. I have to agree with him that the actor in *It's a Wonderful Life* and *Mr. Smith Goes to Washington* could have captured my father's driving personality better than anyone.

9. Ben Armstrong, *The Electric Church* (New York: Nelson, 1979), 89.

10. The lovely arrangements over the television years were done by Ruth and a succession of quartet members: Shorty Yeaworth, Al Black, Bob Brooks, and Neil Fichthorn.

11. Billy Graham letter to Percy Crawford, November 1, 1951 (Billy Graham Center Archives).

12. Armstrong, *Electric Church*, 89.

13. Carl F. Odhner, "Video Info," in (Allentown, Pennsylvania) *Beacon* (February 2, 1950).

14. *Christian Newsette* (October 18, 1951): 21. Quoted from *Hymn Lovers Magazine* (with no citation).

15. *Sunday School Times* (January 27, 1951): 71–72.

16. Percy's initial letter of appeal for the television broadcast announced: "We need over $4000 a week to stay on the air" (October 1949). In the 1950 calendar, he put the figure at "approximately $5000 a week."

17. *Christian Life* (April 1950): 14.

18. January 1951 calendar; *Sunday School Times* (January 27, 1951).

19. *Christian Newsette* 3.3 (September 25, 1952): 31.

20. The 1951 YPCA balance sheet showed that this was one of the few years that losses exceeded gains. "Radio [and television] Gifts" totaled $266,201.22, and the amount "Paid to Radio [and television] Companies" was $285,603.39, for a loss of $19,402.17. The total loss for the year was $20,461.51. But also listed for that year was a cash reserve of $35,000.

21. Joel A. Carpenter, *Revive Us Again: The Reawakening of American Fundamentalism* (New York: Oxford University Press, 1997), 178–81, 184–86 at 185.

22. *Christian Newsette* (October 29, 1953). I have been unable to verify Percy's claim that he would maintain some television broadcasts.

23. *Christian Newsette* (November 26, 1953): 38.

24. Percy Crawford letter to Margaret Dunham (our sitter, "Aunt Margaret"), December 3, 1953.

25. Percy Crawford letter to children, December 12, 1953.

26. Percy wrote later (from Japan): "We are amazed that even through an interpreter the Lord is blessing the message of salvation to the hearts of the Japanese" (*Christian Newsette* [January 21, 1954]).

27. Percy Crawford letter to children, December 9, 1953.

28. Percy Crawford letter to children, December 16, 1953.

29. *Christian Newsette* (January 21, 1954).

30. Percy Crawford letter to children, December 16, 1953.

31. Ruth Crawford letter to Esther Eden, December 26, 1953.

32. *Christian Newsette* (January 21, 1954): 38.

33. Ruth Crawford letter to Esther Eden. This letter was copied (typed) and sent to Percy's office staff. I have made a few minor corrections in spelling and punctuation.

34. *Christian Newsette* (January 21, 1954).

35. Ruth Crawford letter to children, December 25, 1953.

36. Unless otherwise specified, the details of the Korean trip are from Don Robertson's report, "Operation Korea," *Christian Newsette* (February 4, 1954): 22–31.

37. Ruth Crawford letter to Mrs. Thomas Eden, January 13, 1954.

38. Sam Moffett phone interviews, January 19 and 26, 2006. Born in Korea, Moffett returned to the United States for his higher education. He knew of my father through his radio ministry and met him once at Pinebrook. He went back to Korea to teach at the Presbyterian Theological Seminary in 1955, the year after Percy left, but, he said, "they were still talking about him." Moffett is presently emeritus professor of ecumenics and mission at Princeton Theological Seminary and is the author of the definitive study *A History of Christianity in Asia.*

39. Robertson, "Operation Korea," 31.

40. Percy Crawford letter prepared for mailing and signed by Percy, with photo attached, undated, probably written ca. fall 1960.

41. David H. Johnson (general director of The Evangelical Alliance Mission) letter to Percy Crawford, October 2, 1956.

42. Percy Crawford letter to Katharine Bowersox, March 25, 1958.

43. *Youth on the March News* 2.3 (July 1957).

44. *Christian Newsette* (February 12, 1953).

45. The advertising card for this program read (in part): "Again! *Youth on the March* on TV, Channel 12, Sundays 10:00 P.M., Wednesdays 7:15 P.M., Tell Your Friends."

46. Occasionally, Percy would buy television time on various stations scattered about the country, if he could get a good deal. He did this no doubt so that he could legitimately claim to be on television nationally. For example, in the spring of 1956, in addition to putting *Youth on the March* on kinescope on ABC-TV in New York, oddly enough, he was also on stations KBMN-TV in Bozeman, Montana, and KFAR-TV in Fairbanks, Alaska. The radio program was also aired at this time abroad on stations in Guatemala City, Honolulu, and Panama (letter from J. M. Camp and Company [Percy's agent] to N. W. Hunsinger [Kutztown National Bank, Pennsylvania], June 11, 1956).

47. Percy would not have been able to continue the broadcast in the 1958–59 season even if he had wanted to. Channel 12 (now WVUE) went off the air on September 14, 1958.

48. Chuck Pugh letter to author, June 1, 2004.

49. William Drury oral history interview (Billy Graham Center Archives, tape #4).

50. See below, chapter 17.

51. *Youth on the March News,* November 1957, 4.

52. My older brothers' stellar careers at Germantown Academy were interrupted briefly when Percy tried sending them to a Christian boarding school, DuBose Academy in Florida, for better disciplining. The effort failed, however, as the unruly boys managed to get themselves sent home after a few months for missing classes and chapel.

53. Percy was an avid fan of professional boxing and would not miss watching any of the televised championship fights. Although he never attended a live boxing match, he managed somehow to meet up with one champion, who wrote in the flyleaf of my father's New Testament: "Thanks Percy and Lots of luck, Jack Dempsey."

54. *Young People's Church of the Air News* (August 1, 1944): 1.

55. *Christian Newsette* (March 12, 1953): 31.

56. *Youth on the March News* (February 1958): 1.

57. Don Crawford interview, August 2, 2001.

## CHAPTER 16. THE KING'S COLLEGE: THE BRIARCLIFF YEARS

1. "Tidewater Refinery," *Compressed Air Magazine* (June 1956): 160–67.

2. "Prayer Urged against Site of Oil Refinery," Philadelphia Sunday *Bulletin* (September 19, 1954).

3. *King's Life* 2.6 (July 1955).

4. "The King's College Graduate," *King's Life* 4.9 (September 1957).

5. *King's Life* (September 1957).

6. "Purposes of The King's College," *King's Life* 7.4 (April 1960).

7. Ibid.

8. Al Black phone conversations, March 26, 2003, and March 6, 2004. I have not been able to locate the article on doubt that Black referred to in our conversations. According to Black, Percy sent him a note indicating that he liked the article, but cautioned him not to carry the point too far.

9. The Revised Standard Version of the New Testament was published in 1946, the Old Testament in 1952. Many fundamentalists rejected the RSV because they thought it compromised fundamental doctrines. Notably, Donald Barnhouse commended it as one of the best translations ever made; see C. A. Russell, "Donald Grey Barnhouse: Fundamentalist Who Changed," *Journal of Presbyterian History*" 59 (1981): 52.

10. I recall riding into New York City one Sunday afternoon with Bill Willey to hear Tillich give a lecture at Columbia University.

11. This statement of doctrine was included in all the college bulletins from 1939 to 1960.

12. Percy used the phrase *fallacies and misinterpretations* in his December 10, 1959, chapel talk in anticipation of Charles Bauer's visit. In the talk, Percy expressed his own doubts about the RSV's interpretation of "the Virgin birth and the divinity of Christ" and touted Bauer as an expert who had read the Old and New Testaments through four times in the original languages.

13. "Purposes of The King's College," *King's Life* 7.4 (April 1960).

14. Walter Martin questioned whether Black's theology was "in complete agreement" with that of the college. He reported that Black had said, when questioned about the historicity of Adam and Eve "as actual people": "Could be, or perhaps could not be" (minutes of board meeting, May 16, 1960).

15. "Purposes of The King's College," *King's Life* 7.4 (April 1960).

16. Fenton Duvall letter to Percy Crawford (signed "Fenny"), April 15, 1960 (found in Percy's papers).

17. Minutes of board meeting, December 7, 1959.

18. The statement of doctrine, as it was first formulated in the 1939 bulletin, was incorporated into the (amended) Certificate of Incorporation on December 30, 1947, with one change in the fifth doctrine: the phrase "everlasting punishment in Hell [for the unjust]" was replaced by "everlasting conscious torment in Hell." The charter also stipulated that the article containing the doctrinal statement "shall at no time be amended or amendable. Any attempt to amend this Article or this subsection prohibiting amendment shall be tantamount to a request to the State of Delaware to dissolve the Corporation."

19. Phillips took this quotation from Gaebelein's 1952 Griffith Thomas Memorial Lectures, presented at Dallas Theological Seminary. A month after getting Phillips's letter, Percy invited Gaebelein to give the commencement address for the 1960 graduation.

20. John Debrine letter to author, November 13, 2002.

21. Leymon Ketcham letter to Percy Crawford, November 9, 1954.

22. Duvall moved to Waynesburg College that summer as vice president of student affairs and then one year later returned to Whitworth, where he taught history for the rest of his career. Ketcham accepted a position in administration at Gordon College.

23. Richard Rung, assistant professor of history at King's at this time, affirmed this in an interview (April 17, 2004). Rung was another casualty of these doctrinal struggles; he left King's a few years later, fearing that his acceptance of the theory of "theistic evolution"—the view that humans evolved from lower life forms but that God directed the process—made him vulnerable to the conservatives' ax. He took a position at Wheaton, where he taught until his retirement.

24. Minutes of board meeting, June 4, 1960. In the fall, after Dr. Charles Woodbridge had come to the college for a spiritual life week, Percy let the board know that Woodbridge would be acceptable to him.

## CHAPTER 17. A CHRISTIAN BROADCASTING NETWORK

1. "The Editor Chats," *Young People Today* (May 1937): 15.

2. "The Editor Chats," *Young People Today* (March 1938). Percy goes on to state the reason for the Federal Radio Commission's denial: "It seems the Commission denied us the privilege we asked because we refused to take programs of sects which we felt would be detrimental to the Gospel."

3. In any case, those reserve funds dried up quickly: by the spring of 1957, the college was running a $100,000 operational deficit (Leymon Ketcham [assistant to the president] letter "to board of trustees and advisors," "Spring, 57" [handwritten addition]).

4. Percy's two-kilowatt transmitter at the channel 17 station probably had even less coverage.

5. Christopher H. Sterling and John M. Kittross, *Stay Tuned: A Concise History of American Broadcasting* (Belmont, Calif.: Wadsworth, 1978), 324.

6. Ibid., 417.

7. Of the six stations that Percy acquired in his own name, three were purchased (Detroit, Hammond, and Forest Grove) and three (Lancaster, Des Moines, Fort Lauderdale) were obtained by application for new licenses.

8. The 1959 balance sheet showed a net gain of $80,800.

9. Don Crawford interview, August 10, 2005.

10. The backers included Alex Dunlap, realtor and Percy's ubiquitous lieutenant ($15,000), Daniel Fanelle of Star Wrecking Company in Camden, New Jersey ($10,000);

and Paul Johnson, president of a contracting firm in Detroit ($15,000). Even at the fire sale price of $25,000, Percy was hesitant to go it alone, perhaps because he knew there would be more applications and more start-up funds needed. He offered Johnson 50 percent ownership of the station for $12,500, but Johnson turned down the deal because he was wary of a 50–50 partnership with Percy and unsure of the future of FM radio. (Don Crawford letter to author, February 3, 2004.)

11. Dick Gage phone interview, June 2005.

12. Bob Pierce had been the director of the Youth for Christ rally in Seattle and later the founder of World Vision Inc. During this period, he was promoting his work overseas on the radio and in rallies that he held across the nation.

13. Bob Anderson letter to Percy Crawford, October 15, 1959.

14. Percy Crawford letter to Bob Anderson, October 22, 1959.

15. John Adison phone interview, December 13, 2005.

16. Chuck Pugh interview, May 30, 2004.

17. Ben Armstrong (phone interview, May 28, 2005) told me that he attended the dedicatory service with Robertson. Bob Straton (phone interview, July 9, 2008), business manager of WPCA at the time, said he had a vivid recollection of Pat Robertson's presence at the ceremony. Don Crawford does not remember that Robertson was present, but this is not surprising since the young minister was not well known at the time. In correspondence with me (February 16, 2006), Robertson acknowledged that Percy's station was the first Christian television station: ("you are absolutely correct that he started the pioneering Christian television Channel 17 in Philadelphia"); he remembered driving to Philadelphia "to visit the facilities to see what the people were doing," and phoning my father who "gave me some very helpful advice on our efforts to start a new station," but did not recall being a part of the dedicatory service.

18. At the Detroit station WMUZ, which he purchased for $25,000, Percy committed additional funds to upgrade the studios and increase the power (to 115,000 watts), which meant installing a new tower and transmitting equipment. And at WYCA, Hammond/Chicago, after signing a note for $15,000 toward the purchase of the station, it was necessary to jump the power from 3,000 to 30,000 watts (due to its extremely poor coverage) at a cost of $89,000, payable over ten years.

19. Percy disclosed this fact about his finances in his December 10, 1959 chapel talk at King's. I have calculated that approximately three-quarters of this debt ($225,000) was station related. The acquisition of KGGG in Forest Grove (later changed to KWAY) was Percy's worst business decision, as the station proved to be a continual drain on the company and my father's estate until it was finally sold in 1961.

20. The bookstore, ably managed by partner Norm Kellow, was a stable source of income throughout most of Percy's life. On the other hand, the two diners Percy owned at this time were heavily mortgaged and had little or no net value. Pinebrook also owned an apartment in Fort Lauderdale, Florida, which Percy purchased for $6,000 in 1957 and used as a vacation spot for our family and close associates.

21. The only major gift to YPCA that I have been able to trace was a $10,000 grant by the Pew Foundation. Chuck Pugh remembers visiting Mr. Pew with Percy and their getting his attention by pointing out to him that delinquent teenagers were being converted through Percy's ministry.

22. Percy's estimate was not far off; eight months after his death, his estate lawyer, Robert Grasberger, advised Ruth, who was struggling to pay off debt, to hold on to Detroit and Lancaster at all costs, and estimated their "combined sale value" to be $400,000. However Grasberger failed to see the tremendous potential of the Hammond station because, as

he said, it was "so heavily in debt at the time of Percy's death" and "a drain on the capital assets of this estate." (Grasberger letter to Ruth Crawford, June 26, 1961.)

23. Percy Crawford letter to Ruth, January 9, 1959.

24. "I See in My Scrapbook" (1960), 23–34. None of these thoughts were included in the earlier first edition (1958).

25. Don Crawford letter to author, September 10, 2001.

26. Don Crawford created the Crawford Broadcasting Company in 1965 and managed the radio stations (which he increased from three to nine) until 1979, when the company was broken up and the assets distributed among our immediate family. At that time, Don became president and primary owner of Crawford Broadcasting Company, which (in 2006) operated twenty-two Christian stations. WDAC Radio Company became a separate entity and has thrived under the leadership and skillful management of its president, Richard Crawford, Paul Hollinger, who managed the station for forty-five years (1961–2006), and current manager, Doug Myer.

27. A day later, when my brother Dick called him (at the hospital) and asked him for $400 so that his wife, Betsy, and their new baby, Daniel, could be released from the hospital, he had to turn him down, saying, "I don't have it."

28. Barnhouse died Saturday, November 5, five days after my father. Bill Drury told me that Percy had called the hospital to inquire about Barnhouse's condition and said to Bill: "I don't want to die like that; I want to die with my boots on."

29. I have recently been told by a heart specialist that the CPR technique at this time consisted solely in beating on the chest and that the paramedics could easily have fractured one of Percy's ribs and perhaps even punctured a lung (which would explain why he was coughing up blood in the hospital). Ruth gave a full account of Percy's final heart attack and death on a channel 17 television broadcast that our family put on the air the night after Percy died (Tuesday, November 1) (sound track exists in archives). She also discussed his death in an interview with Bill Drury, twenty-one years later (1981) (Ruth Crawford Porter oral history interview, Billy Graham Center Archives).

30. Don Crawford letter to author, September 10, 2002.

31. Audio tape of Billy Graham's message delivered at Percy Crawford memorial service at Town Hall in Philadelphia on November 6, 1960 (family archives).

32. Carl F. H. Henry letter to Ruth Crawford, November 1, 1960.

33. Harold J. Ockenga letter to Ruth Crawford, December 5, 1960.

34. My mother and I did the first musical fifteen minutes from Briarcliff, and Don took the second half and the devotional talk from Philadelphia.

35. I wrote a letter to the board members protesting their action and got twenty-five student leaders to sign it. In the letter, I warned that many of us "feel [we] must transfer, and yet our concern is with a stronger and more effective King's College." I asked that our "honest appeal not go unheeded," but the board ignored it.

## CHAPTER 18. A LIFE FULFILLED

1. *The King's Business* (December 1926): 702.

2. See Robert T. Handy, "The American Religious Depression, 1925–1935," *Church History* 29 (1960): 3–16.

3. Even at the end of his life, when he was having so much trouble financing his radio and television network, he had projects in the offing—The King's Korean Mission and a Christian "home for the elderly" in Florida that he began to advertise as "The Garden of the

Palms." (Mentioned on a morning broadcast, summer 1960 [tape #7 in Don Crawford's YPCA library and included in the Billy Graham Center Archives].)

4. Letter from Torrey Johnson read at Percy Crawford's This Is Your Life dinner, April 24, 1953 (transcribed from cassette tape). Family Archives.

5. "For God so loved the world that he gave his only begotten son, that whosoever believeth in him should not perish, but have everlasting life." Percy invoked this verse countless times in dealing with the lost.

6. Another verse that epitomized Percy's theological beliefs, which he instructed every newly saved person to commit to memory, was John 1:12: "But as many as received him, to them gave he power to become the sons of God, even to them that believe on his name."

7. Charles Woodbridge (see chapter 16, note 24).

# Bibliography

## PRIMARY RESOURCES ON PERCY AND RUTH CRAWFORD

### Magazines

Percy's two magazines, *Young People Today* (January 1934–February 1942) and *Youth on the March/Christian Newsette* (October 1951–February 1954) (title changed to *Christian Newsette,* March 12, 1953) are accessible on microfilm in the libraries of Westminster Theological Seminary and Dallas Theological Seminary, and are in the Percy Crawford Collection (#357) at the Billy Graham Center, Wheaton, Illinois. (*Young People Today* is missing three issues: January 1934, October 1939, and December 1939.)

### Photographs

Additional photographs of Percy and family, YPCA personnel, Pinebrook speakers, etc. are accessible on the Web site ruthandpercycrawford.com. This Web site reproduces the pages of a 101-page booklet produced by Donald B. Crawford (president, Young People's Church of the Air), "Love Wonderful Love: Remembering Ruth & Percy Crawford," which includes over 175 photos and a selection of 51 selected songs from Percy's and Ruth's published songbooks.

### Broadcasts and Music

Donald Crawford has a complete set of the television broadcasts, *Youth on the March* (1949–1953) on DVD. (Some of these are in the Percy Crawford Collection (#357) in the archives at the Billy Graham Center, Wheaton, Illinois.)

Many tape recordings and records of the radio broadcasts have survived, some dating back to the early 1940s. Many of these have been digitalized and are preserved in the "YPCA Heritage CD Masters" collection. Inquiries should be sent to: Donald Crawford, Young People's Church of the Air, Box 3003, Blue Bell, Pennsylvania 19422.

(A few recordings of the YPCA broadcast are stored at the Billy Graham Center (Collection #357), but are currently not available to researchers.)

### Sermons

Over fifty of Percy's printed, but unpublished, sermons are in my possession and will be accessible to the general public on my Web site percycrawford.com in the near future.

## Oral History

I was interviewed on August 3, 2004 about Percy Crawford's ministry and family life by Bob Shuster for the Oral History collection in the archives of the Billy Graham Center at Wheaton College, Wheaton, Illinois (Dan Duvall Crawford, #CN 604).

See also Jack Wyrtzen, Oral History Series, Billy Graham Center Archives, Collection 446, Transcripts 1 & 2.

## Songbooks

Percy and Ruth published thirteen songbooks over a twenty-seven-year period (1932–59):

*The Young People's Church of the Air Hymnbook,* 177 songs compiled by Percy B. Crawford (Philadelphia: n.p., 1932).

*Pinebrook Choruses,* 215 songs compiled by Percy B. Crawford & Ruth D. Crawford (Philadelphia: n.p., 1934).

*New Pinebrook Songs,* 170 songs compiled by Percy B. Crawford & Ruth D. Crawford (Philadelphia: n.p., 1936).

*The King's Songs,* 178 songs compiled by Ruth D. Crawford & Percy B. Crawford (Philadelphia: n.p., 1939).

*Pinebrook Melodies,* 181 songs compiled by Ruth D. Crawford & Percy B. Crawford (Philadelphia: n.p., 1941).

*Pinebrook Praises,* 190 songs compiled by Ruth D. Crawford & Percy B. Crawford (Wheaton, Ill.: Van Kampen Press, 1943).

*Pinebrook Victory Songs,* 191 songs compiled by Ruth D. Crawford & Percy B. Crawford (Philadelphia: Pinebrook Press, 1946).

*Radio Requests,* 79 songs compiled by Ruth D. Crawford & Percy B. Crawford (Wheaton, Ill.: Van Kampen Press, 1947).

*Radio Requests* No. 2, 82 songs compiled by Ruth D. Crawford & Percy B. Crawford (Wheaton, Ill.: Van Kampen Press, 1950).

*Television Tunes,* 74 songs compiled by Ruth D. Crawford & Percy B. Crawford (Wheaton, Ill.: Van Kampen Press, 1952).

*Youth on the March Songs,* 80 songs compiled by Ruth D. Crawford & Percy B. Crawford (Wheaton, Ill.: Van Kampen Press, 1954).

*Mountainbrook Melodies,* 76 songs compiled by Ruth D. Crawford & Percy B. Crawford (Grand Rapids, Mich.: Zondervan Publishing House, 1956).

*Songs of Heaven,* 72 songs compiled by Ruth D. Crawford & Percy B. Crawford (Grand Rapids, Mich.: Zondervan Publishing House, 1959).

Ruth Crawford (remarried, Ruth Crawford Porter) published five additional songbooks after Percy's death:

*Sing My Heart,* 64 songs compiled by Ruth D. Crawford, Singspiration, Inc. (Grand Rapids, Mich.: Zondervan Publishing House, 1962).

*Singing Thru the Years,* 65 songs compiled by Ruth D. Crawford, published by The Estate of Percy B. Crawford (1967).

*How Wonderful and other songs by Esther Eden & Blanche Osborn,* 71 songs compiled and published by Ruth Crawford Porter (1973). (Words by Esther Eden, [Ruth's sister]; music by Blanche Osborn.)

*Hearts in Harmony and other songs by Ruth Crawford Porter & Esther Eden,* 81 songs published by Ruth Crawford Porter (1973). (Words by Esther Eden; music by Ruth Crawford Porter.)

*Singing and Making Melodies,* 85 songs published by Ruth Crawford Porter (1982). (Words by Esther Eden; music by Ruth Crawford Porter.)


## Secondary Literature

Bahr, Robert. *Least of All Saints: The Story of Aimee Semple McPherson.* Englewood Cliffs: Prentice Hall, 1979.

——. *Man With a Vision: The Story of Percy Crawford.* Chicago: Moody Press, n.d. [approx. 1961].

Barnhouse, Donald. "When Winter Comes." *Revelation* (April 1935): 139, 164–166.

Barton, Kelly Damon. "Fundamentalism and Higher Fundamentalism: The MacInnis Controversy at BIOLA." Unpublished essay dated July 22, 1988. In my possession courtesy of Church of the Open Door, Glendora, Calif.

Bechtel, Paul M. *Wheaton College: A Heritage Remembered, 1860–1984.* Wheaton, Ill.: Shaw, 1984.

Blackstone, W. E. *Jesus is Coming.* enl. ed. New York: Revell, 1908 [orig. 1878].

Bollbeck, Harry. *The House That Jack (God) Built.* Schroon Lake, N.Y.: Word of Life Fellowship, 1972.

Carpenter, Joel A., ed. *The Fundamentalist-Modernist Conflict: Opposing Views on Three Major Issues.* New York: Garland, 1988.

———. *Revive Us Again: The Reawakening of American Fundamentalism.* New York: Oxford University Press, 1997.

Clark, David. "Miracles for a Dime: From Chatauqua Tent to Radio Station." *California History* 57 (Winter 1978/79): 354–63.

Cocoris, G. Michael. *70 Years on Hope Street: A History of the Church of the Open Door: 1915–1985.* Los Angeles: Church of the Open Door, 1985.

Cole, Stewart G. *The History of Fundamentalism.* New York: Richard R. Smith, 1931.

Crawford, Donald B. "He was no ordinary man." (printed address given at memorial service of Percy B. Crawford, November 6, 1960.)

Crawford, Percy B. *The Art of Fishing for Men.* Philadelphia: Mutual Press, 1935. Paperback edition, Chicago: Moody Press, 1950.

———. "Can a Person Dance and Be a Christian?" (parts 1 & 2). *Young People Today* (July 1936): 6, 17; (August 1936): 4, 18.

———, ed. *Echoes of Pinebrook: A Series of Timely Messages.* Philadelphia: Young People's Church of the Air, 1941.

———, ed. *Highlights of Pinebrook: Twenty-Four Inspiring Messages Delivered at the Pinebrook Bible Conference.* Philadelphia: Pinebrook Book Club, 1938.

———. "A Modern Revival." *Revelation* (August 1932): 325, 349–50.

———, ed. *Mountaintop Messages* (Thirty inspiring messages delivered at the Pinebrook Bible Conference). Philadelphia: Pinebrook Book Club, 1939.

———. *Salvation Full and Free: A Series of Radio Messages (Preached on 250 Stations Over The Mutual Network).* Philadelphia: Westbrook, 1943.

———. "What I Think of Billy Graham." Audio tape of *Pinebrook Praises* broadcast (approx. September 1959) in family archives.

———. *Whither Goest Thou? A Series of Radio Messages Preached on 250 Stations over the Mutual Network.* East Stroudsburg, Penn.: Pinebrook Book Club, 1946.

———. "Why Another College? (printed radio sermon preached by Rev. Percy Crawford December 6, 1936) in family archives.

Evenson, Bruce J. *God's Man for the Gilded Age.* New York: Oxford University Press, 2003.

Fischer, E. Harlan. "A Challenge for the 90s." *Alpha Gamma Omega, the Christ-Centered Fraternity* (part d), *in Alpha Gamma Omega History.* (Speech presented February 24, 1990). Courtesy of fraternity historian Adam Blauert.

Forbes, Forrest. *God Hath Chosen: The Story of Jack Wyrtzen and the Word of Life Hour.* Grand Rapids, Mich.: Zondervan, 1948.

"From Pulpit on a Plank." *Everybody's Weekly—The Philadelphia Inquirer* (May 19, 1940): 5.

Fuller, Daniel P. *Give the Winds a Mighty Voice.* Waco, Tex.: Word, 1972.

Gasper, Louis. *The Fundamentalist Movement.* The Hague: Mouton, 1963.

*God Hath Spoken: Twenty-five Addresses Delivered at the World Conference on Christian Fundamentals* (1919). Philadelphia: Bible Conference Committee, 1919.

Graham, Billy. "Memorial Service for Dr. Percy Crawford" (printed address). November 6, 1960, Philadelphia Town Hall. (Billy Graham Center Archives). Audio tape of service in family archives.

Guelzo, Allen C. "Barnhouse." In *Making God's Word Plain: One Hundred and Fifty Years in the History of Tenth Presbyterian Church of Philadelphia,* edited by James M. Boice. Philadelphia: Tenth Presbyterian Church, 1979, 63–87.

Handy, Robert T. "The American Religious Depression, 1925–1935." *Church History* 29 (1960): 3–16.

Hangen, Tona J. *Redeeming the Dial: Radio, Religion, and Popular Culture in America.* Chapel Hill: University of North Carolina Press, 2002.

Harkness, Robert. *Reuben Archer Torrey: The Man, His Message.* Chicago: Bible Institute Colportage, 1929.

Head, Sydney W., and Christopher H. Sterling. *Broadcasting in America,* 4th ed. Boston: Houghton Mifflin, 1982 [orig. 1956].

Hart, D. G., ed. *J. Gresham Machen: Selected Shorter Writings.* Phillipsburg, N.J.: P&R, 2004.

Hefley, James. *God Goes to High School.* Waco, Tex: Word, 1975.

Higley, L. Allen. *Science and Truth.* New York: Revell, 1940.

Hilliker, Jim. "History of KSFG: Pioneer L.A. Christian Station Stops Broadcasting After 79 Years" (written for Web site LARADIO.com, 2003).

Hodge, A. A. and B. B. Warfield. "Inspiration." *Presbyterian Review* 2 (April 1881): 225–60.

Hoffman, Bill. "Historical Notes, Alpha Gamma Omega." (Unpublished May 2002 paper, revised February 25, 2004). Courtesy of fraternity historian Adam Blauert.

Hopkins, Paul A. "What Made the Man?" *Eternity* (March 1961): 14–18, 35–43.

Horton, Thomas C. *Personal and Practical Christian Work.* Los Angeles: BIOLA Book Room, Bible Institute of Los Angeles, 1922.

Ketcham, Robert. "Facts for Baptists to Face." Waterloo, Ia.: Walnut St. Baptist Church, 1936 [2nd ed. in 1942].

Kocher, Donald Roth. *The Mother of Us All: First Presbyterian Church in Philadelphia, 1698–1998.* Philadelphia: First Presbyterian Church in Philadelphia, 1998.

Larson, Mel. *Youth for Christ.* Grand Rapids, Mich.: Zondervan, 1947.

Loetscher, Lefferts A. *The Broadening Church: A Study of Theological Issues in the Presbyterian Church Since 1869.* Philadelphia: University of Pennsylvania Press, 1954.

Lothrop, Gloria. "West of Eden: Pioneer Media Evangelist Aimee Semple McPherson in Los Angeles." *Journal of the West* 27 (April 1988): 50–59.

Macartney, Clarence. *The Making of a Minister.* Great Neck, N.Y.: Channel, 1961.

Machen, J. Gresham. *Christianity and Liberalism.* Grand Rapids, Mich.: Eerdmans, 1972 [orig. 1923].

———. "The Sermon on the Mount." In *The Christian Faith in the Modern World* [radio addresses]. New York: Macmillan, 1936.

———. *What is Faith?* New York: Macmillan, 1925.

———. "What is Original Sin?" In *The Christian View of Man* [radio addresses]. Grand Rapids, Mich.: Eerdmans, 1947 [orig. 1937].

Marsden, George M. *Fundamentalism and American Culture: The Shaping of Twentieth-Century Evangelicalism: 1870–1925.* New York: Oxford University Press, 1980.

Marty, Martin. *Modern American Religion, Vol. 1, The Irony of It All: 1893–1919.* Chicago: University of Chicago Press, 1986.

———. *Righteous Empire: The Protestant Experience in America.* New York: The Dial Press, 1970.

Mattson, Vernon Eugene. "The Fundamentalist Mind: An Intellectual History of Religious Fundamentalism in the United States." Ph.D. diss., University of Kansas, 1971.

McLoughlin, William G. *Modern Revivalism: Charles Grandison Finney to Billy Graham.* New York: Ronald, 1959.

McPherson, Aimee Semple. *This is That: Personal Experiences, Sermons, and Writings.* Los Angeles: Echo Park Evangelistic Association, 1923.

McWilliams, Carey. "Aimee Semple McPherson: Sunlight in My Soul." In *The Aspirin Age, 1919–1941,* edited by Isabel Leighton. New York: Simon & Schuster, 1949, 50–80.

Mead, Frank S. "Apostle to Youth." *Christian Herald* (September 1945): 15–17, 51.

Murch, James DeForest. *Adventuring for Christ in Changing Times: An Autobiography.* Louisville: Restoration Press, 1973.

———. *Cooperation without Compromise.* Grand Rapids, Mich.: Eerdmans, 1956.

Murdoch, J. Murray. *Portrait of Obedience: The Biography of Robert T. Ketcham.* Schaumburg, Ill.: Regular Baptist Press, 1979.

Niebuhr, Richard H., Wilhelm Pauck, and Francis P. Miller. *The Church Against the World.* Chicago: Willett, Clark & Co., 1935.

Noll, Mark A. *Between Faith and Criticism: Evangelicals, Scholarship, and the Bible in America.* San Francisco: Harper & Row, 1986.

"Our History." (Rhawnhurst Presbyterian Church document, unpublished.) Courtesy of Enid Milligan, Clerk.

Palmer, George A. "Morning Cheer, Pastor George A. Palmer, 1935." (Booklet, n.p.) Courtesy of Sandy Cove Ministries.

"Pioneer for God: The Biography of Percy B. Crawford" (1954). Typed draft of a biography authorized by Crawford but never completed or published. Author unknown, no pagination but fifty-two pages long. Billy Graham Center Archives.

Rauschenbusch, Walter. *Christianity and the Social Crisis in the 21st Century: The Classic That Woke Up the Church.* Edited by Paul B. Raushenbush. New York: HarperCollins, 2007.

Rice, John R. "What's Wrong with the Dance?" (printed sermon delivered June 1935). Grand Rapids, Mich.: Zondervan, n.d.

Rosell, Garth. *The Surprising Work of God: Harold John Ockenga, Billy Graham, and the Rebirth of Evangelicalism.* Grand Rapids, Mich.: Baker, 2008.

Russell, C. Allyn. "Donald Grey Barnhouse: Fundamentalist Who Changed." *Journal of Presbyterian History* 59 (Spring 1981): 33–57.

———. *Voices of American Fundamentalism.* Philadelphia: Westminster, 1976.

Sandeen, Ernest R. *The Roots of Fundamentalism: British and American Millenarianism: 1800–1930.* Chicago: University of Chicago Press, 1970.

Saunders, Lowell. "The National Religious Broadcasters and the Availability of Commercial Radio Time." Ph.D. diss., University of Illinois, 1968.

Shea, George Beverly. *Then Sings My Soul.* Old Tappan, N.J.: Revell, 1968.

Siedell, Barry C. *Gospel Radio.* Lincoln, Neb.: Back to the Bible Publication, 1971.

Singleton, Gregory. *Religion in the City of Angels: American Protestant Culture and Urbanization, Los Angeles 1850–1930.* Ann Arbor, Mich.: UMI Research Press, 1979.

Smith, Wilbur M., ed. *The Best of D. L. Moody.* Chicago: Moody Press, 1971.

Starr, Paul. *The Creation of the Media: Political Origins of Modern Communications.* New York: Basic Books, 2004.

Stenger, Wallace. "The Radio Priest and His Flock." In *The Aspirin Age, 1919–1941,* edited by Isabel Leighton. New York: Simon & Schuster, 1949, 232–57.

Sterling, Christopher H. and John M. Kittross. *Stay Tuned: A Concise History of American Broadcasting.* Belmont, Calif.: Wadsworth, 1978.

Stonehouse, Ned B. *J. Gresham Machen: A Biographical Memoir.* Grand Rapids, Mich.: Eerdmans, 1954.

Sutton, Matthew A. *Aimee Semple McPherson and the Resurrection of Christian America.* Cambridge: Harvard University Press, 2007.

———. "Between the Refrigerator and the Wildfire." *Church History* 72, no. 1 (March 2003): 159–88.

"Taking Men Alive—By Television: 'Youth on the March' from Coast to Coast." *Sunday School Times* (January 27, 1951): 71–72.

Torrey, Reuben A. *How to be Saved.* New York: Revell, 1923.

———. *How to Bring Men to Christ.* New York: Revell, 1893.

————. *Is the Bible the Inerrant Word of God?* New York: George H. Doran Company, 1922.

————. *What the Bible Teaches.* New York: Revell, 1898.

————. *Why God Used D. L. Moody.* New York: Revell, 1923.

Trollinger, William V. *God's Empire: William Bell Riley and Midwestern Fundamentalism.* Madison: University of Wisconsin Press, 1990.

Vaughn, Gerald F. "Evangelist Percy Crawford and The King's College in Delaware, 1941–1955." *Delaware History* 27, nos. 1–2 (Spring 1996-Winter 1997): 19–41.

Voskuil, Dennis N. "The Power of the Air: Evangelicals and the Rise of Religious Broadcasting." In *American Evangelicals and the Mass Media,* edited by Quentin J. Schultze. Grand Rapids, Mich.: Zondervan, 1990: 69–95.

Ward, Mark. *Air of Salvation: The Story of Christian Broadcasting.* Grand Rapids, Mich.: Baker, 1994.

Weber, Timothy P. *Living in the Shadow of the Second Coming: American Premillennialism, 1875–1925.* New York: Oxford University Press, 1979.

Williams, Robert, and Marilyn Miller. *Chartered for His Glory: Biola University, 1908–1983.* Marceline, Mo.: Herff Jones, 1983.

Wright, J. Elwin. *The Old Fashioned Revival Hour and the Broadcasters.* Boston: Fellowship Press, 1940.

# Acknowledgments

I WISH TO EXPRESS SINCERE THANKS TO THE MANY PEOPLE WHO SHARED with me in long phone interviews and correspondence their personal experiences with my father and reflections on those experiences, and who opened up aspects of his life and ministry that I could not have been aware of as his son. My gratitude to each of them is expressed, I hope, in the way I have tried faithfully to recreate their particular memory of Percy in my text.

Many of those I talked to gave me access to materials that proved invaluable in reconstructing my father's life trajectory in those now distant decades (1930s, 40s, and 50s), especially the late Ray Pritz (calendar books while a member of the YPCA quartet), the late Joe Springer and Alan Forbes (tape recordings of broadcasts), Friedhelm Radandt (King's College records), Paul Hollinger (a complete run of Percy's magazine, *Christian Newsette*), John DeBrine (tapes of Percy's services at *Songtime*), Gerald Vaughn (research materials on The King's College, Delaware campus), Garth Rosell (items from the Ockenga papers), Marjorie Linton (early King's College materials), Dan McDaniel ("Lord of All" film), Adam Blauert (Alpha Gamma Omega fraternity materials), and Mark Crawford (family history).

This biography, like any other, relied heavily on the help of librarians and archivists. Among the many record keepers who assisted me I want to thank especially Grace Mullen at Westminster Theological Seminary (who found a nearly complete run of Percy's magazine, *Young People Today*), Sue Whitehead at BIOLA, Bob Shuster at the Billy Graham Center, Robert Ibach at Dallas Theological Seminary, Judy Cacoris at Church of the Open Door (Glendora, California), Steve Zeleny at The Foursquare Church (for access to the Aimee Semple MacPherson archives), and Freeman Barton at Goddard Library, Gordon-Conwell Theological Seminary.

I have had the unstinting support of my siblings throughout this long process, Donna, Don, Dean, and Dick. Donna and Don had the foresight to save all the family archives (memorabilia, tapes, and kinescopes of the broadcasts, papers, and hundreds of photographs) and shared all of what they had with me; Dean had the computer skills to preserve all of the photographs, greatly enriching the historical record.

My chief conversation partners in writing this book were my uncle Fenton Duvall, my brother Don, and my wife Sidnie. I had many long talks with Fenton who was a key player in the story I tell, having worked closely with Percy practically from day one in 1931. Our dear "Uncle Fenny" died in November 2008, age ninety-six, but fortunately read and made valuable comments on a draft of this entire book before his death. Don worked side-by-side with our father in the final years of his life and knew his entrepreneurial side better than anyone. I profited greatly from his accurate memories and strongly felt reactions to their partnership. My wife Sidnie did not know personally her father-in-law, but could see as clearly as anyone the imprint he left on his five children. Sidnie gave me the idea of writing a full-length book about my father (instead of several journal articles as I had originally thought of doing). Her insightful comments and questions on early drafts of the book prodded me to think more objectively and dispassionately about my father's various roles. Even more, her constant encouragement and readiness to engage in conversation about Percy from her own denominational perspective helped immeasurably in bringing the book to completion.

Finally, I would like to thank the anonymous reviewer from Susquehanna University Press who saw how the story I tell about my father's life could be filled in and improved, and gave constructive guidance toward situating my father within the larger historical development of American evangelicalism.

# Index

Numbers in boldface indicate illustration pages.